HUMAN
SERVICES
AS COMPLEX
ORGANIZATIONS

HUMAN
SERVICES
AS COMPLEX
ORGANIZATIONS

EDITED BY
YEHESKEL
HASENFELD

SAGE Publications
International Educational and Professional Publisher
Newbury Park   London   New Delhi

For information address:

SAGE Publications, Inc.
2455 Teller Road
Newbury Park, California 91320
E-mail: order@sagepub.com

SAGE Publications Ltd.
6 Bonhill Street
London EC2A 4PU
United Kingdom

SAGE Publications India Pvt. Ltd.
M-32 Market
Greater Kailash I
New Delhi 110 048 India

Printed in the United States of America

Library of Congress Cataloging-in-Publication Data

Main entry under title:
Human services as complex organizations / edited by Yeheskel
    Hasenfeld.
            p.   cm.
    Includes bibliographical references and index.
    ISBN 0-8039-4064-5 (cl).—ISBN 0-8039-4065-3 (pb).
    1. Human services—United States—Management.   2. Complex
organizations—United States.   I. Hasenfeld, Yeheskel.
HV95.H75   1992
361'.0068—dc20   92-3060

                    99   00   01   12   11   10   9

  Sage Production Editor: Astrid Virding

Contents

Preface

This book arrives nearly two decades after the publication of *Human Services Organizations*, a book of readings edited by Yeheskel Hasenfeld and Richard English in 1974. The earlier volume marked an important turning point in the history of organizational inquiry in social work and the human services generally. The current book, in its own way, sets the stage for another important era in the analysis of human service organizations.

In the early 1970s, organizational theorists and researchers in the social and behavioral sciences, with a few notable exceptions, had not yet turned their attention to the non-profit social welfare sector. Those who had, looked at what they saw through the prism of their own disciplines and theoretical biases and were more concerned with description and explanation than with change. Therefore, the body of organizational theory that research scholars and practitioners in the human service professions drew on had either been developed in other institutional sectors, or was not in the main concerned with informing practice. The extant organizational literature was helpful to a broad understanding of the dynamics of social and health agencies, but not too useful for illuminating the variant properties and processes of this class of organizations.

One should recall that this was a time when the human service professions were intensely preoccupied with constructing a theory and technology of management practice that was tailored to the demand of organizations in this sector. Such work required a complementary body of research on the structural and social-psychological characteristics of human service organizations. It was essential, then, that there be a literature to explain the behavior of human service agencies in order to inform the development of intervention theories for managers and others.

The Hasenfeld and English volume began to fill this gap by delineating the distinguishing qualities of human services organizations as a class. It laid the basis for thinking about the adaptation of mainstream management technologies to social agencies. Concepts such as "clients as raw materials," "people processing and people changing," goal ambiguity, and "indeterminate technologies," were invented or popularized in this book and have since provided a language used by a generation of scholars and practitioners concerned with organizational behavior.

The current volume, *Human Services as Complex Organizations*, arrives after nearly two decades of concerted efforts to understand and more effectively manage these institutions. While much has been learned, fundamental questions remain. This collection of readings seeks to push our understanding of one of the most basic and elusive of these questions: What determines the nature of service delivery systems in the human services? The book is organized around several broad themes conceptualized as interacting forces that together shape the structure and operation of these organizations.

The book is introduced with two excellent chapters by Hasenfeld. The first updates and extends his now famous essay on the distinctive qualities of human service organizations and the dilemmas that follow. The second chapter presents a comparative analysis of prevailing theories of human service agencies and an assessment of their utility for understanding the nature of human service organizations. While all of the theories are found useful for understanding some problems confronting such agencies, Hasenfeld argues that the most robust explanatory framework grows out of an understanding of the interactions that occur between organizations and their environments. It is in this interaction that policy and program choices are made, intervention technologies chosen, and clientele defined.

More specifically, Hasenfeld develops the notion that the interplay of political and institutional forces may be the essential determinants of how service organizations define and implement their functions. While he acknowledges the utility of other theoretical perspectives for understanding certain kinds of problems, e.g., human relations, rational-legal, and so on, Hasenfeld's own formulation and the perspective that most permeates the book is one that sees delivery systems as accommodations to political power and institutionally imposed rules.

This perspective, which has been emerging in the organizational literature in recent years, is only now coming to be understood or applied by human services practitioners. There has always been a tendency to attribute constraints and flaws in service delivery systems to external "power," but in the final analysis, the inclination among practitioners is to look within organizations to understand why they work well or fail. Thus features such as leadership, interpersonal relations, and decision making have been the variables of interest.

The political-institutional perspective provides an important framework for looking at the effects of external forces. It is especially useful in a time when stakeholders and resource providers are increasingly intent on shaping service agencies to serve specific goals and ideologies. This perspective also suggests that management theory and practice give much more attention to strategic interaction with key groups in the organization's environment. The readings in this book will help to explain how this process occurs and how managers can work to compete for resources, develop influence, and preserve autonomy.

Another critical phenomenon in the human service agency is the belief systems, ideologies, that drive the work of professionals and, therefore, influence the operations of agencies. These ideologies do not exist apart from the political forces mentioned above, but are informed and sometimes shaped by them as professionals seek to accommodate these external influences. Nevertheless, these ideologies become crucial to determining which clients receive service, how problems are defined, the kinds of interventions considered appropriate, and so on. Several chapters provide critical insights into the sometime self-serving, often subjective forces that determine what is done for whom and how.

But this is not solely a book about the role of power in determining the nature of service systems. It is also about those who have little power to influence the terms of their engagement with organizations and the problems that occur in both the delivery and utilization of services when such people remain powerless. One of the characteristics of human service agencies, as Hasenfeld points out, is their reliance on both professional workers *and* consumers to co-produce outcomes. What happens at this interface is critically influenced by the availability of resources, a sense of equity and trust, and opportunities to influence the nature of the service experience. Hasenfeld's prefatory chapters, and many of those in the last half of the volume, underscore the importance of empowering those who typically have little power in these organizations, because it is only when lower participants experience some control of their destinies that trust and commitment (between worker and organization, between client and worker) are developed.

Good outcomes depend on these essential qualities of relationships in the human services.

This book of readings is no dispassionate analysis of human service agencies. While there are important contributions to explanatory theory of organizations, many of the chapters address themselves to change and are intended to inform practice interventions. For example, one section of the book is devoted to building empowerment strategies for women and minorities in social agencies. In this and other respects, this is a volume that will be useful to those who wish to understand organizational behavior and those who wish to change it.

Finally, I was pleased to note the number of professional scholars who, along with social scientists, contributed chapters. This reflects, I think, a growing scholarly capability in the organizational field among human service academics. Twenty years ago it would have been hard to imagine a collection of this quality with so many fine contributions from academics in professional schools. The resulting volume represents the best of scholarship in the service of social change.

—Rino Patti

Acknowledgments

This reader could not have become a reality without the good will and dedication of all the contributors, many of whom generously and cheerfully accommodated my insistent pursuit of a coherent vision for this venture. I want to thank each of them for their patience and perseverance. Helen, Rena, and Rachel deserve special thanks for enduring the many hours I spent away from them while working on this project. Finally, this reader would not have come about without the prodding and insightful suggestions of all my students. I dedicate this book to them.

PART I
Understanding Human Service Organizations

The theme of Chapter 1 is the distinct attributes of human service organizations. These attributes emanate from the fact that these organizations work on people. As a result, they experience particular normative and structural issues the solutions to which give these organizations distinctive qualities. In Chapter 2, I examine some of the dominant organizational theories that have been used to study human service organizations. I assess the appropriateness of each theory, concluding with some thoughts about what theoretical approaches are useful to explain various aspects of these organizations.

1

The Nature of Human Service Organizations

YEHESKEL HASENFELD

The Enigma of Human Service Organizations

[handwritten margin note: ↗ school, hospitals, mental health center]

Despite the ubiquity of human service organizations in the lives of people, and their primary role in influencing our welfare and well-being, they remain an enigma. To the general public these organizations, be they schools, hospitals, mental health centers, or welfare departments, are viewed as symbols of the caring society, a manifestation of the societal obligation to the welfare and well-being of its citizens. But they are also viewed as wasteful, fostering dependency, obtrusive and controlling (Offe, 1984). These contradictions are often manifested in the organizations themselves. Public assistance, for example, serves both to alleviate misery and to deter "undeserving" poor (Handler & Hasenfeld, 1991); schools are set to educate, but spend considerable energy on discipline, often at the expense of education.

To the recipients of their services these organizations are expected to embody the values of caring, commitment to human welfare, trust, and responsiveness to human needs. They often do, but at the same time these organizations also represent formidable bureaucracies burdened by incomprehensible rules and regulations, and where services are delivered by rigid and occasionally unresponsive officials. Gross (1986, p. 139) captures these contradictions in his description of patients' encounters with the Mayo Clinic:

[handwritten margin note: org. human welfare, trust, needs vs. bureaucracy rules regulation]

> When people do come, hoping for, if not a miracle, at least help, there is a rude and quite unexpected shock. They find themselves, very soon, in

3

a large waiting room where . . . dozens of persons like themselves sit waiting hour after hour, even day after day, for their names to be called by white-clad clerks at long counters. For a place of healing, it seems to look highly bureaucratic.

Thus to the recipients human service organizations evoke hope and fear, caring and victimization, dignity and abuse.

To the human service workers these organizations reflect their own commitment and dedication to improve the quality of life of people in need, and offer them the opportunity to practice their professional and occupational skills. They provide them not only with extrinsic benefits but also with the intrinsic rewards that come from helping people. But these organizations also are a source of great frustration, by constraining them from serving their clients in accordance with their professional norms and values, by denying them the resources they need to serve their clients, by burdening them with too many rules and regulations, and by discounting their own views on the best ways to serve clients. For example, in public welfare agencies, workers who experience these contradictions may adapt in several ways: capitulate by feeling that they are doing the best they can for the "deserving" clients; identify with the clients, feeling that the agency creates barriers to meeting their needs; find a niche for themselves by assuming tasks that protect them from the contradictions; withdraw by leaving the agency; or feel victimized themselves by the organization (Sherman & Wenocur, 1983).

How can we account for the apparent incongruities inherent in human service organizations? How can we explain the disparate and contradictory experiences people have in such organizations? I propose that the answer lies, at least in part, in the distinct attributes of these organizations.

People as "Raw Material"

All organizations need raw material as input to produce their products. Human service organizations are distinguished by the fundamental fact that people are their "raw material." By using the term *raw material* in this context I do not wish to imply that the people served by these organizations are merely treated as innate objects without regard to their humanness. Nor does the term imply that the staff who work on people do so without compassion. Rather, I want to highlight the fact that the core activities of the organization are structured to process, sustain, or change people who come under its jurisdiction. For example, when the hospital admits people as patients, it signifies that they become the raw material to be worked on by the medical staff in order to cure their diseases. By designating children as students, the school certifies that they are the raw material for the teachers to work on so that they become educated. It is this *transformation process* to which people are subjected that defines them as the raw material of the organization, and it is precisely what differentiates human service organizations from other bureaucracies. I use the generic term *client* to designate people as raw material.

Having people as raw material or clients confronts human service organizations with several critical issues. As Strauss, Fargerhaugh, Suczek, and Wiener (1985, p. 9) put it, "The product being worked over, or through (!) is not inert, unless comatose or temporarily nonsentient. Two things follow: (1) the patient can react and so affect the work; (2) the patient can participate in the work itself, that is be a worker."

Human Services as Moral Work

Inherent in people work is the fact that it is also *moral work*. Every action taken on behalf of the clients represents not only some form of concrete services such as administering medication, issuing a welfare grant, or counseling the family, but also a moral judgment and statement about their social worth. This is because when we work on people who are themselves imbued with values, our own actions cannot be value neutral. Consider, for example, the fact that when a teacher gives a grade to a student it signifies not only an assessment of mastery of knowledge, but it also conveys a judgment about the student's social worth that inevitably affects one's self-identity. Similarly, when mental health professionals ascribe to their clients certain DSM-III diagnostic labels, they are not merely engaged in a technical activity, because they cannot isolate themselves and their clients from the broader social and hence moral context in which they work and live. In this context, the label conveys a statement of social worth—most likely with a negative connotation. Most importantly, the clients themselves must absorb the moral meanings of the label as a reflection of their own self-identity, which may evoke some sense of personal devaluation. As Estroff (1981) suggests, the administration of medication to the chronically mentally ill, while generally endorsed by the professionals as essential to the functioning of the patient, also has important symbolic meanings, especially that of powerlessness. As she puts it, "these long-term intrusions into clients' inside space may represent exercises of power, legitimated by medical affiliation of the treatment system, which underscore to clients their lack of control over themselves in relation to others" (Estroff, 1981, p. 116).

The very manner in which services are delivered is anchored in a moral context. Should clients be treated as objects or subjects? Who is responsible for the clients' predicament? Who has the right to treat the clients and what qualifications should they have? What clients shall have priority in receiving certain services? Should clients have a voice in deciding about how they are going to be treated? These and other questions, inescapably intertwined in the service delivery process, are not merely technical, but primarily normative and the answers to them represent moral choices. We are often quite unaware that such choices have been made. When the authority of physicians is unchallenged it is not merely a recognition of their technical superiority. It is also an implicit acceptance of their moral superiority (Katz, 1984).

There is another sense in which working on people is inherently moral. Fundamental to such work are decisions about allocation of resources to the clients. These may include money, time, and expertise. Inevitably, the demand for these resources outstrips their supply, resulting in some system of rationing (e.g., first come, first served; clients with greatest need receive priority). Rationing resources to clients is a moral act, because whatever the rationale and merit of the allocation rule may be, fundamentally it conveys an evaluation of social worth, since some clients become more deserving than others (Lipsky, 1980; Prottas, 1979).

The fact that human service organizations engage in moral work tends to be underemphasized since, understandably, our concern is with the actual services they provide. Moreover, seldom are these moral choices made explicit. Because they are embedded in the organizational routines they become part of the "invisible hand" that controls workers' behaviors and actions. Yet, I would propose that it is the moral decisions that determine and justify the actual services that clients obtain. Roth (1972), in his classical study of hospital emergency services, shows that the responsiveness of the medical staff to the patients was greatly influenced by staff perceptions of their social worth (e.g., young were more valuable than old), their assumptions of who is a deserving patient (e.g., drunks were undeserving), and what they considered legitimate demands on their work roles (e.g., emergency room pediatricians complaining about cases of sore throats and snotty noses). Intake workers at the welfare department are also guided by a moral conception of client "need." As noted by Prottas (1979), workers are obviously impressed when applicants have sick children who need a special diet, or when applicants have no place to sleep.

> But when the needs are broadly similar, there remains another sort of need that influences how much personalized attention an applicant will receive. In these roughly comparable cases differences in need reflect the applicant's apparent inability to look out for her own interests and her predilection to accept the worker's help as a gift and not merely her due. . . . Applicants who have these characteristics can generally expect a sympathetic hearing, good quality information, and even a little extra effort from the intake worker. (Prottas, 1979, p. 39)

Being perceived as "deserving" may mean the difference between receiving immediate assistance or being shunted through a bureaucratic maze.

Human Services as Gendered Work

Historically, the care of people has been entrusted to women, and the bureaucratization of human care resulted in the predominance of women as human service workers. Patriarchal ideologies "that see women as nurturers and men as providers within the family wage system rationalize the predominance of women in social welfare " (Dressel, 1987, p. 295). Women predominate in the *direct* service positions in social service agencies, while men tend to occupy administrative and authoritative positions. The same pattern holds true in health services where most positions with limited or no autonomy (e.g., nurses, physical therapists, medical technicians and health aides) are occupied by women (Butter, Carpenter, Kay, & Simmons, 1985). The picture is also replicated in the field of public education.

The fact that most of the frontline workers in human service organizations are women has profound implications on the attributes of these organizations. Ferguson (1984) argues that there is an inherent conflict between the values that women bring to their work environment and the norms of bureaucracy. While women uphold values of caregiving, empathy, nurturing, and cooperation, male dominated bureaucracies reward competition, individualism, and instrumentalism while devaluing "feminist" characteristics. As a result, women assume subordinate and dependent roles in a bureaucracy to protect themselves. According to this perspective, the structure of human service organizations not only inhibits the capacity of women to optimize their caregiving values, but also fails to reward them adequately.

Viewing human services as gendered work suggests that there may be a conflict between a "feminine" and a "masculine" orientation in human service organizations. The task of caring for people is, generally, a nonroutine activity requiring personal and nurturing ties between the caregiver and the client. Caring is done best in primary groups such as family, friends, and neighbors. When the caring function is delegated to a formal organization, there is an inevitable pressure to standardize and routinize the care for the sake of efficiency and economy (Litwak, 1985). The conflict between these two orientations is apparent, for example, in nursing homes as Litwak (1985, p. 59) points out: "If the staff members did decide to provide such individualized services, it would mean neglecting their present standardized tasks, neglecting most residents in favor of a few, and/or working well beyond the limits of a normal work day."

Yet, equating individualized care with "feminine" work and standardized and routinized care with "masculine" work is an oversimplification. Rather, there is a feminist orientation toward human services, not necessarily shared by all women, that espouses organizational values, mode of service and structure not commonly practiced in the human services. Feminist values emphasize "egalitarianism rather than hierarchy, cooperation rather than competition, nurturance rather than rugged individualism, peace rather than conflict" (Taylor, 1983, p. 445). A feminist service orientation focuses on client empowerment: giving the clients a greater sense of power and control over their life circumstances; gaining a better understanding of the broader social and political aspects of their difficult circumstances; and developing skills to use power, both individually and collectively, to change their life circumstances (Gottlieb, Chapter 14, this volume). The structure of the organization, according to the feminist orientation, should be collectivist rather than bureaucratic, participatory democracy rather than hierarchical authority and control (Hyde, 1989; Martin, 1990).

The fact that in many human services both the recipients and the frontline workers are women raises the possibility that the enigma of human service organizations may be rooted, at least in part, in the conflict between the feminist orientation and the current values, practices, and structure of these organizations. Indeed, the failure of human service organizations, especially those predominantly serving women, to embrace a feminist orientation has given rise to alternative feminist organizations especially in such areas as health, domestic violence, and personal counseling (for a discussion of these organizations see Martin, 1990; and Hyde, Chapter 6, this volume).

There is limited research on the conflicts that women as workers experience in human service organizations. Some studies on job satisfaction suggest that women are more likely to feel that their abilities are not being fully utilized in the organization (McNeely, Chapter 11, this volume); and that women give greater value to working relations than men (Himle, Jayaratne, & Chess, 1986; Neil & Snizek, 1987).

There is, however, ample evidence that women do earn appreciably less than men in comparable positions, and are underrepresented in administrative positions (Martin & Chernesky, 1989; York, Henley, & Gamble, 1985, 1987). Moreover, because most human services are female-dominated industries, their wages are appreciably lower than male-dominated industries and occupations (Baron & Newman, 1990; Tienda, Smith, & Ortiz, 1987). As a result, female-based industries have a lower social status.

Such devaluation of women's work, in general, and in human services, in particular, is further exacerbated by the fact that the clients of many human services are also women who are often poor. This is especially the case for women who fail to conform to the domestic code—single mothers who are tenuously attached to the labor force (Abramovitz, 1988). Because they are overwhelmingly poor and their number is growing, these women and their children are in desperate need of human services; yet the human services they are able to use are typically underfunded, not the least because the women are viewed as "undeserving." Thus not only are the workers in these programs undercompensated for the work they do, but they also lack adequate resources to provide the services their clients need. As a result, a vicious cycle is formed whereby lack of resources results in poor services that further reaffirm the low legitimacy of these organizations and their clients, and contributes to the devaluation of gendered work. Of course this pattern is manifested in many human services directed at both women and men who are considered deviant or dangerous (e.g., the chronically mental ill, the substance abuser, the homeless).

The Primacy of the Institutional Environment

Recognizing that human service organizations are engaged in moral and gendered work implies that they are likely to face precarious legitimacy. They must constantly seek support for their moral positions.

They do so by making references to institutionalized moral systems in their environment. That is, they adopt and uphold moral systems that are supported by significant interest groups and organizations. These may include state agencies, professional associations, other human service organizations, and various civic and political associations. In this sense, human service organizations are archetypical of "institutionalized organizations." That is, their growth and survival depends less on the technical proficiency of their work and more on their conformity with dominant cultural symbols and belief systems, that is, institutional rules (Meyer & Rowan, 1977). For human service organizations the primary sources of these institutional rules are the state and the professions. Compliance with state policies and regulations provides the legal foundation for the organization's existence, and a prerequisite to attainment of public funds. The professions, in turn, sanction the service technologies used by the organization.

Thus human service organizations are highly dependent on their institutional environment for legitimacy, and it is the key to garner other resources. Yet the institutional environment in a culturally pluralistic society is both heterogeneous and turbulent. That is, it consists of diverse interest groups upholding conflicting values and norms. Despite the hegemony of the state and the professions, they too embody competing ideologies, resulting in instability and change. Moreover, social forces such as increasing ethnic heterogeneity, the aging of the population, the entry of women into the labor force, and the introduction of new technologies all find normative expressions that contribute to turbulence in the institutional environment. Human service organizations are not only forced to make choices among competing moral systems, but also to accommodate to new ascending moral systems. What was considered an acceptable way of serving people yesterday may rapidly become unacceptable today. For example, the moral precept that gay or lesbian couples are unfit to be foster care or adoptive parents is being seriously challenged; and advances in medical technologies have produced moral dilemmas for health professionals regarding prolonging the life of the terminally ill.

Operating in a turbulent institutional environment means that human service organizations cannot take their legitimacy for granted, and are vulnerable to challenges. The state of "chronic crisis" that many human service organizations find themselves in is often attributed to fiscal uncertainties. While these may be real, typically most human services experience relatively small fluctuations in funding levels from year to year (Gronbjerg, Chapter 4, this volume). Rather, it is the symbolic process of constantly having to justify the budget and to shore up the organizational legitimacy, while satisfying contending ideologies, that generates the aura of a crisis.

At the same time, the organizations themselves, especially those in a powerful position to influence social policy, also act to shape the institutional environment by the very practices that they develop. In other words, human service organizations are also "moral entrepreneurs," influencing public conceptions via the moral categorization of their clients. For example, in contrast to traditional special education programs, the Madison (WI) School District instituted an innovative program in which the parents were viewed as "part of the solution, rather than the problem" (Handler, 1986, p. 92). That is, the parents were seen as important and active partners with the teachers in formulating and implementing educational plans for their children. Thus the school district, acting as a moral entrepreneur, was successful in altering the accepted educational conception of the role of parents.

Moral entrepreneurship, however, also occurs through the day-to-day work with clients. When the State of California instituted, under court order, the 1987 Homeless Assistance Program for welfare recipients, it required welfare workers to give priority to such applicants, and if found eligible to issue them a check to cover up to two months rent. Many welfare workers, however, resented the program not only because it increased their workload, but also because it gave the recipients a relatively large sum of money without extensive verification requirements. From their organizationally driven moral perspective, such a policy was an open-door invitation to cheating on welfare. Welfare workers tended to view the applicants as morally depraved, abusing the system to gain money they did not deserve. These perceptions provided fuel to the critics of the program who sought successfully to delegitimize it[1] (see also Lipsky, 1984).

One of the characteristics of human service organizations is that they experience cyclical legitimacy crises. The organization may be founded as a response to moral entrepreneurship, such as the community mental health movement. As the organization institutionalizes the new moral system through its service system it is gradually taken for granted and the social awareness of the problem may fade into the background. The organization may find that its legitimacy begins to erode, especially when some disappointment sets in that the social problem has not been conquered (Hirschman, 1982; Zucker, 1988), as exemplified in the limited success of integrating the chronically mentally ill into the community. Moreover, changes in the environment, such as the increasing number of homeless chronically mentally ill, may cast a new perspective on the social problem and give rise to contending moral systems that challenge the organizational legitimacy. A legitimacy crisis ensues questioning, for example, the wisdom of community-based care for the chronically mentally ill (e.g., Johnson, 1990). The organization is forced to buttress its legitimacy through renewed moral entrepreneurship and realignment of the moral system that guides its services. Having weathered the crisis, the cycle is bound to repeat itself.

Human Service Technologies as Enactment of Practice Ideologies

Working on people requires human service organizations to select technologies that are socially approved and sanctioned. These technologies must be consonant with dominant cultural beliefs about what is desirable and acceptable to do to people. Hence, the ability of the organization to select a service technology is constrained by its technological environment, namely authoritative sources of technological expertise. These may include other human service organizations, academic and research organizations, certification and accreditation agencies, and professional associations.

There is, clearly, considerable interdependence between the technological and the institutional environments. Institutional rules and enforcement agencies define and constrain the technologies that human service organizations can use, while technological innovations and developments challenge and modify existing institutional rules. Technologies ascend in importance as they gain greater legitimacy in the institutional environment. They do so through their demonstrated capacity to reinforce important values and norms. That is, they can demonstrate effectiveness and efficiency as *defined* by the institutional environment and *practiced* in the technological environment. For example, in the 1980s, efforts to reduce welfare dependency centered on mandating welfare recipients to participate in assisted job search and job clubs. These service technologies gained considerable support and were adopted by many states, because studies showed that they were low-cost technologies, modestly increased employment and earnings, and brought about welfare savings per dollar spent. These measures of effectiveness and efficiency were strongly endorsed by both federal and state legislatures, even though studies also showed that earning gains were mostly from increases in the number of welfare recipients working rather than from improved job quality, and that most recipients remained in poverty and on welfare (Gueron & Pauly, 1991).

Similarly, the use of psychotropic drugs to treat the chronically mentally ill has become the dominant mode of treatment, because they have been shown to reduce clinical relapse, the major criterion of effectiveness adopted by psychiatrists. Effects on quality of patient's life, the impact of side effects, the alternative uses of social therapy, and the feelings of the patients themselves toward the medication, while recognized as significant issues, assume only secondary—if not marginal—importance in the social validation of the technology that is dominated by the medical model (Estroff, 1981).

Organizations are likely to adopt technologies that are sanctioned by the institutional environment. Such sanctions signify the underlying merit of the technology in advancing certain social values. It is in this sense that human service technologies reflect *practice ideologies*, namely they reify certain belief systems about what is "good" for the client, and their efficacy is measured in light of these beliefs. These beliefs provide human service workers with the rationale and justification for their practices.

The attractiveness of the service technology is dependent, in part, on the degree of consensus about its merit. Such consensus is not always present, resulting in technological indeterminacy, that is, lack of certainty and predictability about the effects of the technology. Other factors also contribute to a state of indeterminacy: the knowledge needed to change human attributes, be they physical, economic or psychological, is incomplete; the attributes targeted for intervention vary from person to person; and the attributes interact with others in ways that cannot be readily isolated and controlled (Hasenfeld, 1983). Technological indeterminacy gives the organization considerable leeway in how it can choose and operationalize its own service technology. In the face of technological indeterminacy human service organizations have considerable discretion in making assumptions about the attributes of their clients and the state of their knowledge of how to serve them.

The self-reifying assumptions the organization makes about the attributes of its clients, and about the state of its knowledge and technical know-how constitute its practice ideology. Hence, the service technology is an *enactment* of the organization's practice ideology. Consider, for example, two popular social work interventions technologies, ego-psychological and cognitive. Each is based on a distinct practice ideology. According to Turner (1988), ego-psychological social work

assumes that: ego development is a process of learning and maturation; ego strength indicates neutralization of instinctual energy; people
strive for self-reliance and are rational; people can change through
broadening of coping skills and integrative abilities; the focus of
therapy is on ego functioning and defenses; and the role of the social
worker is to provide support, clarification, ventilation, and insight.
Cognitive therapy assumes that: thinking shapes behavior; individuals are rationally motivated and strive for self-actualization; the person's
nature is neither good nor bad, but can be trained in either direction; people
are highly ration- al; people can change through cognitive reorganization;
the focus of therapy is on teaching and reflective thinking; and the role of
the social worker is to point to cognitive contradictions and to do reality
testing. One can readily surmise how each practice ideology will enact a
very different service technology for people with the same psychological needs.

Similarly, different practice ideologies about nursing care will result
in distinct technologies. In some nursing homes the staff tend to assume
that their residents are all alike, and focus mostly on their common physical
needs. The technology becomes largely custodial with standardized
routines in managing the residents' daily lives. Other homes, in contrast, are more likely to acknowledge and respect the differences among
the residents, and to recognize their psychosocial needs as well. The
technology becomes more complex and treatment oriented with a mix-
ture of standardized and individualized daily management procedures
(Shield, 1988).

Finally, measures of effectiveness in human service organizations
also involve explicit or implicit moral choices that are embedded in the
practice ideologies. What is evaluated includes not only some objective
measures such as reduction in morbidity or prevention of physical
abuse, but also subjective constructs that give moral meaning to these
measures. Measuring reduction in morbidity without attention to the
quality of life of those who survive is a moral choice. Assessing the effectiveness of welfare-work programs in reducing welfare costs without consideration of the psychological costs and benefits to the mothers and their
children casts the objective measures in a particular subjectively constructed moral context. Consequently, measures of effectiveness of human services invariably emanate from the moral systems embraced by the organization (on the issues of measuring effectiveness see D'Aunno, Chapter
16, this volume).

Client Reactivity and Service Trajectory

There is another important source of technological indeterminacy that distinguishes human service organizations, having to do with the ability of the clients to react and participate in the service technology. The reactivity of the clients and their potential capacity to neutralize the effects of the service technology means that the organization cannot take for granted the processes and outcomes of its service technology, even if it is assumed to be highly determinate. The ability of the clients to respond and the need of the staff to react to these very responses is captured in the concept of *service trajectory* (Strauss et al., 1985, p. 8). It denotes not only the course of the client's problem or need itself, but also the entire social organization of the work that is done over that course. It encompasses the responses of the staff to the client as well as to each other as they work with the client; the reactions of the client and significant others (e.g., family, friends); and the subsequent responses of the staff. There are two interrelated features to the service trajectory that must be addressed: the handling of *contingencies* and the management of *client compliance.*

Contingencies arise because neither the reactions of the clients nor the responses of the staff are fully controllable. This is especially the case when (1) the client presents multiple problems or needs, (2) others in the client's social network are involved, and (3) several workers administer to the client. The primary aim of the staff, then, is to manage the contingencies in order to control the service trajectory, and to minimize unanticipated consequences. *Diagnosis* is a key mechanism to control the trajectory, because it provides the staff with a defined course of action. Diagnosis is a process of collecting and assessing information about client attributes in order to typify them into known and "normal" service categories, while discarding what are considered irrelevant attributes. As Abbott (1988, pp. 40-41) puts it, "Diagnosis not only seeks the right professional category for a client, but also removes the client's extraneous qualities. If the client is an individual, such extraneous qualities often include his or her emotional or financial relation to the 'problem.' " Abbott further suggests that the diagnostic classification is constrained by the body of knowledge adopted by the staff and by the availability of treatment schemes. Thus the diagnosis echoes these constraints, and has a reifying quality in that it establishes a set of behavioral expectations for both the clients and the workers. Only when the workers' expectations of the client are not met is the diagnosis questioned and revised.

Isolating the client from "extraneous" factors and compartmentalizing the client problems and needs are additional mechanisms to control the service trajectory. The isolation, at times, may be physical (i.e., hospital, prison), but most likely it is social and psychological. Such isolation takes place by limiting the ability of the client to introduce social relations and attributes not deemed relevant into the service process. For example, students may learn early on that problems at home are of tangential interest to their teachers who isolate these problems from the students' academic performance.

Compartmentalization of the client's needs means that each worker can specialize by attending to a limited set of client attributes, while delegating to other workers client concerns and issues that are not perceived to be within their purview. The total service trajectory becomes fragmented into distinct subtrajectories, each more readily controllable than the whole.

Client Compliance

Clients must be controlled so that their reactions do not neutralize the effects of the technology, and indeed are appropriate and supportive of the workers' activities on their behalf. In many instances the success of the technology hinges on the very active involvement of the clients in their treatment as in the case of renal dialysis. How to achieve client compliance becomes a major concern in managing the service trajectory. Control is initiated at the point of entry by selecting clients who are viewed as amenable to the service technology and by "cooling out" those who are deemed undesirable. For example, a study by Shuptrine and Grant (1988) found that, on the average, 27% of all applications to AFDC in 1985-1986 were denied. Of these denials, 60% were classified as "failure to comply with procedural requirements," and only 21% were due to "excess income." Because states are under federal pressure to reduce eligibility error rates, it is to the advantage of welfare workers to err in the direction of denial of eligibility when applicants fail to conform to strict verification requirements (see also Brodkin, 1986). Control is also exercised through "tracking" the clients into various service trajectories, that, in turn, limit and constrain their options. When teachers track students into "academic," "general," and "vocational" tracks they do so ostensibly to optimize the match between the students' capabilities and the school curricula. However, at the same time, tracking enables teachers to exercise considerable control over the students by "homogenizing" their classrooms, reinforcing their own educational expectations, and narrowing the students' future options (Rosenbaum, 1976).

Once embarked on a service trajectory, various compliance strategies may be employed ranging from constraints to inducements and persuasion (Gamson, 1968). The choice of strategies reflects not only the nature of the technology itself but also the organizational practice ideologies, especially the assumptions staff make about the moral status and the determinants of the behavior of their clients. Yet compliance is never fully assured and, therefore, the service trajectory cannot be completely controlled, thus introducing an element of uncertainty into the technology even when it is quite standard and routine.

In this context it is important to note that by exercising control over their clients, human service organizations also undertake a broader social control function by reinforcing socially sanctioned client roles. That is, by attempting to obtain client compliance with the requirements of its service technology, the organization also signals to its clients what it considers acceptable and desirable behavior on their part. For example, Lorber (1975) found that medical staff responded more favorably to patients who were submissive, uncomplaining and respectful. In doing so, they reinforced a professionally sanctioned conception of the "good patient." Similarly, the tracking of students reinforces cultural conceptions of the "good" student (Kilgore, 1991). By assuming such a social control function, the organization pays homage to the moral systems it adopts to garner and maintain its legitimacy.

The Centrality of Client-Worker Relations

It should become apparent from the discussion thus far that client-worker relations are at the core of human service organizations. These relations are the *primary vehicle* through which information about the client is obtained, assessment of need is made, services are delivered, client responses are evaluated, and client compliance is attained. The quality of client-worker relations becomes paramount when any one —or more—of these conditions exist: (1) clients must have continuous contact with the organization; (2) the technology requires extensive penetration into the client's biographical time and space; (3) interpersonal relations are a major mode of intervention; and (4) the stakes of the intervention are high—it can alter dramatically the client's welfare or well-being.

When any of these conditions prevail, the effectiveness of client-worker relations hinges on their ability to generate client cooperation. From both the perspectives of the organization and the clients, the best form of cooperation is that which is based on *trust.* Cooperation that arises from either fear or manipulation of rewards is neither stable nor efficient. It requires the organization and the clients to maintain constant vigilance and to expend considerable resources in maintaining it. In contrast, cooperation based on trust is more stable and once attained it is intrinsically rewarding.

Trust is an elusive concept. According to Baier (1986), trust means that I rely on the goodwill of another person, which makes me vulnerable to the limits of that goodwill. Such vulnerability creates the potential of being harmed by the other person, yet the essence of trust is that I have confidence that this will not happen. I am willing to put myself in such a state of vulnerability because I need the resources that the other person controls.

In the organizational context, trust tends to be *impersonal,* in the sense that it is based on limited and sporadic contact between clients and organizational agents (e.g., social workers, physicians) who, most importantly, do not share other social ties (Shapiro, 1987). To develop trust in this type of social relationship two important and interrelated issues must be addressed: (a) discretion and (b) power (Handler, 1990). Staff discretion in endemic in human service organizations precisely because the delivery of the services is dependent on client-worker relations. As Lipsky (1980) eloquently points out, discretion cannot be purged even when the organization enunciates detailed rules and regulations. This is because the workers control the flow and interpretation of information (in both directions) between the clients and the organization, and the organization has limited independent capacity to verify the validity of the information transmitted by the workers to either the clients or superiors in the organization. Indeed, the more rules and regulations the organization promulgates the greater the opportunities for the workers to deviate from them, and the greater the difficulty of monitoring them.

Discretion means that the clients become dependent on the goodwill of the workers, and thus vulnerable to abuse. Although administrative due process is designed to protect clients from abuse, Handler (1986) has shown convincingly that reliance on due process to curb discretion is unworkable, especially when clients are dependent on the workers for resources they need and they must transact with the workers on a continuous basis.

This points to a second feature of the social relationship that impersonal trust attempts to regulate—power. By their very nature, human service organizations have considerable power over their clients, because the organization controls vital resources needed by the clients while they, as individuals, seldom control the resources needed by the organization (Hasenfeld, 1987). Such power advantage is translated into an asymmetry of power between workers and clients and is the ultimate basis for client compliance. Such asymmetry is expressed in the workers' control of information, expertise, and access to needed resources.

Human service organizations often rely on a *contract* to regulate these unequal power relations. As Shapiro (1987, p. 632) notes,

> Contracts enunciate the principal's preferences and priorities, disclose the responsibilities and obligations of the agents, explicitly state the procedures agents are to follow and the decision rules they are to employ (thereby limiting agent discretion), plan for contingencies, create incentives for contractual compliance, and specify sanctions to be imposed if agreements are not kept.

But I have already noted that the very nature of work on people makes it next to impossible to explicitly enunciate the conditions of the contract, and it suffers from the same limitations as administrative due process safeguards. Contract also assumes a certain degree of power balance that normally does not exist in client-worker relations.

Thus the development of trusting client-worker relations is seen as the fundamental safeguard and a sign that the worker's power advantage will not be abused. Yet the difficulty with trust is that it can be "blind," that is, the powerless clients are expected to trust the workers because the workers are experts, occupy positions of authority, and subscribe to a code of ethics—in short, because they are indeed in a powerful and privileged position. It is easy, and often expected, to attribute trust to persons in socially sanctioned powerful positions. Katz (1984) describes how physicians prefer what he terms "trust in silence," that is, the willingness of the patient to trust that the physician will make the right decisions without the need for conversation or dialogue.

Therefore, the *basis* for the trust becomes an important consideration in assessing the quality of client-worker relations. Baier (1986) distinguishes between morally decent and morally rotten trust. The former is based on the notion that knowing each other's motives for participating in the relationship will strengthen the entrusting qualities of the relationship. As Handler (1990, p. 103) puts it, such trust arises when "there are mutual respect, common bond, genuine listening, and openness." The problem in developing such trust is that it requires highly personalized relations in an organizational context that, by definition, constrains their development. There are different degrees to which human services organizations can structure their client-worker relations to encourage personalized relationships. Handler (1990) suggests three factors: professional norms that advocate active participation by clients; a service technology whose success hinges on client involvement; and financial incentives that reward the workers (and the organization) for treating clients as subjects rather than objects. Such conditions, however, are not readily enacted. Professional norms may be mostly symbolic and ceremonial; what is defined as success is organizationally constructed; and human services are seldom dependent directly on clients for fiscal resources.

As Shapiro (1987, p. 635) argues "the principles of impersonal trust are vulnerable and impotent," again, because the clients interact with organizational agents whose ability to develop highly personalized relations, needed for morally decent trust, is restricted. Indeed, there may be good reasons to curb personalized relationships in client-worker interactions because they can undermine other important values such as equality of access and treatment, universalism, unbiased judgment, and protection from favoritism. One of the chief strengths of formal organizations is their ability to purge particularism (Perrow, 1986). Encouraging personalized relationships to promote trust heightens the risk, always present, that particularism will take precedence.

In response to this dilemma, human service organizations are embedded in a complex system of internal and external control mechanisms whose purpose is to guard the trustworthiness *and* fairness of the workers' relations with their clients. These include internal mechanisms such as socialization, standard operating procedures, and norms about workers' conduct, record keeping and monitoring and supervision. External mechanisms may include professional accreditation, governmental regulations, liability insurance, and auditing. In general these mechanisms seem to guard impersonal trust reasonably well. Yet, as Shapiro (1988, p. 651) points out, "By increasing agent liability for failure of trust, we foster self-protective acts—unnecessary tests or surgery, unwarranted conservatism." In human service organizations these also include excessive paper work, bureaucratic rigidity, and some degree of distancing from the clients.

In the final analysis, a necessary though not sufficient condition for morally decent trust to emerge is the existence of some degree of power balance between clients and workers (Hasenfeld, 1987). That is, the well-being of the worker is enhanced by investing in the well-being of the client and vice versa. It is such mutual dependence that is most likely to foster mutual respect and trust. That this condition does not normally exist in human service organizations attests to the difficulty in relying on trust to protect the clients. It also explains why the quality of human services is highly stratified by the relative power that clients possess, and it is a key to understanding the enigma of human service organizations.

Note

1. Based on material prepared by Melinda Bird, Western Center on Law and Poverty, December, 1989.

References

Abbott, A. (1988). *The system of professions*. Chicago: University of Chicago Press.

Abramovitz, M. (1988). *Regulating the lives of women: Social welfare policy from colonial times to the present*. Boston: South End.

Baier, A. (1986). Trust and antitrust. *Ethics, 96*, 231-260.

Baron, J. N., & Newman, A. E. (1990). For what it's worth: Organizations, occupations, and the value of work. *American Sociological Review, 55*, 155-175.

Brodkin, E. (1986). *The false promise of administrative reform: Implementing quality control in welfare*. Philadelphia: Temple University Press.

Butter, I., Carpenter, E., Kay, B., & Simmons, R. (1985). *Sex and status: Hierarchies in the health workforce*. Washington, DC: American Public Health Association.

Dressel, P. L. (1987). Patriarchy and social welfare work. *Social Problems, 34*, 294-309.

Estroff, S. E. (1981). *Making it crazy*. Berkeley: University of California Press.

Ferguson, K. (1984). *The feminist case against bureaucracy*. Philadelphia: Temple University Press.

Gamson, W. (1968). *Power and discontent*. Homewood, IL: Dorsey Press.

Gross, E. (1986). "Waiting for Mayo." *Urban Life, 15*, 139-164.

Gueron, J. M., & Pauly, E. (1991). *From welfare to work*. New York: Russell Sage.

Handler, J. (1990). *Law and the search for community*. Philadelphia: University of Pennsylvania Press.

Handler, J. (1986). *The conditions of discretion*. New York: Russell Sage.

Handler, J., & Hasenfeld, Y. (1991). *The moral construction of poverty.* Newbury Park, CA: Sage.

Hasenfeld, Y. (1983). *Human service organizations.* Englewood Cliffs, NJ: Prentice-Hall.

Hasenfeld, Y. (1987). Power in social work practice. *Social Service Review, 61,* 469-483.

Himle, D., Jayaratne, S. D., & Chess, W. A. (1986). Gender differences in work stress among clinical social workers. *Journal of Social Service Research, 10,* 41-56.

Hirschman, A. O. (1982). *Shifting involvements: Private interest and public action.* Princeton, NJ: Princeton University Press.

Hyde, C. (1989). A feminist model for macro-practice: Promises and problems. *Administration in Social Work, 13,* 145-182.

Johnson, A. B. (1990). *Out of Bedlam: The truth about deinstitutionalization.* New York: Basic Books.

Katz, J. (1984). *The silent world of doctor and patient.* New York: Free Press.

Kilgore, S. (1991). The organizational context of tracking in schools. *American Sociological Review, 56,* 189-203.

Lipsky, M. (1980). *Street-level bureaucracy.* New York: Russell Sage.

Lipsky, M. (1984). Bureaucratic disentitlement in social welfare programs. *Social Service Review, 58,* 3-27.

Litwak, E. (1985). *Helping the elderly: The complementary roles of informal networks and formal systems.* New York: Columbia University Press.

Lorber, J. (1975). Good patients and problem patients: Conformity and deviance in a general hospital. *Journal of Health and Social Behavior, 16,* 213-225.

Martin, P. Y. (1990). Rethinking feminist organizations. *Gender & Society, 4,* 182-206.

Martin, P. Y., & Chernesky, R. H. (1989). Women's prospects for leadership in social welfare: A political economy perspective. *Administration in Social Work, 13,* 117-143.

Meyer, J., & Rowan, B. (1977). Institutionalized organizations: Formal structure as myth and ceremony. *American Journal of Sociology, 83,* 340-363.

Neil, C., & Snizek, W. E. (1987). Work values, job characteristics, and gender. *Sociological Perspectives, 30,* 245-265.

Offe, C. (1984). *Contradictions of the welfare state.* Cambridge: MIT Press.

Perrow, C. (1986). *Complex organizations: A critical essay* (3rd ed.). New York: Random House.

Prottas, J. (1979). *People-processing.* Lexington, MA: D. C. Heath.

Rosenbaum, J. (1976). *Making inequality.* New York: John Wiley.

Roth, J. A. (1972). Some contingencies of the moral evaluation and control of clientele: The case of the hospital emergency room. *American Journal of Sociology, 77,* 839-856.

Shapiro, S. (1987). The social control of impersonal trust. *American Journal of Sociology, 93,* 623-658.

Sherman, W. R., & Wenocur, S. (1983). Empowering public welfare workers through mutual support. *Social Work, 28,* 375-379.

Shield, R. R. (1988). *Uneasy endings: Daily life in an American nursing home.* Ithaca, NY: Cornell University Press.

Shuptrine, S., & Grant, V. (1988). *The relationship of the reasons for denial of AFDC/Medicaid benefits to the uninsured in the U.S.* Columbia, SC: Sarah Shuptrine & Associates.

Strauss, A., Fargerhaugh, S., Suczek, B., & Wiener, C. (1985). *Social organization of medical work.* Chicago: University of Chicago Press.

Taylor, V. (1983). The future of feminism in the 1980s: A social movement analysis. In L. Richardson & V. Taylor (Eds.), *Feminist frontiers: Rethinking sex, gender and society.* Reading, MA: Addison-Wesley.

Tienda, M., Smith, S., & Ortiz, V. (1987). Industrial restructuring, gender segregation, and sex differences in earnings. *American Sociological Review, 52,* 195-210.

Turner, F. (1988). *Social work practice theories: A comparison of selected attributes.* Cleveland, OH: Case Western Reserve University, Mandel School of Applied Behavioral Science.

York, R. O., Henley, C. H., & Gamble, D. N. (1987). Sexual discrimination in social work: Is it salary or advancement? *Social Work, 32,* 336-340.

York, R. O., Henley, C. H., & Gamble, D. N. (1985). Barriers to the advancement of women in social work administration. *Journal of Social Service Research, 9,* 1-15.

Zucker, L. (1988). Where do institutional patterns come from? Organizations as actors in social systems. In L. Zucker (Ed.), *Institutional patterns and organizations* (pp. 23-52). Cambridge, MA: Ballinger.

CHAPTER 2

Theoretical Approaches to Human Service Organizations

YEHESKEL HASENFELD

Considering the complexities of human services as a class of organizations, what theoretical approaches are best suited for their study? Morgan (1986) suggests that theories on organizations arise from the images or metaphors we have about them. Yet, these metaphors produce a limited and partial picture of the organization. As a result, the theories themselves, while claiming to be encompassing, only provide a partial, if not biased, understanding of the organization. Such images range from viewing the organization as a rational instrument designed to achieve specific goals to a system determined and driven by powerful environmental forces.

My intention is not to review all the theoretical perspectives on organizations (for such a review, see Perrow, 1986; Scott, 1987), but rather to focus on those that have been particularly salient in the analysis of human service organizations. In reflecting on these theories it is especially useful to consider the assumptions they make about two interrelated issues: The first pertains to the relations between the organization and its environment. Theories vary in their assumptions about the openness of the organization toward its environment, and the impact of the latter on the internal structure and processes of the organization. The second issue refers to the degree to which the organization can control its own destiny. Assumptions range from viewing the organization as purposefully designed system; as an adaptive system; or as a system whose attributes are primarily determined by forces beyond its control (see Astley & Van de Ven, 1983). The theories to be reviewed can be classified along these two axes, as shown in Table 2.1.

Table 2.1 Classification of Organizational Theories

Control of Destiny	Relation to Environment	
	Closed	Open
Purposeful	Rational-Legal	Contingency Theory
Adaptive	Human Relations	Negotiated Order, Political Economy
Reactive		Marxist Theory, Institutional Theory, Population-Ecology

The Rational-Legal Model

The classical image of the organization is that of a goal-oriented, purposefully designed machine. Morgan (1986, pp. 22-23) reminds us that the origin of the word *organization* is derived from the Greek *organon*, which means a tool or instrument. In this theoretical perspective, it is assumed that organizations have a clear and specific set of goals and that the internal structure and processes represent a rational design to attain them. The design is *rational* because the internal division of labor, the definitions of role positions, and the distribution of authority are highly formalized and hierarchical, and can be shown to be the most effective and efficient *means* to achieve the organization's aims. The design is *legal* because the assignments to positions, the distribution of authority, and the rights and duties of each position are based on impersonal rules that are applied universally. Both Taylor's "scientific management" and Weber's model of the rational-legal bureaucracy exemplify such a design. Rationality can be maintained because the organization is viewed as insulated from or functioning in a highly stable environment, its goals are explicit, and the behavior of its staff is fully determined by their formal role prescriptions.

There are many examples in the human services where attempts are made to put such a model of organizations into practice. In my field study of the implementation of work programs for welfare recipients, I found that the implementors assumed a rational model. Having defined a specific set of goals—placing welfare recipients in educational and training programs in order to make them employable—they then developed a careful flowchart of how recipients should be processed through the system, specifying the precise decision rules workers were to follow. They wrote an elaborate manual of procedures that detailed the role of the case managers, and what standard operating procedures they had to follow. A very elaborate management information system was developed to keep track of the clients and of every decision made by the workers, assuring accountability. Clear lines of authority were enunciated. Viewed as a whole, the design seemed to be logically driven by the aim of the program.

In actuality, many elements of the design were put into effect and could be shown to produce some of the desired outputs. However, several limitations of the rational design became quite apparent. External political pressures forced the implementors to contract out the case management, making the delivery of services cumbersome and burdensome. Periodic legislative changes and reduced funding resulted in ambiguities about rules and procedures. Vagueness and disagreements about the goals of the program—emphasis on education versus placement in jobs—resulted in inconsistent operating policies. Uncertainties about availability of services forced case managers to make ad hoc decisions. Difficulties with uncooperative recipients gave rise to informal procedures of handling them, not consonant with the manual. And despite an extensive system of monitoring, the validity and reliability of the information was highly affected by how the case managers and the recipients perceived the situation.

The rational model cannot handle such key factors as the multiple and changing influences of the environment; amorphous and conflicting goals; indeterminate technology; informal relations both among staff and between staff and clients; and constraints on accountability and authority. Especially troublesome are the empirical findings that organizations develop informal structures and relations that could not be accounted for by the formal division of labor, lines of authority, and role prescriptions. Indeed, these informal relations not only supplement but may even deviate from the prescribed and proscribed relations. Studies of mental hospitals, for example, showed that complex and *adaptive* social relationships develop both among the staff and among the patients as well as between the staff and the patients. These relations were formed because the participants needed to adapt to the work situations they encountered as well as to each other's experiences, interests, feelings, values, and norms. Belknap (1956) noted how in the state mental hospital (prior to psychotropic drugs), the attendants assumed most of the management of the patients, even though they were the least educated and the lowest paid. They typically had very negative attitudes toward the patients and often brutalized them. Goffman (1961) described how patients developed their own social organization and "deviant" culture within the hospital to cope with the extensive controls imposed on them. Caudill (1958) described the hospital ward as a "small society" in which staff and patients develop attachments and subtle patterns of communications. When these are disturbed or blocked, patients react by showing signs of regression.

The Human Relations Approach

One theory accounting for the existence of an informal structure has been the human relations school. It emphasizes that job requirements and conditions of work have profound psychological consequences on the staff, especially in terms of their ability to fulfill their own needs (ranging from physical to self-actualization). These, in turn, influence their attitudes toward their work and their co-workers, and ultimately affect how they perform their jobs (Porter, Lawler, & Hackman, 1975). The underlying assumption is that organizational effectiveness is a function of the complementarity and congruency between the goals of the organization and the personal needs of the workers (Argyris, 1962).

There is an accompanying assumption in the human relations school that states that the nature and quality of the organization's leaders are important determinants of the performance and job satisfaction of their subordinates (for a review, see Bargal & Schmid, 1989). Glisson (1989) showed that the power, maturity, and intelligence of the leader influence workers' commitment to the organization. In general, it is assumed that leadership that promotes a democratic atmosphere in the organization will improve workers' productivity.

The human relations approach is particularly important in the human services since it is assumed that the attitudes of the staff to their work situation and their co-workers will have direct consequences to how they relate to their own clients. Eisenstat and Felner (1983) found that mental health settings that created fewer stimulating job environments for their staff also tended to create less stimulating environments for their clients. It is understood that when staff feel alienated, when their personal needs are not met by the organization, and when they are dissatisfied with their job, they will take it out on their clients. This is often labeled as "burnout," namely, the workers become detached and withdrawn from their clients, postpone client contacts, and assume cynical, negative, and inflexible attitudes toward them (see, for example, Cherniss, 1980; Freudenberger, 1980; Maslach & Pines, 1979). The research on "burnout" does seem to support the notion that job satisfaction is associated with jobs that provide autonomy, participation, challenge, promotional opportunities and financial rewards (see Jayaratne & Chess, 1983; Pines & Aronson, 1988).

The linkage between the well-being of the staff and of the clients is an important contribution of the human relations approach. As I have suggested, the core work of human service organization occurs through client-worker relations, and undoubtedly the quality of these relations is influenced by the morale and job satisfaction of the workers. There is also good evidence to suggest that job satisfaction is influenced by the nature of the task and the degree to which workers participate in the decisions affecting their work (see, for example, Glisson & Durick, 1988; Whiddon & Martin, 1989). Leadership also seems to play a significant role in workers' satisfaction.

Nonetheless, the human relations approach suffers from some fundamental limitations, mostly because its level of analysis is social- psychological. The organization is still viewed mostly as a closed system, and the impact of the environment on structure and processes is relegated mainly to the recognition that leaders and workers bring into the organization their own personal dispositions and predilections. Most problematic is the potentially misplaced emphasis on the psychological needs of the workers and on democratic participation as determinants of organizational effectiveness. These factors may pale in the face of strong environmental factors such as political and economic constraints. It is hard to imagine, for example, that democratic participation is going to alter significantly those features of the welfare department that workers find especially alienating such as extensive paper work, inability to respond to the many dire needs of the applicants, pressure to reduce error rates, low wages, and poor working conditions. Nor is it always possible, given the nature of the technology of the organization, to create job conditions that provide for autonomy, creativity, and promotional opportunities. Studies of home care workers, for example, indicate how the inherent attributes of the work itself—low skill, part-time, isolated—coupled with poor wages and benefits create low morale and high turnover. Moreover, demonstration projects to improve the conditions of home care work through job enrichment and training and supervision, while having beneficial results, ultimately failed to alter the organization of home care work because of the basic economic and political forces controlling the home care industry (Feldman, 1990).

Contingency Theory

Shifting the focus from a social-psychological emphasis to a structural perspective, while addressing the limitations of the rational-legal model, researchers have formulated a contingency theory of organizations (Lawrence & Lorsch, 1967; Thompson, 1967). Viewing the organization as an open system, the importance of the environment and the technology on the structure of the organization are recognized. The fundamental assumption is that the effectiveness of the organization is a function of the congruency between its internal structure and the exigencies presented by the environment and technology. That is, there is no one universal effective design as the rational-legal theory or human relations approach would have it, and an effective design must respond to the contingencies presented by these two external conditions.

The environment, consisting mostly of other organizations, varies both in terms of its stability and heterogeneity. A stable and homogeneous environment requires limited unit differentiation and standardized rules while a turbulent and heterogeneous environment requires high unit differentiation and decentralized decision making (Thompson, 1967, pp. 72-73). There is some limited empirical evidence from the human services to suggest that this proposition is at least plausible (e.g., Aldrich, 1979; Leifer & Huber, 1977; Turk, 1977).

Similarly, the effectiveness of the organization's technical system hinges on the design of work units that respond to the technological contingencies. Technologies vary by their task difficulty and variability. These dimensions generate four types of technologies—routine, craft, engineering, and nonroutine (Perrow, 1967). Each technology has different requirements in terms of worker's discretion, power, coordination, and interdependence. The appropriate organizational structure for each of these technologies, respectively, is formal and centralized, decentralized, flexible and centralized, and flexible and polycentered. Again, the empirical evidence from the human services gives some limited credence to this idea (for a review, see Scott, 1990).

The difficulty with contingency theory is its static and mechanistic orientation. The association between environment, technology, and structure is quite dynamic and is mediated by many factors, not the least of which are the ideological, political and economic interests of groups (including clients) within and without the organization. These interests influence organizational choices regarding interactions and exchanges with various elements in the environment (Pfeffer & Salancik, 1978). Moreover, in the case of human service technologies, I have emphasized how they represent enactments of practice ideologies. Thus it is quite possible that internal power relations and negotiations (i.e., structure) within the organization actually determine the nature of the technology (see Glisson, Chapter 9, this volume).

Negotiated Order

An alternative to the contingency theory is to view the organization as a dynamic system in which the nature of the work is evolving and changing, and the structures that emerge to handle the work are a temporal reflection of the "negotiated order" among different actors (staff and clients) who participate in the work (Strauss, Fargerhaugh, Suczek, & Wiener, 1985). Because much of the theoretical model was developed through research on hospitals, it has particular import to the understanding of human services in general. The work that the organization has to do on its clients is a fundamental building block for understanding its evolving structural characteristics. The work, as we have seen, is multifaceted; in the hospital, for example, it includes machine work, safety work, body work, information work, and comfort work—to name a few. While such work has objective attributes (e.g., measuring body fluids, administering medication) it is also, as I noted earlier, socially constructed (e.g., who gets priority, how to interpret the client's reactions). Moreover, such work requires the coordinated participation of various workers who have different levels of training and competence, different values and interests. Also, as work is being done it affects the service trajectory and hence the nature of subsequent work.

"Negotiation enters into how work is defined, as well as how to do it, how much of it to do, who is to do it, how to evaluate it, how and when to reassess it and so on" (Strauss et al., 1985, p. 267). These negotiations are influenced not only by the requirements of the tasks and the skills to carry them out, but also by the interests, ideologies, and social and professional affiliations of the workers and their clients. That is, these negotiations are embedded in the broader social worlds of these actors. These social worlds "include occupational worlds (medicine, physics), ethnic worlds, leisure worlds (ski, tennis), industrial worlds (chemical, oil), and so on (Strauss et al., 1985, p. 287). It is in this sense that the organization is seen as an open system. How the work is done represents the key processes of the organization, and the emerging, yet evolving negotiated order represents its structure.

There is much to be commended by this model of human service organizations, especially because it was developed in such a context. In this approach the clients are prominently included as significant actors. The emphasis on work on people and its socially constructed dimensions is also a significant contribution. The idea that the division of labor reflects processes of negotiations among workers with different skills, ideologies, and occupational affiliations is equally important.

Nonetheless, concepts such as "social world," and "negotiated order" remain quite vague and undifferentiated. The theory focuses on micro-level processes, since the emphasis remains on negotiations among individual actors. At this level the organization qua organization remains understated. Viewed from a macro-level perspective it is clear that organizations develop structures and enforce patterns of interactions that greatly limit the content and nature of these negotiations. Moreover, while the model is of an open system, the role of the environment remains underdeveloped.

Political Economy

The focus on the interactions between the organization and its environment and their effect on its internal dynamics is the cornerstone of the political-economy perspective (Wamsley & Zald, 1976). It recognizes that for the organization to survive and produce its services it must garner two fundamental types of resources: (a) legitimacy and power (i.e., political); and (b) production resources (i.e., economic). I have already indicated how legitimacy is indispensable to the survival of the organization, and power is the means by which authority and influence are distributed in the organization. Production resources (e.g., money, clients, personnel) are essential for establishing and operating the organization's service delivery system and for setting the organization's incentive system.

The political-economy perspective highlights the importance of the environment, especially the task environment, in shaping the organization's service delivery system. The task environment refers to other organizations and interest groups (including clients) who have a potential stake in the organization either because they control important resources needed by it, or because it can advance their own interests. A key feature of the theory is the notion of *resource dependence* (Pfeffer & Salancik, 1978): It proposes that the greater the dependence of the organization on resources controlled by an external element, the greater the influence of that element on the organization. For example, since hospitals are quite dependent on Medicare payments, they must accept the constraints imposed on them by the prospective payment system (i.e., Diagnosis-Related Groups). This has a significant effect on the delivery of medical services, such as the reduction in the length of stay for the elderly.

Moreover, because it is imperative for the organization to ensure a stable flow of external resources while preserving its autonomy as much as possible, it engages in a variety of strategies, ranging from competition to cooptation, to manage its external environment (Benson,

1975). These, in turn, will influence the service delivery system of the organization. For example, it is quite common for social service agencies to obtain governmental contracts to deliver services such as child protection, drug counseling, and mental health case management. To secure these contracts the agencies may undertake several strategies, including "creaming" clients that can demonstrate positive outcomes, using unpaid or low paid staff to save on costs, and including on their board of directors influential persons (Kramer & Grossman, 1987). Most importantly, the handling of the clients themselves is part of the organizational strategy to manage its external relations (Hasenfeld, 1972). The organization may be concerned that it attracts too few clients and embark on a major public relations campaign; or it may find that it attracts "inappropriate" clients and engage in a form of "dumping" (Kramer & Grossman, 1987, pp. 49-50). Thus, as argued by Pfeffer and Salancik (1978, p. 39), "the underlying premise of the external perspective on organizations is that organizational activities and outcomes are accounted for by the context in which the organization is embedded."

Power and economic relations within the organization determine how the service technology is implemented and how decision-making authority is distributed among organizational units. The relative power and control over resources that any organizational unit possesses is, by and large, a function of the importance of the unit in managing the organization's external environment. For example, in their research on universities Salancik and Pfeffer (1974) found that the best predictors of departmental power were, first, its ability to obtain external funding, followed by the number of graduate students, and national ranking. Thus the negotiated order model, discussed above, can be more appropriately explained from this macro perspective.

The political-economy perspective makes a major contribution to our understanding of how the service delivery systems of human service organizations are influenced by both external and internal political and economic forces. Given the high dependence of human service organizations on their external environment, the model is especially cogent in explaining how adaptive strategies to cope with such dependence have major impact on organizational structure and processes. The model also recognizes clients as a significant resource and as a potential interest group, and can make predictions about how the organization will respond to its clients on the basis of the power and resources they possess (Hasenfeld, 1987).

Nonetheless, the political-economy perspective tends to understate the importance of values and ideologies that transcend calculations of power and money in shaping organizational behavior. This is especially problematic in the case of human service organizations where values and ideologies play a key role. As noted earlier, the importance of the institutional environment and the belief systems adopted by members of the organization cannot be overemphasized.

Marxist Theory

Shifting the emphasis to the environment has generated several theories—Marxist, institutional, and population-ecology—that essentially assume environmental determinism. The Marxist approach views organizations, including human services, as *tools* of the capitalist market economy—an economic system based on private ownership of the means of production and market transactions of labor. The owners (i.e., capitalists) are interested in maximizing their accumulation of wealth through the appropriation of surplus value of labor. Surplus value of labor represents the difference between the value produced by labor and the wages it receives. The appropriation of such surplus value is done through the capitalists' ownership of the means of production. To maximize profits, capitalists try to monopolize the means of production while reducing the cost of labor, and they use their accumulated wealth to achieve these aims. In such an economic system, the basic feature of organizations is the control of labor through hierarchy, standard operating procedures, and deskilling of jobs (Braverman, 1974; Edwards, 1979).

Human service organizations are not necessarily designed to produce surplus value, but they still exhibit these attributes because they are "embedded in the structure of capitalist economic criteria" (Clegg & Dunkerley, 1980, p. 488). Accordingly, human service workers lack significant voice or control over the conditions of their work; they are subject to extensive bureaucratic controls; and their jobs are often deskilled (on deskilling of social service jobs, see Pecora & Austin, 1983). Interestingly, the feminist critique of human service organizations paints a similar picture, but attributes it to patriarchal rather than capitalist domination.

More importantly from the Marxist perspective, the state develops human services having several distinct functions in order to support such an economic system. First, they provide benefits, albeit begrudgingly, to labor to ensure a healthy and complacent working class (Offe,

1984). Second, they contribute to the profitability of the capitalists by subsidizing the social benefits that the capitalists would have had to provide to maintain control over labor (O'Connor, 1973). Third, they assume a social control function by marking as deviant and isolating those who might present a threat to the capitalist economic systems (Piven & Cloward, 1971). Thus both the functions and structure of human service organizations are said to be determined by the capitalist market economy, and the interests of the capitalists to preserve their privileged position.

The contribution of the Marxist perspective is in drawing attention to the macro functions of human service organizations in a social system dominated by a capitalist market economy, and how developments and changes in such an economy affect the nature of these organizations (see, for example, Quadagno, 1988). However, the Marxist vision of how such a market economy operates is highly debatable. Moreover, the market economy is only one of several environmental influences over the evolution of human service organizations. Others include competing ideological systems, political interests, electoral dynamics, and the state bureaucracy (see, for example, Weir, Orloff, & Skocpol, 1988).

More problematic is the Marxist view of the structure of human service organizations. Undoubtedly, there are some organizations that fit the Marxist image; this is especially true for those organizations that process the deviant and the poor (e.g., public assistance, child protective services, prisons). There are many others that do not correspond to such an image. In both instances, the reasons for the different structures, as noted above, are more rooted in the complex political economy to which these organizations must adapt than in the simple notion of capitalists' domination.

Institutional Theory

Previously I noted the inadequacy of the political-economy model in addressing the role of both societal and organizational values and norms. The institutional school makes them the driving force of its theory. It proposes that the structure of certain classes of organizations, such as human services, is determined not by technology but by *rules* emanating from the *institutional* environment. Meyer and Rowan (1977, p. 343) put it this way: "Many of the positions, policies, programs and procedures of modern organizations are enforced by public opinion, by the views of important constituencies, by knowledge legitimated through the educational system, by social prestige, by the laws, and by the definitions of negligence and prudence used by the courts." I have already introduced the concept of the institutional environment by noting that key sources of institutionalized rules in modern society are the state, the professions and public opinion.

DiMaggio and Powell (1983) also propose that institutional rules emanate from the network of organizations that constitute an "industry" such as the mental health industry. In such an industry there is hierarchy and dominance, and organizations emulate the practices of the authoritative and powerful organizations in the industry. Moreover, as Zucker (1988) points out, organizations are also an important source of institutionalization when they successfully create new practices or structures. In the human services, this is often manifested in what I have termed *moral entrepreneurship.*

Institutional theorists assume that because organizations want to survive they are forced to uphold these institutional rules because they are the sources of legitimacy, and the avenues to obtain resources. DiMaggio and Powell (1983) suggest three processes by which this is accomplished: (a) coercive, through state and legal forces such as the accreditation of hospitals; (b) imitative or mimetic, following the example of successful organizations such as the adoption of curricula of effective schools; and (c) normative, the transmission of professional norms such as the use of DSM-III by mental health organizations. These processes result in institutional isomorphism. Meyer, Scott, Strang, and Creighton (1988) present data on the increased bureaucratization, formalization and standardization of the U.S. public school systems that they attribute not to centralization of funding but rather to societal forces such as the professionalization of teaching, pursuit of educational equality as a national norm, and the rise of national standards about the proper credentials of teachers and classroom curriculum. Thus institutional isomorphism leads to considerable structural similarity and homogeneity among the organizations in the same industry.

Meyer and Rowan (1983) argue that when institutional rules are embedded in the structure of the organization, the latter becomes decoupled from the actual work or service technology. In the case of schools, for example, the formation of curriculum requirements and the certification of teachers and students are only loosely related to what teachers actually do in their classrooms. Similarly, when mental health professionals use the DSM-III diagnostic labels, these seldom predict the actual therapy therapists will use (see Kirk & Kutchins, Chapter 8, this volume). The structure, then, serves as a buffer between the technology and the environment. This is especially important for organizations whose technologies are indeterminate and their results are uncertain.

In this respect, institutional organizations engage in myths and cere- monies (Meyer & Rowan, 1977): The rules are rationalized myths because they are based on unproven belief systems—such as professional ideologies—yet they are viewed as rational means to achieve desired social ends. The ceremonies are periodic affirmations of these myths through symbolic actions such as certification, accreditation, gradua- tion, and the like.

The institutional school also brings into the analysis the concept of an industry or sector that Scott and Meyer (1983, p. 129) define as "all or- ganizations within society supplying a given type of product or service together with their associated organization set: suppliers, financiers, regulators and the like." This is an exceedingly important concept be- cause it draws our attention away from the single organization to a network of organizations having responsibility for the delivery of a service such as public education, mental health, or child welfare is organized. Again, because the relations within such human service sectors are determined not by market exchanges but by various rules and regula- tions, they are highly institutional. These rules will influence how decision rights within sectors about goals, means, and funding are allocated among the constituent parts. Thus sectors will vary in their degree of de- centralization, fragmentation, and federalization. Sectors will also vary by how the activities of their constituent organizations will be controlled. Thus the institutional approach argues that the structure of individual organizations cannot be understood without reference to the structure of the sector in which they are located.

The institutional perspective adds considerable depth to our under- standing of human service organizations. As indicated earlier, because they engage in moral work human service organizations are the quint- essential embodiment of institutional organizations. Yet, as DiMaggio (1988) points out, the theory is quite mysterious about the process of institutionalization that is at the heart of the theory. He argues that "institutionalization as a *process* is profoundly political and reflects the relative power of organized interests and actors who mobilize around them" (DiMaggio, 1988, p. 13). Moreover, as suggested earlier, organiza- tions themselves are major sources of institutional rules, and they actively shape the institutional environment. Finally, the institutional approach also de-emphasizes the importance of the work to be done and the effects of the institutionalized ways of doing it on the organization of work. Put differently, the distinction between the institutional and technological environment is quite blurred. I noted earlier how technological developments influence institutional rules and vice versa. Thus even in the human services where technologies tend to be indeterminate there are, nonetheless, socially sanctioned ways of delivering the services that are embedded in the structure of the organization.

Population Ecology

The shift in the level of analysis from a single to a collection of organizations is completed in the population-ecology theory. Here, the emphasis is on a *population* of organizations, defined as all organizations that have a *unitary character*, which means that they: (a) share a common dependence on the material and social environment; (b) have a similar structure; and (c) their structure and other characteristics are quite stable over time (Hannan & Freeman, 1988). An example might be all the child-care or all the mental health agencies in a given community. The metaphor is of biological evolution of species in which the processes of variation, selection, and retention define the attributes of the population. The theory is concerned with three fundamental issues—rates of organizational founding, disbanding, and change in a given population. These are important issues in understanding the evolution of human services. In such areas as mental health or child welfare we tend to witness cyclical patterns of rapid expansion to be followed by periods of contraction. Within these cycles we observe the rise of new organizational forms such as the community mental health center, followed by a period of stagnation or inertia. Population ecology attempts to account for these patterns.

Singh and Lumsden (1990, p. 162) state the basic principle of the theory as follows: "once founded, organizations are subject to strong inertial pressures, and alterations in organizational populations are largely due to demographic processes of organizational founding (births) and dissolution (deaths)." The observed cyclical pattern of organizational founding is explained by two processes—density dependence and population dynamics. Initial increase in the number of organizations signals legitimation for their activities and form, thus attracting more founding. But as the number of organizations continues to increase, competition for resources sets in leading to a decline in founding (Hannan & Freeman, 1988). Moreover, when existing organizations disband they create free resources that encourage entrepreneurship, but as the rate of disbanding continues to rise, it signals a hostile environment and discourages additional new ventures (Singh & Lumsden, 1990).

Why do organizations disband? As in biological evolution, organizational forms disappear when they are no longer supported by their environment (e.g., the decline of homes for unwed mothers and orphanages in the United States). Organizations with generalized services are more likely to succeed when the environment is variable and experiences large periodic fluctuations. In contrast, organizations with a specialist strategy are more likely to survive in a relatively stable environment experiencing small and regular fluctuations (Freeman & Hannan, 1983). Organizations also disband because of "liability of newness," namely their inexperience and inability to compete with well-established organizations. Similarly "liability of smallness" results in a high disbanding rate because small organizations have difficulty attracting resources.

Hannan and Freeman (1984) argue that the environment favors organizations whose structures have high inertia. This is because the environment tends to select organizations with a high degree of reliability and accountability. These are organizations that have a well-defined set of reproducible routines. Thus the organization is adaptive or successful because it has specified which routines apply to what situation (e.g., hospitals shifting from normal to disaster situations). It also follows from this argument that as organizations age they become more inert.

The population-ecology perspective has been criticized for inappropriately applying biological evolution models to social organizations (Young, 1988), but most importantly for its inarticulate conception of the environment. The model, as Perrow (1986, p. 213) puts it "tends to be a mystifying one, removing much of the power, conflict, disruption, and social-class variables from the analysis." Although there is an implicit recognition that the environment is socially constructed, the theory is silent about how it is constructed and changed over time. This is in sharp contrast to the institutional and political-economy theories. Aldrich (1979), for example, does recognize the important role of the state in shaping the environment. In the human service, the state is a key player in the environment, and state ideologies, politics, and economics have probably more to do with the founding and survival of human service organizations than any other factor. Indeed, recent studies by Tucker, Baum, and Singh (Chapter 3, this volume) acknowledge that institutional forces, such as the state, may be more important than ecological forces in understanding the founding and disbanding rates of human service organizations.

Also disturbing is the concept of "population" that refers mostly to organizations with a similar product. But this presents only a slice of the complex network of organizations that have different degrees of involvement in the generation of the product. Rather, the concept of "sector" mentioned above seems more promising.

Where Do We Go From Here?

It is clear, even from this cursory review, that no one theory is adequate to explain the structure and processes of organizations in general, let alone human services in particular. In my view, the efficacy of each theory depends on the nature of the organizational phenomena being addressed. Rational theories have a contribution to make if we wish to understand how efficiency is pursued; human relations theories are appropriate for understanding the nature of interpersonal relations in organizations; contingency theories are significant for exploring the impact of technology on structure; the negotiated-order perspective provides insight on how individuals and groups negotiate and carry out their work; political economy is useful in understanding how the organization's strategies to obtain resources influence its service delivery system; Marxist theories draw attention to the impact of the macro economic and political systems on human services; institutional theory is important to understanding how organizations attain legitimacy; and population ecology is appropriate for exploring rates of founding and disbanding of organizations.

Yet to me the most fundamental question to be asked about human service organizations is what determines the nature of their service delivery system. By service delivery system I include such issues as who are the clients to be served, the services to be provided, the manner in which the services will be provided, and, most importantly, the patterns of client-staff relations. I would propose that to address this set of questions, an integration of the political economy and the institutional theories will be most appropriate. I follow DiMaggio's (1988) lead in suggesting such integration. Because I assume that institutional rules arise from political processes, I also refer to the approach articulated by Moe (1990) on the politics of structural choices in public bureaucracies.

Because human services are influenced by institutional rules, it is important, first, to understand how these rules arise and how much influence they possess. I would propose that within any human services sector, institutional rules reflect the outcomes of negotiations among interest groups with differential access and control of power. These interest groups include service organizations, professional associations, funding organizations, political and civic associations, social movements, and the like. Each of these groups has a vested interest in the sector that is reflected in the ideologies it espouses. The relative power of each interest group is a function of how many resources it controls that are essential for the organization and delivery of the sector's services. To protect its interests each group would like to see them expressed in the structure of the service organization(s) in the sector.

But this is a complicated process. First, each group recognizes that it lacks the technical expertise to specify the organization's technology to ensure that it would respond to the human problem in accordance with the group's interests. Second, it recognizes that power relations shift and today's winners are tomorrow's losers. Therefore, following Moe (1990), dominant groups will attempt to articulate institutional rules and embed them in the structure of the organization. These may include regulations about how services must be structured, requirements to employ certain professional expertise, and insulating the organization from political influence through requirements such as adherence to civil service procedures, and subjecting it to judicial review. Thus, according to Moe (1990, p. 137), "The driving force of political uncertainty, then, causes the winning group to favor structural design it would never favor on technical grounds alone."

Second, the existence of various interest groups necessitates processes of coalition formation, bargaining, and negotiations. These generate multiple and often contradictory institutional rules that seek their expression in the structure of the organization. Thus the organization is faced with structural choices, and it is important to understand how these choices are made. I would propose that the extent to which institutional rules are incorporated into the structure of organizations depends on: (a) the resources that they convey, and (b) their enforceability. Organizations are likely to incorporate those institutional rules whose perceived benefits outweigh their perceived costs. When institutional rules are devoid of important resources needed by the organization (or the sector), and cannot be easily enforced, they become truly symbolic and will have little consequences on the actual delivery of service. In reviewing the history of welfare-work programs, for example, Handler and Hasenfeld (1991) found that local communities were able to neutralize the intended aims of these state mandated programs because these institutional rules lacked sufficient attraction or power when they clashed with local ideological, political, and economic interests. Similarly, when institutional rules clash with the political economy of the organization, they are likely to be ignored in the *actual* practices of the organization, unless the rules can be independently enforced. For example, under the Reagan Administration, Social Security ignored its own institutional rules and began to reject an inordinate proportion of disability claims (especially for mental disability) because it was under pressure to reduce government expenditures (Weatherford, 1984). This, despite the fact that the courts found that the majority of the cases were wrongly denied. It finally took a Supreme Court decision to reverse these practices.

To cope with the contradictions among powerful institutional rules, the organization is also likely to create a loosely coupled internal structure so that each institutional rule can find an expression in an organizational component without coming into direct conflict with another rule. For example, mental health centers that wish to continue to obtain public funding for serving the chronically mentally ill, but also want to reach new sources of revenues such as treatment of substance abuse, are likely to develop distinct program components with minimal ties between them. Such loose coupling occurs not only at the organizational level but also at the sector level.

Third, it is also important to emphasize how organizations shape institutional rules as a way of managing their environment and enhance their own interests. To be successful the organization will pursue several strategies (Moe, 1990). It will attempt to nurture exchange relations with specific interest groups. In exchange for support from these groups it will enunciate institutional rules that favor the group. The costs of such a strategy, however, is losing autonomy and attracting opposition. Alternatively, the organization will attempt to insulate itself from environmental pressures by advocating rules that give recognition to its expertise and experience. Universities, for example, retain autonomy by gaining control over degree certification. Mental health organizations maintain autonomy through their authority to define mental illness. Finally, human services organizations form coalitions that regularly lobby for policies, programs and regulations to legitimize practices that they view as protecting and enhancing their interests (Laumann & Knoke, 1987).

I would propose that the interaction between institutional and political-economy processes is a key to understanding how organizational service delivery systems emerge, gain stability, and change over time. In particular, the contradictions found in human service organizations can be explained by the accommodations they make to institutional, political, and economic exigencies. Moreover, the structuring of human services is a perpetual process because interest groups rise and fall, power balances change, new institutional rules ascend in influence and old ones decline, and organizations can never fully accommodate contending institutional rules.

References

Aldrich, H. E. (1979). *Organizations and environment.* Englewood Cliffs, NJ: Prentice-Hall.

Argyris, C. (1962). *Interpersonal competence and organizational effectiveness.* Homewood, IL: Dorsey Press.

Astley, W. G., & Van de Ven, A. H. (1983). Central perspectives and debates in organizational theory. *Administrative Science Quarterly, 28,* 245-273.

Bargal, D., & Schmid, H. (1989). Recent themes in theory and research on leadership and their implications for management of the human services. *Administration in Social Work, 13,* 37-54.

Belknap, I. (1956). *Human problems of a state mental hospital.* New York: McGraw-Hill.

Benson, J. K. (1975). The interorganizational network as a political economy. *Administrative Science Quarterly, 20*(2), 229-249.

Braverman, H. (1974). *Labor and monopoly capital: The degradation of work in the twentieth century.* New York: Monthly Review Press.

Caudill, W. (1958). *The psychiatric hospital as a small society.* Cambridge, MA: Harvard University Press.

Cherniss, C. (1980). *Staff burnout.* Beverly Hills, CA: Sage.

Clegg, S., & Dunkerley, D. (1980). *Organization, class and control.* London: Routledge & Kegan Paul.

DiMaggio, P. D., & Powell, W. (1983). The iron cage revisited: Institutional isomorphism and collective rationality in organizational fields. *American Sociological Review, 48,* 147-160.

DiMaggio, P. J. (1988). Interest and agency in institutional theory. In L. Zucker (Ed.), *Institutional patterns and organizations* (pp. 3-21). Cambridge, MA: Ballinger.

Edwards, R. C. (1979). *Contested terrain: The transformation of the workplace in the twentieth century.* New York: Basic Books.

Eisenstat, R. A., & Felner, R. D. (1983). Organizational mediators of the quality of care. In B. A. Farber (Ed.), *Stress and burnout in the human service professions* (pp. 142-154). Elmsford, NY: Pergamon.

Feldman, P. (1990). *Who cares for them? Workers in the home care industry.* Westport, CT: Greenwood Press.

Freeman, J., & Hannan, M. T. (1983). Niche width and the dynamics of organizational populations. *American Journal of Sociology, 88*(6), 1116-1145.

Freudenberger, H. J. (1980). Burnout: Occupational hazard of the child care worker. *Child Care Quarterly, 6*(2), 90-99.

Glisson, C. (1989). The effect of leadership on workers in human service organizations. *Administration in Social Work, 13*, 99-116.

Glisson, C., & Durick, M. (1988). Predictors of job satisfaction and organizational commitment in human service organizations. *Administrative Science Quarterly, 33*(1), 61-81.

Goffman, E. (1961). *Asylums.* Garden City, NY: Doubleday.

Handler, J., & Hasenfeld, Y. (1991). *The moral construction of poverty.* Newbury Park, CA: Sage.

Hannan, M., & Freeman, J. (1984). Structural inertia and organizational change. *American Sociological Review, 49*, 149-164.

Hannan, M., & Freeman, J. (1988). Density dependence and the growth of organizational populations. In G. Carroll (Ed.), *Ecological models of organizations* (pp. 7-32). Cambridge, MA: Ballinger.

Hasenfeld, Y. (1972). People-processing organizations: An exchange approach. *American Sociological Review, 37*, 256-263.

Hasenfeld, Y. (1987). Power in social work practice. *Social Service Review, 61*(3), 469-483.

Jayaratne, S., & Chess, W. A. (1983). Job satisfaction and burnout in social work. In B. A. Farber (Ed.), *Stress and burnout in the human service professions* (pp. 129-141). Elmsford, NY: Pergamon.

Kramer, R., & Grossman, B. (1987). Contracting for social services: Process management and resource dependencies. *Social Service Review, 61*, 32-55.

Laumann, E. O., & Knoke, D. (1987). *The organizational state: Social choice in national policy domains.* Madison: University of Wisconsin Press.

Lawrence, P., & Lorsch, J. W. (1967). *Organization and environment: Managing differentiation and integration.* Boston: Harvard University, Graduate School of Business Administration.

Leifer, R., & Huber, G. P. (1977). Relations among perceived environmental uncertainty, organizational structure, and boundary-spanning behavior. *Administrative Science Quarterly, 22*, 235-247.

Maslach, C., & Pines, A. (1979). Burnout, the loss of human caring. In A. Pines & C. Maslach (Eds.), *Experiencing social psychology* (pp. 246-252). New York: Random House.

Meyer, J. W., & Rowan, B. (1977). Institutionalized organizations: Formal structure as myth and ceremony. *American Journal of Sociology, 83*, 340-363.

Meyer, J. W., & Rowan, B. (1983). The structure of educational organizations. In J. W. Meyer & W. R. Scott (Eds.), *Organizational environments: Ritual and rationality* (pp. 71-98). Beverly Hills, CA: Sage.

Meyer, J. W., Scott, W. R., Strang, D., & Creighton, A. L. (1988). Bureaucratization without centralization: Changes in the organizational system of U.S. public education, 1940-1980. In L. Zucker (Ed.), *Institutional patterns and organizations* (pp. 139-168). Cambridge, MA: Ballinger.

Moe, T. M. (1990). The politics of structural choice: Toward a theory of public bureaucracy. In O. E. Williamson (Ed.), *Organizational theory: From Chester Barnard to present and beyond* (pp. 116-153). New York: Oxford University Press.

Morgan, G. (1986). *Images of organization.* Beverly Hills, CA: Sage.

O'Connor, J. (1973). *The fiscal crisis of the state.* New York: St. Martin's.

Offe, C. (1984). *Contradictions of the welfare state.* Cambridge: MIT Press.

Pecora, P. J., & Austin, M. J. (1983). Declassification of social service jobs: Issues and strategies. *Social Work, 28*(6), 419-420.

Perrow, C. (1967). A frame work for the comparative analysis of organizations. *American Sociological Review, 32*, 194-208.

Perrow, C. (1986). *Complex organizations: A critical essay* (3rd ed.). New York: Random House.

Pfeffer, J., & Salancik, G. R. (1978). *The external control of organizations: A resource dependence perspective.* New York: Harper & Row.

Pines, A., & Aronson, E. (1988). *Career burnout.* New York: Free Press.

Piven, F., & Cloward, R. (1971). *Regulating the poor: The function of public welfare.* New York: Pantheon.

Porter, L. W., Lawler, E. E., III, & Hackman, J. R. (1975). *Behavior in organizations.* New York: McGraw-Hill.

Quadagno, J. (1988). *The transformation of old age security: Class and politics in the American welfare state.* Chicago: University of Chicago Press.

Salancik, G. R., & Pfeffer, J. (1974). The bases and use of power in organizational decision making: The case of a university. *Administrative Science Quarterly, 19*(4), 453-473.

Scott, W. R., & Meyer, J. W. (1983). The organization of environments: Network, cultural, and historical elements. In J. W. Meyer & W. R. Scott (Eds.), *Organizational environments: Ritual and rationality* (pp. 129-154). Beverly Hills, CA: Sage.

Scott, W. R. (1987). *Organizations: Rational, natural, and open systems* (2nd ed.). Englewood Cliffs, NJ: Prentice-Hall.

Scott, W. R. (1990). Technology and structure: An organizational level perspective. In P. S. Goodman & L. S. Sproull (Eds.), *Technology and organizations.* San Francisco: Jossey-Bass.

Singh, J. V., & Lumsden, C. J. (1990). Theory and research in organizational ecology. *Annual Review of Sociology, 16*, 161-195.

Strauss, A., Fargerhaugh, S., Suczek, B., & Wiener, C. (1985). *Social organization of medical work.* Chicago: University of Chicago Press.

Thompson, J. D. (1967). *Organization in action.* New York: McGraw-Hill.

Turk, H. (1977). *Organizations in modern life.* San Francisco: Jossey-Bass.

Wamsley, G. L., & Zald, M. N. (1976). *The political economy of public organizations.* Bloomington: Indiana University Press.

Weatherford, B. (1984). The disability insurance program: An administrative attack on the welfare state. In A. Champagne & E. J. Harpham (Eds.), *The attack on the welfare state* (pp. 37-60). Prospect Heights, IL: Waveland Press.

Weir, M., Orloff, A. S., & Skocpol, T. (Eds.). (1988). *The politics of social policy in the United States.* Princeton, NJ: Princeton University Press.

Whiddon, B., & Martin, P. Y. (1989). Organizational democracy and work quality in a state welfare agency. *Social Science Quarterly, 70*, 667-686.

Young, R. C. (1988, July). Is population ecology a useful paradigm for the study of organizations? *American Journal of Sociology, 94*(1), 1-24.

Zucker, L. (1988). Where do institutional patterns come from? Organizations as actors in social systems. In L. Zucker (Ed.), *Institutional patterns and organizations* (pp. 23-52). Cambridge, MA: Ballinger.

PART II
Linking the Organization to Its Environment

A key determinant of the organization's service delivery system is the nature of the environment in which it is embedded. The survival of the organization and its capacity to attain its various aims hinge on its ability to obtain needed resources from the environment. The strategies that the organization employs to do so include the very design of its service delivery system. That is, services are organized to respond to environmental constraints, but also to optimize the flow of resources.

In Chapter 3, Tucker, Baum, and Singh show how the founding and disbanding of human service organizations, especially voluntary, are strongly affected by both the ecological and institutional components of the environment. As their research indicates, the institutional environment—especially availability of government support—is a major determinant of the rates of founding and disbanding of voluntary organizations. Moreover, organizational linkages to significant institutional actors are important for the survival of these organizations.

Gronbjerg, in Chapter 4, focuses on a key environmental resource—funding—and shows how the budgeting process serves as a major link between the organization and its fiscal environment. Especially important is her discussion of the strategies that human service organizations use to respond to three challenges: (a) developing good ties with funding sources; (b) maintaining flexibility and cushioning against funding jolts; and (c) maintaining current information about developments in the environment. The strategies themselves, as Gronbjerg emphasizes, have consequences to the nature of the services offered by the organization.

Most of the strategic choices concerning the linkages between the organization and its environment are the domain of the executive leadership. In Chapter 5, Schmid discusses the critical role of executive leadership in human service organizations. One of the disturbing findings from the available research is the limited amount of time executives actually devote to managing the organization's external relations. Internally, executives tend to prefer a centralized decision-making approach. On the basis of these findings Schmid develops a typology of executive leadership and discusses the impact of each type on the linkages between the organization and its environment, and on its internal structure.

CHAPTER 3

The Institutional Ecology
of Human Service Organizations

DAVID J. TUCKER

JOEL A. C. BAUM

JITENDRA V. SINGH

Introduction

The general topic of this chapter is the relationship between human service organizations and their environments. The specific topic addressed deals with the effects of the environment on foundings and disbandings of new human service organizations. The term *environment* is interpreted to include both ecological and institutional components. Ecological components are defined in terms of the availability and distribution of tangible resources. Institutional components are defined to include rules and beliefs about the development and operation of organizations, as well as relational networks of other organizations. When the term *human service organization* is used, it refers to a non-market form of organization that operates with an indeterminate or ambiguous technology, and mainly is concerned with changing, constraining, and/or supporting human behavior.

The specific focus of this chapter is on the interplay between institutional and ecological components of the environment in explaining patterns of vital events (foundings and disbandings) in populations of human service organizations. Drawing on studies of voluntary social service organizations and day-care centers, we argue that institutional effects are dominant in explaining patterns of vital events in populations of human service organizations. Ecological components, though important, play a secondary role. This is in contrast to the generally accepted view that the relationship between institutional and ecological elements is complementary and equal. One contribution of this chapter is in illus- trating that populations of organizations, similar to individual organizations, need to be conceptualized as existing in relation to their social contexts. They are embedded in organizational communities and in society, and the nature of this embeddedness affects their processes and structures in important ways.

Background

Over the past two decades, organization theory has shifted in how it studies organization-environment relations. Earlier approaches analyzed organization-environment relations from the perspective of individual organizations, and explained change mainly in terms of how individual organizations seek to manage or strategically adapt to environmental threats and opportunities (e.g., Pfeffer & Salancik, 1978). In contrast, more recent approaches conceptualize the external environment as the principal agent of change, and treat the internal processes of individual organizations as more of a constant.

Among the recent approaches, ecological and institutional theories of organization have attracted perhaps the widest interest among students of organization (Singh & Lumsden, 1990). Organizational ecology focuses on diversity in populations of organizations, and defines the environment in terms of the availability and distribution of material resources. Studies adopting this approach mainly have examined how environmental conditions influence the founding and disbanding rates of organizations (for reviews, see Carroll, 1984; Singh & Lumsden, 1990).

Institutional theory, on the other hand, conceives of the environment as not only a source of material inputs, but also containing socially created conceptions of appropriate organizational practices, competencies and behaviors that are supported and enforced by a wide range of corporate actors and forces (DiMaggio & Powell, 1983; Meyer & Rowan, 1977; Meyer & Scott, 1983; Tolbert & Zucker, 1983; Scott, 1987). Organizations that reflect the requirements and expectations of the institutional environment in their structures and operation gain the legitimacy and resources needed to survive and grow (Meyer & Rowan, 1977). Institutional environments also promote the founding of new organizations by contributing to the proliferation of components (e.g., professional occupations, legal procedures, systems of accreditation) needed to construct them (Meyer & Rowan, 1977), and by defining formal organizing as a preferred way of dealing with problems (DiMaggio & Powell, 1983; Granovetter, 1985; Tucker, Singh, Meinhard, & House, 1988; Zucker, 1983).

The interrelationship of ecological and institutional theories in explaining dynamic change processes in populations of organizations is currently an important theme in organization theory (Baum & Oliver, 1991; Carroll & Hannan, 1989; Singh & Lumsden, 1990; Singh, Tucker, & Meinhard, 1991; Tucker et al., 1988; Zucker, 1989). Generally, the relationship between them has been treated as complementary, with some scholars proposing that the effects of institutional and ecological elements can be synthesized within a single explanatory framework (e.g., Carroll & Hannan, 1989; Hannan, 1986). Recently, however, reservations have surfaced concerning the efficacy of this view. One telling observation is that ecological theory, by working with a mainly resource-based conception of the environment, has confined the locus of its explanations to within-population processes. Unlike institutional theory, ecological theory has not dealt with questions of how the embeddedness of populations in larger organizational communities and society affects dynamic change processes (Baum & Oliver, 1990; Fombrun, 1986; 1988). This view implies that institutional theory can rightly be regarded as contextual to ecological theory (Granovetter, 1985). Thus the relationship between them is not merely complementary; it is also hierarchical.

While we have some reservations concerning the generality of this view across all classes of organizations, we do think that it has specific relevance for human service organizations. Human service organizations tend to have indeterminate technologies (Singh, Tucker, & House, 1986; Tucker, 1981) and their outputs cannot easily be evaluated in terms of conventional output, efficiency or process criteria (Daft, 1983, pp. 107-108). As well, they are minimalist organizations (Halliday, Powell, & Granfors, 1987), that is, they can be founded and maintained with limited labor commitments and capital (Tucker et al., 1988), and they operate in populations where there are normative pressures away from competition (Baum & Oliver, 1990).[1] Under these conditions, survival is more likely to depend upon the confidence and stability achieved by conforming with the requirements and expectations of higher order collectivities (Meyer & Rowan, 1977; Meyer, Scott, & Deal, 1981; Scott & Meyer, 1983). This suggests that human service organizations are specifically vulnerable to conditions that have their origin in the institutional environment and that their interconnectedness with the external institutional environment significantly affects their survival chances.

Below, we review and discuss a series of studies that have incorporated institutional and ecological variables into analyses of patterns of vital events in two populations of human service organizations. Our approach is to demonstrate how institutional processes affect patterns of foundings and disbandings changes, and consider the extent to which the effects can be considered prior to and causally distinct from ecological effects. We begin with brief descriptions of the two study populations, followed by definitions of some basic terms.

The Study Populations

One population is comprised of all the voluntary social service organizations (VSSOs) that came into existence in Metro-Toronto, Canada, in the period 1970-1982. These organizations all are governed by boards of directors and operate on a nonprofit basis. Population size is 451.[2] Similar to other groups of human service organizations, this population of VSSOs is quite diverse. They range from small organizations using only volunteer staff to large, sophisticated organizations employing professional staff and using computer technology. The services offered range from highly specialized legal, medical and counseling services performed by professional staff to settlement and interpretative services performed by volunteers (Singh et al., 1986, p. 175).

The second study population is also located in Metropolitan Toronto. It is comprised of all licensed day-care centers (DCCs) existing in the period January, 1971, to December, 1989, and numbers 789 (Baum, 1990a, 1990b; Baum & Oliver, 1990; 1991). DCCs are licensed by the Ontario Ministry of Community and Social Services to provide full-time (more than six consecutive hours) collective care to five or more children, ranging in age from newborns to nine years. DCCs vary significantly in the age ranges of children served, some specializing in care to newborns and toddlers, and others specializing in care for school age children. Yet others provide services across a number of age ranges. Associated with these differences are variations in programs, in internal differentiation and complexity, and in the numbers and qualifications of staff. DCCs may operate on either a for-profit or nonprofit basis, and are not restricted by their status from pursuing government contracts or other forms of community support.

Definitions

We study human service organizations at the population level of analysis. A *population* is an aggregate of organizations that share some common unit character, for example, all nonprofit voluntary social service organizations located in Metropolitan Toronto (Carroll, 1984; Singh et al., 1986). Though members of the same population, organizations may differ from each other in important ways. One of the more important differences is whether they are specialists or generalists (Freeman & Hannan, 1983; Hannan & Freeman, 1977). A *specialist organization* has characteristics suited to specific environmental features, and a *generalist organization* has characteristics adapted to a broad range of environmental conditions (Tucker, Singh, & Meinhard, 1990b, p. 155). An example of a specialist organization is a VSSO that operates in a single domain, providing health services for youth, or interpretation service for new immigrants. An example of a generalist organization is a DCC that provides a number of services to children across a range of different age groupings.

The basic objective of the studies reported in this chapter is to explain patterns of foundings and disbandings. A *founding* is defined in terms of a specific act of formalization, the date of legal incorporation for VSSOs, and the date of receipt of an operating license for DCCs. A *disbanding* occurs when an organization discontinues its operation. Dates of disbandings for VSSOs and DCCs were established by examining archival data and through interviews with key informants.

Key concepts used in this chapter to analyze patterns of foundings and disbandings include population density, population dynamics, relational density, institutional linkages, and legitimacy. Population density and population dynamics both deal with aspects of population size (Tucker et al., 1988, p. 151). *Density* refers to the numbers of organizations alive at a given time in the population. *Population dynamics* focuses on numbers of foundings and disbandings (Delacroix & Carroll, 1983). It describes how earlier numbers of foundings and disbandings influence later founding and disbanding rates.

Relational density and institutional linkages characterize the embed-dedness of organizations in larger organizational communities and in society (Baum & Oliver, 1990, 1991). *Relational density* refers to the overall connectedness of a population with its larger institutional context. It is measured by counting the total number of linkages the population has with dominant institutions in its environment at a particular time, for example, numbers of purchase of service agreements a population of day-care centers has with government agencies. Similar to popula-tion density, relational density may increase or decrease over time. *Insti-tutional linkages* refer to direct relationships between individual organi-zations in a population and significant institutional actors in the pop-ulation's environment, for example, a site-sharing arrangement where-by a DCC shares physical facilities with a recognized, well-established, community-based organization. Some organizations maintain several different types of institutional linkages over protracted periods; others do not have any linkages. Yet others may have formed and then lost linkages for a variety of reasons.

The final term we discuss here is legitimacy. Generally, *legitimacy* is conceived of as a conferred status, controlled by forces external to the organization (Pfeffer & Salancik, 1978; Stinchcombe, 1965). It results from congruence between societal values and organizational action (Dowling & Pfeffer, 1975; Meyer & Rowan, 1977). It is dealt with empirically in this chapter in two different ways. First, legitimacy is inferred on the basis of the pervasiveness of an organizational type, that is, increasing num-bers of a particular type of organization indicate its increasing social acceptability and, therefore, its increasing legitimacy. Second, legitimacy is dealt with in terms of endorsements from, and explicit connections with, powerful external actors, for example, government departments, community-based agencies, assumed to reflect dominant societal val-ues and expectations. It is relevant to note here that one of the purposes of research reported in this chapter is to explore the validity of these two approaches to legitimacy in studying patterns of foundings and disbandings.

Organizational Foundings

Different populations of organizations are alike in the sense that their respective patterns of founding show cyclical patterns over time (Carroll, 1984). This similarity across populations has been explained mainly in terms of population dynamics and/or density dependence, which together are referred to as ecological dynamics (Tucker, Singh,

& Meinhard, 1990b). Population dynamics deal with the effects of prior foundings and prior disbandings on current foundings (Delacroix & Carroll, 1983). Initially, disbandings increase foundings because they instantly create free-floating resources that may easily be assembled into new ventures. However, a continued increase in the number of disbandings signals a noxious environment to entrepreneurs, resulting in a decline in foundings. Similarly, an initial increase in the creation of new organizations encourages the subsequent creation of others because it is interpreted as indicating a supportive environment. However, unrestrained entrepreneurial activity results in a saturated and competitive market, suggesting that even higher levels of foundings restrict the frequency of subsequent foundings.

Density dependence explains fluctuations in organization foundings in terms of the overall size of the population (Carroll & Hannan, 1989; Hannan, 1986; Hannan & Freeman, 1989). According to this argument, initial increases in the numbers of a particular type of organization legitimates the organization form itself and/or the activity of creating organizations. This helps to further increase the number of foundings. However, as the number of organizations continues to increase, the legitimacy process is dominated by the competitive process, resulting in a decrease in foundings.

Figures 3.1 and 3.2 show respectively the patterns of foundings by quarter for VSSOs and by year for DCCs. The observation period for the VSSOs extends from January, 1970, to December, 1982. For the DCCs, it extends from January, 1971, to December, 1989. As might be expected, given the findings from other research, the data show cyclical patterns of foundings for both populations.

In attempting to explain the patterns of foundings described in Figures 3.1 and 3.2, findings from earlier research suggested that the influence of population dynamics and density dependence should be considered. However, we also considered it essential to incorporate measures of institutional processes into the analyses because of the susceptibility of human service organizations to influences emanating from the institutional environment. Based on this, as well as other considerations, the central questions posed for VSSOs were how change in the institutional environment affected the ecological dynamics of organization foundings, and whether it varied across organizational forms. For DCCs, the central question was whether density dependence or relational dependence (a number of connections with governments and community institutions) accounts for how legitimation affects patterns of foundings.

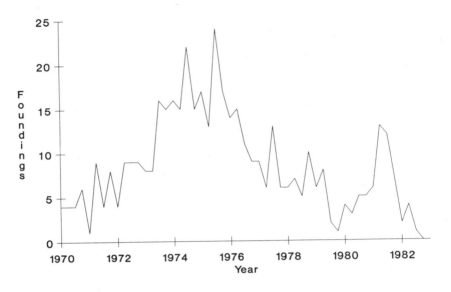

Figure 3.1. Quarterly Foundings of VSSOs, 1970-1982

Institutional Change and Organizational Foundings

Based on the view that the institutional environments can be conceptualized in terms of the decisions and activities of a few powerful institutional actors (Rowan, 1982; Tolbert & Zucker, 1983), Tucker et al. (1988) argued that the state, through its respective agencies and programs, is a significant actor in the environments of VSSOs. This significance of the state is based in its control over the authoritative allocation of values and resources (e.g., Aldrich, 1979; Brown & Schneck, 1979; Freeman, 1979). This seems particularly true for the voluntary social services sector because it has historically had a close association with the state, frequently being regarded as complementary to, or in some circumstances, an appendage of state-operated service systems (e.g., Kramer, 1981; Wilensky & Lebeaux, 1957).

Specific arguments dealing with the nature of institutional changes and their effects on patterns of VSSO foundings concern the occurrence of two historical events, the Opportunities for Youth period (OFY), lasting from 1971 to 1975, and the Provincial Restraint period (RES), lasting from 1976 to 1981. OFY corresponds to a period of favorable institutional change, when the Canadian Federal Government elaborated

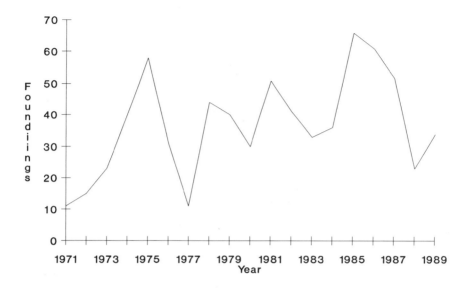

Figure 3.2. Annual Foundings of DCCs, 1971-1989

and enforced a new institutional rule that promoted the legitimacy of dealing with social problems by creating new organizations (Best, 1974; Houston, 1972; Looney, 1977; Wharf & Carter, 1972). RES corresponds to a period of unfavorable institutional change. It was characterized by fiscal restraint (McKeough, 1975, 1976; Miller, 1980; Puckett & Tucker, 1976) with sharply increased emphasis on increasing the productivity of existing organizations as opposed to legitimating the creation of new ones (Economic Council of Canada, 1976, 1977).

Generally, the results provide clear evidence that favorable institutional change altered how prior foundings and prior disbandings affected current founding patterns (Singh et al., 1991). Also, both favorable and unfavorable institutional changes altered how changes over time in the number of organizations affected patterns of organizational foundings. Restated in more explicit terms, the results show that for this population of VSSOs as a whole, the effects of major institutional change altered the predicted curvilinear effects of prior foundings and prior disbandings on current foundings. Prior foundings were found to have only a linear effect on current founding, and prior disbandings were found to have no effect. Also, increases in overall numbers of organizations had a curvilinear effect on patterns of foundings only under conditions of favorable institutional conditions. This suggested the interesting interpretation that favorable institutional conditions increased foundings to such an extent that competition increased, leading to a down turn in numbers of foundings.

Tucker, Singh, and Meinhard (1990b) investigated further the relationship between institutional changes and ecological dynamics by asking whether the findings above held for subpopulations of specialist (single domain) and generalist (multiple domain) organizations. The results showed that, as hypothesized, the founding patterns of specialists and generalists were significantly different. Prior foundings and prior disbandings, density, and institutional changes had significant effects on specialist foundings, but not on generalist foundings. Most significantly, institutional changes altered the density dependent (competitive) dynamics of specialist foundings, but had no effect on generalist foundings. This suggests that the effects of institutional change on competitive processes in populations may vary by organizational form.

Field Structuration and Organization Foundings

In their study of the founding patterns of DCCs, Baum and Oliver (1990) question the validity of the theory that cyclical patterns of organizational foundings reflect the legitimating and competitive effects of the number of organizations in the population. They propose an alternative hypothesis wherein the operation of legitimating and competitive effects is explained in terms of "relational density," or the interconnectedness of the population with superordinate community agencies and government departments.

Drawing on Dill (1958) and Fombrun (1986, 1988), Baum and Oliver portray organizations as embedded in task environments comprised minimally of a population structure and population suprastructure.[3] *Population structure* refers to interdependencies among organizations that produce similar products or services. *Population suprastructure* refers to interconnections between a population and surrounding institutions. An important limitation of the density dependence argument is that because it explains population dynamics in terms of changes over time in population density, it mainly focuses on population structure and pays little attention to the evolution of relationships with population suprastructure. However, where relations with community and government are dense, the forces in a population for the founding of new organizations may be altered because community and government organizations exert considerable influence over the conditions that regulate competition for scarce resources and legitimacy.

The above characterization of the contexts of populations raises doubts about the efficacy of population size as the key mediating variable of the effect of legitimation and competition processes on patterns of organizational foundings and disbandings. Suprastructural considerations should also play a role. This is particularly true when government or community endorsements are crucial to the public's willingness to consume services provided by members of a population, and when population members depend heavily on the suprastructure for material support. Suprastructural considerations should also be crucial when a population's collective administrative and regulatory mechanisms grow more quickly than its numbers, and when success depends more on being legitimated by powerful institutional actors than on achieving high standards of efficient internal production. When these conditions are satisfied, it is likely that population suprastructure dominates population structure in explaining the effect of legitimation and competition processes on patterns of foundings and disbandings.

Suprastructural effects were measured by relational density, the number of connections population members had with relevant government departments and community agencies. Density dependence effects were measured using the conventional approach of counting the numbers of organizations extant for each observation period. The analysis contrasted the effects of relational and population densities on the founding rates of DCCs. The findings showed that, with relational density modeled simultaneously, population density had a negative linear effect on founding frequencies. Thus population density worked only to decrease foundings by enhancing competitive processes. Relational density, on the other hand, had a curvilinear effect, meaning that it worked to both increase and decrease foundings. Initial increases in relational density stimulated the founding of new DCCs by promoting the creation of supportive institutional structures. However, at higher levels, competition among DCCs for resources and endorsements from the suprastructure increased, resulting in a decreasing number of foundings. The clear implication, therefore, is that relational density plays a dominant role in explaining legitimation effects in the population of DCCs, and an important role in explaining competition effects.

Overall, we think the above results for the founding patterns of VSSOs and DCCs strongly suggest that the embeddedness of populations of human service organizations in a larger institutional context has an important influence on the dynamics of foundings.

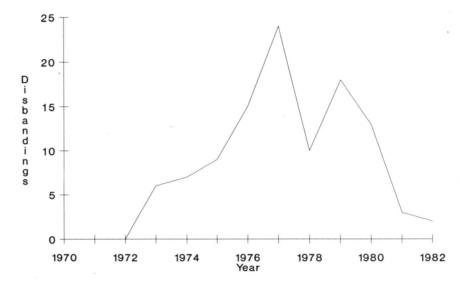

Figure 3.3. Annual Deaths of VSSOs, 1970-1982

Organizational Disbandings

Figures 3.3 and 3.4 show the annual number of disbandings in the VSSO and DCC populations respectively. For the VSSO population, the period covered is 1970-1982. The number of disbandings recorded is 106. For the DCC population, the period is 1971-1989, and the number of disbandings recorded is 171. The disbanding pattern for the VSSO shows that there were no disbandings in the first three years. After that, the number of disbandings increased each year to 1977, and then declined steadily until 1980 when the number increased again. For DCCs, the data in Figure 3.4 show that after the first year, the number of disbandings increased each year to 1976. They declined the following year and stayed at a fairly constant level until 1984. After that they increased steadily each year until 1989.

We have investigated processes underlying the disbanding patterns described in Figures 3.3 and 3.4 using five different arguments—population dynamics and density dependence, the liability of newness, institutional linkages, the liability of smallness, and the impact of founding conditions. This section reviews both the theoretical arguments and

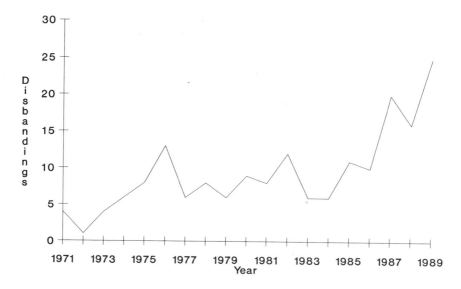

Figure 3.4. Annual Deaths of DCCs, 1971-1989

empirical evidence for each argument, considering particularly the comparative explanatory significance of institutional and ecological variables.

Population Dynamics and Density Dependence

The preceding section on foundings described how, in our earlier studies (Baum & Oliver, 1990b; Singh et al., 1991; Tucker, Singh, & Meinhard, 1990b; Tucker et al., 1988), we investigated institutional, population dynamics and density dependence arguments in studying founding patterns. We used the same general approach in studying organizational disbandings. In Tucker et al. (1988) and Singh et al. (1991), our purpose was to examine whether institutional changes, as manifested in changes in government policies and programs, influenced disbanding rates by how they affected intrapopulation imitation and replacement effects, proposed by population dynamics, and competition effects, proposed by density dependence arguments. The results suggested a negative answer. Unlike foundings, there was no effect on disbanding rates of the interaction between institutional changes and ecological dynamics. However, the results did show strong evidence for the main effects of ecological dynamics—prior foundings and disbandings and density—and institutional changes—favorable and unfavorable policies by the state—on disbanding rates.

A key purpose of the Baum and Oliver (1990) study was to explore the validity of competing explanations for the basis of legitimation and competition effects on disbanding rates. Density dependence proposes that the legitimation and competition effects are regulated by population size (Carroll & Hannan, 1989; Hannan, 1986). Initially, increasing numbers of organizations imply increasing legitimacy of the organizational form and, thus, decreasing disbandings. However, with increasing population size, competitive pressures take over, resulting in increasing disbanding rates. In contrast, Baum and Oliver's relational density hypothesis proposes that, subject to certain contingencies, initial increases in relational density, not population density, account for legitimation effects. This will be shown by the fact that early increases in relational density will decrease disbanding rates for organizations with links to the population suprastructure, but will increase disbanding rates for organizations without such links. Contrary to density dependence predictions, the effects of population density on disbanding rates will be linear and positive, meaning that it affects competition but not legitimation processes.

Baum and Oliver (1990) argue further that as relational density continues to increase, competition for legitimacy and resources from the institutional environment increases among organizations highly embedded in the population suprastructure, resulting in increasing disbanding rates. However, the dynamics underlying the effects of high relational density on the disbanding processes of organizations with no or minimal connections is somewhat different. Increasing relational density implies a more dense, highly organized population suprastructure and, thus, the potential for more pervasive community and government endorsements. In such a context, the legitimacy of all population members is enhanced, regardless of whether they have direct ties to institutional actors in the suprastructure. Although this "legitimacy by association" improves the disbanding rates of detached population members, that is, organizations without direct ties to institutional actors in the suprastructure, it does not fully compensate for the survival advantage of direct ties to the suprastructure. Nonetheless, the implication is that high relational density affords detached organizations some increased survival advantage. Therefore, they have lowered disbanding rates compared to those sustained by embedded organizations.

The analysis strongly supports Baum and Oliver's arguments. Population density had a positive linear effect on disbanding rates, meaning that it worked only to increase disbandings by enhancing competitive processes. It did not affect the legitimation processes. Relational density, on the other hand, had a strong curvilinear effect on the disbanding rates of DCCs embedded in the suprastructure, meaning that it worked both to increase and decrease disbandings. For detached organizations, disbanding rates were analyzed in relation to the disbanding rates of embedded organizations. The results showed that disbanding rates increased at low levels of relational density but decreased at higher levels. This indicates that detached organizations were disadvantaged at low levels of relational density, compared to embedded organizations, due to low legitimacy resulting from having no connections with the population suprastructure. However, they were less disadvantaged at high levels because of the acquisition of "legitimacy by association."[4] Overall, these findings indicate that, similar to the above conclusions for foundings, relational density plays a dominant role in explaining legitimation effects on disbanding rates, and an important role in explaining competition effects.

Liability of Newness

Newer organizations tend to die more quickly than older organizations (Stinchcombe, 1965). This liability of newness occurs because young organizations have to learn new roles as social actors, coordinate new roles for employees, and deal with problems of mutual socialization and trust. Also, they must overcome the competitive disadvantages of having to attract clients who are familiar with and deal with existing organizations, and who may be resistant to change.

Studies of the disbanding patterns of VSSOs (Singh, Tucker, & House, 1986) and DCCs (Baum & Oliver, 1991) provide evidence to indicate that the liability of newness does have relevance in understanding processes underlying the differential survival of these types of human service organizations. Also, these studies point to importance of considering the role played by institutional factors. The central question asked about VSSOs was whether the higher propensity of young organizations to die was primarily due to external factors such as low levels of legitimacy and the organizations' inability to develop strong exchange with key environmental constituencies, or whether it was due to internal processes such as members having to learn mutual coordination of roles processes and establish routines and patterns of work. In this regard, the study investigated how the acquisition and loss of external legitimacy, and the occurrence of internal change and reorganization, each affected the disbanding rates of VSSOs. The findings show more support for the external legitimacy than for the internal coordination argument.[5] External legitimacy depressed organizational disbanding rates, whereas internal organizational changes generally were unrelated to death rates.

In a similar vein, a question asked about DCCs (Baum & Oliver, 1991) was whether interorganizational linkages to legitimated institutions reduced the disbanding rates more for younger than for older organizations. The underlying argument was that the liability of newness may not apply to new organizations able to negotiate such linkages because the resources and legitimacy resulting from the linkages compensates for the disadvantages of organizational inexperience. The findings show support for this argument. New DCCs with institutional linkages had significantly lower failure rates than new DCCs without the advantage of such relations. Notably, the disbanding rate of DCCs without linkages declined significantly with increased age whereas the disbanding rate for DCCs with linkages did not. Overall, a plausible conclusion from these two studies is that the lack of external institutional support experienced by young human service organizations is one important reason underlying the liability of newness in this type of organization.

Institutional Linkages and Organizational Disbanding

Institutional and ecological theories of organization assert that an organization's life chances improve if it can establish itself as legitimate in that its purposes and behaviors conform with the norms and social expectations of the larger society. Institutional theory bases its claim on the view that by developing ties to well-established societal institutions, an organization signals its preparedness to adhere to institutional prescriptions of appropriate conduct. This brings with it a variety of rewards, including easier and more predictable access to higher levels of resources, enhanced status, and less vulnerability to critical questioning (Aiken & Hage, 1968; Aldrich & Auster, 1986; DiMaggio, 1988; DiMaggio & Powell, 1983; Meyer & Rowan, 1977, 1983; Meyer & Scott, 1983; Pfeffer & Salancik, 1978; Scott & Meyer, 1983; Selznick, 1947). The overall effect is an improvement in an organization's life chances because the basis of its operation is stabilized, and it obtains increased protection from environmental threats and uncertainty.

For ecological theory, the proposition that legitimacy reduces the likelihood of organizational failure has two sources. First, the density dependence argument (Carroll & Hannan, 1989; Hannan, 1986; Hannan

& Freeman, 1989) proposes that increasing numbers of a particular type of organization initially depress disbanding rates because the increasing pervasiveness of the organizational type itself signals its increasing social acceptability and, thereby, its increasing legitimacy. Second, Hannan and Freeman (1984, 1989) argue that to survive in modern societies, organizations must satisfy the external requirements of reliability and accountability. In this regard, several theorists (Aiken & Hage, 1968; DiMaggio, 1988; DiMaggio & Powell, 1983; Pfeffer & Salancik, 1978; Selznick, 1947) have noted that linkages to significant actors in the institutional environment increase an organization's stability and resource predictability. Since these factors are likely to engender at least the appearance of increased reliability and accountability, it is plausible that organizations with connections to the institutional environment have lower disbanding rates than organizations without such connections.

Baum and Oliver (1991) explored the validity of these views using data on the population of DCCs. They proposed that DCCs with connections to government and community agencies have significantly lower failure rates than those without such connections. Specifically, DCCs with institutional linkages are able to provide more reliable service than DCCs without such linkages because, in a context characterized by high turnover of personnel, they have increased ability to attract and retain qualified staff. Relatedly, in exchange for increased legitimacy and other resources, institutionally linked DCCs are likely to accept minimum standards of performance. This implies more limited variation in performance across organizations and, thus, greater reliability. Finally, consumers and other constituents tend to attribute accountability to institutionally linked DCCs because such organizations are likely to be seen as operating in compliance with norms of rational and acceptable behavior.

The analyses confirm Baum and Oliver's arguments. DCCs with established institutional relations to government and community institutions had significantly lower failure rates than those that did not. In addition, and of key importance to this chapter, institutional relations were found to be most beneficial under conditions of intense competition. Possessing institutional linkages reduced by more than 50% the competitive effect of increases in population density on disbanding rates. Thus as competition increased and as environmental resources became increasingly scarce, institutionally linked DCCs demonstrated a markedly superior ability to survive, compared to their nonlinked competitors.

Liabilities of Smallness

Based on Halliday et al. (1987), we asserted earlier that human service organizations are minimalist organizations, thereby implying that on average they will be fairly small. Current theory proposes that, for a number of reasons (Aldrich & Auster, 1986; Freeman, Carroll, & Hannan, 1983), smaller organizations are likely to have significantly higher disbanding rates than larger ones. It is logical, therefore, that the question of how an organization's size affects its survival chances is important for human service organizations.

In an earlier study, Tucker, Singh, House, and Meinhard (1985) examined how size at founding affected the survival chances of VSSOs. They proposed that the smaller the number of persons involved with VSSOs at founding, the higher the disbanding rate. The main reason for this is that larger VSSOs are likely to have a greater capacity to attract and retain resources due to higher visibility in the community, more extensive access to a larger pool of potential supporters (Provan, 1980, p. 229), and more contacts with other groups, and the larger system, via common memberships (McPherson, 1983, p. 1050). Organizational size was measured by counting the number of persons serving on a VSSOs board at the time of its founding.[6] Results showed that smaller VSSOs had higher initial death rates than larger VSSOs, thereby indicating support for the liabilities of smallness argument. Significantly, later studies (Singh, Tucker, & Meinhard, 1988, 1991; Tucker, Singh, & Meinhard, 1990a) reconceptualized board size as an indicator of external legitimacy, arguing that differences in the size of organization's boards of directors at founding reflect important differences in the way organizations are able to relate to institutional components of their environments. These studies all found that VSSOs with larger boards of directors at founding have lower disbanding rates than VSSOs with smaller boards.

Baum and Oliver (1991) have investigated the question of how organizational size affects disbanding rates, using data on the population of DCCs. They wanted to understand if institutional processes mediate the effects of liabilities of smallness on disbanding rates. Building on arguments that institutional linkages are effective in sheltering young organizations from the risk of failure, Baum and Oliver propose that institutional linkages will have differential effects on disbanding rates, depending upon whether the organizations involved are large or small. Institutional linkages improve an organization's chances for survival by providing the organization with cultural and resource support. Also, they facilitate the acquisition of legitimacy, which, in turn, improves an organization's capacity to attract clientele and skilled labor, and to mobilize resources. These conditions are likely to be especially helpful to small organizations. This implies that, all other things being equal, institutional linkages are most effective in reducing the failure rates of small organizations. The findings support this argument. The failure rate among small DCCs without institutional linkages was high, but declined with increases in size. On the other hand, the failure rate of small DCCs with linkages was low, and declined only moderately with increasing size.

Overall, the results reported in this section point to the importance of considering the effects of both institutional and ecological processes in explaining patterns of disbandings for human service organizations. Of key significance here are results which show how external legitimacy and institutional linkages play significant roles in reducing disbanding rates for both VSSOs and DCCs. The analyses also highlight several important conditions under which external legitimacy and institutional linkages may be most effective in reducing the disbanding rates of human service organizations. Finally, the findings suggest that external legitimacy and institutional relations may contribute significantly not only to explaining how organizational characteristics such as age, size, and strategy affect disbanding rates, but also to supporting the view that, for human service organizations, institutional processes may work to alter how ecological processes affect disbanding rates.

Conclusions

In this chapter we have argued that the interrelationship of ecological and institutional theories of organization in explaining the dynamics of organizational populations should take account of their embeddedness in larger organizational communities and in society. Whereas ecological theory generally has confined the locus of its explanations to within-population processes, institutional theory has maintained a broader view, incorporating attributes and activities of higher order collectivities. Following from this, we think that the relationship between the two perspectives can be construed as hierarchical, with institutional theory occupying the more encompassing position. This is contrary to the generally accepted view of the relationship as complementary and equal.

Our review of the studies conducted on the VSSO and DCC populations has demonstrated that, for these types of human service organizations, the view of ecological processes as hierarchically embedded in institutional processes is a valid one. Briefly, the empirical evidence we reported showed that institutional changes altered the role of density dependent competition in the founding patterns of VSSOs.

Relational density was shown to play a stronger role than population density in explaining legitimation effects on patterns of foundings and disbandings in the DCC population, and to be equally significant in explaining competition effects. External legitimacy and institutional linkages were found to play a very significant role in reducing the disbanding rates for both VSSOs and DCCs. Finally, it is significant that all studies found that when ecological and institutional processes were modeled together, the independent effects of institutional processes on founding and disbanding rates were neither altered nor eliminated.

One very important area of study not discussed in this chapter due to space limitations is organizational change. However, several studies have been conducted on organizational change in VSSOs and DCCs. Briefly, four studies (Baum & Oliver, 1990a; Singh, Tucker, & Meinhard, 1988, 1991; Tucker, Singh, & Meinhard, 1990a) examine processes underlying patterns and origins of change in human service organizations, and two (Baum & Oliver, 1991; Singh, House, & Tucker, 1986) deal with the relationship between organizational change and disbandings. Overall, the results of these studies offer additional support for the central thesis of this chapter concerning the relatively greater significance of institutional components of the environments in explaining the behavior of human service organizations over their life spans.

We think it would be interesting and relevant to investigate other macro-level questions about human service organizations, in addition to questions about foundings and disbandings and patterns of organizational change. Three potentially significant areas of investigation come to mind. The first is organizational diversity. Are there increasing numbers of different kinds of human service organizations, or are human service organizations becoming increasingly alike? In perhaps the only study of the dynamics of diversity, Baum (1990b) examined the validity of a series of hypotheses about the effects of competitive and institutional pressures on the occurrence of diversity in the core features of organizations (Hannan & Freeman, 1984). The findings show that competitive and institutional pressures have specific and contradictory effects, promoting increased similarity in features across DCCs under some conditions, and increased diversity in features under other conditions.

The second area focuses on the nature of organization-environment linkages, and asks how differences across linkages affect the life-cycle behavior of organizations. In one of the very few studies to address this issue, Baum and Oliver (1990) examine the influence of institutional linkages on the differential survival of nonprofit versus for-profit

DCCs. They argue that because nonprofit DCCs are perceived as more socially acceptable than for-profit DCCs (e.g., Social Planning Council of Metro-Toronto, 1984), linkages between for-profit DCCs and government and community institutions will receive negative social evaluations. This implies that nonprofit DCCs will receive significantly more survival value than for-profit from such linkages, based on the theory that the social validity of institutional linkages affects organizational survival. The findings support this prediction.

The final area of investigation we highlight is a variation on the theme explored in this chapter, namely, is it possible that ecological processes produce change in certain aspects of the institutional environment (Singh et al., 1991). Earlier case studies by Warren (1973), and by Warren, Rose, and Bergunder (1974) of the behavior of community decision organizations explored the relationship between the emergence of intrapopulation competition and institutional change. Among other things, the findings suggest that increasing competition among groupings of human service organizations may result in these organizations working to define interorganizational coordination strategies as the institutionally correct strategies so as to limit competition, and help ensure that they obtain new allocations from funding sources.

Extending the types of investigations initiated by Baum (1990b) and Baum and Oliver (1990), and by Warren (1973) and Warren et al. (1974) is important for both theoretical and applied reasons. For example, the ability of groupings of human service organizations to change or control certain aspects of their institutional environments has been associated with avoidance of public accountability (e.g., Hurl, 1984), and with a lowered propensity to innovate (Hurl & Tucker, 1986). By the same token, it is frequently advocated that human service organizations need to increase their control of their institutional context if they are to serve their constituencies adequately. Alternatively, if we look at questions such as how children are cared for organizationally in modern societies, there appears to be increasing diversity. Children are cared for in their families, private home day care, day-care centers, foster homes, group homes, institutions, and so on. Moreover, at least some of this caring seems to be taking place under increasingly competitive conditions. While a fair amount has been written about approaches to caring within these organizational forms, little attention has been given to the nature and origins of this overall diversity, the ecological dynamics involved, or the long-term implications. In sum, applying ecological and institutional theories of organization to human service organizations suggests a rich and diverse research agenda which, if implemented, would not only further understanding of this important subclass of organizations, but also would contribute to the development of policies and strategies for more effective enactment at community and societal levels.

Notes

1. This "normative press away from competition" (Halliday, Powell, & Granfors, 1987, p. 457) is well documented for human service organization. For a historical overview, see Rogers and Mulford (1982) and Hurl and Tucker (1986). Assessments pertaining to more current circumstance can be found in Warren (1972) and Warren, Rose, and Bergunder (1974).

2. This number of 451 differs from the 389 VSSOs studied in the analyses of disbanding rates (e.g., Singh et al., 1986). The 389 VSSOs were the number founded during the 1970 to 1980 period. Updated death data were not obtained for VSSOs founded in 1981 and 1982.

3. As originally conceived by Dill (1958), the task environment of an organization consists of all external factors relevant to organizational goal setting and goal attainment. More recently, Scott (1987) has refined this quite inclusive definition by reconceptualizing task environments as containing four major groups of external actors—customers, suppliers, competitors, and regulatory groups. Viewed from this perspective, task environments here are seen as encompassing both population structure and population suprastructure, with the former incorporating ecological components of the environment and the latter incorporating institutional components.

4. It is important to note here that embedded DCCs had a lower failure rate across the entire range of relational density.

5. Interestingly, the measures of external legitimacy used in this study—that is, acquisition of tax-exempt status, listing in the community agencies directory—can be interpreted as types of institutional linkages. As we shall see below, institutional links play an important role in explaining the disbanding rates of human service organizations.

6. Use of the number of board members as a measure of size was based first on the position that boards are particularly important to organizations at their genesis (Zald, 1969, p. 107) and, in the case of small voluntary organizations, are likely to do much of their work. In addition, in the case of the VSSO study population, more than 80% did not have financial resources at founding. Thus, they could not retain paid staff. Further, since emphasis was on founding size, it would have been premature to use other indicators of size, such as size of membership (e.g., McPherson, 1983), or number of active volunteers, since in general, neither would have been developed to any degree.

References

Aiken, M., & Hage, J. (1968). Organizational interdependence and intraorganizational structure. *American Sociological Review, 33,* 912-931.

Aldrich, H. (1979). *Organizations and environments.* Englewood Cliffs, NJ: Prentice-Hall.

Aldrich, H., & Auster, E. R. (1986). Even dwarfs started small: Liabilities of age and size and their strategic implications. In B. M. Shaw & L. L. Cummings (Eds.), *Research in organizational behavior* (pp. 165-198). Greenwich, CT: JAI Press.

Baum, J. A. C. (1990a). Adaptive and inertial patterns of organizational change. In L. R. Jauch & J. L. Wall (Eds.), *Academy of Management best paper proceedings,* 165-169.

Baum, J. A. C. (1990b). Why are there so many (few) kinds of organizations? A study of organizational diversity. In K. Kirchmeyer (Ed.), *Proceedings of the Administrative Sciences Association of Canada meetings,* part 5, pp. 1-10.

Baum, J. A. C., & Oliver, C. (1990). *Field structuration and the dynamics of organizational populations.* Unpublished manuscript, Stern School of Business, New York University.

Baum, J. A. C., & Oliver, C. (1991). Institutional linkages and organizational mortality. *Administrative Science Quarterly, 36,* 187-218.

Best, R. S. (1974). Youth policy. In G. B. Doern & V. S. Wilson (Eds.), *Issues in Canadian public policy* (pp. 137-165). Toronto: Macmillan.

Brown, J. L., & Schneck, R. (1979). A structuralist comparison between Canadian and American industrial organizations. *Administrative Science Quarterly, 24,* 24-47.

Carroll, G. R. (1984). Organizational ecology. *Annual Review of Sociology, 10,* 71-93.

Carroll, G. R., & Hannan, M. T. (1989). Density dependence in the evolution of populations in newspaper organizations. *American Sociological Review, 54,* 524-541.

Daft, R. L. (1983). *Organization theory and design.* New York: West Publishing.

Delacroix, J., & Carroll, G. R. (1983). Organizational foundings: An ecological study of the newspaper industries of Argentina and Ireland. *Administrative Science Quarterly, 28,* 274-291.

Dill, W. (1958). Environment as an influence on managerial autonomy. *Administrative Science Quarterly, 2,* 409-443.

DiMaggio, P. J. (1988). Interest and agency in institutional theory. In L. G. Zucker (Ed.), *Institutional patterns and organizations: Culture and environment* (pp. 3-21). Cambridge, MA: Ballinger.

DiMaggio, P. J., & Powell, W. W. (1983). The iron cage revisited: Institutional isomorphism and collective rationality in organizational fields. *American Sociological Review, 48,* 147-160.

Dowling, J., & Pfeffer, J. (1975). Organizational legitimacy. *Pacific Sociological Review, 18,* 122-136.

Economic Council of Canada. (1976). *People and jobs: A study of the Canadian labour market.* Ottawa: Information Canada.

Economic Council of Canada. (1977). *Into the 80s.* Ottawa: Information Canada.

Fombrun, C. J. (1986). Structural dynamics within and between organizations. *Administrative Science Quarterly, 31,* 403-421.

Fombrun, C. J. (1988). Crafting an institutionally informed ecology of organizations. In G. R. Carroll (Ed.), *Ecological models of organizations* (pp. 223-239). Cambridge, MA: Ballinger.

Freeman, J. H. (1979). Going to the well: School district administrative intensity and environmental constraint. *Administrative Science Quarterly, 24,* 119-133.

Freeman, J. H., Carroll, G. R., & Hannan, M. T. (1983). The liability of newness: Age dependence in organizational death rates. *American Sociological Review, 48,* 692-710.

Freeman, J. H., & Hannan, M. T. (1983). Niche width and the dynamics of organizational populations. *American Journal of Sociology, 88,* 1116-1145.

Granovetter, M. (1985). Economic action and social structure: The problem of embeddedness. *American Journal of Sociology, 91*, 481-510.

Halliday, T. C., Powell, M. J., & Granfors, M. W. (1987). Minimalist organizations: Vital events in state bar associations, 1870-1930. *American Sociological Review, 52*, 456-471.

Hannan, M. T. (1986). *A model of competitive and institutional processes in organizational ecology* (Tech. Rep. No. 8613, July). Ithaca, NY: Cornell University, Department of Sociology.

Hannan, M. T., & Freeman, J. (1977). The population ecology of organizations. *American Journal of Sociology, 82*, 929-964.

Hannan, M. T., & Freeman, J. H. (1984). Structural inertia and organizational change. *American Sociological Review, 49*, 149-164.

Hannan, M. T., & Freeman, J. (1989). *Organizational ecology.* Cambridge, MA: Harvard University Press.

Houston, L. F. (1972). The flowers of power: A critique of OFY and LIP programmes. *Our Generation, 7*, 52-61.

Hurl, L. F. (1984). Privatized social service systems: Lessons from Ontario's children services. *Canadian Public Policy, 10*, 395-405.

Hurl, L. F., & Tucker, D. J. (1986). Limitations of an act of faith: An analysis of the Macdonald commission's stance on social services. *Canadian Public Policy, 12*, 606-621.

Kramer, R. M. (1981). *Voluntary agencies in the welfare state.* Berkeley: University of California Press.

Looney, M. (1977). The political economy of citizen participation. In Leo Panitch (Ed.), *The Canadian state: Political economy and political power* (pp. 346-372). Toronto: University of Toronto Press.

McKeough, W. D., The Hon. (1975). *Ontario budget 1975.* Toronto: Ministry of Treasury, Economics and Intergovernmental Affairs.

McKeough, W. D., The Hon. (1976). *Ontario budget 1976.* Toronto: Ministry of Treasury, Economics and Intergovernmental Affairs.

McPherson, M. (1983). The size of voluntary organizations. *Social Forces, 61*, 1044-1064.

Meyer, J. W., & Rowan, B. (1977). Institutional organizations: Formal structure as myth and ceremony. *American Journal of Sociology, 83*, 340-363.

Meyer, J. W., & Rowan, B. (1983). The structure of educational organizations. In J. W. Meyer & W. R. Scott (Eds.), *Organizational environments: Ritual and rationality* (pp. 71-98). Beverly Hills, CA: Sage.

Meyer, J. W., & Scott, W. R. (1983). Centralization and the legitimacy problems of local government. In J. W. Meyer & W. R. Scott (Eds.), *Organizational environments: Ritual and rationality* (pp. 199-215). Beverly Hills, CA: Sage.

Meyer, J. W., Scott, W. R., & Deal, T. E. (1983). Institutional and technical sources of organizational structure: Explaining the structure of educational organizations. In J. W. Meyer & W. R. Scott (Eds.), *Organizational environment: Ritual and rationality* (pp. 45-70). Beverly Hills, CA: Sage.

Miller, F. S., The Hon. (1980). *Ontario budget 1980.* Toronto: Ministry of Treasury and Economics.

Pfeffer, J., & Salancik, G. R. (1978). *The external control of organizations.* New York: Harper & Row.

Provan, K. G. (1980). Board power and organizational effectiveness among human service organizations. *Academy of Management Journal, 23*, 221-236.

Puckett, T., & Tucker, D. J. (1976). Hard times for Ontario's social services. *Canadian Welfare, 52,* 8-11.

Rogers, D. L., & Mulford, C. L. (1982). The historical development. In D. L. Rogers & D. A. Whetten (Eds.), *Interorganizational coordination* (pp. 32-53). Ames: Iowa State University Press.

Rowan, B. (1982). Organizational structure and the institutional environment: The case of public schools. *Administrative Science Quarterly, 27,* 259-279.

Scott, W. R. (1987). *Organizations: Rational, natural and open systems.* Englewood Cliffs, NJ: Prentice-Hall.

Scott, W. R., & Meyer, J. W. (1983). The organization of societal sectors. In J. W. Meyer & W. R. Scott (Eds.), *Organizational environment: Ritual and rationality* (pp. 129-153). Beverly Hills, CA: Sage.

Selznick, P. (1947). *TVA and the grass roots: A study in the sociology of formal organization.* Berkeley: University of California Press.

Singh, J. V., House, R. J., & Tucker, D. J. (1986). Organizational change and organizational mortality. *Administrative Science Quarterly, 31,* 587-611.

Singh, J. V., & Lumsden, C. J. (1990). Theory and research in organizational ecology. *Annual Review of Sociology, 16,* 161-195.

Singh, J. V., Tucker, D. J., & House, R. J. (1986). Organizational legitimacy and the liability of newness. *Administrative Science Quarterly, 31,* 171-193.

Singh, J. V., Tucker, D. J., & Meinhard, A. (1988, August). *Are voluntary organizations structurally inert? Exploring an assumption in organizational ecology.* Paper presented at the Academy of Management National Meetings, Organization and Management Theory Division, Anaheim, CA.

Singh, J. V., Tucker, D. J., & Meinhard, A. (1991). Institutional change and ecological dynamics. In W. W. Powell & P. J. DiMaggio (Eds.), *The new institutionalism in organizational analysis.* Chicago: University of Chicago Press.

Social Planning Council of Metropolitan Toronto. (1984). *Caring for profit.* Toronto: Social Planning Council of Metropolitan Toronto.

Stinchcombe, A. L. (1965). Organizations and social structure. In J. G. March (Ed.), *Handbook of organizations* (pp. 142-193). Chicago: Rand McNally.

Tolbert, P., & Zucker, L. G. (1983). Institutional sources of change in the formal structures of organizations: The diffusion of civil service reform. *Administrative Science Quarterly, 28,* 22-39.

Tucker, D. J. (1981). Voluntary auspices and the behavior of social service organizations. *Social Service Review, 55,* 605-627.

Tucker, D. J., Singh, J. V., House, R. J., & Meinhard, A. G. (1985). *Age dependence, heterogenity, and organizational mortality.* Unpublished manuscript, School of Social Work, McMaster University.

Tucker, D. J., Singh, J. V., & Meinhard, A. G. (1990a). Founding characteristics, imprinting and organizational change. In J. V. Singh (Ed.), *Organizational evolution: New directions* (pp. 182-200). Newbury Park, CA: Sage.

Tucker, D. J., Singh, J. V., & Meinhard, A. G. (1990b). Organizational form, population dynamics and institutional change: The founding patterns of voluntary organizations. *Academy of Management Journal, 33,* 151-178.

Tucker, D. J., Singh, J. V., Meinhard, A., & House, R. J. (1988). Ecological and institutional sources of change in organizational populations. In G. R. Carroll (Ed.), *Ecological models of organizations* (pp. 127-152). Cambridge, MA: Ballinger.

Warren, R. L. (1972). The concerting of decisions as a variable in organizational interaction. In M. Tuite, R. Chisholm, & M. Radnor (Eds.), *Interorganizational decision making* (pp. 20-32). Chicago: Aldine.

Warren, R. L. (1973). Comprehensive planning and coordination: Some functional aspects. *Social Problems, 20,* 355-364.

Warren, R. L., Rose, S. M., & Bergunder, A. F. (1974). *The structure of urban reform.* Lexington, MA: Lexington Books.

Wharf, B., & Carter, N. (1972). *Planning for social services: Canadian experiences.* Ottawa: Canadian Council on Social Development.

Wilensky, H., & Lebeaux, C. (1957). *Industrial society and social welfare.* New York: Free Press.

Zald, M. N. (1969). The power and functions of boards of directors: A theoretical synthesis. *American Journal of Sociology, 75,* 97-111.

Zucker, L. G. (1983). Organizations as institutions. In S. B. Bacharach (Ed.), *Research in the sociology of organizations* (vol. 2, pp. 1-47). Greenwich, CT: JAI Press.

Zucker, L. G. (1989). Combining institutional theory and population ecology: No legitimacy, no history. *American Sociological Review, 54,* 542-545.

CHAPTER 4

Nonprofit Human Service Organizations
FUNDING STRATEGIES AND PATTERNS
OF ADAPTATION

KIRSTEN A. GRONBJERG

Nonprofit organizations constitute critical links in the provision of human services in the United States. While the public sector directly controls and administers most systems of cash assistance, nonprofit organizations provide a large proportion of all human *services,* especially outside the health field (where proprietary agencies increasingly dominate). The importance of nonprofit human service organizations derives in part from their large numbers and the amount of organizational resources they control,[1] but they also occupy strategic intermediary positions in the complex system of interorganizational relationships through which human services are delivered in the United States. They deliver large proportions of human services that are financed

AUTHOR'S NOTE: A revised version of this chapter was presented at the National Conference of the American Society for Public Administration, Panel on "Partnerships for Excellence in Human Services," Los Angeles, California, April 9-12, 1990. Parts of this paper were originally published in *Nonprofit and Voluntary Sector Quarterly, 20* (1). ©1991 by Josey-Bass Inc. and is used here with permission; the analysis is the subject of a forthcoming book on *The Structure and Management of Funding Relations in the Nonprofit Sector: The Case of Human Services* (Jossey-Bass).
   Grants from the Joyce Foundation, the Program on Non-Profit Organizations at Yale University, the Chicago Community Trust, the Woods Charitable Fund, and Loyola University of Chicago have supported the research. Some data were collected as part of a Chicago Urban Policy Seminar at the University of Chicago. I acknowledge the participation by students in that course and by Susan Waldhier, Jing Zhang, Jack Harkins, Carol Dragon, and Christine Wiegand of Loyola University of Chicago. In addition, the executive directors of the participating organizations, scholars at the University of Minnesota and at Case Western Reserve University, Dennis Young, Joseph Galaskiewicz, Zeke Hasenfeld, and Gerald Suttles provided valuable feedback on the data and analysis.

through public expenditures,[2] provide *all* human services that are financed through donations (i.e., with indirect public funding in the form of foregone tax revenues because of the tax-deductibility of donations), and deliver at least some human services financed through private individual or third-party payment systems (e.g., insurance).

Obviously, the entire interorganizational human service system involves the participation of all levels of government, numerous nonprofit organizations, a significant number of proprietary service organizations (especially in the day-care and homemaking fields) as well as independent, individual providers (i.e., homemakers, foster parents, counselors). When fully articulated, these interorganizational relationships take a variety of forms, including collaborative needs assessment, joint development of social service models, client referrals, coordinated advocacy efforts, and—most explicitly—formalized partnerships in the form of grants and contractual arrangements among consenting organizations for the delivery of human services.

Because these relationships often involve the exchange of key organizational resources, that is, access to clients, technology, or legitimacy, they tend to be highly politicized and to dominate management efforts. These features are most obvious in the case of funding relationships because it is through the effective management of these relationships that nonprofit organizations obtain their most critical organizational resources: the revenues that allow them to operate, employ staff, and provide services to clients.

Relying on case studies of nonprofit social service organizations with distinctive funding profiles, I examine how such organizations secure and manage three major types of funding available to them (fees, donations, and government grants and contracts); the effects of these activities on nonprofit agency overhead, planning, and program development; and the variety of mechanisms nonprofit organizations employ in managing and attempting to control their respective funding sources. I also speculate on how these efforts impact on clients and on the structure of the available human service system.

Managing Nonprofit Funding Relations

Nonprofit funding sources differ in how institutionalized, predictable, and controllable they are and in whether they separate clients (service recipients) and customers (sources of funds). According to the resource dependency perspective, the composition of such funding structures provide the critical context within which organizational decision making takes place (Dess & Beard, 1984; Pfeffer & Leong, 1977; Pfeffer & Salancik, 1978; Provan, Beyer, & Kruytbosch, 1980). For nonprofit organizations several key features stand out. First, nonprofit organizations generally do not exercise direct control over the continued availability of their funding sources. In contrast to government agencies, nonprofit organizations can rarely point to legally mandated services that *they* must provide and for which legislators *must* allocate tax dollars. That limits the conditions under which they can participate in the political process in order to protect themselves against charges of lobbying and maintain their tax-exempt status.

In contrast to for-profit businesses, nonprofit organizations rarely have ready access to customers who are able and willing to pay the entire cost of the services they provide. Advertisements, sales strategies, and other attempts to manipulate demand will therefore have limited impact and uncertain or diffuse consequences for earned revenue. And when nonprofit organizations do attempt to seek access to financially competent customers, or develop marketable goods or services, they face charges of "unfair competition" from the business sector (Bennett & DiLorenzo, 1989).

Second, most nonprofit organizations rely on a great variety of funding sources. For example, they may receive public grants and contracts directly from government or administered through other nonprofit agencies; donations in the form of foundation grants, corporate support, direct individual giving, United Way funds, church donations, federated funding, and bequests; earned income from dues, fees, service charges, rent, and product sales; and other income from endowments, investments, and special events.

Each of these types of revenue reaches a significant proportion of nonprofit organizations. In 1982, an estimated two-thirds of Chicago area nonprofit service organizations received funding from government, from a combination of fees, dues or service charges, or from direct individual donations; two-fifths obtained foundation grants and/or corporate support; one-quarter had revenues from United Way, from endowments and other investments, or from fund-raising and sales of products; and one-fifth received support from religious and other federated funders (Gronbjerg, Kimmich, & Salamon, 1985, p. 41).

In order to secure funding from these sources, nonprofit organizations must perform specific tasks: write grant proposals, enter contractual relationships, solicit donations, meet United Way membership requirements, market themselves to fee-paying clients, collect dues, invest endowments, organize special events, and so forth. Most funding sources (e.g., restricted grants and contracts, earned revenues) also require agencies to provide specific services or undertake particular activities in return for the funding.

The particular tasks vary from one revenue source to the next and create highly specific funding relationships that differ greatly, even among similar types of funding. Most of these relationships link the recipient organizations directly or indirectly to a large and diverse number of other organizations and present them with an ongoing series of strategic opportunities and contingencies. Nonprofit administrators must manage these with some degree of effectiveness and understanding of how they combine and interact, if the organization is to continue to function.

Finally, all organizations must also secure and manage resources under conditions that reflect the environment in which they operate, particularly the industry or service sector to which they belong. Major nonprofit service industries, such as social services, health, education, arts and culture, not only have different products and technologies, but also differ in the size and composition of the industry, the presence of for-profit competitors, and in the extent and nature of linkages to the public sector (Gronbjerg, 1987).[3] In addition, the nonprofit status itself carries certain organizational imperatives (e.g., assumptions about purposes and goals) and mandates particular institutional procedures (e.g., accounting and reporting practices).

These institutional practices create distinctive "normative climates" (J. W. Meyer & Scott, 1983, p. 14) and inter-organizational relational structures (DiMaggio & Powell, 1983; Hannan & Freeman, 1977, 1984), which in turn set parameters for the nature of funding relationships and the delivery of human services. Social service organizations exist in a dense organizational environment in which many linkages connect a large number of active organizations in a system of mutual dependence focused around the cooperative production of services (Gronbjerg, 1987). Public and private actors control key aspects of this environment because they shape the types and magnitude of problems that nonprofit service organizations attempt to address and set parameters for the models they pursue.

Research Approach and Methodology

My approach examines how nonprofit organizations relate to specific funding sources and manage the challenges these present. Here I present selected findings from six social service nonprofit organizations with distinctive resource profiles. They represent three types of *funding composition* (primary reliance on government funding, on mixed public and donation funding, or on fees) and illustrate how differences in resource dependency and the composition of funding streams influence organizational structure and work.

The effectiveness of specific resource strategies and management choices are likely to vary by type of resource (Hall, 1987; Kimberly, 1975; Rowan, 1982; Ylvisaker, 1987). I selected two patterns of *funding stability* (turbulence and stability) to identify the strengths and weaknesses of strategies for the different types of resource dependencies. Two of the "turbulent" organizations included in this chapter experienced sustained growth, rather than a combination of growth and decline.

The combination of these criteria produces six profiles. I identified a suitable social service candidate for each profile from an existing data base on Chicago nonprofit organizations (Gronbjerg, 1986), but limited my selection to medium-sized organizations, defined as organizations with 1986 revenues of at least $200,000 (to insure a relatively high level of organizational stability) and less than $1.5 million (to manage the data collection). As Table 4.1 shows, the selected organizations pursue fairly typical missions.

For each of the selected organizations, we analyzed a wide range of documents (e.g., audit statements, annual reports, board minutes, correspondence with donors, grant and contract files). We sought to document changes in funding sources over time (4-11 years) and to analyze efforts to develop, secure, and manage fees, donations, and restricted grants and contracts over one fiscal year. We also interviewed the executive director and other key staff persons in order to examine resource strategies.

Managing Nonprofit Funding Streams

The general analysis confirms a basic hypothesis from the resource dependency model—that resource relationships become institutionalized over time (Pfeffer & Salancik, 1978). All six human service organizations showed great continuity in their overall reliance on particular funding streams, although they differed in their efforts and abilities to control them. Such institutionalization occurs because it is less costly to organizations to continue to manage funding relationships with which

Table 4.1 Description of Participating Agencies

Agency Profile	Mission/Target Population	1988 Revenues	Average % (1984-1988) from		
			Public	Donations	Fees
Public-Stable	Alcoholism Treatment	$319,000	82	3	6
Public-Growth	Hispanic Youth	965,000	89	9	0
Mixed-Stable	Minority Youth	1,429,000	48	44	3
Mixed-Growth	White Ethnic Population	584,000	42	29	11
Fee-Stable	Minority Search	560,000	0	25	67
Fee-Turbulent	Christian Therapy	111,000[a]	1	18	77

NOTES: a. Down from $265,000 in 1987.
  Percentage distributions do not add to 100 for each agency. Remaining revenues come from interests, special events, and other miscellaneous sources.
  The Alcoholism Treatment Agency provides substance abuse services and treatment to adults and youths. The Hispanic Youth Agency provides substance abuse treatment, pregnancy prevention, employment and training, and community organizing to Hispanic youth. The Minority Youth Agency provides counseling, prevention, employment, and arts involvement to minority students in inner-city schools. The White Ethnic Agency provides immigration services, counseling for battered women, shelter for homeless males, food pantry for the elderly, and employment services for refugees. The Minority Search Agency recruits and trains promising minority college students and places them in internship positions with major corporations. The Christian Therapy Agency provides therapy within a Christian framework to individual clients.

they have developed familiarity than to meet the overhead costs and uncertainty involved in exploring new funding relationships. In addition, organizational members develop vested interests in continuing existing funding relationships: contacts and skills (and hence status in the organization) that are appropriate to one type of funding source may not easily translate to other sources.

Detailed analysis of each of three major types of nonprofit funding sources (fees, donations, and government grants and contracts) reveals important differences among them in terms of predictability, controllability, and the nature and amount of management work. However, the analysis also shows that there are equally important variations among specific funding streams within each major type of funding.

Marketing Services to Clients

Fees and other sources of earned income share important resource characteristics that make them very attractive to nonprofit human service organizations. Specifically, client-paid fees allow organizations to control directly the allocation of staff resources (who should do what) and the content, structure, and timing of management tasks (what kinds of organizational records to maintain and over what time frame). However, the importance of such resource flexibility must be balanced against the corresponding uncertainty that stems from lack of control over the supply and characteristics of clients and over the number and capacities of competitors. In general, patterns of growth or decline in fee income reflect the organization's ability to develop and manage a client market or product line, safeguard the market against competitors, and position itself for changes in client supply and service demands.

Five of the six social service organizations have income from client-paid fees (see Table 4.1), and two of them rely heavily on fees. Detailed fundings document that these two organizations differ markedly on their abilities to secure fees on a continuing basis, and in related programmatic and structural changes. I interpret these differences as reflecting how the two organizations have sought to market themselves in the human service environment.

The analysis suggests that the most critical elements in generating stable, predictable fee revenues for nonprofit human service organizations involve the extent to which such organizations are able fully to equate their market niche and organizational mission, establish predictable client relationships, and maintain control over staff and other organizational resources. Specifically, organizations seeking to create relatively predictable client relationships will find it preferable to develop long-term client relationships, seek high proportions of repeat clients, focus on fiscally competent clients, and pursue organizational rather than individual clients.[4] However, such efforts may endanger organizational missions if the latter include service and outreach to low-income clients.

More generally, fee-reliant organizations need to maintain tight management control over organizational resources to prevent staff members from using their service expertise to compete directly with the organization. This involves control over staff work assignments and over access to and management of clients, as well as efforts to create loyal staff members by promoting compensation and career development.

Identifying and Cultivating Donor Sources

Like fees, most sources of donations constitute relatively flexible funding sources for nonprofit human service organizations. Unrestricted donations especially would seem to allow nonprofit managers to plan their allocation of staff, space, and activities with some flexibility and direct control. All six of the participating organizations received donations from two or more types of sources.

The participating organizations pursue diverse strategies for generating donations. Most of these involve efforts to market the organization to a variety of publics that are thought to be potential sources of donations. Organizations that develop multiple donation sources spread the risks associated with each source and are able to maintain a relatively high reliance on donations. However, this strategy requires demanding efforts, especially by board members, and is not easily sustained. It also favors the selection of board members on the basis of affluence or personal access and easily diverts the board from serving other functions.

Several of the organizations identify and target specific marketing segments from whom to solicit donations in order to obtain better access to donors and develop more customized scripts. However, most social service agencies have only a limited constituency who are loyal contributors, consisting largely of individuals with a personal belief in the agency's moral mission, or of foundations whose charters or priorities match that of the organization. Several of the organizations also use formalized and systematic fund-raising efforts in order to make the donation relationships more predictable and controllable. However, only the most institutionalized relationships (e.g., with United Way and religious funding federations) provide reliable and continuous donations.

In general, while agencies may devote a high level and a variety of efforts to seeking donations, few strategies result in predictable or growing sources of revenues. Rather, donations change in volatile and unpredictable ways from year to year and these fluctuations occur whether or not the organizations have systematic development efforts or the opportunity to build on natural constituencies.

Although both fees and donations provide flexible funding, the findings suggests that fees may be more controllable (at least under some conditions) than are most forms of donations. I interpret these findings as reflecting the fact that donations, in contrast to fees, separate customers (donors) from clients (service recipients) and that organizations have no effective leverage over donors or ability to generate donation funding by restructuring their own service efforts. The lack of control explains why donations rarely drive organizational service activities or programmatic strategies as explicitly or forcefully as do fee revenues or government grants and contracts.

Securing and Managing
Public Grants and Contracts

In contrast to fees and some sources of donations, most public grants and contracts subject recipient organizations to considerable outside control in the form of deadlines and mandatory reporting requirements that limit discretion and impose a wide range of management tasks. However, the ongoing nature of public funding (at least in the social services field) makes the relationships predictable and organizations can adjust to them by institutionalizing particular management practices. Four of the participating organizations have sufficient public funding to examine how public funding relationships operate and interact with other funding sources.[5]

The analysis reveals that government grants and contracts constitute complex and demanding funding structures. Each individual grant or contract usually involves transfer of funds between several different levels of government and at times passes through nonprofit intermediary organizations as well. The structure imposes obvious transaction costs because each organizational participant adds its own layer of objectives and must track decisions at all other levels in order to determine its own resource opportunities.

Figure 4.1 illustrates the complete funding structure for one of the four agencies, including additional grants and contracts it received from the United Way and 37 different foundations and corporate giving programs. As the figure shows, many public funding paths involve three separate organizations before they reach the agency that actually delivers the services. Although most grants and contracts for social services are administered by state agencies (at least in Illinois), the four organizations also tracked policy decisions at the federal and local levels of government in order to position themselves for future funding opportunities or changes in current requirements.

Overall, the four organizations received 46 separate grants and contracts directly or indirectly from public funding sources through 85 separate funding transactions that involved 36 different organizations. However, the analysis (and the example illustrated in Figure 4.1) oversimplifies the funding structure, since each grant and contract also connects recipient organizations indirectly to other service providers with similar grants and contracts from the same funding source and program. Obviously, the overall efficiency and effectiveness of the human service system depends on how these funding networks operate.

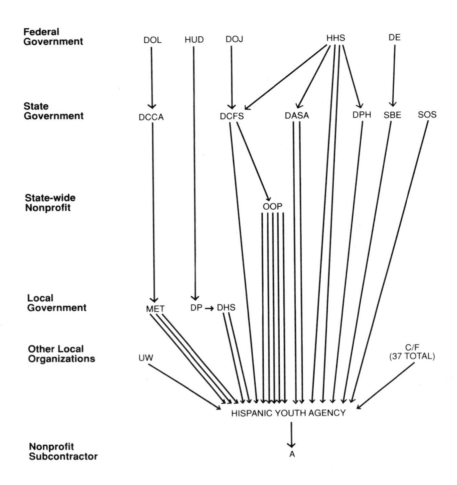

Figure 4.1. Fiscal Year 1988 Funding Relations, Hispanic Youth Agency
NOTE: *Federal Government:* DOL—Department of Labor; HUD—Housing and Urban Development; DOJ—Department of Justice; HHS—Health and Human Services; DE—Department of Education.
    State Goverment: DCCA—Department of Commerce and Community Affairs; DCFS—Department of Children and Family Services; DASA—Department of Alcoholism and Substance Abuse; DPH—Department of Public Health; SBE—State Board of Education; SOS—Secretary of State.
    State-Wide Nonprofit: OOP—Ounce of Prevention.
    Local Government: MET—Mayor's Employment and Training; DP—Department of Planning; DHS—Department of Human Services.
    Other Local Organizations: UW—United Way; C/F—Corporations/Foundations;
    Nonprofit Subcontractor: A—Local nonprofit.

Although important, monitoring funding networks and tracking potential sources of new grants and contracts took less time and effort for the agencies than managing the individual grants and contracts active over the fiscal year. We documented high levels of management efforts in both the proposal/contract phases and in the operating/reporting phases. These phases, and the associated tasks, do not appear to relate in predictable ways to the size of the grant or the level of government involved. Rather, the type and amount of work, and the nature of decisions that nonprofit organizations face in managing these funding relationships differ considerably depending on how restrictive the funding source is and also on whether the contract or grant is new or continuing.

The number, diversity, and idiosyncratic timing of these tasks create further complexity and complicate coordination and planning. The restricted grants and contracts that were active during one fiscal year averaged 24 coordinated management tasks per grant spread over 30 months for the four agencies. Moreover, during any fiscal period agencies manage activities related to three consecutive program cycles: winding up reporting and reimbursement activities for the past period; delivering services, reporting, and tracking contract performance for the current period; and preparing proposals for the next period.

The public grants and contract system also impose special fiscal contingencies in the form of cash-flow problems and high levels of accounts receivables. For example, until agencies receive the finalized contract they cannot bill their services. But if agencies temporarily curtail service efforts they may encounter staff problems and also fail to meet the service "numbers" specified in the contract. In turn, that may endanger their overall performance record and ability to recover or salvage the full grant amount. In addition, only the United Way and very small public grants provide agencies with up-front funding for service activities, the rest impose a system of post-effort and delayed payments that in effect provide fiscal relief and interest free loans to public treasuries. Such practices place a premium on access to reserve funds and mean that agencies will likely use more flexible funding, such as donations, to supplement or bridge efforts mandated under restricted grants and contracts. In effect, private funding and the nonprofit agencies themselves subsidize the public sector.

In spite of the efforts and difficulties involved in managing the government grants and contract system, agency directors view these funding sources quite positively because they provide ongoing and predictable funding from year to year. The dominant pattern is one of continuing grants and contracts over the 1984-1988 period, with increases in public funding primarily through the addition of new (but small) grants and contracts that the agencies gained access to and expected to keep. However, the ongoing grants and contracts rarely provided cost of living increases. Their flat or declining nominal values from year to year required agencies to meet ongoing or increasing service needs and costs with declining values of resources. The addition of new *and* smaller grants also added disproportionately to management overhead because each grant or contract requires its own management schedule and processing. All four agencies also encountered government grants and contracts with increasingly diverse program periods that no longer matched their own fiscal years, further complicating their ability to manage and coordinate programs.

Nevertheless, the greater continuity in and predictability of government grants and contracts (compared to donations) make them particularly attractive to social service agencies. That, along with the increasing complexity of securing and managing them, means that they easily come to dominate agency activities, even if the organization receives other funding as well. In addition, the intricacy and timing of these efforts complicate the ability of agencies to engage in effective planning and program development of their own.

Strategies and Patterns of Adaptation

The analysis summarized above points to a number of organizational problems that nonprofit organizations face when they attempt to manage their funding relationships and participate in the delivery of publicly funded human services. I have discussed specific contingencies associated with each of three major funding streams. However, the case studies also identify a number of more general strategies and patterns of adaptations that nonprofit organizations may pursue in managing funding sources and the contingencies these present. The list of problems and strategies also includes more accidental observations from my wider fieldwork. While I have some documentation for all of the strategies discussed below, I present them as types of adaptations that in some cases go beyond what we observed in the individual agencies.

Nonprofit service agencies must attempt to address a number of general management challenges that relate directly or indirectly to contingencies associated with particular funding sources and efforts to manage the external environment. They must decide: How to link the priorities of funding sources to agency missions and client or community needs; how to develop resource flexibility and cushion themselves against funding jolts; and how to engage in networking and other boundary spanning activities in order to develop and maintain resources.[6] Table 4.2 summarizes specific strategies (and their respective limitations) for meeting each of these major challenges.

Challenge: Link Funding Priorities to Agency Mission and Client/Community Needs

The effective delivery of human services requires fairly tightly coupled relationships between nonprofit service providers and public funders in order to insure that funder priorities reflect client or community needs as closely as possible, and that agency missions are consistent with both of these. Our cases studies suggest that such coordination and linkages are especially difficult to create if agencies rely on a variety of funding sources or on multiple grants and contracts from public funding sources.

The Bottom-Up Approach. Agencies may seek to use a "client-driven" approach, in which the agencies seek to maintain close communication between service-level staff and key administrators with central responsibility for the development of grant and contract proposals. Such communication structures may help agencies overcome the tendency towards a decoupling of service delivery activities from the maintenance of funding relationships. Otherwise, the short lead times associated with grants and contract work interferes with the use of more formalized needs assessments (or other mechanisms for determining client needs) to guide decisions about how to restructure proposals for existing funding relationships or develop approaches to new funding sources.

Even so, the bottom-up approach seems to be followed intermittently, at best, and is easily compromised. It demands a high level of commitment to maintaining effective communication and sharing decision making and consumes a great deal of staff time.[7] The approach seems to be easiest to follow when the agency has unrestricted private funding available and can use these funds to initiate new program developments. It is instructive that we encountered no contract amendments that reflected changing client needs and that most proposals seemed to contain only minor modifications of the agency's previous proposal for the same program.

Table 4.2   Nonprofit Management Challenges and Strategies

Challenge—Link Funder Priorities, Mission, Needs	
Strategy	Caveats
Bottom-up, "client-driven" approach	Easily disrupted or subverted
Marketing approach to repackage activities	Costly if revealed to funders
Selection approach to match mission	Threatens missions, client needs, resources
Accidental approach	Unanticipated directions

Challenge—Create Flexibility, Cushion Funder Jolts	
Strategy	Caveats
Develop private funding	Uncontrollable donations
Seek markets for commercial services	Secures organizational control
Expand existing public grants/contracts	Requires funder trust
Combine grants/contracts	Requires narrow, priority target populations
Centralize control over reporting	Encourages errors or abuse
Disaggregate files, customize reporting	Staff training, assessments, abuse
Cash-flow crises procedures	Cost, long-term impact

Challenge—Expand Networking, Boundary-Spanning Activities	
Strategy	Caveats
Seek political contacts	Legitimacy and high-level efforts
Seek contacts with funder staff	Competent staff
Seek referral networks with other nonprofits	Demanding if fully implemented
Create joint programs with other nonprofits	Complex, difficult to evaluate
Copy features from other nonprofits	May not meet client needs

The Marketing Approach. In one version of the marketing strategy, the agency takes what it is currently doing and repackages it with new terminology that fits "hot" funder priorities or emerging market demands. If centrally controlled and conducted separately from the service staff, this approach may have only little impact on what the agency actually does and thus preserves agency mission. However, new funder initiatives or program developments then may be new in name only, not in approach, service structure, or client outcomes. Several of the agencies pursued this strategy with considerable funding success. To the extent that agencies follow this approach, funders will find it difficult accurately to document the effectiveness of new program initiatives.

In the more common version of the strategy, the agency uses its perceptions of market demands, whether those of funders or of fee-paying clients, to select among the array of funding possibilities. In principle, the agency uses its mission to guide its choices, but our analysis suggests that this type of marketing approach may easily take on a life of its own. While likely to be successful at least in the short run, agencies seem to find it difficult to maintain the primacy of their mission and the strategy may therefore endanger agency mission and ability to meet client needs. In turn, either or both of these failures may threaten the agency's access to other resources, such as client referrals or community support (e.g., donations).

The Accidental Approach. Agencies may simply happen to be in the right place at the right time, e.g., serving ethnic groups with large numbers of illegal aliens eligible for publicly funded legalization services. Or agencies may obtain funding before programs have been fully developed because of opportunities coming its way. As a result (and similar to the second version of the marketing approach), the agency may easily find itself pursuing new directions with which its staff and/or board may not feel comfortable. For those reasons, the strategy may also create problems in meeting program performance expectations.

Challenge: Provide Flexibility and Cushioning Against Funding Jolts

Fiscal contingencies associated with the restricted grants and contract system place a high premium on access to flexible funding and funding reserves to cushion against funding jolts (A. D. Meyer, 1982). Differences in the predictability and controllability of funding sources also mean that nonprofit managers must continuously explore a variety of short- and long-term resource strategies. We identified a number of such strategies, ranging from attempts to increase non-public funding sources to efforts to overcome specific problems associated with government grants and contracts.

Develop Unrestricted Private Funding. Agencies may use unrestricted private funding to subsidize public grants and contracts, as bridge funding, to compensate for failures to claim the entire contract amount (eliminate salvage), or to support efforts for which no public funding is available. However, as discussed above, our cases studies reveal that agencies may have limited success in controlling donations and that even sophisticated and formalized donation strategies may not result in predictable revenues.

That is because corporations, foundations, individual donors, and other sources of private donations tend not to be subject to outside resource controls (except in the form of volunteer decision makers). In contrast to public funders, donors are not legally mandated to insure continuity of specific efforts and have less reason to provide ongoing funding or impose detailed management tasks on grantees. Under these circumstances agency leverage originates less in its own service efforts than with the contacts it can establish with outside resource decision makers who have little or no investment in the agency itself.

Staff, board members, or consultants devote considerable efforts to building such access, but uncertainties and high failure rates encourage agencies to insulate their central core from these fund-raising activities. We found that agencies relegate donation efforts to special subunits within the organization (development departments), to more peripheral units (consultants, auxiliaries, or busy board members), or engage in them only sporadically. As a result, these funding sources rarely drive agency developments.

Seek New or Predictable Markets for Commercial Services. Agencies may seek fees and other forms of earned revenues as ways to reduce the impact of high failure rates of fund-raising or up-front management efforts associated with public grants and contracts. Fees and earned income also provide agencies with a market test of their services and allow them to exploit their service efforts and capacities to generate resources directly. In addition, management practices and efforts associated with fees are less obviously shaped by institutional actors outside the agency than is the case for government grants and contracts. As a result, management efforts for fee-dependent organizations are less standardized and more closely intertwined with internal features of the organization than is the case with government funding.

Our analysis of fee-dependent social service agencies reveals dramatic differences in their ability to secure fees on a continuing basis and in the extent of related programmatic and structural changes. Their experiences demonstrate the importance, but difficulty, of efforts to link missions and market niches and of creating loyal clients and staff in order to secure organizational control over this particular revenue source.

Seek Expansion of Existing Public Grants and Contracts. Agencies may use a variety of mechanisms to seek expansion or prevent reductions in existing grants and contracts with public agencies. For example, all four agencies with public grants and contracts submitted proposals that would have increased funding levels over the prior year. Most of these "expansion" proposals were fairly close to prior year funding levels, although the Alcoholism Treatment Agency submitted one proposal that would have more than tripled the contract *and* its own size. Such expansion efforts were rarely successful, but agency administrators thought of them as important strategies for preventing cuts and as bases for future negotiations with the funding source by building a claim for increased client needs and for high levels of agency service capacity.

A closely related strategy involves attempts to manipulate unit costs of services, and therefore the agency's competitive edge in future grant and contract proposals. Such strategies include decisions about quality and costs of staff, how broadly to define program efforts (and thus costs), and which overhead costs to include. In all cases, the analysis suggests that agencies must cultivate relationships with funders over a period of time in order to develop sufficient trust and credibility to succeed in these strategies.

Combine Grants and Contracts. Agencies may combine grants from several sources by packaging them around concepts that appear to be salable to a variety of funders so that services will be provided consistently even if funders change. This is easiest to do if the agency focuses on narrowly defined target populations with high funder priorities (such as low-income, minority youths). It is a much more difficult strategy to follow if the agency aims to serve a variety of different, non-overlapping client groups with different service needs (e.g., clients include battered women, older alcoholic males, illegal aliens, *and* officially recognized refugees).

Centralize Control over Reporting. Agencies may institute systems of centralizing control over reporting to insure that it matches funder expectations and contract requirements as closely as possible. This allows the agency to overcome a variety of common problems, such as changes in the levels of funding or service activities required by other contracts, staff vacancies, or events that bar access to program facilities (such as strikes). The strategy is most likely to be needed if the agency has a very high reliance on very restrictive funding sources. However, such a system of centralized reporting is difficult to carry out conscientiously because of the complexity of reporting requirements and is therefore subject to error.

Disaggregate Reporting and Data Files. Whether or not agencies chose to exercise central control over the actual reporting, they may maintain separate files and reporting systems for each funding source in order to customize funding relationships. This practice has special implications for how staff are trained to report and file service statistics and may prevent the agency from developing coherent perspectives on its own activities. Like the strategy to centralize reporting, the strategy to disaggregate reporting will impede the ability of a funder to determine how its funded activities relate to the agency's other activities, should it want to do so, and both may in extreme situations open the door to agency abuse.

Establish Cash-Flow Crises Procedures. Agencies may develop crisis mechanisms for dealing with cash-flow problems, such as delaying the payment of bills, establishing a line of credit, delaying paychecks selectively for some staff members (usually central administrative staff), and borrowing against endowments. However, any of these solutions are likely to have adverse long-term impacts, such as limiting opportunities for future credit, the disaffection of staff, and the loss of earned interest.

Some agencies see the development of marketable products or services as strategies for insuring relatively stable cash flow, as may the purchase of real estate to house tenants who can pay rent as well as the agency itself. However, each of these efforts involves direct expenditures, expands the range of tasks and scope of management responsibilities, and may therefore detract from efforts to meet client needs and pursue organizational missions.

Challenge: Expand Networking and Other Boundary Spanning Activities

To develop and maintain resources nonprofit human service agencies must maintain good, current information about the institutional environment in which they operate. The large number of organizations active in the human services field, the multiple sources of funding available, and the short response time under which many of these operate, make networking and other boundary spanning activities especially important. We found that most of these activities centered around efforts to protect existing funding relationships and develop opportunities for new ones. We did encounter some networking and other boundary spanning efforts that served to develop effective coordination and integration of services. But these were fewer in number and less vigorously pursued.

Seek Political Contacts. Agencies may attempt to develop contacts that serve the explicit purpose of providing information about funding (especially new) and protect existing funding relationships. For public funding, these efforts appear most effective if they involve contacts with elected officials who can pull the right strings. The resource control that legislative bodies can exert over public agencies constitute points of vulnerability for them and provide nonprofits with leverage. However, it is a strategy that only relatively few nonprofits can use successfully or persistently. It is also a strategy that requires high-level agency efforts, usually that of the executive director, more rarely board members. This strategy thus serves to maintain central control and power in the hands of the executive director. It also leaves the agency vulnerable to turn-overs in executive directors—as the director leaves, so may the contacts.

Seek Contacts with Funder Staff. Agencies may focus on developing working relationships with funder staffs, usually at the program level. This serves to establish the credibility and legitimacy of agency service performances and serves to forewarn agencies about impending changes in funding levels or program requirements. These contacts also greatly facilitate the resolution of problems that may occur in documenting agency performances. However, it requires a relatively high level of competency among staff members to insure that such contacts with funders enhance, rather than endanger, the agency's credibility.

Seek Referral Networks with Other Nonprofits. Agencies may seek to establish networks with other nonprofits for referral purposes. Such networking is required or strongly encouraged by several funding sources and some agencies see them primarily as pro forma requirements that they need to document for resource opportunities. It is unclear how much referral actually takes place. A number of studies suggest that few agencies are likely fully to implement effective referral networks because the fragmented service system requires extensive efforts to insure that clients actually receive the services for which they are referred and because effective referral systems threaten professional autonomy (Bush, 1988; Jacobs, 1990).

Develop Joint Programs with Other Nonprofits. We encountered several examples of joint programs with other nonprofits. Some of these joint program structures are very complex and would appear difficult to evaluate. The effectiveness of such joint ventures appears most problematic when the cooperation is created specifically to secure a particular funding source. The relationships may be easiest to institute if the participating agencies have unrestricted funding available and do not need to compete for funding at all costs. One of our agencies engaged in several such relationships with smaller agencies and views most of them as successful. It sees these efforts as strengthening the nonprofit sector and as part of its own service to the larger community. Another of our agencies resists such relationships except for the explicit purpose of allowing it to provide the full range of services that contractual obligations require.

Copy Features from Other Nonprofits. We found several examples where agencies adopt program models or administrative features from other agencies. This strategy appears to be effective if used carefully. For example, it may be easier to adopt a particular fee schedule from an agency that provides similar services than to replicate a program from an agency that serves a different ethnic group. Such strategies require agencies to know about available models and to choose to adopt models developed by others rather than formulate their own. These approaches provide agencies with ready-made legitimacy of service models and thus strengthen their efforts to secure resources, but may also encourage them to adopt service approaches that do not necessarily meet the needs of their own clients.

Nonprofit Funding Relations: Decoupling the Human Service System

I have described the management problems and contingencies nonprofit human service organizations encounter when they seek to generate independent funding streams from client-paid fees and service charges, when they attempt to cultivate private donors to subsidize their service activities, and when they participate as formal partners in the public funding network that dominates the delivery of human services in the United States. I have also described the strategies available to them in addressing major organizational challenges that derive from efforts to manage funding relationships and the external environment more generally, and I have identified some of the limitations associated with these strategies.

Because of the critical, intermediary role nonprofit organizations play in the delivery of human services, the overall efficiency and effectiveness of the human service system depend on how these organizations manage their funding relationships. The case studies document the driving force of public funding. When nonprofit human service organizations have such funding beyond a token amount, it absorbs and dominates management efforts. Sometimes referred to as "third-party government" (Salamon, 1981, 1989) the public-nonprofit relationship carries major advantages for its participants. For government funders, it reduces program start-up costs by accessing existing extragovernmental infrastructures, increases flexibility by making it easier to reallocate resources, allows them to cater to demands for local control, and maximizes control over resources while minimizing responsibilities for direct administrative supervision (Rehfuss, 1989).

For nonprofit social service agencies, the system provides access to stable, predictable, and significant sources of funding. It also confers legitimacy because it allows nonprofit agencies to contribute directly to "collective goods" (Douglas, 1983, 1987), that is, program activities that have received sufficiently broad political endorsements to receive tax allocations. In addition, to the extent that funding sources reduce resource uncertainty, agencies will find them attractive in spite of the control, management difficulties, and work they may impose. Intense and prolonged relations with funding sources give agencies opportunities to learn how to negotiate the system and circumvent or adjust to customer (funder) demands.

Agencies with high reliance on government funding or other prolonged relationships with fee-paying institutions scored highest on standard measures of organizational success. They had consistent surpluses and growing fund balances, while agencies with mixed funding or less controllable fee relationships showed closely balanced revenues and expenditures and small or declining fund balances. We interpret these findings as reflecting the greater predictability of public funding and, more generally, the greater opportunity for agencies to centralize organizational control over long-term, institutionally-based resources.

However, the structure under which human services are financed and delivered imposes obvious transaction costs and also separates, or "uncouples" (J. W. Meyer & Scott, 1983), responsibility for implementing policy decisions from the actual delivery of those services (Williams, 1980). Nonprofit intermediaries in particular seem to buffer their nonprofit subcontractors. This allows for considerable flexibility, but at the risk of disengagement by any of the participating organizations. Moreover, because each link in the system adds its own program objectives and mode of implementation, the service system assumed to operate may bear little relationship to the one that actually exists. This complicates efforts to coordinate services. The development of comprehensive approaches and coordination occurs primarily at the service delivery level and only with difficulty, if at all, because of the organizational contingencies these grants and contracts impose on nonprofit participants.

Decoupling also occurs because few funders (public or private) are able or inclined to evaluate agency performances fully, even for the subset of activities they support. Numerous revisions in proposals, contracts, and reporting requirements reflect more general patterns of accommodation and informal understandings between funders and providers. Agencies also encounter unpredictable enforcement and monitoring efforts by funding sources, directed mostly at fiscal accountability and technical compliance with reporting obligations. The manner in which these relationships operate creates a world of uncertainty and ambiguity that easily lends itself to goal displacement and may compromise both agencies and funder objectives. Finally, both donations and public funding also tend to separate clients (service recipients) and customers (funders) and present agencies with potential conflicts between satisfying the demands of either. On this dimension, donations and public fundings are inherently more difficult resources to manage than are fees and other forms of earned income. The latter provide at least some direct market tests of how effective services are.

The case-study findings thus raise a number of larger policy issues about the role of nonprofit service providers in the delivery of human services in the United States. For example, the high level of transaction and planning costs associated with the current system raises important questions about whether it is possible systematically to implement new policies and assess the impact of existing policies.

Second, the diverse funding structures under which human service agencies operate raise important questions about what services are available, to whom, and at what costs. Inevitably, services are unevenly available to different clients, irrespective of client needs or public mandates. Inevitably, the costs are high, because they include not only direct tax dollars used for the purchase of goods and services, but also the loss of unrealized tax revenues from the exclusion of donations on individual and corporate tax returns, and the direct and indirect administrative costs associated with the complex system of grants and contractual relationships.

Finally, our findings suggest that as participants in "third-party" government (Salamon, 1989), nonprofit service organizations may easily come to share in the broad decline of public confidence in government. The "third-party" government structure allows public agencies to externalize their problems onto the nonprofit sector, including fiscal shortfalls, staff turnover, limited career mobility, and visible responsibility for the (often inadequate) delivery of mandated public services (Sosin, 1990). Nonprofit organizations that rely heavily on government grants and contracts risk becoming part of an "organizational sink" in which government submerges its problems. As the general public recognizes this, nonprofit agencies may be unable to attract other sources of funding, especially sources that come from donors with a moral commitment to collective goods.

Notes

1. For example, the Chicago metropolitan area had an estimated 2,400 nonprofit human service organizations in 1982 (exclusive of hospitals and educational institutions), with combined revenues of about $2.3 billion (Gronbjerg, Kimmich, & Salamon, 1985).

2. In 1984, nonprofit agencies received an estimated $177 million in public grants and contracts to deliver social services in the Chicago-Cook County area, about 47% of total public spending by all levels of government for those purposes. Comparative data on other communities also document high levels of reliance on nonprofit organizations for the delivery of public human services (Salamon, Musselwhite, Holcomb, & Gronbjerg, 1987).

3. For example, nonprofit organizations in the community development and social service fields tend to be relatively small and numerous compared to nonprofit organizations in the education and health fields. On the other hand, the social service and education fields have relatively few for-profit competitors, compared to the health and community development fields. Finally, the public sector transfers a significant proportion of its own resources to nonprofit service providers in the social service and health fields, but less so in the education and community development fields.

4. Reliance on organizational clients allows for more formalized negotiations about what services to provide, to whom, at what cost, and reflects a range of institutional interests. Such client relationships are more fateful in terms of revenues, but also more resilient and less easily interrupted than relationships with individual clients.

5. These are described in greater detail in Gronbjerg (1990, 1991).

6. We also identified a range of strategies for managing internal resources, such as matching staff skills with program demands, establishing organizational leadership and structure, and developing agency philosophy and role of the board.

7. One of our participating agencies reserves 20% of all staff time (one full day per week) for staff training and communication about program needs.

References

Bennett, J. T., & DiLorenzo, T. J. (1989). *Unfair competition: The profits of nonprofits.* Lanham, MD: Hamilton Press.

Bush, M. (1988). *Families in distress: Public, private and civic responses.* Berkeley: University of California Press.

Dess, G. G., & Beard, D. W. (1984). Dimensions of organizational task environments. *Administrative Science Quarterly, 29,* 52-73.

DiMaggio, P. J., & Powell, W. W. (1983). The iron cage revisited: Institutional isomorphism and collective rationality in organizational fields. *American Sociological Review, 48,* 147-160.

Douglas, J. (1983). *Why charity: The case for a third sector.* Beverly Hills, CA: Sage.

Douglas, J. (1987). Political theories of nonprofit organizations. In W. W. Powell (Ed.), *The nonprofit sector: A research handbook* (pp. 43-54). New Haven, CT: Yale University Press.

Gronbjerg, K. A. (1986). *Responding to community needs: The missions and programs of Chicago nonprofit organizations* (Report). Prepared under The Urban Institute Nonprofit Sector Project.

Gronbjerg, K. A. (1987). Patterns of institutional relations in the welfare state: Public mandates and the nonprofit sector. *Journal of Voluntary Action Research, 16,* 64-80.

Gronbjerg, K. A. (1990). *Managing nonprofit funding relations: Case studies of six human service organizations* (Working Paper No. 156, Institution for Social and Policy Study, Working Paper No. 2156). New Haven, CT: Yale University, Program on Non-Profit Organizations.

Gronbjerg, K. A. (with S. Waldhier & J. Zhang). (1991). Managing grants and contracts: The case of four nonprofit organizations . *Nonprofit and Voluntary Sector Quarterly, 20,* 5-24.

Gronbjerg, K. A., Kimmich, M. H., & Salamon, L. M. (1985). *The Chicago nonprofit sector in a time of government retrenchment.* Washington, DC: Urban Institute.

Hall, P. D. (1987). Abandoning the rhetoric of independence: Reflections on the nonprofit sector in the post-liberal era. *Journal of Voluntary Action Research, 19,* 11-28.

Hannan, M. T., & Freeman, J. (1977). The population ecology of organizations. *American Journal of Sociology, 82,* 929-964.

Hannan, M. T., & Freeman, J. (1984). Structural inertia and organizational change. *American Sociological Review, 49,* 149-164.

Jacobs, M. (1990). *Screwing the system and making it work: Juvenile justice in the no-fault society.* Chicago: University of Chicago Press.

Kimberly, J. R. (1975). Environmental constraints and organizational structure: A comparative analysis of rehabilitation organizations. *Administrative Science Quarterly, 20,* 1-9.

Meyer, A. D. (1982). Adapting to environmental jolts. *Administrative Science Quarterly, 27,* 515-537.

Meyer, J. W., & Scott, W. R. (Eds.). (1983). *Organizational environments: Ritual and rationality.* Beverly Hills, CA: Sage.

Pfeffer, J., & Leong, A. (1977). Resource allocation in United Funds: Examination of power and dependency. *Social Forces, 55,* 775-790.

Pfeffer, J., & Salancik, G. (1978). *The external control of organizations.* New York: Harper & Row.

Provan, K. G., Beyer, J. M., & Kruytbosch, C. (1980). Environmental linkages and power in resource-dependence relations between organizations. *Administrative Science Quarterly, 25,* 200-224.

Rehfuss, J. (1989). *Contracting out in government: A guide to working with outside contractors to supply public services.* San Francisco: Jossey-Bass.

Rowan, B. (1982). Organizational structure and institutional environment: The case of public schools. Administrative Science Quarterly, 27, 259-279.

Salamon, L. M. (1981). Rethinking public management: Third-party government and the changing forms of government action. *Public Policy, 29,* 255-275.

Salamon, L. M. (1989). *Beyond privatization: The tools of government action.* Washington, DC: Urban Institute.

Salamon, L. M., Musselwhite, Jr., J. C., Holcomb, P. A., & Gronbjerg, K. A. (1987). *Human services in Chicago: The changing roles of government and private providers* (Research Report). Washington, DC: Urban Institute.

Sosin, M. R. (1990). Decentralizing the social service system: A reassessment. *Social Service Review, 64,* 617-636.

Williams, W. (1980). *Government by agency: Lessons from the social program grants-in-aid experience.* New York: Academic Press.

Ylvisaker, P. N. (1987). Foundations and nonprofit organizations. In W. W. Powell (Ed.), *The nonprofit sector: A research handbook* (pp. 360-379). New Haven, CT: Yale University Press.

CHAPTER 5

Executive Leadership in Human Service Organizations

HILLEL SCHMID

The study of leadership in organizations in general, and in human service organizations in particular, is central to research on the management and administration of social systems. Numerous attempts have been made to define the term *leadership* and to analyze the leader's functions and roles, his or her commitment to the organization and its members, and the ways and means of meeting organizational goals. Research on executive leadership has examined the programs, priorities and administrative patterns of executives, considering the degree to which they plan activities, take initiative, and adapt their style of management to changing environments.

This chapter focuses on the behavior, roles and characteristics of executive leadership in human service organizations. The reference is to those men and women who hold executive roles in these organizations, particularly roles that are analogous with those of these executives in other organizations.

The chapter presents the prevailing approaches discussed in the literature, as well as criticism of those approaches. The reference is to research findings on: the behavior of executive directors, the relationship between patterns of management and organizational structures, and interrelations between these patterns and the unique characteristics of the external environments in which human service organizations operate.

Central Theoretical and Empirical Trends Regarding Executive Leadership

For many years, researchers tended to assume that executive directors are equipped with innate characteristics that make them suitable for leadership roles. Studies conducted in the 1930s and 1940s led to the creation of long lists of traits that were believed to predict organizational effectiveness (Stogdill, 1974), although there was no support for the assumption of a relationship between these traits and effectiveness. More recent studies found that effective executives have a higher than average level of intelligence, a high degree of self-confidence, high achievement motivation, are able to express themselves well verbally and aspire to attain power (Campbell, Dunnette, Lawler, & Weick, 1970; Ghiselli, 1963; Korman, 1968). Here too, however, the relationship between these traits and organizational effectiveness was found to be weak, and the traits were not found to be reliable predictors of administrative behavior.

Other theories (Bales & Slater, 1955; Fleishman, 1953) have attempted to attribute effectiveness to executive behavior, examining the relationship between the director's activities and his or her subordinates' emotional reactions (satisfaction) and behavior (performance). The most significant research in this vein has pointed to varying leadership styles (White & Lippit, 1960), identifying several categories of executive behavior, such as "consideration" and "initiating structure." However, as it was difficult to reveal consistent relationships between management styles and worker productivity, attempts were made to determine the styles that best fit specific organizations and enhance their functioning in given situations. This led to the formulation of the "contingency theory," based on the assumption that organizational effectiveness is contingent on a "fit" between the executive's behavior and the specific situation in which he or she operates (Evans, 1970; Fiedler, 1964; Fiedler & Chemers, 1967; House, 1971; Vroom & Yetton, 1973).

Another prevalent trend has been the normative approach, which focuses on the classical roles the executive should fulfill and how he or she should perform them (Fayol, 1949; Guilick & Urwick, 1937; Mahoney, Jerdee, & Carrol, 1965; Muller-Thym, 1960; Strong, 1965). Some studies have examined administrative styles adopted in the face of environmental exigencies (Adizes, 1976; Blake & Mouton, 1964; Hersey & Blanchard, 1977), while others have dealt specifically with the management skills required of executives at various organizational levels (Katz, 1974). This literature was primarily devoted to a conceptual description of executive roles, and empirical evidence was not provided to support arguments regarding the roles executives should fulfill.

Yet another research trend, which gained impetus in the 1970s (Kotter, 1982a, 1982b; Kurke & Aldrich, 1983; Mintzberg, 1973; Stewart, 1967), documents the executive's behavior and performance in a number of spheres. These studies described and analyzed the role of the executive per se, rather than the individual performing the role, and were specifically concerned with what executives do. They delineated the main activities in the executive's daily routine, his or her main working priorities, and the allocation of his or her time. They analyzed the ways that information flows in the decision-making process, and they described the executive's organizational network. Differences between executives were ascribed to their personalities, professional background and organizational differences (size; socio-economic, political, technological, and demographic-geographic conditions; resource distribution; nature of the task environment). Similar research has been conducted in human service organizations; notable are studies of social welfare agencies (Patti, 1977; Wolk, Way, & Bleeke, 1982), community service organizations (Schmid, Bargal, & Hasenfeld, 1991), self-help groups (Yoak & Chesler, 1985) and the school system (Galley, 1982; Martinko & Gardner, 1984). A unique issue addressed in this context is the relationship between leadership and organizational culture (McClelland, 1975; Schein, 1985); it was argued that the executive creates and changes his or her group's culture. Other studies investigated the relations between leadership and satisfaction (Burns, 1978; Katerberg & Hom, 1981; Lord, DeVader, & Alliger, 1986; Nord, 1976; Vecchio, 1982). Yet another study (Glisson, 1989) supports the argument that leadership is an important factor in creating a positive organizational climate that enhances the morale and commitment of human service workers.

Examination of the above research trends elicits a number of questions regarding executive leadership in human service organizations. In comparison to the considerable material documenting and describing the roles of executives, specifying their priorities and analyzing their work schedules, little attention has been paid to normative issues. No attempt has been made to present a model of normative performance that suggests how executives in human service organizations should behave. Nor have researchers examined the points of similarity and difference between described executive roles and normative performance. Finally, the literature does not distinguish between these executives at different organizational levels.

Existing studies also have limitations, the most significant being methodological. Some lack adequate samples and do not rely on systematic observation of executive behavior. Those studies employing the observational method focus on behaviors—conversing, reading, reviewing documents, writing—that are merely the input and output of neuropsychological activities. Yet, the executive's work is largely mental in nature (Carroll & Gillen, 1987, p. 43), and "mental" time differs from "physical" time. The functioning of the human mind, which works rapidly and can deal with a number of subjects simultaneously, cannot be measured or quantified. Moreover, an observational study cannot assess the relative subjective importance that executives attribute to the various aspects of their work or the psychic energy they invest in them.

Discussion of ethical questions relating to the role of executive leadership is also lacking in the literature. In contrast to the extensive material on questions relating to the process of management, there is little research on substantive issues relating specifically to professional management in human service organizations. The literature has disregarded the unique professional infrastructures underlying the job of the executive or ideology of human service organizations (see also Zaleznik, 1990), that is, the values transcending superficial symbols and sentiments. Human service organizations are bound, more than their counterparts in business or industry, by environmental constraints determined by morals, ethics, and values. Demands for productivity, effectiveness and efficiency in human service organizations may conflict with demands for humane treatment, attention to clients' problems and demands. Yet this salient topic has not been addressed. Our analysis considers executive management styles along two continua—centralized versus decentralized authority and internal versus external orientation (see Figure 5.1; Quinn & Rohrbaugh, 1983). The former continuum refers to the extent to which the executive director involves other staff members in decision making (Hage & Aiken, 1967). The latter refers to whether emphasis is placed on management of the organization's internal processes or whether it is placed on management aimed at external environments. (Austin, 1989, also applied this model in his analysis of the executives' roles.)

The two continua in the model are based on the unique characteristics of human service organizations and the context in which they operate. These organizations operate in turbulent environments with a relatively high degree of political and economic instability. They are highly dependent on external interest groups and donors because they do not have their own capital. Competition for resources in the external environment is fierce, especially since the social services have been struggling to gain legitimacy and face continuous budget cuts. Given the importance of the environment and its influence on the executive's functioning, the "Internal Versus External Orientation" continuum indicates which direction the executive must move toward in his efforts to establish the organizational domain and ensure its survival. The second

Toward Centralization

I. Centralized-internal. Geared toward defending the organizational domain, stabilizing the formal structure, and maintaining regular management procedures. Does not involve own staff in decision making or delegate authority; emphasis on one "best way" to achieve results and attain efficiency. Management style is reactive, characterized by close supervision.

III. Centralized-external. Geared toward outside environments so as to ensure legitimation of the organizational domain and resource recruitment. Director holds full power and authority to make decisions. Administrative and professional staff is not encouraged to suggest innovative ideas and new strategic options that might suit changing environments.

*Internal Orientation*_____*External Orientation*

II. Decentralized-internal. Focuses on organization's internal problems; delegates authority regarding technical areas of functioning and decision making in subsystems, such as maintenance, management of human resources, budgeting, and resource allocation.

IV. Decentralized-external. Emphasis on developing mechanisms for adapting to changing environments so as to maximize organizational effectiveness. Directs efforts at new options and at developing administrative and professional staff which has the power to make decisions. Management style is pro-active; seeks new opportunities, yet identifies risks.

Toward Decentralization

Figure 5.1. Four Patterns of Executive Management: Centeralized Versus Decentralized Management and Internal Versus External Orientations

continuum, "Centralized Versus Decentralized authority," relates particularly to organizations where most of the staff is professional. Professionals employ nonroutine technologies and aspire toward personal and professional fulfillment. It is important to determine whether a director has adopted an orientation toward centralization or decentralization of his or her authority in order to understand the relationship between the executive's input, satisfaction of professional staff and organizational effectiveness.

Behavioral Characteristics of Executives: Findings and Analysis

Almost all of the research conducted thus far on the functioning of executives has shown that their approach fits the features described in the first quadrant of Figure 5.1 (the centralized-internal pattern of management). The main findings on the nature of managerial work relate to the following areas (this section is from Schmid & Bargal, 1988a):

Planning the Executive's Activities

The planning process varies from one organizational context to another. Some studies have found that executives prefer planning to implementation, while others indicate that executives do not plan their activities or time (Kurke & Aldrich, 1983; Mintzberg, 1973; Stewart, 1967). With respect to community centers, Schmid, Bargal, and Hasenfeld (1987) found that 75% of the activities of directors are short term and ad hoc. Their thinking is superficial, providing solutions for the "here and now" without adopting any specific plan. Research on social service organizations (Patti, 1977) suggests that administrators tend to spend more time in organizational maintenance and control than in such goal-oriented activities as planning, research procurement, innovation and representation.

The Nature of the Executive's Job

Research has shown that the executive's job is characterized by brevity, variety, and fragmentation. His or her work generally consists of numerous episodes in which information and issues requiring extensive consideration and decision making are crowded into very short periods of time, and the amount of time devoted to management activity is minimal. Wolk et al. (1982) report that most of the activities of the directors of social service agencies last less than nine minutes; Martinko and Gardner (1984) found that some of the executive's activities are as brief as five minutes; Schmid et al. (1987) report that an average of five minutes is devoted to specific administrative activities; and Mintzberg (1973) found that 50% of the executive's activities last less than nine minutes and only 10% last as long as an hour. As Kotter (1982b) has suggested, executives operate very efficiently, and even seemingly inefficient behavior can be characterized by a certain efficiency, which Mintzberg (1973) defines as "proficient superficiality."

Patterns of Communication

Most studies have found verbal communication to be the prevalent form of communication used by executives. Executives prefer unmediated contacts and receive most of their information from conversations with their own staff or people outside of the organization (Mintzberg,

1973). Schmid et al. (1987) report that 66% of the information reaching the executive is based on informal meetings and conversations. Galley (1982) reports that 82% of all executive exchanges are verbal—65% are devoted to intimate conversations held in his or her office, and 17% are telephone conversations. Minimal attention is paid to written material.

In most cases, the executive serves as the main source of formal and informal communication in the organization. Wolk et al. (1982) report that 73% of the communication in organizations is channeled through the executive director; Martinko and Gardner (1984) report 80%; Mintzberg (1973) reports 78%; and Stewart (1967) reports a percentage ranging from 66% to 80%. Kotter (1982a) argues that executives use such patterns of frequent interaction and communication to develop a network of cooperative relations through which they can influence many aspects of the organization.

Contact with Own Clientele and External Agents

Studies have shown that executives tend to devote relatively little time to their clientele. School principals devote 11.2% of their time to students and parents (Galley, 1982); business executives devote 20% of their time to clients (Mintzberg, 1973); and directors of community service organizations devote 11.5% of their time to the center's clientele (Schmid et al., 1987).

Most of the executive's time is devoted to internal management; relatively little is spent managing the external environment. Executives of community service organizations devote about 70% of their time to internal activities, such as finance management, human resources, and general administration and maintenance. In contrast, only 23% of their time is devoted to contact and negotiation with representatives of organizations and suppliers of legitimation and resources (Galley, 1982; Schmid et al., 1987).

Initiation of Activities

Research findings indicate that a considerable proportion of organizational activities are initiated by the executive. Galley (1982) reports that the executive initiates half the organization's administrative activities. A study of community center directors (Schmid et al., 1987) found that half the center's activities are initiated by the director, another third are initiated by other community center employees, and the remainder are initiated jointly.

Local Centralization

Studies have also revealed that the activities of executives are primarily executed in their office. This is where 83% of all the activities of school principals (Galley, 1982; see also Edwards, 1979; Sproull, 1981; Willis, 1980) and 67% of all the activities of community center directors (Schmid et al., 1987) were found to take place.

Considering the above findings as a whole, one can infer that executives in various sectors would rather engage in administration and maintenance of the organization than in management (i.e., policy-making, leading the organization toward goal achievement, developing mechanisms that enhance effective operation). They prefer short-term projects, since long-range goals are considered vague and indeterminate. As they are accountable to constituencies and interest groups, they strive to attain visible, immediate outcomes that gain them legitimation and ensure the flow of resources to the organization. Indeed, it seems that executives who concentrate on internal problems and maintenance of the organization without planning for the future have no choice but to adopt a style of management geared toward crisis management—solving immediate problems and removing obstacles as they arise.

The research has also indicated that executives tend toward centralization, concentrating decision-making authority in their own hands and preventing employees from functioning autonomously or reaching decisions in their domains of responsibility. This trend has been attributed to a wealth of objective and subjective factors, within and outside of the organization, such as lack of management know-how and skills, inability to motivate employees, reluctance to take risks, intolerance of ambiguity, and preference for a "one man show." Sometimes centralization evolves out of the executive's lack of self-confidence and professionalism. In such instances, the concentration of information and decision-making authority is aimed at making others dependent upon them. Conversely, it can be ascribed to a lack of confidence in the ability of one's staff to operate independently (Schmid, 1990). This causes the executive to enforce tight control over subordinates rather than control in accordance with results.

Centralized, internally oriented patterns of management described in the research can be explained by the researcher's perception of the organization as a closed system where the laws of physics and engineering are applicable and that operates in a stable and certain environment. This perspective tends to ignore the environmental constraints affecting the organization and assumes that there is one best way the organization can achieve its goals. According to this approach, the organization is an independent, self-sustaining entity and most of its problems relate to its internal structure rather than to external exigencies. As external environments are not considered influential factors, processes of scanning and gathering information on opportunities and risks in these environments are not developed. Moreover, emphasis is placed on the fixed, static aspects of the social structure rather than on the changes taking place within it (Emery & Trist, 1960). Along these lines, the executive is considered responsible for running a rational system that will maximize efficiency. Specifically, he or she is expected to enforce efficient administrative procedures, a strict system of regulations and a routine that should protect the organization and its employees from unexpected events or potential turmoil.

The second quadrant refers to human service organizations with an internally oriented, decentralized pattern of management. This style is particularly suited to organizations in the second stage of their life cycle, which is called the "development" stage (Hasenfeld & Schmid, 1989b). During this stage, the perceived environment becomes slightly more stable as a result of increased familiarity with its elements. As the organization continues its efforts to stabilize its domain and structure, there is a trend toward role differentiation and specialization. Patterns of communication become more structured, developing primarily in a horizontal direction, and coordination is based on procedures. Some functions become professionalized—especially those related to development of service technologies. Executives seek increased cooperation from the staff and encourage participation and collaboration as they focus their efforts on developing and expanding the staff. The dominant method of problem solving also changes, since the executive begins using more techniques based on achievement of consensus and relies less on exerting authority. Power once centralized solely among executives (see Figure 5.1, quadrant I) is now divided among the executive staff, which begins to crystallize within the organization and shares responsibility for policy and decision making.

Patterns of Executive Management
Under Conditions of Changing External
Environments and Organizational Structures

In contrast to closed systems, social service organizations operate as open systems that negotiate with external environments in order to obtain the resources they need to provide services. They act in an "arena in which various interest groups, external and internal, possessing resources needed by the organization, compete to optimize their values through it" (Hasenfeld, 1983, p. 44). These environments, which are characterized by a high level of politicization, have undergone significant changes in recent years, and these changes have affected the nature of management and the scope and quality of services provided for the target population. Such trends have generated a loss in legitimation for social services, which has in turn led to budget cuts.

Changes have also occurred in the classical structure of the "social market," leading to the creation of a mixed economy. The private, profit-making sector functions alongside such providers of social services as the government, voluntary organizations, employers and informal social systems (the family, self-help groups). Consequently, competition over scarce resources has intensified.

The hierarchical structure of organizations, in which directives and communications flow only through formal channels and activity initiation is the exclusive domain of the executive, does not lend itself to changing political environments. This elicits a need for transformation into a more flexible, organic pattern that is open to changes and creates new strategic options. The source of authority in this structure is expertise, and communication flows openly through a variety of channels. The strength of this pattern lies in its flexible division of labor and authority and its ability to make the staff mobile. Rather than demanding rigid conformity with formal channels according to a fixed hierarchy, this perception of the organizational structure seeks to circumvent the formal structure by activating informal elements and deviating from routine while constantly striving for increased efficiency, innovation, and the ability to keep up with changes in the external environment. This trend conforms with the tendency of human service organizations to develop organizational structures based on the "loosely coupling" principle (Orton & Weick, 1990; Weick, 1976). In such a structure, the units operating within the organization are relatively autonomous, with little coordination between them; communication is sporadic, brief, and frequent; and supervision and control are generally diffused and decentralized (Hasenfeld, 1985; Hasenfeld & Schmid, 1989a). This structure is most suitable for organizations that need to respond to various interest groups in the task environment.

The classical bureaucratic structure is also being replaced, to some extent, by an organizational structure based on small task forces. This ad hoc structure ensures operational flexibility, adaptation to changes, and reception of immediate, direct feedback from suppliers, and clients. It

allows for autonomous functioning of organizational units, whose ability
to survive is determined by their capacity to adapt to the conditions of
the external environment. The roles of the executive director in this type
of structure change, and the extent of his or her success or failure is measured on the basis of actual achievements.

The increasing proportion of professionals in human service organizations is another factor affecting the nature of management. Professionals demand more autonomy and strive for delegation of authority
and involvement in decision making. Under a rigid, centralized hierarchical system, they cannot fulfill themselves or achieve their professional goals. Hence they seek to attain authority and power that will enable them to make professional decisions and utilize their skills. Loyalty to the organization, which characterizes the bureaucratic system,
is thus being replaced by professional loyalty, which emphasizes professional development. When the staff is primarily professional, there
is high mobility of workers within and between organizations. In such
cases, formal barriers are broken and strategic options are created that
make it possible for the organization to achieve innovation and growth
(Kanter, 1983).

These structural developments accelerate the process of decentralization in the organization, encourage local action, increase staff participation in the setting of management goals, and heighten the staff's
responsiveness to the needs of their clientele. In such organizations,
planning is "bottom-up" rather than "top-down"; that is, ideas emanate from the lower echelons, which are in close contact with clients
and seek to satisfy the clients' needs.

Decentralized Management
Oriented Toward External Environments

Changing environments and structures divert executive leadership
in human service organizations toward a decentralized-external pattern
of management (see quadrant IV of Figure 5.1), while the centralized-
external pattern (quadrant III) is particularly appropriate for organizations that operate under conditions of economic uncertainty, shortage of resources and continuous budget cutbacks. Under such conditions, executives direct their efforts toward the task environment in
an attempt to raise capital and increase the organization's revenue
while adopting a centralized pattern of management. This pattern enables

executives to adopt aggressive policies in several areas—that is, determining the organization's goals; centralizing power and decision-making authority regarding allocation of resources; setting priorities without consulting staff members. In this case, since executives are working under critical conditions, they tend to refrain from involving the staff in decision making and believe that the way to increase the staff's productivity and enhance organizational effectiveness is centralization of authority.

A different management pattern is presented in quadrant IV. In this case, too, the executive's orientation is toward managing the external environment. At the same time, however, he delegates his authority and involves others in decision making, recognizing the importance of the environment as the main supplier of resources for the organization. The environment itself is characterized by a struggle for scarce resources, as each organization attempts to increase its involvement in control of resources. This is also reflected in the organization itself, where interest groups and coalitions compete for resources that can give them relative power over others and allow them to dictate policy according to their interests. In the course of the struggle, the organization seeks to free itself of external agencies and to make others dependent on it. Under these circumstances, the role of the executive is political and power based, in an attempt to formulate and adopt strategies that will reduce external dependence. The executive manages dependencies in order to ensure a steady flow of resources, negotiates with competitors and maintains a balance between interest groups.

An orientation toward external environments also entails mapping of the task environment and achieving legitimation of the organization's domain. It means forming alignments with other human service organizations, with community leaders and with business organizations. It also means involving the professional staff in lobbying efforts and representing the organization before community and government officials. Furthermore, it entails the development of intelligence systems, which brings about organizational learning in terms of how to adjust defensively to reality and how to use knowledge defensively to improve the "fit" with environments (Hedberg, 1981).

Management of external environments affects organizational effectiveness. In light of recent research (Schmid & Bargal, 1988b), which found a positive relationship between external orientation and service effectiveness and a negative one between internal orientation and effectiveness, there are grounds to argue that executives who seek to increase organizational effectiveness should direct their efforts toward recruiting support from external agencies that control the resources necessary for the organization's survival. This is particularly true of human service organizations, which lack their own capital and have to generate resources from their task environments. These implications of the external orientation strengthen the contention of Aldrich and Pfeffer (1976, p. 83) that "administrators manage their environments as well as their organizations and the former activity may be as important or even more important than the latter."

An external orientation is complemented by decentralization of authority, especially in human service organizations. In these organizations, the "raw material" is people who are imbued with moral values, and this affects their technologies, which are indeterminate and nonroutine. Moreover, complete information on cause and effect relations cannot be obtained in these organizations and it is therefore difficult to determine how to attain desired outcomes (Hasenfeld, 1983, p. 9). Under these conditions, a centralized-authoritative pattern of management might not be effective. Rather, a decentralized, participative style of management may be required—especially when it comes to gathering information and making decisions on interventions. Delegation of authority is clearly necessary in the unstable political milieu of human service organizations. In these environments, which challenge the legitimacy of the organizations and limit the resources at their disposal, a cooperative effort is needed on the part of all of the staff members in order to achieve the desired goals. Involvement of staff in administrative processes strengthens the organization, enabling it to struggle for the resources it needs in order to survive. Delegation of authority to lower levels of the hierarchy creates commitment to those who delegate it. Decentralization promotes tolerance of ambiguity among the administrative and professional staff and widens the director's span of control. It relieves the director of routine management duties, enabling him or her to engage in innovative thinking and strategic planning, creating new challenges, and adopting patterns of management by exceptions.

The relationship between decentralization of authority and other structural properties has been discussed in several studies based primarily on Weber's (1947) bureaucratic model (e.g., Hage & Aiken, 1967; Hall, 1968; Pugh, Hickson, Hinings, & Turner, 1969). A recent study (Schmid, in press) found that the higher the degree of perceived decentralization, the greater the perceived autonomy of the professional staff. A positive relationship was found between decentralization of authority and perceived coordination, indicating that the closer the professional staff is to the foci of power and decision making, the more willing they are to coordinate their activities. This reduces the need for mechanisms of close supervision over their activities, since participation in decision making strengthens the staff's commitment to the organization. In this way, control becomes built into the process and the decisions become the agreed standards for control and evaluation of planned activities.

Research on the relationship between decentralization and organizational effectiveness has produced contradictory results. Several studies (e.g., Morse & Reimer, 1956) have found that overall productivity increases in centralized decision-making structures, and research on human service organizations has revealed that a highly centralized structure of authority is the most powerful, direct determinant of productivity and efficiency (Glisson & Martin, 1980; Weinman, Grimes, Hsi, Justice, & Schoolar, 1979). In contrast, some researchers maintain that a decentralized, participatory form of organization is most conducive to effectiveness, both for organizations and employees (Argyris, 1972; Likert, 1967; Pennings, 1976). Other studies have supported these findings, indicating that service improves when staff members are actively involved in decision making (Cummings & Berger, 1976; Ellsworth, Maroney, Klett, Gordon, & Milieu, 1971; Holland, 1973; Holland, Konick, Buffum, Smith, & Petchers, 1981; Martin & Segal, 1977; Prager & Schnit, 1985/1986; Sherman, 1988; Whiddon & Martin, 1987). In addition, studies conducted in business organizations (Kanter, 1983) show that productive forms of organizational power increase when superiors share power and responsibility with subordinates. Similar conclusions were reached by Peters and Waterman (1982) and Miller and Friesen (1984), who found that organizations excelling in performance offer flexibility and autonomy to executives and employees alike.

The transition from leadership styles described in the first quadrant of Figure 5.1 (centralized-internal) to those described in the fourth quadrant (decentralized-external) signify a move from transactional leadership to transformational leadership (Burns, 1978). The former is an "exchange leadership," in which the needs of "followers" are met if their performance measures up to the terms of the contract with the leader. The transactional leader defines the tasks of employees, delivers rewards for performance and promises rewards for further efforts. In contrast, transformational leadership

> occurs when one or more persons engage with others in such a way that leaders and followers raise one another to higher levels of motivation and morality. Their purposes, which might have started out as separate but related, as in the case of transactional leadership, become fused.

Power bases are linked not as counterweights but as mutual support for a common purpose. (Burns, 1978, p. 20)

The changes transformational leaders invoke in their followers are not as drastic as those invoked by transactional leaders, but they are of a higher order. The transformational leader actively engages in the intellectual stimulation of followers, gearing his or her behavior toward influencing their thoughts, perceptions, attitudes, and values. Moreover, he or she treats each follower individually, catering to each one's emotional and personal needs in an attempt to further the follower's growth and self-fulfillment (Bargal & Schmid, 1989). This behavior is likely to raise the consciousness of followers regarding specific issues, changing attitudes or altering the contextual framework of the organization.

The transformational leader creates a vision for the organization. He or she has the capacity to develop and communicate a clear and compelling picture of the desired state of affairs that will enable the organization to mobilize resources and generate commitment to its espoused goals (Bennis & Nanus, 1985). This leader can and must develop a mental image of the future state of the organization in the form of a clear statement, a dream, or a tentative plan. Once formulated, the vision must be clarified and communicated to directors, board members, and key members of the organization. They must understand and commit themselves to the vision before ideas—that are sometimes vague and general—can be translated into concrete organizational structures and administrative processes and before the lower echelons can take responsibility for personally implementing them.

Conclusion

The chapter points to the emergence of new patterns for managing executive leadership in human service organizations (see Table 1). The functions of management delineated in the past no longer fit the situations that have arisen as a result of changes in the following areas:

(1) Turbulent, uncertain environments characterized by a high degree of politicization, a crisis of legitimation affecting social services, lack of resources, intensification of the trend toward changing public services into private services, and a target population with a high level of consumer consciousness and high demands.

Table 5.1 Comparison Among Patterns of Executive Leadership in Human Service Organizations, By Nature of Management and Executive's Orientation

Characteristic	Centralized Management and Internal Orientation	Decentralized Management and External Orientation
1. Centralized/ decentralized authority	Centralization of authority	Delegation of authority
2. Organizational orientation	Internal orientation	Management of external environment
3. Perception of the organization's goals	Operational efficiency	Organizational effectiveness
4. Leadership objectives	Satisfaction of the individual's and organization's needs	Attainment of power and control of resources
5. Nature of management	Ad hoc, "proficient superficiality"	Comprehensive and strategic management
6. Focusing on the subsystem	Production, maintenance	Adaptation and development
7. Strategies of adaptation	Domain defensive	Domain offensive
8. Openness to new options	Relatively little	Considerable
9. Patterns of leadership	Transactional	Transformational

(2) Structural changes that have a profound effect on the organization's structure and the role of management and that lead to "flattening the organizational chart."

(3) A professional staff that seeks personal development, professional fulfillment, and autonomy and that demands to participate in policy making and decision making.

(4) A stronger orientation among constituencies toward visible, measurable effects that are significant for the target population.

These changes obligate executive leaders of human service organizations to develop patterns of management based on decentralization of authority and an external orientation. They must direct their approach toward management of an environment where competing organizations are involved in a struggle for power. This type of management requires the director to ensure the ongoing management and maintenance of the organizational system, delegating the task to an executive staff. Such a system requires development of human resources, encouragement of initiative, tolerance of failure, and encouragement of innovation. Only under such conditions can executives ensure that their staff will be professional and skilled, and that they will be able to direct their efforts toward external relations, competing with other organizations over scarce resources.

References

Adizes, I. (1976). Management styles. *California Management Review, 19*(2), 5-20.

Aldrich, H., & Pfeffer, J. (1976). Environments of organizations. In I. Inkeles (Ed.), *Annual review of sociology* (Vol. II, pp. 79-105). Palo Alto, CA: Annual Review.

Argyris, C. (1972). *The applicability of organizational sociology.* New York: Free Press.

Austin, D. M. (1989). The human service executive. *Administration in Social Work, 13,* (3/4), 13-36.

Bales, R. F., & Slater, P. E. (1955). Role differentiation in small decision making groups. In T. Parsons et al. (Eds.), *Family, socialization and interaction process.* Glencoe, IL: Free Press.

Bargal, D., & Schmid, H. (1989). Recent themes in theory and research on leadership and their implications for management of human services. *Administration in Social Work, 13*(3/4), 37-55.

Bennis, W., & Nanus, B. (1985). *Leaders.* New York: Harper & Row.

Blake, R. R., & Mouton, J. (1964). *The managerial grid.* Houston: Gulf Publishing.

Burns, J. M. (1978). *Leadership.* New York: Harper & Row.

Campbell, J. P., Dunnette, M. D., Lawler, E. E., & Weick, K. E. (1970). *Managerial behavior performance and effectiveness.* New York: McGraw-Hill.

Carroll, S. J., & Gillen, D. J. (1987). Are the classical management functions useful in describing managerial work? *Academy of Management Review, 12*(1), 38-51.

Cummings, L., & Berger, C. (1976). Organization structure: How does it influence attitudes and performance? *Organizational Dynamics, 3,* 34-49.

Edwards, W. L. (1979, October). The role of principal in five primary schools in New Zealand: An ethnographic perspective. *Journal of Educational Administration, 17*(2), 248-254.

Ellsworth, R., Maroney, L., Klett, L., Gordon, H., & Milieu, G. R. (1971). Characteristics of successful psychiatric treatment programs. *American Journal of Orthopsychiatry, 41,* 427-441.

Emery, F. E., & Trist, E. L. (1960). Socio-technical systems. In *Management sciences models and techniques* (Vol. 2). London: Pergamon.

Evans, M. G. (1970). The effects of supervisory behavior on the path goal relationship. *Organizational Behavior and Human Performance, 5,* 277-298.

Fayol, H. (1949). *General and industrial management.* London: Pitman.

Fiedler, F. E. (1964). A contingency model of leadership. In L. Berkowitz (Ed.), *Advances in experimental social psychology.* New York: Academic Press.

Fiedler, F. E., & Chemers, M. M. (1967). *Leadership and effective management.* Glenview, IL/Brighton, England: Scott, Foresman.

Fleishman, E. A. (1953). The description of supervisory behavior. *Journal of Applied Psychology, 37*, 1-6.

Galley, J. (1982). *The evaluation component: An exploratory study in educational administration.* Unpublished doctoral dissertation, University of California, Santa Barbara.

Ghiselli, E. E. (1963). Managerial talent. *American Psychologist, 18*, 631-642.

Glisson, C. (1989). The effect of leadership on workers in human service organizations. *Administration in Social Work, 13*(3/4), 99-116.

Glisson, C., & Martin, P. Y. (1980). Productivity and efficiency in human service organizations as related to structure, size and age. *Academy of Management Journal, 23*(1), 21-37.

Guilick, L., & Urwick, L. (1937). *Papers on the science of administration.* New York: Institute of Public Administration.

Hage, J., & Aiken, M. (1967). Relationship of centralization to other structural properties. *Administrative Science Quarterly, 12*, 73-92.

Hall, R. H. (1968). Professionalization and bureaucratization. *American Sociological Review, 33*, 92-104.

Hasenfeld, Y. (1983). *Human service organizations.* Englewood Cliffs, NJ: Prentice-Hall.

Hasenfeld, Y. (1985). Community mental health centers as human service organizations. In R. Scott & B. Black (Eds.), *The organization of mental health services* (pp. 133-146). Beverly Hills, CA: Sage.

Hasenfeld, Y., & Schmid, H. (1989a). The community center as a human service organization. *Non-Profit and Voluntary Sector Quarterly, 18*(1), 47-61.

Hasenfeld, Y., & Schmid, H. (1989b). The life cycle of human services organizations: An administrative perspective. *Administration in Social Work, 13*(3/4), 243-269.

Hedberg, B. (1981). How organizations learn and unlearn. In P. C. Nystrom & W. H. Starbuck (Eds.), *Handbook of organizational design* (pp. 3-27). Oxford: Oxford University Press.

Hersey, P., & Blanchard, K. (1977). *Management of organizational behavior.* Englewood Cliffs, NJ: Prentice-Hall.

Holland, T. P. (1973). Organizational structure and institutional care. *Journal of Health and Social Behavior, 14*, 241-251.

Holland, T. P., Konick, A., Buffum, W., Smith, M. K., & Petchers, M. (1981). Institutional structure and resident outcomes. *Journal of Health and Social Behavior, 22*, 433-444.

House, R. J. (1971). A path goal theory of leadership. *Administrative Science Quarterly, 16*, 321-339.

Kanter, R. M. (1983). *The change masters: Corporate entrepreneurs at work.* London: Allen & Unwin.

Katerberg, R., & Hom, P. W. (1981). Effects of within-group and between-group variation in leadership. *Journal of Applied Psychology, 66*, 218-223.

Katz, R. L. (1974). Skills of an effective administration. *Harvard Business Review, 52*(1), 90-102.

Korman, A. K. (1968). The prediction of managerial performance: A review. *Personnel Psychology, 21*, 295-322.

Kotter, J. P. (1982a). *The general managers.* New York: Free Press.

Kotter, J. P. (1982b). What effective general managers really do. *Harvard Business Review, 60*(6), 156-167.

Kurke, L. B., & Aldrich, H. E. (1983). Mintzberg was right: A replication and extension of the nature of managerial work. *Management Science, 29*, 975-984.

Likert, R. (1967). *The human organization*. New York: McGraw-Hill.

Lord, R. G., DeVader, C. L., & Alliger, G. M. (1986). A meta-analysis of the relation between personality traits and leadership perceptions: An application of validity generalization procedures. *Journal of Applied Psychology, 71*(3), 402-410.

Mahoney, T. A., Jerdee, T. J., & Carrol, S. J. (1965). The job of management. *Industrial Relations, 4*, 97-110.

Martin, P. Y., & Segal, B. (1977). Bureaucracy, size and staff expectations for client independence in halfway houses. *Journal of Health and Social Behavior, 18*, 376-390.

Martinko, M. J., & Gardner, W. L. (1984). The observation of high performing educational managers: Methodological issues and managerial implications. In J. G. Hunt, D. M. Haskins, E. A. Shriesheim, & R. Stewart (Eds.), *Leaders and managers* (pp. 142-162). Elmsford, NY: Pergamon.

McClelland, D. C. (1975). *Power: The inner experience*. New York: Irvington.

Miller, D., & Friesen, P. H. (1984). *Organizations, a quantum view*. Englewood Cliffs, NJ: Prentice-Hall.

Mintzberg, H. (1973). *The nature of managerial work*. New York: Harper & Row.

Morse, N., & Reimer, E. (1956). The experimental change of major organizational variables. *Journal of Abnormal and Social Psychology, 52*, 120-129.

Muller-Thym, B. J. (1960). *Practices in general management: New directions for organizational management* (Paper No. 60, WA-59). New York: American Society of Mechanical Engineers.

Nord, W. R. (Ed.). (1976). *Concepts and controversies in organizational behavior*. Santa Monica, CA: Goodyear.

Orton, D. J., & Weick, K. E. (1990). Loosely coupled systems: A reconceptualization. *Academy of Management Review, 15*(2), 203-223.

Patti, R. J. (1977). Patterns of management activity in social welfare agencies. *Administration in Social Work, 1*(1), 5-18.

Pennings, J. M. (1976). Dimensions of organizational influences and their effectiveness correlates. *Administrative Science Quarterly, 21*, 688-699.

Peters, T., & Waterman, R. (1982). *In search of excellence: Lessons from America's best run companies*. New York: Harper & Row.

Prager, E., & Schnit, O. (1985/1986). Organizational environments and care outcomes decisions for elderly clientele. *Administration in Social Work, 9*, 49-62.

Pugh, D. S., Hickson, D. J., Hinings, C. R., & Turner, C. (1969). The context of organization structures. *Administrative Science Quarterly, 14*, 91-114.

Quinn, R. E., & Rohrbaugh, J. (1983). A spatial model of effectiveness criteria: Toward a competing values approach to organization analysis. *Management Science, 29*, 363-377.

Schein, E. H. (1985). *Organizational culture and leadership*. San Francisco: Jossey-Bass.

Schmid, H. (1990). Staff and line relationships revisited: The case of community services organizations. *Public Personnel Management, 19*(1), 71-83.

Schmid, H. (in press). Relationships between decentralized authority and other structural properties in human service organizations: Implications for service effectiveness. *Administration in Social Work*.

Schmid, H., & Bargal, D. (1988a). The functioning of executives: Findings, analysis, and implications to human service organizations [in Hebrew]. *Society and Welfare, 9*(2), 185-198.

Schmid, H., & Bargal, D. (1988b). *Patterns of management and organizational effectiveness among executives and program directors in community services organizations.* Jerusalem: Hebrew University of Jerusalem, Paul Baerwald School of Social Work.

Schmid, H., Bargal, D., & Hasenfeld, Y. (1987). *The community services organization's executive—Areas of function and activity.* Jerusalem: Hebrew University of Jerusalem, Paul Baerwald School of Social Work.

Schmid, H., Bargal, D., & Hasenfeld, Y. (1991). Executive behavior in community services organizations. *Journal of Social Service Research, 15* (1/2) 23-39.

Sherman, J. D. (1988). *Dysfunctional effects of centralization in a voluntary organization.* Paper presented at the Academy of Management Meeting.

Sproull, I. S. (1981, Summer). Managing educational programs: A micro-behavioral analysis. *Human Organization,* 113-122.

Stewart, R. (1967). *Managers and their jobs.* London: Macmillan.

Stogdill, R. M. (Ed.). (1974). *Handbook of leadership.* New York: Free Press.

Strong, E. P. (1965). *The management of business: An introduction.* New York: Harper & Row.

Vecchio, R. P. (1982). A further test of leadership effects due to between-group variation and within-group variation. *Journal of Applied Psychology, 67,* 200-208.

Vroom, V. H., & Yetton, P. W. (1973). *Leadership and decision-making.* Pittsburgh: University of Pittsburgh Press.

Weber, M. (1947). *The theory of social and economic organizations.* New York: Free Press.

Weick, K. E. (1976). Educational organizations as loosely coupled systems. *Administrative Science Quarterly, 21,* 1-19.

Weinman, M., Grimes, R., Hsi, B., Justice, B., & Schoolar, J. (1979). Organizational structure and effectiveness in general hospital psychiatry departments. *Administration in Mental Health, 7*(1), 32-42.

Whiddon, B., & Martin, P. Y. (1987). *Quality of staff performance in a state welfare agency.* Unpublished manuscript, Florida State University.

White, R. K., & Lippit, R. (1960). Leader behavior and member reaction in three social climates. In D. Cartwright & A. Zander (Eds.), *Group dynamics* (pp. 318-335). New York: Harper & Row.

Willis, Q. (1980). The work activity of school principals: An observational study. *The Journal of Administration, 18,* 27-54.

Wolk, J. L., Way, L. F., & Bleeke, M. A. (1982). Human service management: The art of international relationships. *Administration in Social Work, 6*(1), 1-10.

Yoak, M., & Chesler, M. (1985). Alternative professional roles in health care delivery: Leadership patterns in self-help groups. *Journal of Applied Behavioral Science, 21*(4), 427-444.

Zaleznik, A. (1990). The leadership gap. *The Executive, 4*(1), 7-22.

PART III
Ideology, Professional Work, and Technology

Because human service organizations engage in moral work, ideologies become a driving force in shaping and giving credence to their service technologies. Ideologies are belief systems about the nature of the clients to be served, how they should be served, and what the desired outcomes should be. The dominant ideologies in the organization serve as a guiding framework in selecting and shaping the service technology. Based on a study of four feminist health organizations Hyde, in Chapter 6, shows the crucial role ideologies play in shaping both the services and the internal structures of these organizations. More importantly, she analyzes how, in the face of a hostile environment, these ideologies underwent significant changes in order to provide the organizations with a more adaptive framework to reorganize their services and internal structures. Such changes were not opportunistic, however, but were consistent with the original ideologies.

In addition to ideologies, human services organizations also rely on professionals to implement and justify their service technologies. At the same time, the professionals use the organization as a vehicle to buttress their own professional claims. As Abbott points out in Chapter 7, the work of the profession, be it medicine or social work, has both objective and subjective foundations. The objective foundations emanate from the nature of the work to be done, but the subjective foundations emanate from the claims of the profession for exclusive jurisdiction over the work. Abbott goes on to analyze the major elements of professional work—diagnosis, treatment and inference, and to show how these are shaped by the efforts of the profession to protect its niche.

Using professional knowledge such as diagnosis to advance the interests of professionally dominated human services organizations is illustrated in

Chapter 8. Kirk and Kutchins examine the use of DSM-III as a diagnostic tool by mental health organizations. They demonstrate that even though such a diagnostic scheme is fraught with ambiguities and has a dubious relation to the actual treatment, it is, nonetheless, widely used. They propose that DSM-III is used not to diagnose but to regulate client flow, to protect clients from harm, to acquire fiscal resources, to rationalize decision making, and to advance the jurisdictional claims of psychiatry.

Finally, Glisson, in Chapter 9, examines the complex issue of the relationship between technology and structure. Noting the contradictory findings about the effects of technology on structure, he proposes that, at least in the case of human service organizations, the relationship may be reversed. Because human service technologies are enactments of belief systems, these may indeed emanate from the structure. Glisson offers an alternative approach that distinguishes between design and implementation phases. In the design phase, the available technology is matched with a designed structure. The implemented structure, however, is more likely to reflect the actual skills of the workers. It is also likely to be influenced by other environmental forces such as institutional isomorphism and organizational inertia. Therefore, how the workers actually go about doing their work will ultimately determine the implemented technology.

CHAPTER 6

The Ideational System of Social Movement Agencies
AN EXAMINATION OF FEMINIST HEALTH CENTERS

CHERYL HYDE

I know that everyone who works here, and this is what makes us feminist, has an analysis of patriarchy and has a platform for change . . . that has to do with empowering women, ethnic minorities, lesbians, and differently abled people. The ideology is what makes us truly feminist . . . and to be involved in something political, programs that improve the quality of women's lives. That's the bottom line.

—Pam, Community Health Clinic

When we think of a human service agency, the image that often comes to mind is the professional, perhaps impersonal, bureaucracy that delivers services to a targeted population with assumed needs. And when we think of a social movement organization, typically we picture a vanguard group making impassioned and seemingly unrealistic demands on the state through protest and mass mobilization strategies. Human service and social movement orientations often are viewed as being at odds or in conflict with one another (Withorn, 1984). One can pursue revolution or provide programs, but to try both is to court chaos, co-optation, or worse, failure.

AUTHOR'S NOTE: The author extends her thanks to Yeheskel Hasenfeld for his helpful insights on and suggestions for earlier drafts.

121

Yet what of those organizations that both engage in social change and serve a client population? These organizations may be labeled *social movement agencies.* Social movement agencies are hybrid organizations in which the explicit pursuit of social change is accomplished through the delivery of services. Such agencies are part of a broader political legacy rooted in the settlement house movement for social and economic justice (Ehrenreich, 1985; Garvin & Cox, 1979; Withorn, 1984). Their hybrid nature is captured in an ideational duality that encompasses both social movement and human services orientations.

This chapter explicates the dynamics of these organizations so as to underscore how this ideational duality serves as a bedrock for survival. Relationships between movement and agency ideational components (ideologies and goals), the ideational system and other intraorganizational characteristics, and the organization and selected environmental factors are examined. Particular combinations of movement and agency ideational tendencies facilitated organizational transformations necessary for survival in politically and economically hostile environments. This is illustrated through the analysis of three feminist health centers and their encounters with New Right actions.

The Ideational System

An organization's ideational system is composed of its ideologies and goals. Organizational ideologies convey fundamental values, needs, and aspirations; suggest appropriate problem analyses; provide rationales for joining; promote group cohesion; and guide responses to environmental forces (Ahrens, 1980; Beyer, 1981; Meyer, 1982; Riger 1984). Organizational ideologies may be stated explicitly, as in public pronouncements or manifestos, or conveyed implicitly through ceremonies, language, structure, and technology (Meyer, 1982; Riger, 1984). Despite exceptions, such as Gusfield's analysis of the Temperance Union's ideological purity and its subsequent failure to adapt to environmental shifts (Gusfield, 1963), ideology has been a relatively neglected topic in organizational studies. Recent works such as the intellectual roots of cooperative workplaces (Rothschild & Whitt, 1986), the influence of founding group ideology on alternative services (Reinharz, 1984), ideological shifts in professional reform organizations (Helfgot, 1981), and the interactions between and changes in ideologies, structure, and strategic repertoires in feminist movement groups (Staggenborg, 1989) suggest that the ideological aspect of organizational life is receiving increased attention.

In contrast to the study of ideology, organizational goals are frequent analytical foci. Goals suggest intended outcomes and provide organizational direction, standards for evaluation, and legitimacy (Lauffer, 1984). In recognition that organizations often act in ways not necessarily congruent with publicly stated aims, various goal classifications have been proposed (cf. Etzioni, 1964; Mohr, 1973; Perrow, 1961). For our purposes Mohr's distinction is most helpful:

> An organization may have two distinct types of goals: a "transitive" externally oriented, or functional goal, and a "reflexive," internally oriented or institutional goal. (Mohr, 1973, p. 475)

Transitive goals are suggested by organizational activities in the environment, specifically programs and services. *Reflexive goals* are manifested through various maintenance activities such as governance procedures or personnel development. Theoretically, both goals are co-equal in that they exert influence on one another. In actuality, organizations may emphasize one over another at different points in time (Hasenfeld, 1983; Mohr, 1973). Much attention has been paid to the tensions that exist between different types of goals, and the extent to which an organization becomes more conservative when reflexive goals predominate (cf. Jenkins, 1977; Michels, 1949; Scott, 1967; Zald & Ash, 1966). The inevitability and consequences of goal displacement, however, remain empirical questions.

Organizational ideologies and goals shape one another. Specifically, an ideological framework serves as a philosophical rubric that informs other components of the organization. Thus, goals should flow from ideology. Yet while aligned with ideologies, goals are distinct in that they specify a plan and operationalize the larger vision (Beyer, 1981). Over time, the fulfillment or pursuit of goals may alter the ideological framework.

As an ideational system, ideologies and goals influence and are influenced by other internal properties (e.g., governance, outputs) and environmental relations (e.g., funders, opposition). Figure 6.1 depicts the interactional nature of organizational life. Note that environmental connections occur through output activities, in particular, and with the entire organization, in general.

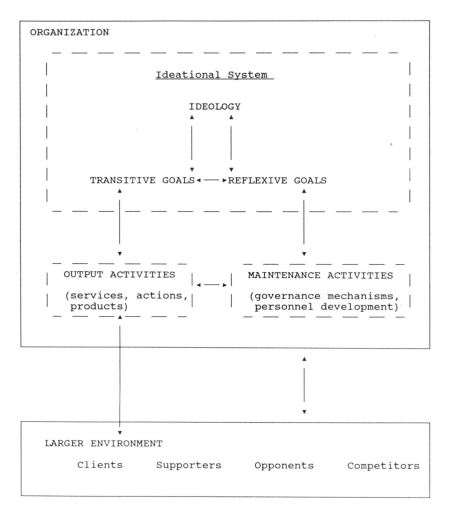

Figure 6.1. The Interaction Patterns of an Organization and Its Enviornment

Organizational transformation is conceptualized as a dynamic process through which the organization attempts to manage, control, or adapt to its environment. Resulting changes depend on environmental factors *and* the particular mix of intraorganizational characteristics.

As noted in the introduction, two ideational orientations or tendencies are of concern: social movement and human service agency. A social movement orientation encompasses those values, beliefs, and objectives that focus on societal change by challenging, altering, or overthrowing current economic, political, cultural, and social systems. An agency orientation encompasses those values, beliefs, and objectives that focus on approaches to the caring for and servicing of clients and consumers. It is possible that social movement and agency tendencies blend, particularly on the ideological level. It also is conceivable that transitive and reflexive goals exist for both movement and agency orientations (e.g., movement-oriented reflexive goals or agency-oriented transitive goals). The changing nature of the relationships between ideology and goals, and between movement and agency tendencies is of critical concern in this chapter.

Case Studies: Feminist Health Centers

Case studies of three feminist health centers serve as the empirical base for discussion.[1] These centers are social movement organizations within the reproductive rights wing of the feminist movement and service agencies, as they offer gynecological and family planning programs. Thus the health centers contained both movement and agency tendencies in their ideational systems. The health centers are the:

Cooperative Health Project (CHP): founded in the early 1970s as a referral group to help women obtain abortions prior to nation-wide legalization. It now offers abortions, gynecological care, birth control, and AIDS screening and counseling. There are 10 full-time collective members, 5 part-time contract workers, and a "paper" board.

Community Health Center (CHC): founded in the mid-1970s. It offers a gynecological clinic, lesbian health clinic, fertility awareness class, AIDS screening, INS [Immigration and Naturalization Service] exams, bilingual outreach programs. It does not offer abortions, but does provide counseling and referral. There are 10 paid staff, 10 board members, and 40 volunteers.

Self-Help Clinic (SHC): founded in the late 1970s as a self-help group for women. Developed into a comprehensive medical center that provides gynecological care, birth control, abortion, AIDS screening, and donor insemination. Offers community education programs and legislative testimony. There are 50 paid staff and 6 board members.

Data gathered during field visits of 7 to 10 days at each site, consist of interviews with past and current participants and organizational documents.

These health centers changed dramatically during the 1970s and 1980s. Their earliest orientations were toward revolution: a revolution based on women having complete control over their bodies. The traditional medical establishment in particular, and misogynistic societal practices in general, would be swept away. Over the years, however, this *explicit* call to revolution waned. These organizations still provide alternative, woman-centered health programs and still maintain a commitment to transformative politics, yet as one CHC member stated, "the clinic lost its socialist-feminist identity that had been clear when we started."

Understanding the reasons for, extent of, and implications of this broadly painted transformation is the heart of this analysis. It was not a simple matter of goal displacement, though some of that occurred. Nor was it merely the presence of an opposition that forced certain changes, though to some extent that happened. Moreover, even though this general loss of revolutionary fervor was present in all three centers, it materialized in very different ways. Only by understanding the dynamics within the ideational system, the relationships between the ideational system and other organizational properties, and the connections between the organization and the environment, can the reasons for the distinct changes, as well as the general transformation, be understood. This section traces the basic patterns of organizational transformation, by first discussing the ideational systems in the formative years, then introducing key environmental factors, and concluding with resulting ideational shifts.

Formative Years

During the formative years, the three health centers exhibited a number of important similarities. There also was considerable compatibility among the various components of their ideational systems. All of the centers embraced versions of socialist feminism, an ideology that locates female subordination in the intersection of class and gender relations (Riger, 1984; Weil, 1986). The centers' approaches to health care critiqued patriarchy and capitalism:

> We of the CHC, as socialist feminists, want to join with the rest of the anti-imperialist movement in the United States in expressing our great joy at your victory and our solidarity and support for your continued struggle against imperialism, sexism, racism and for the building of

socialism. . . . The CHC fosters socialist ideas by offering medical care for women, meeting one of the basic needs common to all people. . . . In all of our work we show women that there are basic contradictions under capitalism that can never be rectified until we have a socialist revolution. (CHC, 1975 letter to Viet Cong women)

We are in the process of struggling through an anarchist/socialist/feminist analysis and applying that to the functioning and structure of the clinic. We are always defining and redefining our position in a patriarchal society. Our commitment to women's health care comes from the fact that in medicine, as in most aspects of our culture, women are treated like second class citizens. (CHP, 1978 newsletter)

Above all we have a feminist political commitment. We take ourselves seriously, are anti-imperialistic and anticapitalistic. (SHC, 1980 annual report)

It is clear that the provision of services by and for women was linked to larger movement forces. Thus in terms of ideology, movement and agency tendencies were fused.

This feminist ideology primarily was manifested through the practice of self-help, an essential vehicle for revolutionizing women's health care. Self-help, a consumer-oriented service delivery strategy, was and is the backbone of their programs. Usually done in a group setting, it combines principles of consciousness raising, empowerment, and education, all in keeping with socialist-feminist values (Rothschild & Whitt, 1986; Weil, 1986). The clinics emphasized demystified language in discussions of medical problems, designed patient advocacy systems, and engaged the consumer as much as possible in preventive and holistic treatment. While primarily the guiding method to health service delivery, the self-help approach permeated all aspects of these centers as this example suggests:

The Self-Help Educational Project . . . focuses on our community outreach functions. The basic concept of self-help is learning and change through sharing experiences, information, and resources. People can educate themselves to become better aware of their own health needs, and how and where to best meet these needs, thereby learning to be healthier. Through [the] sharing of our experiences and information we help each other in this process. . . . We have incorporated this concept of self-education into our programs. (CHC funding application, 1976)

The self-help component reflects the transitive goals of these organizations. It also indicates how movement orientations influence agency tendencies.

Governance mechanisms, which suggest reflexive goals, also were compatible with the overarching ideologies. Adherents to socialist feminism advocate the development of cooperative work and authority arrangements (Rothschild and Whitt, 1986; Weil, 1986). All three health centers began as collectivist organizations. Consensus was used in decision making, work was rotated, hierarchy was minimal or nonexistent, and communal accountability was emphasized. This approach to governance fused movement and agency tendencies. It represented a conscious effort to create a kind of organization fundamentally different from traditional or mainstream organizations. And, it influenced the approach to client care in terms of the organization of labor, particularly its reinforcement of egalitarian relationships between patient and provider.

There were, however, important differences between the centers; differences that accounted for some of the divergence in later change trajectories. First, the Self-Help Clinic also embraced another feminist framework, that of cultural feminism. Cultural feminism contends that the denial or subordination of a female nature and the devaluation of female attributes are the reasons for women's oppression (Alcoff, 1988). In practice, cultural feminists claimed that successful women-centered businesses and institutions were the route to revolution as they provided refuge from the hostile patriarchal world and affirmed the intrinsic talents of women. To some extent, SHC founders promoted this vision: they adopted a more entrepreneurial stance in terms of service delivery than did the other two clinics. They also asserted that democracy and business could be combined and that feminists had to recognize and develop leaders (1979 Annual Meeting minutes); views antithetical to socialist feminism. Thus, during SHC's formative years an uneasy co-existence between socialist and cultural feminism was manifested in all components of the ideational system.

A second difference concerned the degree to which collective governance mechanisms were developed. While all three centers professed support for the collectivist structure, the Cooperative Health Project and the Community Health Center instituted policies and procedures that insured its actualization and continuance more so than the Self-Help Clinic. Both used versions of a job contract, which was viewed as:

> a way of assuring accountability of each woman to the collective. We, as a collective decide what work we want to do. . . . The process of individual re-evaluation of our work and collective feedback about our work is an invaluable part of our collective commitment to consciously evaluate the effectiveness of the CHC and our feelings about the work we do. (CHC, 1977 newsletter)

Another mechanism, "strokes and constructive criticisms," guided collective praise and feedback and furthered accountability to the larger group. Typically this was done at the close of a meeting, as supportively as possible to other collective members and occasionally to oneself. Some examples from the Cooperative Health Project:

> There were some strokes about the preparation of the workshop for Jean and Kim. . . . The criticism was made that Jean and Kim should have used the "checking in" at the beginning of the meeting. There were some discussions about the pros and cons of the checking in procedure at the beginning of a meeting, that it was good to know what frame of mind people were attending the meeting in and that it took too much time sometimes. (Workshop on chairing meetings, July 1979)

> I criticize myself for being so damned impatient about the doctor situation. I'm glad we . . . slowed this process down. Guess I was getting too emotionally involved. Sorry—Maura. (Gynecology clinic meeting, November 1979)

Collective members from the CHC and CHP were trained in these, and other, procedures and viewed them as critical to the functioning of the collective. This commitment to a collectivist vision was especially strong in the Community Health Project. In contrast, the Self-Help Clinic used neither job contracting nor stroke/criticism procedures (suggestive of the constraints of cultural feminism), which contributed to the comparably swift demise of its collectivist form of governance.

A third difference concerned the ways in which these centers understood and operationalized their relationships with the larger movement. Even though the Cooperative Health Project and the Community Health Center placed themselves within a larger global struggle (see excerpts above), clinic members believed that this was achieved best by addressing community level needs. Thus their transitive goals were guided by a grassroots lens. This was particularly salient for the Community Health Center. In contrast, the Self-Help Clinic drew much of its identity from being a member of a national feminist health clinic alliance. This alliance, which largely subscribed to the values of cultural feminism, influenced the nature of the clinic's service delivery.

To summarize, all three health centers exhibited versions of socialist feminism. This was conveyed in ideological pronouncements, the nature of service delivery (transitive goals), and governance mechanisms (reflexive goals). In a broad sense, there were similarities across the health centers and compatibility among the components within the ideational systems. There also were important differences, mostly in terms of emphasis. While all the centers practiced self-help, the Self-Help Center differed in that its approach was shaped in part by the entrepreneurial values of cultural feminism. While all the centers emphasized collectivism, actual commitment was stronger in the Community Health Center and especially in the Cooperative Health Project. And, while all embraced a global struggle, for the Cooperative Health Project and especially for the Community Health Center, this struggle was fought on the grassroots level. In contrast, the Self-Help Clinic drew much of its identity from membership in a national health center alliance. While relatively minimal during the formative years, these differences became increasingly important during the transformation period of the 1980s. These changes were due in part to interactions with the New Right, which is the subject of the next section.

Environmental Factors: The New Right

While feminist organizations always have encountered opposition, the late 1970s through the 1980s proved to be a particularly contentious period. Much of this can be traced to the rise and coalescence of the New Right. This movement developed both a solid grassroots base and strong ties with local, state, and national government. The New Right espoused an antifeminist and antihuman service philosophy, and thus the health centers were particularly vulnerable (Hyde, 1991). While other environmental factors no doubt contributed to organizational change, this section summarizes the role of the New Right.

Three types of New Right activities were experienced by the health centers. Legislatively, all contended with increasingly punitive antichoice laws and regulations. The restricted use of Medicaid for abortion and gynecological care, parental and spousal notification and consent bills, circumscribed zoning ordinances for abortion clinics, and continuous introduction of various human life amendments on state and federal levels limited the functioning of these centers. Fiscally, the centers found it increasingly difficult to remain solvent. They had trouble getting foundation support and lost government funds. At the same time, insurance and personnel costs rose dramatically. Finally, the clinics either witnessed or withstood direct actions by the New Right. These were in the form of clinic invasions, picketing and sidewalk "counseling," vandalism, and protest rallies. Such actions generated considerable fear and anxiety among the centers' staffs.

The Self-Help Clinic felt the wrath of the New Right most viciously and extensively. This organization was subjected to continuous New Right activity from 1982 to 1986. Right-to-life protestors often surrounded the clinic, blocking its entrance and harassing clients and staff. A number of invasions were attempted. Bomb threats, which necessitated clinic evacuation, were made. At one point, the clinic was vandalized. These New Right activities exacerbated the difficulties already posed by the highly competitive market within which the SHC operated. No fewer than six nonfeminist, for-profit abortion clinics existed in its catchment area.

The Cooperative Health Project also withstood direct attacks by the New Right. Picketers were present, particularly on anniversaries for *Roe v. Wade* (the 1973 Supreme Court case that legalized abortion). Right-to-lifers sponsored a billboard that named CHP staff and local NOW (National Organization for Women) leaders as murderers. Yet a more devastating environmental factor threatened the very survival of the CHP. While all three clinics experienced difficulties in getting and paying for insurance coverage, the CHP lost its insurance in 1986 and nearly closed. This insurance disaster can be attributed to the New Right, as its actions created a high-risk climate unsuitable to insurance companies.

The Community Health Center experienced right-wing actions earlier than did the other two clinics. In the mid-1970s, a conservative medical board shut down the clinic. This forced lock-out was largely due to alternative gynecological and abortion approaches offered by the clinic. Upon its reopening, the center decided not to offer abortion services (as other more traditional clinics had filled that market niche), and this decision no doubt spared it from direct actions (though they did happen at other area clinics). However, the CHC experienced severe economic damage at the hands of local right-wing government. In the late 1970s, conservative controlled state and county revenue boards eliminated funds to the center. These funds were reinstated a few years later, though at an insufficient level. This overtly hostile economic climate influenced center dynamics throughout the 1980s.

As is evident from these summaries, the nature of New Right attacks varied in terms of type and intensity. To some extent, these differences were important in the organizational changes that occurred during the 1980s. Yet also important was the way in which the New Right presence generated a shared rallying cry that focused on the protection of and access to woman-centered services. Both aspects of New Right influence, and larger transformation patterns, are discussed in the next section.

Organizational Transformations

As noted earlier, the explicit declaration of socialist feminism all but disappeared from these three health centers during the 1980s. While at first glance it appears that the ideational systems in these organizations became more conservative, that would be an oversimplification. The clinics maintained commitments to transformative movement politics and to the provision of woman-centered health programs—albeit in new and differing ways.

To some extent, challenges by the New Right elicited public declarations to feminist principles. These examples typify the impassioned feminist, anti-right rhetoric:

> Reagan is hazardous to your health. The current administration is jeopardizing the health and livelihood of millions of people both in the U.S. and abroad. From the Human Life Amendment to nuclear weapons development, basic human rights and respect for the individual are being threatened and ignored. (CHC newsletter, June 1981)

> There is a war going on—a war between a woman's right to choose and fetal rights, between women's right to self-determination and fetuses' "right to life." This war takes many forms including Medicaid payment cutoffs, parental consent requirements, Reagan's state of the Union address, picketing, marches on Washington, and clinic violence.... Our biggest challenge is to swing the momentum away from the anti-abortion perspective, away from the "silent scream" of the fetus to the woman's pain of an unwanted pregnancy and her need for privacy in such a personal matter. We must not compromise on abortion. . . . We must speak up for each woman's right to control her body and decide her future. (SHC director's speech to the National Lawyer's Guild, 1985)

During the formative years, movement orientation guided agency orientation: social change through service provision. Encounters with the New Right altered this equation, however, as the desire to protect services (agency orientation) informed movement analysis and action. The two orientations remained compatible, yet the balance shifted.

The New Right also inspired organizing activities. While none of these organizations saw direct actions (transitive goal) as central to their missions, they participated in and in some cases organized anti-New Right events. For example:

> The anti-choice group is getting a parade permit for January 22 for the clinic. The permit will be limited to 2-10 people, but we know that they

will be on our friendly and supportive neighbors' yards. We discuss whether or not we should have a[n abortion] clinic or our own rally. We decide to cancel the clinic and organize our own rally to celebrate 10 years of safe and legal abortions! We decide that rather than be confrontative we will have a march and rally downtown. We will march from downtown to [local restaurant] and have a celebration with refreshments and speakers and entertainers. Advantages: not being here will be the ultimate insult for the misogynist picketers, we will be indoors rather than outdoors, they have selected CHP as their turf so we will select all of [our city] for our turf! (Abortion committee meeting, December 1982)

The Self-Help Clinic, in particular, engaged in extensive lobbying activities against restrictive legislation and organized various public education forums (press releases, workshops, rallies). Here again, the desire to protect services guided activities usually associated with movement organizations. As with ideological analyses, responding to the New Right facilitated a new fusion between movement and agency tendencies within some of the transitive goals.

Most importantly, the centers maintained the goal of offering self-help programs and services. These quotes suggest the salience of self-help throughout the 1980s:

[The CHP] . . . was founded so that feminist self-help ideals and practices could be introduced to our community through health service clinics, active education and client participation. It is our goal to promulgate these ideals or participatory health care, informed medical consumerism, patient's rights, women-oriented health care delivery and the larger ideals of the feminist philosophy: political, economic and social equality and the right to choose our vocations and our life-styles. (CHP, 1984 statement of purpose)

The CHC stresses the empowerment of women to make decisions about their treatment, self-help, health education and preventative care. The CHC is committed to serving the traditionally medically underserved in our community. (CHC, 1985 grant application)

Keeping in practice with introducing self-help and the SHC to women in the community, the SHC hosted a group of nine women from [a local] college. (Community relations report, 1986)

This commitment, however, was compromised by harsh political and economic realities. The most telling aspect of this compromise was the introduction of individual clinic sessions:

> In an effort to increase our business, we changed the structure of our Well Woman clinic. Women can now come on Mondays and Wednesdays and are seen on an individual basis by a health worker and nurse practitioner. It seems as though more women are coming for services, and they are definitely here for a less amount of time, but we recognize the amount of [political] "turf" we have given up to increase our business. (Clinic team report, 1983)

The "turf" that was given up was a group setting within which to educate and politicize consumers. In addition, the centers reduced or eliminated some programs that did not generate needed income; though the extent of such measures varied considerably. The advent of individual clinics, and other "business" decisions, laid the groundwork for political conflicts between reflexive goals and other components of the ideational systems. The presence and extent of this conflict, indicative of goal displacement in the conventional sense, is important in understanding the different change trajectories experienced by the health centers.

The center that changed the least was the Cooperative Health Project. This may have been due to its insistence that collectivist governance (reflexive goals) continue to serve movement ends; a commitment much stronger in this rather than the other centers. During the 1980s, the general trend was the downsizing of staff and programs due to fiscal difficulties. As already indicated, some of its self-help clinics were offered on an individual basis. It eliminated its positive pregnancy program and reduced its community relations program to maintenance activities. However, it retained the gynecological clinic even though it was and is not a "money-maker":

> The staff has chosen to retain gynecology services despite its narrow financial margin. The service draws mostly local residents as clients (unlike other services), which establishes a base of local support for the CHP in a generally hostile political atmosphere. It helps familiarize clients with the CHP encouraging their expanded use of other services when needed. (Business plan, 1985)

The CHP maintained its desire to be a supportive environment. Encounters with the New Right reinforced the closed, collective nature of this organization:

> [The consultant] was asked why [he lowered his fee] and this is the summary. He really has been impressed by how we work together and what we have accomplished over the years. . . . He then went on to say

that he was glad to happen to have come here on a day we had picketers. He was immediately aware of the difference in attitude at the clinic; our focus had narrowed and we were obviously dealing with the problem at hand. It was clear to him that we had pulled together to take care of ourselves and the clinic. . . . For the first time since the beginning of the project [he] felt like an outsider again when he saw our bonding around the picketing issue. (Central committee meeting, July 1984)

The protective or cocoon nature of collectivism assisted the participants in coping emotionally with the New Right threat. Yet this reinforced the insular quality of the organization that made growth and expansion very difficult.

The Community Health Project re-affirmed its identity as a cooperative workplace. Even when engaged in business and market planning, the centrality of worker-control remained:

CHP is owned by membership: members being limited to staff. All excess revenues (e.g., profits) are used for further corporate growth, as stated in the company by-laws. When an employee is hired, she automatically becomes a member-owner of the Clinic. Any staff personnel that leaves employment gives up her ownership rights. (Business plan, 1985)

This business plan signified an important turning point for the center. While it may seem antithetical for a collective to undertake a systematic analysis of marketing needs and strategies, in this case it was the key to its survival. It succeeded because it was embedded in the larger movement-oriented ideational context of collectivism. Because of this planning, the CHP weathered the financial storm caused by the loss of insurance until a new doctor agreed to work for the clinic on his own insurance plan. Currently, it operates as a "modified" collective[2] with 10 full time collective members and a battery of nonmember contract workers who work in the abortion clinic but do not participate in planning and governance. The CHP suggests that the fusion of movement and agency orientations can remain viable through carefully constructed reflexive and transitive goals. Moreover, that aspect of the organization that was strong during its formative years, collectivism, was accentuated during encounters with the New Right and in the subsequent changes.

The Community Health Center changed substantially in the early 1980s, moving from a collective to a participatory organization with a board and administrator. In many respects this transformation is the result of the center's strong commitment to the local community. The

CHC operated as a collective through the early 1980s, yet a collective typically is homogeneous and exclusive in membership. These qualities clashed with the center's increased desire to serve a diverse community population. As one member stated:

> We realized that everything about us was about white, middle class women. It was the language we used, it was the structure, it was doing strokes and constructive criticism, it was having this collective with members that necessarily were excluded because they weren't part of how we traditionally took people in. . . . There was a kind of intimacy that came from who we were and the fact that we . . . had shared our victimization as women that wasn't necessarily the same shared experience for women of color who dealt with issues of poverty and being single parent households, being farmworkers. (Ann)

That aspect of socialist-feminism that emphasized a coalition-based struggle guided the CHC through the transition to a participatory workplace. Internal and external multiculturalism took precedent over collectivism. In this case, the ideological commitment to diversity informed changes throughout the organization. Thus the fusion between movement and agency orientation remained.

This process was not, however, without conflict. While the collective agreed to be 50% women of color, economic hardships necessitated that this be accomplished through layoff rather than expansion. The clinic already was under financial siege from revenue cuts that occurred in the late 1970s. The response at that time was to downsize staff:

> As a result of losing County Revenue Sharing Funds in 1978, a realistic and painful view of our finances evolved and hit hard. At that point there were 25 women in the collective, 17 of whom were paid. We decided that it was in our best interest to pay 4 to 5 women an adequate wage—which meant that 12 women, whose work was integral to the collective, had to be laid off. It was an emotionally painful and draining time for us. . . . We lost many women who were involved in the work of the collective, yet we were committed to continuing the community services we offered. (1981 newsletter)

The turmoil generated by this fiscal volatility raised stress levels and resulted in staff burnout. It was in this organizational context that the clinic pursued its multicultural mission.

In order to survive Right Wing fiscal damage and to pursue its broader agenda, the center diversified and expanded its offerings. The clinic initiated bilingual services and community outreach programs during this tumultuous time. A coalition with other community agencies attempted a collaborative approach to area foundations and in general the center broadened its base of community support. The clinic participated in a network to protect undocumented workers from INS raids and most recently offered low cost INS exams to women, children and men. This grassroots emphasis captured both movement and agency orientations, and also helped the clinic negotiate the hostile environment.

The clinic constituted a community-based board, yet had difficulty in turning over the power so that the board could make the necessary decisions. Because financial solvency became a critical problem, the center hired an administrator with fund-raising experience in 1984. Despite best intentions, it was difficult to break old habits of collective decision making. Yet even with turmoil that resulted in staff turnover, positive internal changes occurred. After considerable chaos, there currently is a solid structure, good planning and accountability mechanisms, clarified personnel policies, updated educational materials, monthly reports, and a salary and benefit system. Many on staff are bilingual, and there is continued commitment to hiring women of color. Thus the reflexive goals, while considerably different from those of the formative years, were compatible with and supportive of the multicultural ideology and transitive goals.

The Self-Help Clinic underwent the greatest transformation, shifting from a small collective to a bureaucratic medical care facility with a million dollar budget. This dramatic change was the result of several potent and mutually reinforcing factors: the ascendance of cultural feminism, particularly the entrepreneurial values; the overwhelming hostility of the New Right; and the competitive health center market. Clinic survival was embedded in a drive to become more businesslike, while still maintaining an overarching commitment to woman-centered health care. Within this transformation process, developments in 1983 and 1984 proved most telling. In 1983, the SHC instituted individual clinic sessions to a much greater extent than did the other two centers, and with a clearer indication that this was a "business" decision. In 1984, the SHC formalized structural changes that had been occurring gradually. These changes included increased job specialization and stratification, such as the creation of new supervisory positions, and the standardization of financial procedures and personnel policies. These developments occurred primarily for reasons of greater efficiency and task clarity. The director felt that these changes merely reflected the reality of the clinic at that time. With these changes, management became more entrenched; an oligarchy comprised of clinic founders and close allies solidified. The staff increasingly referred to the center as a health care business.

The New Right was a factor in these changes. Its toll on the clinic was extensive:

> Overall, the increased anti-abortion activity has added new stress to the entire staff and their families. . . . [With the arrival of anti-choice activist Joe Scheidler] we started to feel what other clinics around the country were experiencing—paranoia (grounded in reality), frustration, shock and amazement at the fanaticism and perseverance of possessed, organized anti-abortion people. (Clinic report, 1985)

The clinic organized patient escorts, held frequent news conferences, and tried to alleviate the stress felt by workers and their families through workshops and counseling. In 1985 the director estimated that $150,000 went to security and legal expenses. Considerable resources were channeled into clinic defense to the detriment of other projects. The SHC was particularly sensitive to fluctuations in consumer needs. In a discussion of client demands, individualized clinics, and a dress code (only the SHC had one), the director noted:

> We had to add on additional abortion clinics to generate money. We also had to appeal to a middle-class clientele that could pay. These women wanted privatized health care. They weren't interested in self-help or group education. We changed. The spiffier the clients, the spiffier we had to get.

Thus the entrepreneurial values of cultural feminism both shaped and were enhanced by encounters with the New Right.

This is not to suggest that the SHC abandoned feminist ideals. The current personnel manual still reflects a strong commitment to reproductive rights: "The SHC philosophy is pro-abortion. Staff must agree with women's right to abortion and reproductive control." The director indicated that she refused to hire three prospective candidates for health worker positions because they would not learn self-help techniques. In addition to previously mentioned political activities, the center expanded its offerings to include more clinic hours, second trimester abortions, and more comprehensive educational programs including special workshops on women and AIDS. While the clinic now considers itself a health business, which means downplaying once explicit anticapitalistic themes, it maintained its essential identity as a defender of reproductive rights. During this time of transformation, cultural feminism solidified as the guiding ideology. As such, reflexive goals dominated transitive goals since maintenance through entrepreneurship was the primary concern. An agency orientation, highly compatible with cultural feminism, shaped the movement orientation in that political work was done to protect health services.

To summarize, there were some similarities in the changes that occurred during the 1980s. There was a waning of explicitly stated socialist feminism, yet this was replaced by more general transformative political analyses. The New Right did inspire some public outcry and political events, which suggest that feminist analysis remained at the core of these centers' identities. In all three clinics, agency orientations shaped movement orientations, a reversal of the relationship between these tendencies during the formative years. There also were important differences. The Cooperative Health Project reaffirmed its collectivist approach to governance, the Community Health Center emphasized a multicultural, grassroots approach, and the Self-Help Clinic stressed cultural feminism with its attendant entrepreneurial values. Each of these points of emphasis shaped and were enhanced by the challenge posed by the New Right. Moreover, these points of emphasis also were the distinctive features of each center during its formative years. Table 6.1 provides a summary of organizational characteristics during the formative and transformative periods.

Implications and Conclusion

These transformations not only have implications for organizational theory and practice, but also for the participants who experienced them. Most participants understood that the realities of the situations necessitated certain compromises. These quotations capture the thoughts held by most members:[3]

> The process of changing our structure from a more collective one to a hierarchical structure has been occurring in women-controlled clinics throughout the country. Each health center is responding to the increased conservatization of our society. Our response is pragmatic, yet optimistic—to change and move forward and continue to grow. (SHC executive director's report, 1984)

> We had to make these changes. We wouldn't have survived otherwise. . . . [Do you think the organization is still feminist?] Yes I do. The staff has always been real dedicated to the work we do and to the women

Table 6.1   Characteristics and Key Changes of Three Health Centers

	Cooperative Health Project	Community Health Center	Self-Help Clinic
Formative Period			
Ideology	Socialist-feminism	Socialist-feminism	Socialist and cultural feminism
Transitive Goals	Self-help clinics with grassroots focus	Self-help clinics with grassroots focus	Self-help clinics with membership in national alliance
Reflexive Goals	Collectivism with clear procedures	Collectivism with clear procedures	Belief in, but no support for, collectivism; Belief in some hierarchy
New Right Actions	Direct actions; Loss of insurance	Shut down early in history; Loss of funding	Severe direct actions; Increased competitive market
Transformations			
Ideology	Worker ownership	Multiculturalism	Cultural feminism, entrepreneurship
Transitive Goals	Streamlined offerings, maintained self help including some individual clinics	Diversified offerings, maintained self help including some individual clinics; Community coalitioning	Expanded offerings, more so than other centers offered individual clinics; Engaged in various political actions
Reflexive Goals	Reaffirmed collectivist governance and worker ownership	Moved to participatory democracy; Diversified staff development	Hierarchical governance; Business oriented mechanisms for accountability

who come in. We still radicalize and politicize the women who use our services. (Teresa, CHP)

My idealistic side misses what collectivity is. Spending lots of time listening, discussing, processing. And ensuring through the collective process that everyone is heard because anyone can stop a collective decision. And I miss the intimacy that brought in the sense of empowerment to all those involved. I think that we wouldn't have survived with it and so the part of me that values what we do and that we exist and need to exist sadly says goodbye to the collective and gladly embraces what we have now. (Ann, CHC)

In many respects, the participants understood that trade-offs were necessary for survival.

This suggests that those who criticize the "lack of purity" of some feminist organizations neither appreciate the environmental constraints that influence these organizations nor the ways in which these organizations reconstruct feminism and continue to challenge society (e.g., Ferguson, 1984). Indeed, given the impact of the New Right and the high rate of mortality for alternative organizations, it is remarkable that these health centers survived. Based on these cases, we can understand how organizational responses to environmental opposition are based on accentuating different aspects of the ideational systems. This does not imply that the loss or decline of revolutionary ideas, such as the waning of socialist feminism, is a superficial development. Yet the experiences of these health centers suggest that feminism, in particular, and transformative politics, in general, assume many forms, are manifested in many ways, and are best understood within the larger ideational context.

Thus, goal displacement, as conventionally analyzed in social movement and organizational theory (Zald & Ash, 1966), did not occur in these health centers. While maintenance actions associated with reflexive goals were emphasized during the 1980s, such processes occurred within broader ideational systems. To argue that goal displacement occurred because the Community Health Center ended collectivism, the Cooperative Health Project designed business plans, or the Self-Help Clinic became increasingly entrepreneurial, is to ignore the CHC's decision to be more ethnically diverse, the CHP's rededication to worker ownership, and the SHC's creative medical, political, and educational expansion. Rather than goal displacement, which has conservative connotations for organizational development, these three centers exhibited creative goal reconfiguration in the face of hostile environmental forces.

Finally, these case studies also suggest that agency and movement orientations need not be incompatible. As Withorn (1984) correctly observes, there is a tendency to force a choice between service and social change perspectives. Studies typically assert that service delivery co-opts the social change objectives of the organization. The literature on both feminist and alternative organizations is replete with case studies on co-opted organizations (e.g., Ahrens, 1980; Ferraro, 1983; Morgenbesser et al., 1981; O'Sullivan, 1978). Yet for these health centers, service provision has been and continues to be an essential feature of these organizations. The service component was not an "add-on," but was and is the primary vehicle of social change. Indeed, the protection of these services during the 1980s became the rallying point for movement oriented analysis and action. Emphasis on services, therefore, should not be an automatic indication of co-optation. It is possible, as in these health centers, that service orientations guide movement orientations (and vice versa) and as with goal displacement, this only is understood fully when the larger ideational system is examined. This dynamic represents the heart of social movement agencies.

The feminist movement is not the only social movement to pursue a social change mission through service provision. Examples abound from the civil rights, welfare rights and labor movements and represent a fertile ground for theory, practice and research. The analysis of these organizations can help those who seek social change through service delivery by indicating the various dilemmas that challenge the very survival of these organizations. Future studies also may indicate or substantiate different organizational housing paradigms. Most importantly, serious treatment of social movement agencies may help to piece together the puzzle of creating truly revolutionary services that address basic needs and change the world.

Notes

1. These three case studies are part of a larger research project on the impact of the New Right on change in feminist social movement organizations from 1977 to 1987 (Hyde, 1991).

2. This is a term used by Harvey (1985) to describe a minimal hierarchy (2 tiers) with high degree of participation.

3. Not all members understood or sympathized with these developments. Only SHC members, however, indicated that agency ideologies ended the feminist dream, and they were in the minority. For example: "We aren't feminists. Feminist and business, never the twain shall meet. And we are in the health center business." (Suzanne)

References

Ahrens, L. (1980). Battered women's refuges: Feminist cooperatives vs. social service institutions. In J. Ecklein (Ed.), *Community organizers*. New York: John Wiley.

Alcoff, L. (1988). Cultural feminism versus post-structuralism: The identity crisis in feminist theory. *Signs: Journal of Women in Culture and Society, 13*, 405-436.

Beyer, J. M. (1981). Ideologies, values, and decision making in organizations. In P. C. Nystrom & W. H. Starbuck (Eds.), *Handbook of organizational design*. New York: Oxford University Press.

Ehrenreich, J. (1985). *The altruistic imagination*. Ithaca, NY: Cornell University Press.

Etzioni, A. (1964). *Modern organizations*. Englewood Cliffs, NJ: Prentice-Hall.

Ferguson, K. (1984). *The feminist case against bureaucracy*. Philadelphia: Temple University Press.

Ferraro, K. (1983). Negotiating trouble in a battered women's shelter. *Urban Life, 12,* 287-306.

Garvin, C., & Cox, F. (1979). A history of community organizing since the Civil War. In F. Cox, J. Erlich, J. Rothman, & J. Tropman (Eds.), *Strategies of community organization* (pp. 45-75). Itasca, IL: F. E. Peacock.

Gusfield, J. R. (1963). *Symbolic crusade: Status politics and the American temperance movement*. Urbana: University of Illinois Press.

Harvey, M. R. (1985). *Exemplary rape crisis programs: A cross-site analysis and case studies* (DHHS Pub. No. ADM/85-1423). Rockville, MD: National Institute of Mental Health.

Hasenfeld, Y. (1983). *Human service organizations*. Englewood Cliffs, NJ: Prentice-Hall.

Helfgot, J. H. (1981). *Professional reforming*. Lexington, MA: Lexington Books.

Hyde, C. (1991). *Did the New Right radicalize the women's movement? A study of change in feminist social movement organizations, 1977-1987*. Unpublished doctoral dissertation, University of Michigan.

Jenkins, C. J. (1977). Radical transformation of organizational goals. *Administrative Science Quarterly, 22,* 567-586.

Lauffer, A. (1984). *Understanding your social agency*. Beverly Hills, CA: Sage.

Meyer, A. D. (1982). How ideologies supplant formal structures and shape responses to environments. *Journal of Management Studies, 19,* 45-61.

Michels, R. (1949). *Political parties: A sociological study of the oligarchical tendencies of modern democracy*. New York: Free Press.

Morgenbesser, M., et al. (1981). The evolution of three alternative social service agencies. *Catalyst, 11,* 71-83.

Mohr, L. (1973). The concept of the organizational goal. *American Political Science Review, 67,* 470-481.

O'Sullivan, E. (1978). What has happened to rape crisis centers? A look at their structures, members and funding. *Victomology: An International Journal, 3,* 45-62.

Perrow, C. (1961). The analysis of goals in complex organizations. *American Sociological Review, 26,* 856-866.

Reinharz, S. (1984). Alternative settings and social change. In R. Price et al. (Eds.), *Psychology and community change* (chap. 9). Homewood, IL: Dorsey Press.

Riger, S. (1984). Vehicles for empowerment: The case of feminist movement organizations. *Prevention in Human Services, 3,* 99-117.

Rothschild, J., & Whitt, J. A. (1986). *The cooperative workplace: Potentials and dilemmas of organizational democracy and participation*. Cambridge, MA: Cambridge University Press.

Scott, R. A. (1967). The factory as a social service organization. *Social Problems, 15,* 160-175.

Staggenborg, S. (1989). Stability and innovation in the women's movement: A comparison of two movement organizations. *Social Problems, 36,* 75-93.

Weil, M. (1986). Women, community and organizing. In N. Van Den Bergh & L. Cooper
    (Eds.), *Feminist visions of social work*. Silver Springs, MD: National Association of
    Social Workers.
Withorn, A. (1984). *Serving the people: Social services and social change*. New York: Columbia
    University Press.
Zald, M., & Ash, R. (1966). Social movement organizations: Growth, decay, and change.
    Social Problems, 44, 327-341.

CHAPTER 7

Professional Work[1]

ANDREW ABBOTT

Objective and Subjective

There are in fact several types of objective foundations for professional tasks. Some of them are technological. I have earlier noted the railroad as a technological system generating a variety of problems for experts. Computers are an excellent contemporary example. Another objective source of such tasks is organizations. Social work and teaching are professions based on such organizational foundations; neither would exist in its present form without the current mass welfare and educational systems. Psychiatry similarly looks back to its foundation as the profession of mental hospital superintendents. A third source of objective qualities lies in natural objects and facts. The body and the universe, water and weather, are all objective aspects of the work of medicine, astronomy, hydrology, and meteorology. The case of medicine to the contrary, the strength of natural objects as objective foundations should not be overestimated. For a long time it was not hydrologists but foresters who dominated American water resource management. Finally, there are, as I have noted, slow-changing cultural structures that have an objective character. Often these have passed through periods of rapid flux to a later objective existence. The concept of private property, a fundamental work area for the legal profession in England and America, once caused wild debates among narrators and other early English legal professionals. But it has been an objective aspect of Western legal work since the late Middle Ages.[2]

A profession is always vulnerable to changes in the objective character of its central tasks. Thus, in the immediate postwar period, computer professionals were generally electrical engineers or programming specialists expert in the hardware peculiarities of particular machines. The development of compilers and other forms of fixed software has freed computing professionals to develop rapidly toward the much more open applied software jurisdiction. The development of UNIX and other hardware-impervious operating systems will allow complete emancipation. Other examples are common—the removal of the psychiatrists from the financially pressed mental hospitals, the feminization of American teaching as education ballooned into a mass institution, the death of the railroad professions. In each case, autonomous change in the objective character of the task transformed the profession.[3]

A task also has subjective qualities. Like its objective ones, these too may make it vulnerable to change, although the change comes from a different place. Not the vagaries of external forces, but the activities of other professions impinge on the subjective qualities. Moreover, while the objective qualities of tasks may be discussed as if they existed in themselves, subjective qualities may not. The subjective qualities of a task arise in the current construction of the problem by the profession currently "holding the jurisdiction" of that task. The subjective qualities of alcoholism, which define it for the readers of popular magazines, are created by the work of the medical and psychological professions with the task. To investigate the subjective qualities of jurisdictions is thus to analyze the mechanisms of professional work itself.

In their cultural aspect, the jurisdictional claims that create these subjective qualities have three parts: claims to classify a problem, to reason about it, and to take action on it; in more formal terms, to diagnose, to infer, and to treat. Theoretically, these are the three acts of professional practice. Professionals often run them together. They may begin with treatment rather than diagnosis; they may, indeed, diagnose by treating, as doctors often do. The three are modalities of action more than acts per se. But the sequence of diagnosis, inference, and treatment embodies the essential cultural logic of professional practice. It is within this logic that tasks receive the subjective qualities that are the cognitive structure of a jurisdictional claim.[4]

Diagnosis

Diagnosis not only seeks the right professional category for a client, but also removes the client's extraneous qualities. If the client is an individual, such extraneous qualities often include his or her emotional or financial relation to the "problem." If the client is a group, they include irrelevant internal politics, financial difficulties, and so on. (A diagnosed problem may still be ambiguous, but the ambiguity will be profession-relevant ambiguity—ambiguity within the professional knowledge system.) Thus, diagnosis first assembles clients' relevant needs into a picture and then places this picture in the proper diagnostic category. Following Whewell, I shall call these two processes colligation and classification. Colligation is the assembly of a "picture" of the client; it consists largely of rules declaring what kinds of evidence are relevant and irrelevant, valid and invalid, as well as rules specifying the admissible level of ambiguity. Classification means referring the colligated picture to the dictionary of professionally legitimate problems. A classification system is a profession's own mapping of its jurisdiction, an internal dictionary embodying the professional dimensions of classification.[5]

Like the larger pairing of diagnosis and treatment, colligation and classification are often tied together in strange ways. Classification can, for example, determine colligation; a diagnostic classification of psychosis leads psychiatrists to disregard further client evidence altogether. More importantly, the actual sequence of colligation is often dictated by the classification scheme, since the ultimate object of colligation is a classifiable object. When a doctor suspects a common disease, he or she asks a series of leading questions aimed at establishing its existence. So also generals must ask leading questions of civilian politicians who "don't know what they want," or architects make similar advances when their clients are similarly uncommitted. Although logically distinct, colligation and classification are seldom separate in practice.[6]

Colligation is the first step in which the professional knowledge system begins to structure the observed problems. For example, rules of relevance are often strict. A divorce lawyer does not want to hear about a client's lingering love for an estranged spouse; that is for the counselor, clergyman, or psychiatrist. (Not all professionals can enforce their relevance structures; an architect does not want to hear about costs but often does.) Rules of evidence may also be strict; for example, doctors make a careful distinction between symptoms, which a patient reports, and signs, which are externally verifiable.[7]

Information passing these exclusion rules is assembled into a picture that can be classified. The diagnostic classification system to which it is referred is of staggering complexity. Unlike most biological taxonomies, it is not organized in a simple hierarchical structure. If it were, there would be a standard sequence of questions, a proliferating diagnostic key, that would allow problems to be properly classified without colligation and indeed without reference to experts at all. But the classification system cannot be organized that way. The information available may be inevitably ambiguous or incomplete; a key without built-in redundancy will then mistake diagnoses. Yet even once the professionally irrelevant information is excluded, much of the information remaining will prove unimportant in a given case. There are, moreover, likely to be several plausible colligations. The art of diagnosis lies in finding which is the real one. This holds as much for a financial planner ascertaining a client's true financial picture as for a doctor divining a patient's illness. There are further problems with a key model. Within the classification system itself, there may be large areas of unclassified, residual problems. Problems may fall under several classifications simultaneously, or may be able to change from one classification to another. More importantly, many or even most clients lie in relatively few classifications, and so the majority of steps in a key approach to diagnosis can usually be skipped. Indeed they must be if service is to be efficient. A profession's diagnostic classification system is therefore actually organized not as a logical hierarchy from the common to the esoteric. As it moves toward the esoteric, however, the system becomes more and more logically structured. This gradient causes a classic pattern of misdiagnosis in professions. A patient is discovered, after many diagnostic attempts, to have an esoteric disease absolutely identifiable by two or three unusual and easily accessible symptoms or signs. The successful diagnostician cannot understand why these were not discovered earlier in the process. The reason, of course, is precisely that early diagnosis is *not* key-based, and therefore skips many tests that "ought to be" performed if a key approach were followed from the start.[8]

The diagnostic classification system has two external relations that constrain it. First, it is related to the abstract foundations of professional knowledge, normally maintained by academic professionals who impose a logical clarity that belies the muddle of practice. Second, it is constrained by the treatment system, which classifies problems implicitly by lumping together problems that share similar treatments. This treatment classification is usually complex and probabilistic, and in absolutely pragmatic professions may dictate the diagnostic or academic one.

When coupled with internal complexity, these external constraints make diagnosis a very complex matter. Medicine, which provides the metaphor of diagnosis and treatment, offers excellent examples. The explicit separation of classification and colligation is illustrated by the statement that "pancreatic cancer (a disease classification) often presents as a personality change (a symptom picture). "The well-known complexity of medicine's diagnostic classification is illustrated by its diverse ways of labeling diseases: by the location and type of pathology (multiple sclerosis), by leading symptoms (epilepsy), by etiology (amoebic dysentery). A common by-product is that one disease usually has several names; thus, infantile paralysis = anterior sclerosis = poliomyelitis. Diseases are constantly shifting around in classification. The endocrine diseases, whose chief symptoms defined them as nervous diseases at the turn of this century, are now amorphously classified as functional diseases with anatomical bases. As one might expect, the medical diagnostic system is dominated by the treatment classification. Thus, when lithium carbonate turned out to treat many patients diagnosed by the old psychiatric classification system as manic-depressive, the disease was essentially reconceptualized as lithium insufficiency, and response to lithium treatment became its identifying sign. The century-old diagnostic entity of manic-depression simply disappeared, even though it is quite possible that there is a disorder presenting this picture but not generated by lithium insufficiency. Such cases are now considered mistaken diagnoses. As a by-product of this dominance of diagnosis by treatment, those aspects of a disease unknown when an efficacious treatment is discovered are never studied.[9]

The classification system, too, affects the openness of the jurisdiction. Vulnerability begins not with the most commonly treated professional problems, but with the peripheral ones. Diagnostic classification implicitly claims any problems sharing features with the standard professional problems and, more generally, any problems identifiable by the underlying dimensions of the diagnostic classification system. Such implicit claims often include vast areas of residual problems not conceptualized in clear types like the standard professional problems, but loosely labeled as "nervous exhaustion," "emotional difficulties," "marital troubles," "financial difficulties," "tax problems," or whatever. These residually conceptualized areas are a standard site of interprofessional poaching. Since they are not claimed explicitly by a specific picture on the main list of professional tasks, but rather implicitly by the dimensions of professional jurisdiction, they are held only weakly. Redefinition under a new system of abstractions can easily remove them.[10]

Diagnosis, then, begins to assign subjective properties to the objective problems with which professions work. The problems become more than simply objective tasks. They are related to various underlying conceptual dimensions, guarded by rules of evidence and of relevance, and located at the ends of various diagnostic chains. The clarity, the strictness, and the logic of these subjective definitions of the problem make it more-or-less open to the intervention of other professions. But the properties assigned in diagnosis are only part of the subjective aspect of jurisdiction. A different set of properties arises in treatment.[11]

Treatment

The effects of treatment parallel those of diagnosis. Like diagnosis, treatment imposes a subjective structure on the problems with which a profession works. Like diagnosis, treatment is organized around a classification system and a brokering process. In this case brokering gives results to the client, rather than takes information from the client; colligation is replaced by prescription.

The treatment classification system occupies a space defined by the various possible treatments. Problems are clumped together if they share a common treatment. This classification often differs from the diagnostic one, although, in some ultimate sense, the aim of every profession is to reconcile the two. Thus, excessive vomiting and schizophrenia are quite different diseases diagnostically, but may involve similar drug treatments. Again, whatever may be the cause that takes a lawyer to litigation, the formalities of civil procedure are invariant across them all. Professions are ambivalent about the isomorphism of diagnosis and treatment classifications. On the one hand, identifying the two would clarify and simplify professional work, at the same time making it more comprehensible to outsiders. Yet it would also make professional work more easily downgraded.[12]

In many cases, of course, the two systems coincide. Like the diagnostice classification system, the treatment system is organized around the common cases that make up the majority of professional work—bacterial infections, wills, preparation of IRS Form 1040, amplifier design. Most of these problems have trivial diagnoses, and for each the profession involved has a purely conventional treatment. Often the treatment is delegated to subordinates, as conveyancing is by solicitors to managing clerks in England, as working drawings are by architects to draftsmen, as much of primary care is by doctors to nurses and others. Beyond these conventional cases, however, the treatment system and the diagnostic system are not isomorphic. Indeed, the treatment system often suggests a combination of treatments for a particular diagnosis, or a sequence of treatments conditional on prior results.[13]

The treatment classification not only lumps together problems with similar treatments, it also associates with each problem a likelihood of successful outcome under a given treatment. For some standard problems, this likelihood is near 1.0; such treatments are uniquely tied to antecedent diagnoses. In most problems, the chance of success is much lower, and often much less clearly known. In medicine, the literature specifies formal morbidity, mortality, and complication rates for all sorts of procedures, often specified by age, sex, and other qualities of the patient. A good lawyer has an equally solid, if less universal, sense of the probabilities associated with settling a case or trying it, often specified by which side he is on, which judge he is likely to get, and how proficient the opposing counsel is, as well as by the facts and legal merits of the case.[14]

Clearly many properties of this treatment classification system influence the vulnerability of professional jurisdiction to outside interloping. I have already noted that too absolute an association between diagnoses and particular treatments may lead to demands for delegation or deprofessionalization. Another variable, of course, is efficacy itself. Treatment failure obviously makes a jurisdiction vulnerable, although a variety of forces, as we shall later see, weaken this effect.

Another variable affecting vulnerability is the measurability of the results. As results become less and less measurable, there is less and less need to prefer one treatment to another, and thus a weaker professional hold on the problem area. Since the results of psychotherapy are famously difficult to measure, psychotherapeutic schools have become interchangeable and the problems they treat have become an interprofessional battleground. On the other hand, results that are too easily measurable lead to easy evaluation from outside the profession and consequent loss of control. They may also make it easier for competitors to demonstrate treatment superiority if they have it (see Lesse, 1968; Stiles, Shapiro, & Elliott, 1986).

Treatments, like diagnoses, can range from very general to very specific, and this too influences the amenability of the jurisdiction to seizure. "Get lots of rest" is one kind of injunction; "take two of these tablets three times a day, give up alcohol and cheese aged over ninety days, and see me in two weeks" is quite another. Normally, the more specialized a treatment is, the more a profession can retain control of it. Control over certain kinds of treatment may be central to a profession's jurisdiction, as law and medicine's monopolies of litigation and drugs make

very clear. That control of treatment may be central and that specialized treatments are easier to protect suggests that professions may
defend jurisdiction by specifying treatments even where the results of
specification may be unmeasurable and where general treatments in
fact suffice. For example, at the turn of this century, treatments proposed for nervous diseases were arranged in concentric circles, from
general treatments aimed at the overarching "predisposing causes" to
highly specific (and quite dubious) ones aimed at the particular "precip-
itating" cause, which was more often than not unknown. The complete
lack of efficacy for the specialized treatments did not prevent their
elaboration, which indeed was competitively necessary to protect
medicine's control over these problems from the incursions of the faith
healers.[15]

The professional interested in effective treatment must worry about
many client characteristics that influence treatment efficacy. Just as the
diagnostic system removes the human properties of the client to produce a diagnosed case, so also the treatment system must reintroduce
those properties to make treatment effective for real clients, human or
corporate; this is the process of prescription. Sometimes the client cannot
comply; schizophrenic outpatients are given long-lasting shots of flu-
phenazine because they will not remember to take daily dosages of
shorter-lasting drugs. Sometimes a client's daily routines oblige prescription; doctors schedule pills around minimizing their side effects (e.g.,
sedation during the day) as much as around maintaining blood titer. The
same decisions must be made by a lawyer who knows what his client
will look like "in the box" or by the architect who knows how his client
is likely to alter the building after it is designed. Who the client is thus
determines much of what he or she gets. And most professions—American medicine is the great exception here—have treatment cost as a
central problem in prescription. Each treatment fits uniquely into the
life of a particular client, and that in part must determine whether it is
preferred.[16]

The impact of client characteristics on prescription and treatment is
felt both within the profession itself and in its relations with competitors. Within the profession, the ability of clients to handle prescriptions
is an important stratifying mechanism. One factor that makes certain
clients more attractive to professionals is their ability on the one hand
to prediagnose their problems and on the other to understand their
treatment in relatively professional terms. For example, this quality
makes upper class people more attractive clients for psychotherapists.
A similar difference makes corporations more attractive than individ-

uals as clients for lawyers. Brokering, whether in diagnosis or prescription, is a dirty business, and intraprofessional status often reflects the amount of it a professional must do.[17]

But client ability to handle prescription also has effects on interprofessional competition. These effects are analogous to the effects of rules of relevance in diagnosis. A profession clearly derives general social prestige from meeting clients on *its* own, rather than on *their* own, grounds, just as it derives prestige from strictly enforced rules of relevance. But a profession that forces clients to take treatment completely on its own terms risks heavy competition from those who talk to the clients in their own language. Many of medicine's nineteenth-century competitors followed this approach, as does chiropractic today. Only when a profession possesses absolute monopoly can it afford to ignore this arena of competition. Even the British barristers, whose clogged courts monopolize legal dispute settlement, have seen administrative tribunals emerge to handle disputes to the expeditious liking of corporations, unions, and other social groups. So it is that many professions meet clients on their own grounds—phrasing their treatments in common language, offering advice on professionally irrelevant issues, indeed promising results well beyond those predicted by the treatment structure itself. If they didn't do it, clients would take their problems to someone who would. A similar process forces professions to keep a weather eye to treatment costs. Professions can easily piece themselves out of markets, as psychoanalysts have discovered over the last few decades.[18]

The move from diagnosis to treatment is not necessarily one-way. As I noted at the outset, treatment is often a means to diagnosis; its failure may falsify the diagnosis on which it was based. Yet professions vary in their temporal structuring of diagnosis and treatment. Many professions allow an unlimited sequence of diagnoses and treatments; psychotherapists and clergymen get a second or third or fourth chance. A few professions, like forestry and other renewable-resource specialists, get an infinite number of chances, since their work is to manage a relatively constant situation. For law and architecture, however, there is one chance and one only. In both cases, of course, the reality is much more complex. A good lawyer can switch treatments in mid case, just as a good architect can correct some problems even after a building is completed. But in principle, there is only one chance. Doctors are in the same position when they work with precarious cases.

The time structure of the diagnosis-treatment relation determines the resort to the intermediate, purely professional task of inference. Where costs of failure are low and the professional is assured of a second chance, he or she prescribes the most likely treatment and sees what happens. It is curious that this approach, common among professionals, is held by many to be a definitive sign of nonprofessionalism in the stereotypical nonprofession of automobile repair. Even though careful professional inference is possible in car repair, the costs of failure are low—failure is indeed profitable to the expert—and there is nearly always a second chance. As a result, the standard diagnostic procedure in expert auto repair is to replace something. But where costs are prohibitive or there is no second chance, a professional must set a strategy of treatment from the outset. Only professional inference can do this.

Inference

Professional thinking resembles chess. The opening diagnosis is often clear, even formulaic. So also is the endgame of treatment. The middle game, however, relates professional knowledge, client characteristics, and chance in ways that are often obscure. Nonetheless, like diagnosis and treatment, this middle game—professional inference—has qualities that make a professions' work more or less accessible to competitors.[19]

Inference is undertaken when the connection between diagnosis and treatment is obscure. The composite of diagnostic and treatment classification cannot narrow the range of outcomes acceptably. Acceptability depends, of course, on the costs and reversibility of failure on first trial. High costs and near-total irreversibility make inference a necessity in military tactics. Minor chronic illnesses demand less of it.

Inference can work by exclusion or by construction. Medicine, for example, tends to work by exclusion. If a case is unclear, doctors maintain a general supportive treatment while ruling out areas by using special diagnostic procedures or watching the outcomes of "diagnostic" treatments provided beyond the general maintenance. Classical military tactics, on the other hand, work by construction. The tactician hypothesizes enemy responses to gambits and considers their impact on his further plans. Since in general the flow of forces can be affected only marginally once a battle is begun, the tactician constructs a plan allowing as many winning scenarios as possible. Sometimes, of course, a tactician is mainly interested in not losing—like Jellicoe at Jutland—but there too the emphasis is on constructing possible battles ahead of time, rather than on fighting little ones to find out what doesn't work.[20]

As these examples show, reasoning by exclusion is a luxury available only to those who get a second chance. The impact of reasoning by exclusion on a profession's vulnerability to outside interference is thus conditional on the effects of time structuring. Multichance time structuring, curiously, is more vulnerable. Other things being equal, an incumbent profession with several chances to work on a problem will have more failures than will a profession that gets only one chance. For multichance professionals may be conservative, taking short-run failure in exchange for a greater chance of long-run success (which will help them in terms of the efficacy competition). Even where a profession makes its best effort from the start, there will be more failures with multichance problems from simple probability. Given one hundred clients and a success rate of 50 percent, a profession generates fifty failures on the first chance, twenty-five on the second, and so on. Even if the success rate rises with the number of trials, there will still be more failures in absolute numbers when there are more trials. Since treatment failure is the first target of attacking professions, professions with multiple chances are generally more vulnerable, ceteris paribus.

Within the world of multichance problems, however, there are clear differences in vulnerability by type of inference, although again we must distinguish two cases. Incumbents' rate of success can be measured either by successes achieved or by catastrophes avoided. There is no question that exclusion is a more effective strategy under the latter measure. It will not, however, reach success as fast as constructive strategies. To the extent that nonfailure is the dominant measure, then, exclusion protects an incumbent's jurisdiction over a problem. After a problem has bewildered a profession for some time, however, it tends to become fair game for outsiders, because nonfailure no longer satisfies. Success is demanded. Both early neurology and chiropractic founded themselves on jurisdictions largely made up of patients who had bewildered the regular medical profession despite repeated attempts at therapy.[21]

Inference also varies in the length of the logical chains it permits. Again, in the case of one-time problems, these chains are "as long as they need to be." Tacticians or architects, who must construct decisions no matter what, extend inferences until they afford conclusions. Like doctors or social workers, they associate with each step a probability of error or difficulty, and with the whole chain a total probability compounding these single probabilities. Doctors and social workers, however, have a freedom tacticians and architects lack. They can terminate any chain in which the total likelihood of error reaches a certain level, waiting for further information and following up other chains in the meantime. The higher this tolerated level, the more open a profession's jurisdiction is to outside interference. This is true not only because higher errors imply lower probabilities of success, but also because higher overall errors reflect longer chains, which allow more places for outsiders to intervene.

Another aspect of inference that influences the course of external poaching is the use of stopgaps. Each profession has had some well-recognized problems for which it knows it lacks effective treatment. Since these are very vulnerable to external attack, they are secured in various ways. They often become the province of elite consultants, or are academicized as "crucial anomalies." The academicization may be connected with a conveniently vague public labeling, which serves as a stopgap against dangerous questioning. The study of viruses, for example, is an important and advanced area of medical research. Nonetheless, the common culture believes with some reason that physicians label "viral" a wide variety of diseases whose chief common property is their therapeutic intractability. While such stopgap labels protect a profession's jurisdiction in the short run, they are often signs of long-run weakness.

The most important aspect of professional inference in determining jurisdictional vulnerability is actually external to inference itself; it is the degree to which inference predominates, rather than the routine connection of diagnosis and treatment without inference. Any profession has rules dictating when a professional must resort to complex inference, and learning these rules is central to learning the profession. Yet whatever these rules may be, either too little or too much use of inference will ultimately weaken jurisdiction.

Too little inference is a familiar part of the larger phenomenon of routinization. Of course, routinization occurs not only to the diagnosis-treatment connection, but also to once-esoteric diagnostic and therapeutic procedures; palpation, sight testing, administration of medicine, and preparing working drawings were once specialized procedures for dominant professionals. Indeed professions sometimes routinize whole procedures, from diagnosis to treatment; conveyancing and preparation of certain kinds of audits are examples. While such procedures are sometimes delegated to subordinates, to the extent that they are not they are an obvious target both for poaching by other professions and for compulsory deprofessionalization by the state. The only defense is the argument that such routine cases may be indistinguishable from less routine ones, an argument long used by psychiatrists to protect their jurisdiction against incursion by lay psychotherapists, who "might not recognize organic brain syndrome." No such argument was available to protect the railroad auditing work of CPAs when the Interstate Commerce Commission imposed a rigid "scientific" account structure on the railroads. Much of the work has been done by government-paid nonprofessionals since the 1910s.[22]

But just as professions doing mostly routine work risk jurisdiction incursions, so also do professions that refer nearly all their cases to formal inference. For one thing, the claim that all problems are nonroutine does not persuade external critics. For another, the profession cannot reinforce its legitimacy by showing how, in simple cases, the professional knowledge system leads ineluctably from diagnosis to treatment. While it may successfully demonstrate efficacy, a profession that is purely esoteric has trouble demonstrating the cultural legitimacy of the basis for that efficacy.

For example, in the early days of American psychiatry, Adolf Meyer and others argued that each case had its own unique logic. After dominating American psychiatry in the 1920s, this system was gradually destroyed by the Freudian one, which made some problems more routine than others and offered relatively clear rules for the decision to invoke formal inference. Freudianism succeeded because the routine aspect of the system made it comprehensible to laymen, while the nonroutine aspect justified the creation of a specialized corps to apply it. To an outsider, Meyer's system seemed like a mass of personal judgments, well-informed, but ultimately idiosyncratic. It was effective, to be sure, but only because Meyer and those he trained were good therapists individually. There was no abstractable, portable system independent of those individuals, and hence no scientifically legitimate basis for efficacy.[23]

Like diagnosis and treatment, then, professional inference has a number of qualities that help subjectively define a profession's area of work and thereby shape the jurisdiction it exercises over its tasks. These properties are closely related to the temporal structuring of professional work, in particular to whether a profession gets one or many chances with its problems. Professions with only one chance per task approach it constructively, developing chains of inference that choose a single treatment that maximizes chances of success or minimizes chances of failure, depending on the context. Professions that get second chances can minimize failure by exclusionary reasoning, which may protect their jurisdictions to some extent, but this strategy ultimately opens certain jurisdictions—those for which they have no answers—to direct attacks. Irrespective of the mode of inference or the temporal structuring of the problem, long chains in professional inference seem more vulnerable than short ones. Finally, it seems clear that professions cannot afford to invoke either too much or too little inference. Too little makes their work seem not worth professionalizing. Too much makes their work impossible to legitimate. In either case, their jurisdiction is weakened.

Notes

1. Excerpt from Abbott, A. (1988). *The system of professions*. Chicago: The University of Chicago Press. Used by permission.

2. Outstanding works on the organizational foundations of teaching are Katz's books (1968, 1971). On the similar foundations of social work, see Lubove (1969). On psychiatry, see Grob (1973). On forestry and hydrology, see Hays (1975). On narrators and on property, see Plucknett (1956).

3. On computer history generally see Moreau (1984), and on languages in particular see Wexelblat (1981). On psychiatrists leaving hospitals, see Grob (1983) and Abbott (1982), and on feminization in teaching, see Sugg (1978).

4. The idea of treating diagnosis and prescription as modes of thought (or alternatively the idea of labeling those modes, with which we are familiar, with these terms) comes from Levine (1971), who, I believe, got it from Richard McKeon. A splendid discussion of the medical knowledge system itself is Freidson's classic work of 1970a, part 3.

5. I first encountered the term *colligation* in McCullagh (1978). Whewell coined it in *The Philosophy of Inductive Science*, in 1847.

6. On medical diagnosis, see Freidson (1970a, chap. 12). For a discussion of the celebrated civil-military situation of the Second World War, see Huntington (1957). On the actual practice of architecture, see Gutman (1983) on the use of formulaic designs, and Blau (1984) on practice conditions in firms. There is not, to my knowledge, a case study of small-scale firms equivalent to, say, Carlin's (1962) excellent study of the actual work of solo lawyers. For personal information about small architectural firms, I am indebted to Richard Kalb of Cone and Kalb, AIA. A brilliant and entertaining fictional account can be found in Creswell (1964).

7. On divorce practice, see O'Gorman (1963), and for a German comparison, Schumann (1985). Carlin (1962, pp. 91 ff.), however, presents his solo lawyers as enjoying their "marriage broker" roles. The class and type of clients may of course affect colligation; see, for example, Kadushin (1962, 1966). Murphee (1984) discusses the screening of "dirty work" by subordinate personnel, while both B. K. Rothman (1983) and Loseke and Cahill (1984) discuss screening by professionals themselves. Professions sometimes *expand* areas colligated. See for example, K. Jones's (1985) discussion of the inclusion of family in child psychiatric diagnosis, and Duhart and Charton-Brassard (1973) on "nursing diagnosis."

8. For an interesting (but nonsociological) discussion of the diagnosis process in management systems, see McCosh, Rahman, and Earl (1981). Diagnosis is often inaccurate; B. Moore (1984) has a brief historical review of relevant studies on medical diagnosis.

9. On the endocrine diseases as nervous diseases, see chapter 10 in Abbott (1988). Having identified manic depression with a biological marker, researchers are now announcing it to be hereditary (Kolata, 1987). The earlier redefinition of it as a lithium insufficiency was openly visible to me throughout my fieldwork both in clinic and hospital.

10. On chiropractic as specializing in medical residuals, see Cleary (n.d.). Another paper on a residual population in Brumberg's (1982) discussion of "chlorotic girls."

11. There are professions specializing in diagnostic work: clinical psychology in its early days, optometrists, and others. Such groups generally seem to be subordinates in divisions of labor. The "information professions," however, represent a new approach to such specialization.

12. The treatment system of nineteenth-century British psychiatry illustrates lumping by treatment type (Scull, 1975b). Hyperemesis and schizophrenia are both treated by phenothiazine drugs, although of considerably different strengths in the two cases.

13. For information on law practice, I am indebted to Scott Thatcher.

14. On the danger of nonspecific treatments in, for example, nursing, see Reinhard (1986). A similar conflict between highly mathematicized and naturalistic treatments separates geophysicists from the geologists they are invading (personal communication, Roger Revelle). On measurability, see, for example, Geison (1980) on medicine. Rosenkrantz (1974) discusses the decline of public health medicine once results become less measurable. On efficacy itself, there is a surprisingly small literature. See Grob (1973, 1983) on nineteenth-century-American psychiatry, and Scull (1975a) on nineteenth-century-British, McKeown (1979) on medicine generally, Cleary (n.d.) on chiropractic, Roeber (1979) on colonial lawyers, and again, Rosenkrantz (1974) on public health medicine.

15. In most professions, cost is a central dimension aspect of treatment decisions. Like medicine with its third-party insurance, law, too, has to some extent avoided the cost problem with the contingent fee. But in most professions—accountancy, psychoanalysis, social work, and above all in industrially employed professions like engineering—cost of treatment is a central issue. Yet if cost has been an absent factor in American medicine, other "professionally irrelevant" client factors—age, general health, emotional outlook, family support—have been as powerful in reshaping treatment there.

16. The correlation of client status and professional status is taken up in chapter 5 of Abbott (1988). More generally, see Abbott (1981). On prediagnosing, see, for example, Kadushin (1962, 1966). Despite the distractions of brokering, it is extremely necessary, and individual professionals sometimes pride themselves on the sophistication of their brokering knowledge. Schumann (1985) deals with brokering, both in colligation and prescription, among German lawyers.

17. On patient understanding and its impact on medical treatment, see F. Davis (1960) and McKinlay (1976). On costs see, for example, Rothstein's (1972) discussion of competitors underselling regular medicine in the nineteenth century. Client relations in psychotherapy are discussed in Henry, Sim, and Spray (1971).

18. There are surprisingly few studies of actual professional inference—ethnographic accounts of professionals thinking about problems and defining them. Examples are B. K. Rothman (1983), Loseke and Cahill (1984), and Latour and Woolgar (1979). Most writing about professional inference is of course written by professionals themselves. Schön (1983) is an ethnographic and comparative account, but somewhat

romanticized. It takes inference as the dominant process in professional work, which belies virtually all other data on practice.

19. On tactics, see R. Holmes (1976), Koening (1975), Fuller (1961); and on strategy more generally, see Earle (1966). Churchill is said to have remarked that Jellicoe was "the only man on either side who could lose the war in an afternoon."

20. On chiropractic, see Wardwell (1952) and Cleary (n.d.). On neurology, see chapter 10 in Abbott (1988).

21. The literature on routine work and deprofessionalization is extensive. See Ritti et al. (1974) on parish assistants, Denzin (1968) on pharmacists, Coe (1970) on anesthesiology, Previts and Merino (1979) on accounting (the ICC issue is discussed on p. 162; see also Carey, 1969, pp. 57, 60), and Johnstone and Hopson (1967) on lawyers. The psychiatrist quote is from my own fieldwork. The theoretical literature on this subject is discussed in chapter 5 of Abbott (1988), but the classic citation has been Jamous and Peloille (1970) on the "indeterminacy/technicality ratio."

22. On Meyer, see Abbott (1982, pp. 388-393). The occult professions have foundered over precisely this problem. Mediums, astrologers, and other occult professionals have generally held that every problem must be handled in its own special way. There is no simple system that can be applied by laymen to professionally trivial cases to illustrate how effective the professional knowledge system is. As a result, occult professions have gradually lost control of jurisdiction over predicting the future, an area in which they were once prominent, to state councillors and, latterly, policy scientists, whose knowledge systems are more easily legitimated, if not always more successful.

References

Abbott, A. (1981). Status and status strain in the professions. *American Journal of Sociology, 86,* 819-835.

Abbott, A. (1982). *The emergence of American psychiatry.* Unpublished doctoral dissertation, University of Chicago.

Abbott, A. (1988). *The system of professions.* Chicago: University of Chicago Press.

Blau, J. (1984). *Architects and firms.* Cambridge: MIT Press.

Brumberg, J. J. (1982). Chlorotic girls, 1870-1920. *Child Development, 53,* 1468-1477.

Carey, J. L. (1969). *The rise of the accounting professions* (vol 1). New York: American Institute of Certified Public Accountants.

Carlin, J. (1962). *Lawyers on their own.* New Brunswick, NJ: Rutgers University Press.

Cleary, P. D. (n.d.). Chiropractic use. New Brunswick, NJ: Rutgers University, Graduate School of Social Work.

Coe, R. (1970). The process of the development of established professions. *Journal of Health and Social Behavior, 11,* 59-67.

Creswell, H. B. (1964). *The honeywood file.* Winchester, MA: Faber & Faber.

Davis, F. (1960). Uncertainty in medical prognosis: Clinical and functional. *American Journal of Sociology, 66,* 41-47.

Denzin, N. K. (1968). Incomplete professionalization: The case of pharmacy. *Social Forces, 46,* 375-381.

Duhart, J., & Charton-Brassard, J. (1973). Reforme hospitalière et soin infirmier sur ordonnance médicale. *Revue française de sociologie, 14*(Suppl.), 77-101.

Earle, E. M. (Ed.). (1966). *The makers of modern strategy.* New York: Atheneum.

Freidson, E. (1970). *Profession of medicine.* New York: Dodd Mead.

Fuller, J. F. C. (1961). *The conduct of war.* London: Eyre & Spottiswoode.

Geison, G. (1980, May 9). *Science and efficacy in the history of professions.* Paper presented to the Shelby Cullom Davis Center for Historical Studies, Princeton University.

Grob, G. N. (1973). *Mental institutions in America.* New York: Free Press.

Grob, G. N. (1983). *Mental illness and American society, 1875-1940.* Princeton, NJ: Princeton University Press.

Gutman, R. (1983). Architects in the home building industry. In J. R. Blau, M. LaGory, & J. S. Pipkin (Eds.), *Professionals and urban form* (pp. 204-223). Albany: SUNY Press.

Hays, S. P. (1975). *Conservation and the gospel of efficiency.* New York: Atheneum.

Henry, W. E., Sim, J. H., & Spray, S. L. (1971). *The fifth profession.* Ann Arbor, MI: Books on Demand.

Holmes, R. (1976). *Epic land battles.* Secaucus, NJ: Chartwell.

Huntington, S. P. (1957). *The soldier and the state.* New York: Vintage.

Jamous, H., & Peloille, B. (1970). Changes in the French university hospital system. In J. A. Jackson (Ed.), *Professions and professionalization.* Cambridge, UK: Cambridge University Press.

Johnstone, Q., & Hopson, D. (1967). *Lawyers and their work.* Indianapolis: Bobbs-Merrill.

Jones, K. (1985, April). *Straightening the twig.* Paper presented to the Organization of American Historians, Bloomington, IN.

Kadushin, C. (1962). Social distance between client and professional. *American Journal of Sociology, 67,* 517-531.

Kadushin, C. (1966). The friends and supporters of psychotherapy. *American Sociological Review, 31,* 781-802.

Katz, M. B. (1968). *The irony of early school reform.* Boston: Beacon.

Katz, M. B. (1971). *Class, bureaucracy, and the schools.* New York: Praeger.

Koenig, W. (1975). *Epic sea battles.* Secaucus, NJ: Chartwell.

Kolata, G. (1987). Manic depression. *Science, 232,* 576-577.

Latour, B., & Woolgar, S. (1979). *Laboratory life.* Beverly Hills, CA: Sage.

Lesse, S. (1968). *An evaluation of the results of the psychotherapies.* Springfield, IL: Charles C Thomas.

Levine, D. N. (1971). *Facing our calling: Sociology and the agon of liberal education.* Paper presented at the American Sociological Association, Denver. [MONTH?]

Loseke, D. R., & Cahill, S. E. (1984). The social construction of deviance: Experts on battered women. *Social Problems, 31,* 290-310.

Lubove, R. (1969). *The professional altruist.* New York: Atheneum.

McCosh, A. M., Rahman, M., & Earl, M. J. (1981). *Developing managerial information systems.* New York: John Wiley.

McCullagh, C. B. (1978). Colligation and classification in history. *History and Theory, 17,* 267-284.

McKeown, T. (1979). *The role of medicine.* Princeton, NJ: Princeton University Press.

McKinlay, J. B. (1976). Who is really ignorant—Physician or patient? *Journal of Health and Social Behavior, 16,* 3-11.

Moore, B. (1984). Historical notes on the doctor's work ethic. *Journal of Social History, 17,* 547-572.

Moreau, R. (1984). *The computer comes of age*. Cambridge: MIT Press.

Murphee, M. C. (1984). Brave new office: The changing world of the legal secretary. In K. B. Sachs & D. Remy (Eds.), *My troubles are going to have trouble with me* (pp. 140-159). New Brunswick, NJ: Rutgers University Press.

O'Gorman, H. (1963). *Lawyers and matrimonial cases*. New York: Free Press.

Plucknett, T. F. T. (1956). *A concise history of the common law*. Boston: Little, Brown.

Previts, G. J., & Merino, B. D. (1979). *A history of accounting in America*. New York: John Wiley.

Reinhard, S. (1986). *Is nursing's jurisdiction eroding or expanding?* [Course paper.] Rutgers University, Department of Sociology.

Ritti, R. R., Ference, T. P., & Goldner, F. H. (1974). Professions and their plausibility. *Sociology of Work and Occupations, 1*, 25-51.

Roeber, A. G. (1979, April 27). *Justices and lawyers in Virginia*. Paper presented to the Shelby Cullom Davis Center for Historical Studies, Princeton University.

Rosenkrantz, B. G. (1974). Cart before horse: The practice and professional image in American public health. *Journal of the History of Medicine and Allied Sciences, 29*, 574.

Rothman, B. K. (1983). Midwives in transition. *Social Problems, 30*, 262-271.

Rothstein, W. G. (1972). *American physicians in the nineteenth century*. Baltimore, MD: Johns Hopkins University Press.

Schön, D. A. (1983). *The reflective practitioner: How professionals think in action*. New York: Basic Books.

Schumann, C. (1985). La gestion juridique de problèmes emotionnels. *Annales de Vaucresson*, No. 23, pp. 115-135.

Scull, A. (1975a). From madness to mental illness. *Archives européenes de sociologie, 16*, 218-251.

Scull, A. (1975b). Mad-doctors and magistrates. *Archives européenes de sociolgie, 17*, 279-305.

Stiles, W. B., Shapiro, D. A., & Elliott, R. (1986). Are all psychotherapies equivalent? *American Psychologist, 41*, 165-180.

Sugg, R. (1978). *Motherteacher*. Charlottesville: University Press of Virginia.

Wardwell, W. I. (1952). A marginal professional role: The chiropractor. *Social Forces, 30*, 339-348.

Wexelblat, R. L. (1981). *History of computer languages*. New Haven, CT: Yale University Press.

CHAPTER **8**

Diagnosis and Uncertainty in Mental Health Organizations

STUART A. KIRK

HERB KUTCHINS

During the last three decades, the mental health industry in America greatly expanded and diversified. There has been a vast expansion in the number of mental health professionals (Goleman, 1990), the number of caregiving episodes (Schulberg & Manderscheid, 1989), the number of mental health organizations providing services, and, not surprisingly, the costs of mental health care (Mechanic, 1980). Accompanying this expansion has been a transformation in the delivery of services from a system of large public mental hospitals where most psychiatric services took place, supplemented by a few private clinics and psychoanalysts, to a diverse array of public, not-for-profit, and for-profit inpatient facilities and clinics, supplemented by a great number of private practitioners from many disciplines. From a system in which the majority of treatment facilities were public institutions of last resort for the impoverished, elderly and mentally disabled, we now have a fragmented, multi-tiered, diversely sponsored and financed array of services for those who have various levels of impairment, many of whom voluntarily seek help from those who dispense the popular psychotherapies (Specht, 1990). Mental health care has evolved into a much more complex system of services in which mental health service providers face increasing uncertainties in their internal and external environments. Within any societal sector, rapid growth, by itself, can create instability. Within

163

the mental health field, uncertainties stem from other characteristics of the enterprise as well.

Uncertainty and Mental Health Organizations

For starters, mental health agencies are founded on a concept that many think is of dubious merit: that there are discrete "disorders" that are "mental." There is little agreement among mental health experts that "disorders" can be easily or clearly separated from nondisorders. Even more divisive among scholars is the notion that the "mental" can be separated clearly from the physical, behavioral, social, or moral. The fundamental concepts of mental health and mental illness (or disorder) have been hotly contested for decades. Mental health organizations operate despite or, some might be tempted to argue, because of these fundamental ambiguities.

The primary tasks of mental health organizations—to treat mental illness effectively—involves working with people as the "raw materials." Clients follow a variety of routes in arriving at a mental health agency, come at times and in numbers that may not conform to the organization's capacities or work flow, present with a bewildering array of personal and interpersonal troubles, and possess all manner of idiosyncratic personal histories.

The tasks of mental health organizations, like those of other human service agencies, are made more difficult because the raw material—the client—is also simultaneously the consumer and an active participant in the process. The client has a major role in determining what the desired outcome should be and how the goal will be accomplished. Despite the clients' active role, they frequently do not know what they want or how to get it. They are usually in emotional pain for which they seek relief, but are not certain about the proper remedy. Their confusion is often shared by the clinic's staff. The precise nature of a client's trouble is frequently ambiguous, its causes obscured by a lifetime of personal experiences, environmental stresses, and psychological confusion.

The services that may be offered to the client consist largely of a special relationship with a clinician, making the relationship itself a primary part of the service technology. Given the uniqueness of both client and clinician and the ambiguities surrounding the nature of the problem, the intervention itself introduces additional uncertainties into the helping process. This is particularly so because there may be no widely shared or scientifically established best method of effectively helping the disturbed client.

Finally, there are different perspectives about what would actually constitute the desired client outcome. For example, the client, the family, the neighbors, the mental health professionals, and the health insurance companies might have different preferred treatments or outcomes for a client with a serious and persistent disorder. Evaluating success from the standpoint of any of these parties could not be easily determined by using a simple profit margin.

Despite these inherent difficulties, managers strive to make their organizations appear to be carefully coordinated and efficient efforts in pursuit of some established, legitimate purpose or mission. In other terms, managers want to make their organizations "rational" or to appear to be rational. Whatever the agency goals, the activities of the organization should appear to contribute in some way to those objectives. By establishing objectives, structuring production or service procedures, developing rules and procedures, allocating resources, hiring and training staff, and monitoring outcomes, managers attempt to make their organizations' actions purposeful and effective. Developing successful plans and courses of action are much easier when there are few uncertainties within the organization or in its external environment.

All organizations abhor environmental uncertainty and devise ways of minimizing it or buffering themselves from its currents (Thompson, 1967). Uncertainty is endemic for mental health organizations and a common enemy for those who work in them. There are many methods by which human service managers try to reduce the external uncertainties they face. For example, they create boundary units, like screening, intake, and referral services, to buffer their organizations from fluctuating client demand. Waiting lists are developed because they are flexible devices for stock-piling demand. Information and referral procedures are established to send clients elsewhere, which eliminates excess pressure for service. When there are shortages of clients, agencies advertise their services and increase their service domain to cover more geography, clients, or problems. Through active lobbying, grantsmanship, and fund-raising, managers attempt to diversify their fiscal base, maintain a steady source of funds, and buffer themselves from unpredictable budget cuts.

Within the mental health organization, uncertainties are usually more easily, and less visibly, managed. Trained professionals are hired because they are supposed to know what to do with clients and how to do it, usually behind closed doors. Even if they do not know how to resolve the problems that clients present, they will at least act in a predictable way, usually by making diagnoses and providing medication or the talking cure; the predictability of the therapist's responses reduces uncertainty. Furthermore, internal organizational structures and procedures are created to clarify who is responsible for what tasks so there will be a minimum of confusion and conflict. Intake units monitor the nature of the "raw material" and make decisions about what clients to assign to which clinicians or programs. Clients are enrolled, given service, and discharged, often without demonstrable change in their condition. And all these activities are accompanied by a blizzard of paperwork explaining, justifying, and certifying what was done.

Although environmental uncertainties are always troublesome, internal uncertainties about clients and the services they need, that is, technological ambiguities, frequently present opportunities. Paradoxically, uncertainty within mental health organizations can be very useful to them. If uncertainty is great, so are the limits of organizational discretion. To be sure, not every organization can benefit as much from uncertainty. For example, NASA has clearly defined and visible goals to get a shuttle into space and back again without damage or injury. If there is too much uncertainty about how to achieve this objective successfully or their attempts end in observable failure, the agency will have to submit to greater oversight by other organizations such as Congress or Presidential Commissions.

But since the goals of mental health organizations are not as clear or visible as those of the space agency, uncertainty over how or whether the objectives are achieved is a basis for greater organizational latitude. If there is ambiguity about what they should do in regard to clients, then there is also room for creativity and negotiation. If there are few specific organizational actions that will predictably produce specific outcomes for clients, then many organizational actions are permissible. Uncertainty for mental health organizations has the advantage of allowing wide latitude in internal decision making. Nowhere is this more apparent than in the first step of client processing—in the diagnosis of mental disorder.

Diagnosis as Technical Rationality

Mental health organizations are "professional bureaucracies" (Mintzberg, 1981). Many of their employees are educated in the professions of medicine, social work, psychology, and nursing. As professionals, they are expected to apply the knowledge and skills of their respective disciplines in assisting clients; they are technically expert. Among the hallmarks of many professions is the claim that their practitioners will consciously and carefully apply specialized scientific knowledge to specific cases and circumstances with the objective of solving particular problems. Professional practice, in this view, is providing service in specific circumstances through the application of general scientific principles. Professional knowledge is specialized, firmly bounded by purpose, rooted in science, and standardized in application. Schön (1983, p. 21) refers to this process where "professional activity consists in instrumental problem solving made rigorous by the application of scientific theory and technique" as "*technical rationality.*" Although not all professions are grounded in "scientific" theory (e.g., law, journalism), all of the mental health professions, psychiatry, psychology, nursing, and social work, maintain that they apply scientific principles to professional practice. The view that action is a deliberate application of scientific knowledge is one of the distinctive claims of these professions. Mental health professionals and the organizations in which they work, explain many of their decisions and behaviors as the expression of technical rationality.

A well-known psychiatrist, Robert Jay Lifton, has analyzed therapeutic activity in similar terms:

The technicist model in psychiatry works something like this:

A machine, the mind-body function of the patient, has broken down; another machine, more scientifically sophisticated—is called upon to "treat" the first machine; and the treatment process itself, being technical, has nothing to do with place, time or individual idiosyncrasy. It is merely a matter of being a technical-medical antagonist of a "syndrome" or "disease." Nor is this medical-technical model limited to physicians— nonmedical psychoanalysts and psychotherapists can be significantly affected by it. (Lifton, 1973, p. 423)

Diagnosis is the presumed, crucial starting point of the technical-rational system that is used by mental health workers. The very concept of "diagnosis" connotes systematic problem solving. In medicine, clinicians develop a hypothesis about the nature of a person's disease after observing the patient or being told about the symptoms or interpreting biological tests about a person's health. Facts are objectively gathered and, based on the clinician's expert knowledge, a disease or disorder is inferred. This inferred disease is considered to be the underlying cause of the observed manifestations of illness. Clinical intervention is then directed primarily at the underlying disease, with the assumption that the symptoms will disappear when the disease is effectively treated. Beyond what the physician can see and feel, diagnosis is increasingly aided by high technology probes into heretofore unobservable phenomena: biological tests of urine and blood samples, X-rays, electrocardiogram (EKG), electroencephalogram (EEG), various genetic screening tests, computer assisted tomography (CAT), magnetic resonance imaging (MRI) and positron emission tomography (PET) (Nelkin & Tancredi, 1989).

Judging by the vast expansion of diagnostic tests and procedures in American life, identifying "abnormalities" has become big business. A *New Yorker* cartoon (reprinted in Nelkin & Tancredi, 1989) shows cars lined up at Joe's Drive-Thru Testing Center, where customers can be quickly checked for emissions, drugs, intelligence, cholesterol, polygraph, blood pressure, soil and water, steering and brakes, stress and loyalty. Although testing and diagnostic practices are always presented as grounded in science and technology, they are frequently inaccurate and often meaningless. Moreover, there are many chilling stories—for example about racial and class inferiority—about the way that evidence for the validity of such tests is fabricated, and how they are used to assert ideological and racist perspectives (Gould, 1981). The significant and growing role of diagnosis and testing in American society suggests that we should be attentive both to their purported purpose as well as to how they are actually used by organizations and interest groups. The practice of psychiatric diagnosis is no exception.

The connection between science and professions provides a powerful framework for mental health organizations to describe the process of diagnosing mental disorder. Diagnosis, a first step in the multistage process of servicing mental health clients, is described as the product of a science-based assessment process that uncovers the nature of the client's internal "disorder." The disorder is inferred by clinicians who are supposed to use objective diagnostic criteria and prescribed decision rules in applying scientific standards and procedures to the client's condition. For example, for children who are "argumentative with adults, frequently lose their temper, swear, and are often angry, resentful, and easily annoyed by others" the current psychiatric nomenclature provides a diagnosis of Oppositional Defiant Disorder. To use that diagnosis, clinicians are instructed to apply a series of inclusion and exclusion criteria. These criteria and procedures are presented with a psychiatric language that exudes the spirit of technical rationality. The diagnosis comes with its unique code number; references to other complex concepts, such as "mental age"; specifications about precise duration (six months) and the number of symptoms needed; vague references to unspecified research about "discriminating power" and national field trials; and defined levels of severity. Through these criteria embedded in symbols of science, common, everyday behaviors of children are transformed into objective symptoms of disorder.

Once the diagnosis has been made, the client is referred to the proper service unit, program, or clinician who will use the technically appropriate treatment to achieve the desired outcome. Diagnosis is the first scientific step in the organization's technological process of transforming a person with an ambiguous complaint into a client who will be a member of the organization with a defined mental disorder to be remedied. Despite the pivotal role that diagnosis plays in mental health practice, it has had a very troubled history. Since the concept of mental illness itself has been troublesome, it should be no surprise that the practice of identifying specific psychiatric illnesses has been for many decades the target of pointed criticism. Many observers found evidence that psychiatric diagnoses were of questionable validity and reliability and suggested that the practice of psychiatric diagnosis often was a haphazard exercise in pseudoscience, rather than the clear expression of scientific knowledge. It is understandable that this problem was particularly threatening to the profession of psychiatry, since it struck at the heart of its scientific claims to technical rationality.

These concerns were among the major reasons why the American Psychiatric Association (APA) undertook a major revision of its diagnostic manual during the 1970s and published a revolutionary new version in 1980, the *Diagnostic and Statistical Manual of Mental Disorders, Third Edition,* or DSM-III for short (APA, 1980). Seven years later, another revision of the manual (DSM-III-R) was published (APA, 1987). DSM-III was hailed by its developers and the APA as a new scientific approach to diagnosis that resolved many of the serious problems with psychiatric diagnosis (particularly the problems of unreliability). Leaders in mental health, lauding the new manual, called it a "tour de force," a brilliant document (Sabshin, 1990), a tremendous scientific achievement in mental health (Klerman, 1984).

Our concern in this chapter is not with the veracity or details of those claims, they are extensively reviewed elsewhere (Kirk & Kutchins, in press; Kutchins & Kirk, 1986), but with the fact that a major public effort was made by the APA to defend itself against critics by attempting to make diagnosis more scientifically credible, to make it appear to conform more closely with the image of technical rationality. The APA's objective is understandable. How could treatment planning for clients, the development of new services, the assessment of the prevalence of mental disorder in communities, or claims on the allocation of scarce resources be made rationally, if there is substantial disagreement about the definition, nature, or procedures to be used to identify mental health problems? Attempting to improve the diagnostic classification system was one approach to reducing uncertainty in the identification and processing of clients and making organizational and professional decision making appear to be less haphazard and more the application of science.

Diagnosis as Rationalization of Action

Psychiatric diagnosis as an expression of technical rationality conforms closely to the conventional views of both professions and bureaucratic organizations. With each there is an emphasis on goal-directed behavior. An explicit organizational mission is established, specific goals that achieve that mission are set, objective information is gathered, alternative courses of action are considered, rational decisions are made, action is carried out, and progress is evaluated.

But there are other strikingly different views of organizational behavior that have special salience for human service organizations, particularly those that provide mental health care. These alternative views question conventional wisdom about the nature of organizational goals (Lipsky, 1980; Perrow, 1978, 1986) and the underlying assumption that they are rationally pursued as part of some generic problem-solving method. Organizational goals, instead of serving as the focus of action, may be the least important explanation of organizational behavior (Perrow, 1978). Instead, human service organizations can be analyzed as collections of individuals and groups that are in a never-ending struggle for survival, security, power, discretion, and autonomy. Moreover, the publicly espoused goals are often highly ambiguous and may obscure myriad objectives that are disparate or in conflict. Organizational behavior, it has been suggested, is more accurately described as a struggle for power among contending interests than as a cooperative endeavor among those striving for a shared, cherished objective (see, for example, Hasenfeld, 1983; Lipsky, 1980; Morgan, 1986; Perrow, 1986). One has merely to point to the resistance shown by staff of state mental hospitals (and their employee unions) to the transfer or discharge of patients to illustrate the multiple and often conflicting objectives of members of such facilities.

Furthermore, if goals are multiple, ambiguous, and in conflict, decision-making discretion among organizational members is greatly broadened. If no precise goal is established, if there is incomplete understanding of how to achieve vague objectives, and if there are few systematic methods of monitoring organizational outcomes, then staff and managers have considerable leeway in explaining what they do. Some organizational theorists have proposed that instead of viewing organizational behavior as an attempt to develop solutions to problems, that it may be more informative to view staff as having available a drawer full of solutions that they use to scan a large pool of potential problems in search of one that will justify their course of action (Cyert & March, 1963; Cohen, March, & Olsen, 1972). This "garbage can model" of organizational behavior views decision making as attempts to rationalize past actions, actions that are stimulated by a host of private, personal, and technical developments, rather than by a collective desire to rationally pursue some over-arching explicit goal.

If one recognizes the ambiguities involved in organizational life, then one more easily recognizes the latitude enjoyed by mental health organizations. Mental health practitioners and the organizations that employ them have considerable discretion in selecting, defining, and processing their clients (Lipsky, 1980). Moreover, mental health clients arrive at agencies with problems that are undifferentiated. Professionals can define clients' problems in a variety of ways: on the basis of presenting complaint, observed symptoms, inferred causes, or prognosis. These ambiguities allow mental health staff considerable discretion in the type of diagnosis they can impose on the client (see, for example, Freidson, 1960; Greenley & Kirk, 1973; Lipsky, 1980; R. A. Scott, 1969). It was, in fact, a major purpose of the development of DSM-III to restrict just such discretion among clinicians, to bind them to criteria-based decisions. The developers of DSM-III wanted to ensure that as a result of the use of the new manual, diagnosis would be more scientific or at least more predictable. Since such bold claims have been made about the new scientific basis for psychiatric diagnosis, it is worth noting some evidence that suggests that technical rationality does not fully explain diagnostic practices. We will then suggest that because technical rationality is less than complete, diagnoses are used for less obvious organizational purposes.

Continuing Diagnostic Unreliability

The central assumption of the view of diagnosis as technical rationality is that mental health professionals will arrive at the same diagnostic conclusion when assessing the same client. To promote this, DSM goes to great length in offering explicit criteria and formal decision-making rules for diagnoses. When using these criteria and rules, clinicians are supposed to reach the same conclusion; evidence of reliability was to be the proof of the success of technical rationality in psychiatric diagnosis.

Much evidence suggests that no matter what changes have been introduced in the diagnostic manual, there continue to be serious problems in obtaining consistent agreement about diagnoses (Kutchins & Kirk, 1986). The reliability issue is difficult to address because there have been few broad tests of the reliability of DSM-III, except for the initial data gathered by the developers themselves who had reason to be sanguine about equivocal findings (Kirk & Kutchins, in press). When the manual was revised in 1987, there were no studies of its reliability and there have been none since its publication. More pertinent, many reliability studies are conducted in the contrived context of "a reliability study." Few studies of psychiatric diagnosis have actually examined what practicing clinicians do in mental health organizations to reach an official DSM-III diagnosis. What studies exist indicate that diagnosis in mental health may not conform well to the view of diagnosis as the precise application of science.

For example, surveys have found that in arriving at diagnoses, psychiatrists do not fully conform to the decision criteria explicitly required by DSM-III (Lipkowitz & Idupugnati, 1983, 1985). Among 301 psychiatrists there was little agreement about the signs and symptoms of schizophrenia, including the ones recommended by DSM-III. Only one clinician in their sample used all six DSM-III criteria as prescribed. Other researchers (Lipton & Simon, 1985) reviewed the hospital charts of 131 patients diagnosed as schizophrenic at Manhattan State Hospital in New York and found that the chart information often did not support the diagnosis given, at least according to DSM-III criteria.

Ironically, some of the innovative features in DSM-III added new reliability problems while trying to solve old ones. DSM-III introduced a multiaxial approach to diagnosis in which clients are rated on five dimensions or axes. Skodal (1989), who has been closely associated with the developers of the manual, admits that even though the multiaxial approach is widely taught in training programs, it appears to be used clinically only on a relatively limited basis. Furthermore, the few research reports about the multiaxial system are not encouraging to its proponents.

There have been consistent difficulties with the actual use and the reliability of each of the dimensions. Even the developers acknowledged that there are serious reliability problems with Axis II, personality disorders, where some 40% of diagnoses are made (Skodal, 1989; Williams & Spitzer, 1988). Problems with Axis III, medical problems, are even more severe. The only study of Axis III (Maricle, Leung, & Bloom, 1987) reported that documented physical problems were not accurately conveyed in diagnostic formulations using the DSM-III format. The problem has been especially pronounced among nonphysician clinicians who are fearful of charges of malpractice if they make medical assessments of the clients (Williams & Spitzer, 1982).

The other two axes also have their share of technical problems. New Zealand researchers (Rey et al., 1988) concluded that the available data "casts some doubt" on the reliability of Axis IV ratings of the severity of psychosocial stressors. They note the lack of specific guidelines for obtaining basic information and express concern that tinkering with the ratings or the aggregation process is likely to create an impression of statistical objectivity but to have no practical benefits. The problems with Axis V, a rating of the highest level of adaptive functioning, were even more severe (Fernando et al., 1986), and as a consequence, the scale was jettisoned in the 1987 revision and replaced with a single item assessment of functioning. This has compounded the problems with diagnosis since the new scale also measures psychological functioning, and so it assesses many of the same factors evaluated on Axis I (Skodal, 1989).

These various problems in conceptual clarity, reliability, and actual use of DSM-III undermine the claims of psychiatry that diagnosis is now an expression of the application of scientific procedures. While some of the unreliability of diagnosis and some of the departures from the established diagnostic criteria can be dismissed as simple, random error that exists in all measurement or classification efforts, there is evidence that the problems are more profound. For example, in one national survey of clinical social workers, 55% indicated that DSM-III diagnoses did not, in their opinion, accurately reflect clients' problems, 45% said it obscures individual differences, and only a third felt it was very helpful for treatment planning, one of the major tenets of the technical rationality view of diagnosis. Only half (49%) of the respondents thought that DSM-III serves the purposes of their profession. More revealing, perhaps, were the views of 57% who described DSM-III more as a management than a clinical tool (Kutchins & Kirk, 1988). What they appeared to be suggesting was that the use of official diagnoses as provided in DSM is frequently not determined by the clinical needs of the client or the treatment planning activities of the therapist, but by the organization's need to manage service delivery.

If clinicians have or take considerable latitude in decision making, particularly in diagnosis, for what organizational purposes is discretion used? Five such purposes will be described. With each, we will indicate how diagnosis is used to help fulfill those purposes. These purposes, although by no means unique to mental health organizations, have special expressions within them. The five purposes are: to regulate client flow, to protect clients from harm, to acquire fiscal resources, to rationalize decision making, and to advance a broader political agenda.

Regulating Client Flow

Clients can be a source of resources or a burden to psychiatric facilities. Clients bring legitimacy as indicators of the community's need for the agency's services. They also bring financial resources through fees paid by themselves, government agencies, or insurance companies. On the other hand, they consume agency resources by using staff time and scarce facilities. Consequently, mental health organizations have an understandable concern about serving clients and, at the same time, meeting the needs of the organization.

Psychiatric diagnosis plays a pivotal role in allowing mental health organizations to choose the number and type of clients they serve. The ambiguities involved in using (or ignoring) DSM diagnostic criteria allow agencies discretion and a rationale for accepting, rejecting, or referring an applicant for service. A clinic offering a special program for people with "mood disorders" may need to operationally liberalize their application of the criteria for them when they are in need of clients and narrow it when their caseloads are full. This is possible since the specific diagnostic criteria often depend on considerable subjective judgments. For example, the criteria for Major Depressive Episode include depressed mood, markedly diminished interest in all activities, psychomotor agitation, loss of energy, diminished ability to think, and so forth. Although the purpose of DSM is to prevent flexibility in applying these criteria, they all permit considerable subjective judgment on the part of the clinician. In general, mental health organizations will narrow diagnostic or eligibility requirements to restrict their service domains when there is an excess demand for service and broaden them when they need more clients (Greenley & Kirk, 1973; Lipsky, 1980).

When an applicant is accepted for services, diagnostic labeling is a way of defining the client's problem in the most favorable manner for the organization. For example, one mental hospital observed by the authors, sometimes uses Axis V—the global assessment of functioning (GAF)—to determine whether a client requires emergency, involuntary hospitalization. This hospital adopted the policy of only admitting clients who received GAF scores of 40 or less (on a 99-point scale), indicating relatively low functioning. When emergency room personnel wanted to admit someone to this facility, they made certain that the patient was given a rating of 40 or less, even though the score they should have given was higher. Similarly, some hospitals require evidence of improvement before a client is discharged. Knowing this, clinicians who want to discharge a patient may add 20 points or more to the admitting GAF score, whether or not this rating is appropriate. In this way, the diagnostic system provided by DSM-III, while appearing to provide a technically rational way of assessing clients, is easily manipulated by staff to control client flow into and out of facilities.

Protecting Clients From Harm

Ironically, in making diagnoses, clinicians frequently want to use "the least noxious diagnosis," acknowledging the well-recognized iatrogenic nature of psychiatric labeling. Clinicians do this to minimize communicating damaging confidential information to insurance companies and others, to avoid the labeling effects of more severe diagnoses, and to limit the adverse impact on the client's self-esteem if the client becomes aware of the diagnosis. Such underdiagnosing is very common among clinicians. Of a national sample of clinical social workers, 87% indicated that a less serious diagnosis than is clinically indicated was used sometimes to avoid labeling (Kirk & Kutchins, 1988), and the majority of those who were aware that this occurred said that it happened frequently. Seventy-eight percent said that on some occasions only the least serious of several appropriate diagnoses was used on official records, and more than half of the respondents who acknowledged this practice indicated that it happened frequently. Eighty-two percent admitted that "Adjustment Disorder" is sometimes used when a more serious diagnosis might be more accurate and more than a third of them reported that this practice occurred frequently. Only a small fraction of respondents were unaware of any occurrence of these types of deliberate misdiagnoses. Brown (1987) made similar observations of underdiagnosis in a community mental health center. He documented a variety of ways in which clinicians coped with the demands to make diagnoses "on paper" in the face of a variety of clinical uncertainties. Organizational and interorganizational factors were often decisive in choosing diagnoses.

In a major study of the accuracy of diagnostic information submitted to insurance companies by psychiatrists, investigators found that diagnostic information sent to insurance companies was considerably different from information provided in an anonymous survey (Sharfstein, Towery, & Milowe, 1980). Diagnoses of neuroses were submitted three times more frequently to insurance companies than the more serious disorders reported in other independent surveys. Clinicians appear to distort official diagnoses frequently to protect clients. Undoubtedly, the concerns of clinicians are genuine; they don't want to harm in the act of trying to help.

Nevertheless, such protectiveness may not always benefit clients. False diagnoses create their own problems. They establish a written record of professional "scientific" judgments that affirms that clients meet criteria for disorders that they, in fact, do not have. Whatever the disadvantages of more severe but accurate diagnoses, they at least have the benefit of someone's best judgment about a clinical condition. A deliberately false diagnosis, whatever the merits of the motivation behind it, officially labels a client as suffering from a mental disorder that he in fact does not have. A chain of such false diagnoses over the years hardly enhances the meaningfulness of a person's or an organization's official medical records.

Deliberately underdiagnosing, however, does indirectly serve some organizational interests. To the extent that people are aware of the potentially stigmatizing labels that clinicians can affix to personal medical records, they may be appropriately reluctant to seek service voluntarily from those facilities. By practicing underdiagnosis on a broad scale, agencies signal to clients that the stigmatization will be minimized; that they are there only to help. By thus encouraging clients to seek help when they might otherwise be reluctant, mental health practitioners reduce one barrier for clients and thereby promote a demand for their services. Diagnosis in these circumstances represents the application of a political calculation about the negative effects of diagnosis within some ambiguous technical constraints. These widespread practices depart significantly from the conventional view that psychiatric diagnosis is an objective, scientific decision.

Acquiring Fiscal Resources

All human service organizations need resources, particularly money that can be used flexibly in exchange for other things. In mental health, fiscal resources are increasingly coming from fees paid by clients, or more commonly, by their private insurance companies, or government programs such as Medicaid. Clearly, clients bring important resources to a mental health organization. Third-party payers for mental health services, however, require that the person being serviced have a mental disorder and very often have one of a particular set of mental disorders; not all mental disorders are equally reimbursable. Reimbursement directly to the client or the agency is tied to particular psychiatric diagnoses, often the more serious ones. Personality disorders, family problems, or routine adjustment difficulties may not be reimbursable. Thus the acquisition of fiscal resources is tied directly to the clinician's decision about the nature of the client's mental disorder.

Mental health practitioners and their agencies are very aware of this connection. More importantly, they admit that it affects their use of diagnosis. In the survey mentioned above (Kirk & Kutchins, 1988), there is evidence of widespread "overdiagnosis" in which clinicians use a more serious diagnosis than warranted in order to qualify the client or the agency for reimbursement from third parties. For example, 72% believed that there were occasions when a more serious diagnosis was used than was warranted clinically in order to help clients qualify for reimbursement for treatment. More than half of the respondents who acknowledged the existence of these practices felt that they occurred frequently. Since reimbursement is rarely available for family problems, 86% admitted that a diagnosis for an individual was used even when the primary problem was in the family system. More than half said this was done frequently.

Another study of clinicians (Brown, 1987) found that they coped with these diagnostic dilemmas by using humor and sarcasm to express their dissatisfaction with the requirement to make official diagnoses in order to fulfill external organizational requirements. Frequently the requirements of the referring agency or the client's social needs dominated the diagnostic outcome. One staff member quipped that a client's DSM-III diagnosis was "insurance claim."

Rationalizing Decision Making

The ostensible clinical purpose for making a formal psychiatric diagnosis is to guide the choice of therapeutic intervention. Pneumonia, take penicillin. Flu, take an antibiotic. Manic-depressive psychosis (bipolar affective disorder in the DSM-III-R technical-rational lexicon), take lithium. In these cases the diagnosis precedes and determines the choice of treatment. In mental health, under- and overdiagnoses suggest that diagnoses are sometimes determined by considerations other than the clinical condition of the client and often by factors external, but important, to the organization.

Nevertheless, it could be argued that despite the use of a deceptive official diagnosis, the treatment used was based on the "real," if unofficial, diagnosis. For example, a family with communication problems may receive family therapy, although the problem had been diagnosed officially as if the mother alone had a disorder. Thus it could be said that the diagnosis (the unofficial, not the official one) led to treatment. However, many third-party payers insist that treatment conform to the diagnosis. In the example just given, once a diagnosis is made on the mother, an insurer might refuse to pay for family therapy, and reimburse only individual treatment.

There are also circumstances in mental health organizations where the treatment determines diagnosis or where it is simply irrelevant to treatment. In the former instances, diagnosis is used to justify treatment that has already occurred. Social workers in one agency told the authors that with some clients the consulting psychiatrist was unable to figure out what the diagnosis was, but would sequentially prescribe different medications until one seemed to work. The diagnosis would then be changed to reflect the clinical condition that the drug is supposed to treat. If it was pounded by a hammer, it must have been a nail.

At another social agency, the staff explained that diagnosis was the art of "making distinctions without differences." Psychiatrists would frequently debate the fine points about the correct diagnosis for a disturbed client, but always would prescribe Haldol regardless of the outcome of the diagnostic debate. In cases like these, precise diagnostic classification, instead of leading to specific differential actions, is largely irrelevant. DSM-III, in this light, provides for 200 carefully developed categories of inaction.

Using diagnoses that are largely irrelevant to subsequent decisions is not unique to mental health organizations. Such ritualistic use of diagnosis occurs regularly in higher education. Almost all the nation's colleges require high school students to take the SAT given by the Educational Testing Service (ETS), under the assumption that the assessment of "scholastic aptitude" will make a difference in admissions decisions. The fact is, however, many colleges (and many graduate schools as well) accept virtually all their applicants, regardless of their SAT scores. Moreover, the few highly selective colleges that do select students from a large pool of applicants would make essentially the same admissions decisions on the basis of high school grade point average and other information, without the SAT scores (Owen, 1985). Thus thousands of students are encouraged to spend millions of dollars to have the ETS provide reified scholastic information to colleges that do not really need it. Although this is an example of unnecessary testing, it does serve an important symbolic function for colleges that can then present themselves as basing decisions on standardized, objective, scientific information. This permits both the accepted and rejected applicants to believe that their fate is tied directly to test scores.

Sometimes diagnoses are simply ignored or concealed when they interfere with the agency functions. In one mental health agency, known to the authors, the staff tries to find shelter for the homeless mentally ill. The staff knows that some available housing facilities will not admit mentally ill clients who have problems with substance abuse. Consequently, the staff will occasionally make a diagnosis, but avoid making the warranted diagnosis of substance abuse when doing so would jeopardize the client's chance for admission to housing. Consequently, an incomplete and inaccurate formal diagnosis is used to describe the client. In situations like these, the inaccurate official diagnosis becomes the instrumentally appropriate label that can be used to achieve an organization objective—getting housing for clients.

Advancing a Political Agenda

Diagnosis marks the boundaries of psychiatry and the other mental health professions that use the psychiatric diagnostic system, DSM-III-R; it is, to some extent, a political claim. A narrow definition of mental disorder, strict diagnostic criteria, and few diagnostic categories would greatly limit the scope of the mental health field, would encourage fewer people to seek services, would provide reimbursement for fewer human troubles, and would require fewer clinicians to be trained and employed. A broad, flexible approach lends itself to expansionary interests. Thus what is included or not included in the diagnostic manual has implications beyond those pertaining to the clinical condition of any individual client. It reflects what the society is willing to designate as mental illness. The shape of the diagnostic manual and the use that is made of it involves strategic choices for psychiatry, some of them very controversial.

In the last 15 years, the American Psychiatric Association has battled groups of individuals who wanted certain conditions withdrawn from the DSM list of mental disorders. Homosexuality is the most celebrated case of a controversial diagnosis that psychiatrists were forced to discard in 1974 (Bayer, 1981). More recently, in 1985, several diagnoses pertaining specifically to women created another major political flap during the revision of DSM-III. The women argued, less successfully than gay activists a decade earlier, that such diagnoses as self-defeating personality disorder would be used against abused women (Kutchins

& Kirk, 1989). As a political compromise, these controversial diagnoses were placed in the appendix of the revised manual.

Publicized instances of attempts to remove diagnostic categories are in stark contrast to the relatively quiet way in which most diagnostic categories are revised, split, combined, or created for the official psychiatric manual. The first version of DSM (1952) contained 106 different categories, DSM-II (1968) had 182, DSM-III (1980) offered 265, and its revision, DSM-III-R (1987), increased them to 292. It would be a mistake to believe that all potentially affected groups try to keep their conditions out of the diagnostic manual. After years of work, Vietnam veterans and their advocates succeeded in inserting a new Post-Traumatic Stress Disorder into DSM-III (W. J. Scott, 1990). And many mental health clinicians and some clients would like to see diagnoses expanded to include marital and family problems, so that a broader array of therapeutic services would be reimbursable. In fact, the expansion of the psychiatric domain is limited by little else than the political judgment of the American Psychiatric Association.

The expanding scope of mental health, advanced through an ever-growing list of official diagnoses of mental disorders, produces two important political gains for psychiatry. First, if increasing numbers of people have definable mental disorders, the mental health professions can argue that increasing funds should be allocated to conduct research and provide treatment for them. An expanded scope allows more claims on society for legitimation and support. Second, an expanding list of mental disorders that contains everything including low intelligence, tobacco dependence, antisocial personality, schizophrenia, caffeine intoxication, and childhood misconduct is offering an ideology for understanding a potpourri of dysfunctional or disvalued behaviors as medical "disorders" rather than as a diverse forms of social deviance. This trend to "medicalize" deviance has a long and thorny history. Here we simply note that diagnostic decisions routinely made in mental health organizations for reimbursement purposes are institutionalizing this medicalization in a way that cannot be easily reversed.

Diagnostic Conclusions

Diagnoses in mental health organizations serve many functions. Sometimes they conform to the conventional view by classifying people and their problems so that they can be properly treated. At other times and in other situations, diagnoses provide the rationalization for organizational processing decisions already made or dispositions that are readily available. When the goal of diagnosis is to support organizational needs rather than to determine what treatment clients need, the process is often distorted and frequently involves intentional misdiagnoses. Diagnoses in these latter situations, that is, where deliberate misdiagnosis occurs, are rarely recognized in the literature on diagnostic "errors." In fact, even viewing these occurrences as "errors" imposes on the situation a model of diagnostic rationality that fails to recognize that clinicians often deliberately use diagnosis for organizational purposes, not primarily for clinical ones. If the goal is to place a homeless person who abuses drugs into housing, then a diagnosis that conveniently overlooks a significant clinical reality reveals the many instrumental uses of psychiatric assessment. The goal may be laudable, but the process distorts diagnostic activity and calls into question its scientific assumptions.

Diagnostic practices function to screen clients into and out of organizations, to sort clients into programs and services that are available, and to label prospective clients in such a way as to make the referral decision appear to be clinically, rather than organizationally, motivated. The inherent uncertainties involved in assessing clients' problems and determining what to do about them allows organizations to buffer themselves against fluctuating client demands and to keep or dispose of them as desired. In so doing, mental health organizations are merely practicing what has been widely recognized as processes of "creaming," "dumping," and "typifying" clients. Moreover, because of the structure of third-party reimbursement for certain psychiatric diagnoses, the clinical ambiguities involved present mental health organizations with irresistible opportunities to gain fiscal resources by merely labeling and mislabeling clinical conditions. These organizational maneuvers can be accomplished while the agency appears, through the use of the much acclaimed DSM-III, to be rigidly applying technical rationality to the assessment of human pain.

There is much about these processes that is still not well understood. Because psychiatric diagnosis has been narrowly viewed as the application of scientific procedures, most attention has been given to developing technical procedures and criteria that will constrain the behavior of clinicians in making diagnoses. Comparatively little attention has been given to how diagnosis is actually accomplished by clinicians working within the constraints and demands of mental health organizations. Broadening the analysis of diagnosis to include the organizational context in which it occurs points to an underdeveloped topic for future research.

References

American Psychiatric Association. (1980). *Diagnostic and statistical manual of mental disorders* (3rd ed.) (DSM-III). Washington, DC: Author.

American Psychiatric Association. (1987). *Diagnostic and statistical manual of mental disorders* (3rd. ed., rev.) (DSM-III-R). Washington, DC: Author.

Bayer, R. (1981). *Homosexuality and American psychiatry*. New York: Basic Books.

Brown, P. (1987). Diagnostic conflict and contradiction in psychiatry. *Journal of Health and Social Behavior, 28*, 37-50.

Cohen, M. D., March, J. C., & Olsen, J. P. (1972). A garbage can model of organizational choice. *Administrative Science Quarterly, 17*, 1-25.

Cyert, R. M., & March, J. C. (1963). *A behavioral theory of the firm*. Englewood Cliffs, NJ: Prentice-Hall.

Fernando, T., et al. (1986). The reliability of Axis V of DSM-III. *American Journal of Psychiatry, 143*(6), 752-755.

Freidson, E. (1960). Client control and medical practice. *American Journal of Sociology, 65*, 374-382.

Goleman, D. (1990, May 17). New paths to mental health put strains on some healers. *The New York Times*, pp. 1, B12.

Gould, S. J. (1981). *The mismeasure of man*. New York: W. W. Norton.

Greenley, J. R., & Kirk, S. A. (1973). Organizational characteristics of agencies and the distribution of services to applicants. *Journal of Health and Social Behavior, 14*, 70-79.

Hasenfeld, Y. (1983). *Human service organizations*. Englewood Cliffs, NJ: Prentice-Hall.

Kirk, S. A., & Kutchins, H. (1988). Deliberate misdiagnosis in mental health practice. *Social Service Review, 62*, 225-237.

Kirk, S. A., & Kutchins, H. (in press). *The selling of DSM: The rhetoric of science in psychiatry*. Hawthorne, NY: Aldine de Gruyter.

Klerman, G. (1984). The advantages of DSM-III. *American Journal of Psychiatry, 141*, 539-542.

Kutchins, H., & Kirk, S. A. (1986). The reliability of DSM-III: A critical review. *Social Work Research and Abstracts, 22*, 3-12.

Kutchins, H., & Kirk, S. A. (1988). The business of diagnosis: DSM-III and clinical social work. *Social Work, 33*, 215-220.

Kutchins, H., & Kirk, S. A. (1989). DSM-III-R: The conflict over new psychiatric diagnoses. *Health and Social Work, 34*(4), 91-103.

Lifton, R. J. (1973). *Home from the war*. New York: Simon & Schuster.

Lipkowitz, M. H., & Idupugnati, S. (1983). Diagnosing schizophrenia in 1980: A survey of U.S. psychiatrists. *American Journal of Psychiatry, 140*, 52-55.

Lipkowitz, M. H., & Idupugnati, S. (1985). Diagnosing schizophrenia in 1982: The effect of DSM-III. *American Journal of Psychiatry, 142*, 634-637.

Lipsky, M. (1980). *Street-level bureaucracy: Dilemmas of the individual in public services*. New York: Russell Sage.

Lipton, A., & Simon, F. S. (1985). Psychiatric diagnosis in a state hospital: Manhattan State revisited. *Hospital and Community Psychiatry, 36*(4), 368-372.

Maricle, R., Leung, P., & Bloom, J. (1987, November). The use of DSM-III Axes III in recording physical illness in psychiatric patients. *American Journal of Psychiatry, 144,* 1484-1486.

Mechanic, D. (1980). *Mental health and social policy* (2nd ed.). Englewood Cliffs, NJ: Prentice-Hall.

Mintzberg, H. (1981, January-February). Organization design: Fashion or fit? *Harvard Business Review*, pp. 103-116.

Morgan, G. (1986). *Images of organizations.* Beverly Hills, CA: Sage.

Nelkin, D., & Tancredi, L. (1989). *Dangerous diagnostics: The social power of biological information.* New York: Basic Books.

Owen, D. (1985). *None of the above: Behind the myth of scholastic aptitude.* Boston: Houghton Mifflin.

Perrow, C. (1978). Demystifying organizations. In R. C. Sarri & Y. Hasenfeld (Eds.), *The management of human services* (pp. 105-120). New York: Columbia University Press.

Perrow, C. (1986). *Complex organizations: A critical essay* (3rd. ed.). New York: Random House.

Rey, J., et al. (1988). DSM-III Axis IV revisited. *American Journal of Psychiatry, 145,* 286-292.

Sabshin, M. (1990). Turning points in twentieth-century American psychiatry. *American Journal of Psychiatry, 147*(10), 1267-1274.

Schön, D. A. (1983). *The reflective practitioner: How professionals think in action.* New York: Basic Books.

Schulberg, H. C., & Manderscheid, R. W. (1989). The changing network of mental health service delivery. In C. A. Taube & D. Mechanic (Eds.), *The future of mental health services research* (pp. 11-22). Washington, DC: U.S. Department of Health and Human Services.

Scott, R. A. (1969). *The making of blind men: A study in adult socialization.* New York: Russell Sage.

Scott, W. J. (1990). PTSD in DSM-III: A case in the politics of diagnosis and disease. *Social Problems, 37*(3), 294-310.

Sharfstein, S., Towery, O., & Milowe, I. (1980). Accuracy of diagnostic information submitted to an insurance company. *American Journal of Psychiatry, 137*(1), 70-73.

Skodal, A. E. (1989). *Problems in differential diagnosis.* Washington, DC: American Psychiatric Press.

Specht, H. (1990). Social work and the popular psychotherapies. *Social Service Review, 64*(3), 345-357.

Thompson, J. D. (1967). *Organizations in action.* New York: McGraw-Hill.

Williams, J., & Spitzer, R. (1982). Focusing on DSM-III's multiaxial system. *Hospital and Community Psychiatry, 33,* 891-892.

Williams, J., & Spitzer, R. (1988). DSM-III and DSM-III-R: A response. *Harvard Medical School Mental Health Letter, 5*(4), 3-6.

CHAPTER 9

Structure and Technology in Human Service Organizations

CHARLES GLISSON

The optimal structuring of work activities has occupied a central position among the concerns of organizational theorists since the turn of the century. It was not until the middle of the century, however, that theorists abandoned the search for the "one best way" to structure and directed their attention to identifying and understanding the contingencies upon which the optimal structuring of particular work activities depend. For example, Woodward's (1958, 1965) seminal work identified the core technology of an organization as the most important contingency, and spawned three decades of research into the relationship between structure and technology.

The core technology of an organization is comprised of the raw materials, knowledge, skills, techniques, and hardware that create the product or provide the service that is the organization's raison d'être. The general thrust of the structure-technology research has been to confirm that less routine and more complex core technologies require organizational structures that are less hierarchical and more flexible, and that more routine and less complex technologies require structures that are more hierarchical and less flexible. A portion of the structure-technology research has concerned human service organizations. This research has attempted to show that what human service workers do in their efforts to affect clients (i.e., technology), is related to the nature and patterns of relationships that exist among the workers, their co-workers and supervisors (i.e., structure).

Recent reviews describe two problems that have hampered progress in understanding the structure-technology relationship (Barley, 1990; Scott, 1990; Weick, 1990). First, the relationship described in this literature is implicitly static, with little attention given to the process by which the association between structure and technology develops. The understanding of this process is essential to understanding the malleability or vulnerability of the types of soft technologies found in the human services. Second, the orientation to technology tends to be materialistic, emphasizing hardware and the technical requirements of production systems while ignoring the activities, interpretations, and intentions of humans who use the technology. This is a particularly serious problem for understanding the relationship between technology and structure in human service organizations where the technology itself consists of human interactions and the raw material is human beings. Although hardware may be important to some human service activities, such as the use of personal computers in monitoring client functioning and case management, most human service technologies are characterized by human interactions, interpretations, and intentions rather than by hardware and technically based production systems.

As a result of these types of problems, Barley (1990) concludes that two important questions have remained unanswered. First, why are similar technologies associated with different structures? Second, how are macrosocial and microsocial phenomena entwined in the relationship between structure and technology? Answers to these questions require alterations of existing structure-technology models to include, among other things, the ways in which technology assumes a dependent role in its relationship with structure. This dependent role emerges when the types of vulnerable technologies found in many human services are molded by the organizational structures in which they are embedded. Consequently, this chapter addresses these and related issues using an alternative model of the structure-technology relationship. With modifications, the underlying tenets of the technology-based contingency model first proposed by Woodward are used to explain the link between the structure and the effectiveness of human service organizations.

Core Technology

As described in the previous section, the core technology of any organization includes the raw materials, knowledge, skills, techniques, and hardware that create the product or provide the service for which the organization is remunerated. In human service organizations, the problem or need addressed by the service, the clients who receive the service, the interventions that are applied, and the skills and equipment used in those interventions are all part of the core technology.

From its inception, the comprehensiveness and complexity of the concept of technology have created a number of problems for theorists. One problem that plagues the work of Woodward (1958, 1965), Thompson (1967), and subsequent writers who have attempted to characterize entire technological systems, is the "unrationalized categorization" of multiple technological variables under a single broad category (Stanfield, 1976). Such category labels as long linked, continuous process, mediating, intensive, and batch have been used to characterize entire production or service systems. This has led to the categorization of very different technological activities under the same label. For example, a construction firm and a hospital are both described as having the same type of core technology (e.g., Thompson, 1967, p. 17).

In contrast, other theorists have encountered problems by narrowing their focus to the individual worker in the technological core. Beginning with Perrow (1967), Hage and Aiken (1969), and Hunt (1970), writers have used the extent to which individual workers identify and handle exceptions in the processing of raw material as the factor that characterizes core technologies. In the human services, technology researchers have defined this factor as the extent to which workers perceive clients as individuals who each have unique problems, and use interventions that are individually tailored for specific clients (Glisson, 1978).

In focusing on the individual worker, however, there is disagreement and vagueness in the writers' explanations of the variance in the workers' identification and handling of exceptions. Perrow (1967) attributes this variance to the "organization's" perceptions of the raw material, allowing for differences among organizations that incorporate the same technology. Unfortunately, the concept of an "organization's" perceptions has little explanatory value for understanding individual perceptions, because an organization's perception is simply an aggregate of the perceptions of certain individuals in the organization. Although Hunt (1970) adopts Perrow's definition of technology, he uses Woodward's system-level term, *complexity*, to describe the dimension of technology he examines. And, in contrast to Perrow, Hunt explains the variance in the identification and handling of exceptions as a function of cognitive plans that have been internalized by individual workers. However, he fails to explain how these plans are internalized and provides for no individual variation in the cognitive plans of workers who use the same technology.

One of the most serious problems that is associated with the confusion surrounding the operationalization of technology is the failure to specify exactly what separates structure from technology. Stanfield (1976) documents overlapping definitions and operationalizations that can result in different researchers actually using the same instrument to measure both constructs. This is frequently a problem when technology is defined at the individual level, but measured at the subunit or organizational level. In these cases, the definition of technology at the individual worker level may appear to be clearly distinct from structure, while the actual approach used to measure technology at the system level may confound the two constructs. This is because it is difficult to measure technology at system levels without describing the nature of the relationships among workers, and the nature of relationships among workers also comprises many measures of structure. One example of this problem is Hage and Aiken's (1969) use of items from Hall's (1963) division of labor scale to measure Perrow's (1967) technology construct in a sample of human service organizations.

Another example of the confusion surrounding levels of analysis can be found in Rousseau's (1978) work. She defines a dimension of technology at the individual level as, "how much discretion is required of the individual operator," but on the same page she operationalizes technology at the departmental level: "Since dimensions of structure and technology refer to properties of entire organizational units in this study, they are measured at the departmental rather than the individual level" (p. 524). This disparity results in her measuring individual discretion using Thompson's (1967) system-level descriptions of core technologies. Although she believes that Thompson explicitly linked his three types of system-level technologies (long-linked, mediating, and intensive) to increasing amounts of individual discretion, this is not evident in the work she cites. While a reader might surmise that varying levels of individual discretion are associated with the organizational examples that Thompson gives of the three types of technologies (i.e., assembly lines, insurance firms, and construction firms, respectively), that association is neither explicit nor certain.

The types of problems that faced the early theorists, regardless of whether they conceptualized *technology* at the system or individual level, have continued. Barley (1990) attributes the tenacity of these problems to writers having only a "distant knowledge" of the technologies they study. This leads to the use of ambiguous terms that may refer to anything from hardware to cognition. Despite the early documentation of these types of problems by Mohr (1971), Khandwalla (1974), and Stanfield (1976), writers have continued to use discrepant definitions, incongruent operationalizations, and unrationalized categorizations of core technologies.

Organizational Structure

Fry (1982) argues that in comparison to that of technology, there is more agreement among structure-technology theorists about the definition and measurement of the most salient dimensions of structure. He identifies complexity, formalization, and centralization as the three structural dimensions that dominate the first 15 years of this research. Structural *complexity* refers to the amount of vertical and horizontal differentiation, that is, the number of divisions and layers in the organization. *Formalization* refers to the amount of red tape, procedural specifications, and rules; and *centralization* refers to the extent to which the power in the organization is narrowly distributed. Furthermore, he concludes that findings are consistent despite differences in operationalizations, including agreement between findings based on objective and subjective measures of these structural dimensions.

Barley's (1990) more recent analysis is less positive, finding that ambiguous terminology plagues structural as much as technological variables. He points out that structure may refer to something as concrete as the repetitive features of the day-to-day activities of individual line workers or to something as abstract as global institutional arrangements characteristic of large bureaucracies. However, Barley's criticisms of the use of the term *structure* seem more directed at social scientists generally than at those who focus specifically on structure-technology relationships. Moreover, Barley actually increases the ambiguity and confusion by suggesting the use of multiple terms with overlapping definitions to refer to different types and levels of intraorganizational relationships. For example, it is not clear that his definition of *structure* as abstract relational patterns or social networks is distinct from his definition of *social order* as a social pattern or regularity (Barley, 1990, p. 65).

The point at which Fry (1982) and Barley (1990) do agree is on the confusion caused by generalizations across levels of analysis. This occurs when findings concerning one level, such as the pattern of interactions among individual workers within a department, are applied to conclusions about another level, such as the arrangements among subunits of an organization. For example, the effects of the centralization of departmental power into the hands of a relatively few workers in a single department might be generalized to conclusions about the centralization of organizational power across departments. This parallels the confusion caused by the system- versus individual-level conceptualizations of core technologies discussed earlier. Fry concludes that differences in findings across individual, subunit, and organizational levels of analysis account for a significant portion of the discrepancies in the findings of structure-technology research.

Levels of analysis are also related to the failure of structure-technology theorists to consider adequately alternative sources of structural variation and stability. Scott (1990) describes the need for macro levels of analysis that offer explanations of structural variation that compete with those associated with technology. Attributing structural characteristics solely to the dictates of technology, the so-called technological imperative, fails to explain why different structures may be associated with the same technology, an implied requirement of contingency models of effectiveness. For example, the technological imperative does not explain why one residential mental health institution may be highly centralized and formalized while another mental health institution that treats similar patients, is not. Promising alternative macro explanations of structural variation and stability include: institutional isomorphic models of organizational mimesis, which argue that organizations that share a given environment become increasingly similar because their managers mimic each other in their efforts to reduce uncertainty (DiMaggio and Powell, 1983; Galaskiewicz & Wasserman, 1989); and population-ecology models of structural inertia that argue that individual organizational structures become increasingly rigid and entrenched, and that new structural forms emerge only with new organizations (Hannan & Freeman, 1984; Keats & Hitt, 1988). These explanations will be developed in a later section.

A related issue is that the technological imperative also fails to explain how technology can assume other than an independent relationship with structure. For example, if structural characteristics depend only on the nature of the technology, it is unclear how it is possible that what human service workers do with their clients in the technological core can be affected by the structure of the organization in which they work.

Finally, understanding structural variation also requires that structure be viewed in dynamic, as well as static, terms and that it be examined as a process of structuring rather than as simply form (Barley, 1990; Scott,

1990; Weick, 1990). In particular, the roles played by organizational designers and the social interactions of workers who implement the designs are sources of structural variation that have received limited attention in the structure-technology literature.

The Technological Imperative

Most of the structure-technology research that has followed Woodward's (1958, 1965) earlier work has been undertaken to confirm the existence of the technological imperative. However, from Woodward's initial hypothesis that an organization's structure must complement or "fit" its core technology, this imperative has been interpreted in two distinct ways. First, most researchers have examined simply the extent to which there is, in fact, a relationship between structural and technological variables. For these researchers, although their studies tend to be correlational, the intent is to determine the extent to which the characteristics of an organization's structure are a function of the characteristics of its core technology. For example, less formalized and centralized structures are expected to be associated with less routinized and more complex technologies.

In human services research, this has been interpreted to mean that structures that give more authority and discretionary power to workers are associated with human service technologies that are more individualized and less routinized in serving clients (Glisson, 1978). This is because the individualization of services involves more worker decisions and more worker interactions that cannot be preprogrammed or anticipated. As a result, individualized service requires a less centralized and less formalized structure. With some exceptions, reviewers are in agreement that research findings support this type of structure-technology consonance (Fry, 1982; Scott, 1990). Some writers have labeled this interpretation of the technological imperative the congruent proposition to distinguish it from the second interpretation, labeled the contingent proposition (Scott, 1990).

The contingent proposition is that organizational effectiveness is contingent upon the fit between the organization's structure and the core technology. Using the previous example from the human services, this would mean that the extent to which an organization's structure gives authority and discretionary power to workers who provide more individualized and less routinized services, is the extent to which the services will be effective. With a few exceptions, this type of contingent proposition has been ignored by researchers. Moreover, given the findings surrounding the congruent proposition, it might appear that the contingent proposition need not be pursued. In other words, if there tends to be an association, or fit, between structure and technology for organizations generally, the ability of this fit to explain meaningful differences in effectiveness is limited. However, there are two reasons why the contingent proposition should be explored further.

First, the strength of the association, or fit, between structure and technology varies among those studies that find support for the relationship. Therefore, there could be implications of the strength of that association for effectiveness. Second, and most important here, the observed association may result from technology being in a dependent role with structure. That is, characteristics of the technology may conform to fit the characteristics of the structure in which it is imbedded. In other words, it may be that human service workers recognize and address the individual nature of their clients' problems because they work within an organizational structure that allows more worker discretion, rather than vice versa as assumed by the traditional model (Glisson, 1978). Although this is a radical departure from the thinking of most writers, Perrow (1967) introduced the possibility of such a proposition early in the literature. Twenty years later, however, Glisson's (1978) study remained the only work that Hall (1987) could identify that placed technology in a dependent relationship with structure. In support of Glisson's (1978) positive empirical findings, both Weick (1990) and Scott (1990) have recently reemphasized the importance of this alternative view of the structure-technology relationship.

Glisson (1978) placed technology in a dependent position by distinguishing between two organizational phases: design and implementation. In the design phase, structure is placed in the traditional dependent role. Management designs an organization's structure to complement management's design of the technology that is to be used. For example, if the clients who are to receive a particular service are perceived by management as having very similar characteristics and problems requiring very similar interventions and solutions, management designs a technology that prescribes repetitive, routine intervention and problem-solving activities. To complement this technological design, management designs a structure that has strict divisions of labor, specific rules and regulations to guide worker interactions, and allows relatively little worker discretion.

In the implementation phase, management translates the structural design into the actual structure that is experienced by the workers, which in this example would be highly centralized and formalized. Most importantly, in the implementation phase technology assumes a nontraditional dependent role. This is because the intervention and problem-solving activities of the workers, that is, the implemented technology, must conform to the implemented structure in which the workers function. Thus the implemented structure "fits" the implemented technology because the implemented technology conforms to the implemented structure.

Using the design and implementation phases suggested by Glisson (1978), a synthesis of the congruent and contingent interpretations of the technological imperative can be developed. This requires the identification of two distinct and separate technologies: (1) the available, state-of-the-art technology that is theoretically accessible to any organization engaged in the type of work addressed by the technology, and (2) the technology that is actually implemented by the organization. The available technology is characterized by the existing, up-to-date knowledge of the raw material, the state-of-the-art techniques used to change it, and the degree to which outcomes can be predicted using the available techniques. In contrast, the implemented technology describes what workers in a specific organization actually do in producing the product or delivering the service. The implemented technology in the organization may or may not reflect the characteristics of the available technology.

The implemented technology is the usual referent for testing the congruent hypothesis. Therefore, the frequently observed association between structure and technology is explained in this alternative view as the result of the malleable characteristics of the implemented technology. This is, congruence is accomplished in the implementation phase by the implemented technology conforming to the implemented structure, rather than the other way around. However, the fit between the implemented technology and the implemented structure may have little to do with effectiveness. Effectiveness is contingent upon a different fit, the fit between the implemented structure and the available state-of-the-art technology. If a human service requires an available technology that is highly routinized, for example, then a highly centralized and formalized structure "fits" the available technology and effectiveness is maximized. However, if effectiveness requires an available technology that addresses the unique needs of individual clients using individually tailored interventions, a highly centralized and formalized implemented structure would not fit the available technology and effectiveness would be jeopardized.

Thus this alternative view of the technological imperative provides a synthesis of the congruent and contingent propositions. Most importantly, this view includes design and implementation processes that provide the basis for a dynamic model of structuring that includes the activities, interpretations, and intentions of humans who use the technology. As described by Barley (1990), these have been the missing characteristics of previous theoretical models that have left unanswered two major questions: (1) Why are similar technologies associated with different structures? and (2) How are macrosocial and microsocial processes entwined in the relationship between structure and technology? In the following sections, these questions are answered using a sociotechnical model that incorporates this alternative view of the technological imperative.

The Alternative Model

Sociotechnical models generally depict an organization as a work system of interrelated components that include a technology to transform raw material into output and a social structure to link workers to the technology and to each other (Perrow, 1967; Thompson, 1967). More recent applications of these models have emphasized the conceptual separation of job characteristics from technology (Glisson & Durick, 1988; Rousseau, 1977, 1978). The importance of this distinction is that it separates within the core technology the technical foundation of work from job activities that are defined in part by social structure. The technical foundation of work is determined by the actual nature of the raw material, the existing knowledge of the raw material, and the state-of-the-art techniques that are used to process it. In other words, the technical foundation of work is equivalent to the available technology described in the previous section. In contrast, job characteristics describe what a worker actually does and experiences in completing assigned work tasks within the technological core. These include, for example, the skills actually used by the worker and the roles assumed by the worker in creating the product or providing the service. Thus, job characteristics are determined by both the available technology and the social structure in which the worker functions. As a result, it cannot be assumed that workers share similar job characteristics simply because their work could be accomplished using the same available technology. Rather, it is both the technical and social components of the system that determine the characteristics of the jobs performed by workers (Glisson & Durick, 1988; Rousseau, 1978).

The distinction made in the sociotechnical literature between technology and job characteristics is the same as the distinction made in the previous section between the available technology and the implemented technology. Previous writers have not explicitly equated job characteristics with the term *implemented technology*, but the connection is implicit. For example, Rousseau (1978) defines a dimension of technology as "how much discretion (decision making) is required of the human operator" (p. 524) and defines a dimension of job characteristics as "the opportunity to use a variety of skills or to make decisions" (p. 525). She is distinguishing between a requirement of the [available] technology and what actually occurs in the actual implementation of that technology.

Therefore, the implemented technology is presented here as a function of both the available technology and the social structure within which the technology is implemented. In other words, what a worker actually does in the technological core, say the extent to which a child welfare worker provides an individualized and comprehensive array of services to an abused child, is determined by the relevant, available knowledge and techniques, and by the demands and constraints of the social structure in which the work is completed. The mechanisms by which each affects what a worker does (i.e., the implemented technology) can be explained in the context of a theoretical model that includes the design and implementation phases introduced by Glisson (1978).

The proposed, theoretical model is shown in Figure 9.1. It describes the relationships among three "types" of technology and two "types" of structure. In the model, T_a refers to the available technology. In the human services, this consists of the state-of-the-art knowledge and intervention techniques, the actual characteristics of the clients, and the types of outcomes that can be expected from using those techniques. T_d refers to the technology designed by management. This is comprised of the interventive strategies and techniques that management intends for workers to use, management's view of the salient client characteristics to which they expect workers to attend, and management's expectations of outcomes. T_i refers to the implemented technology. This is comprised of the interventive strategies and techniques actually used by workers, their perspectives of their clients, and the outcomes of their interventions. The first type of structure shown in the

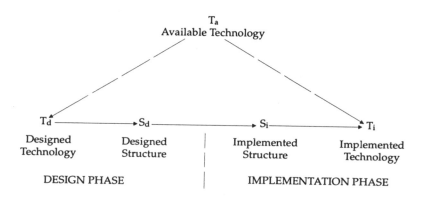

Figure 9.1. An Alternative Model of the Structure-Technology Relationship

model, S_d, refers to the structure designed by management to support T_d. S_d includes the hierarchy of authority, participation in decision making, division of labor, and procedural rules prescribed by management to complement their technological design. The second type of structure, S_i, refers to the implemented structure. This is the actual structure that the workers experience and within which they must function.

The congruence version of the technological imperative is tested most frequently by examining the relationship between S_i and T_i. However, in direct contrast to this alternative model, previous researchers who have examined this relationship have assumed they were observing the effect of technology on structure. In comparison, the contingent version of the technological imperative has rarely been tested, but using the proposed model, such a test would consist of an examination of the extent to which the fit between T_a (rather than T_i) and S_i predicts organizational effectiveness. This is because the fit between T_a and S_i will determine the extent to which the implemented structure supports those available, state-of-the-art technological processes that maximize effectiveness. Therefore, the fit between T_a and S_i also determines the congruency between T_a and T_i. The more that T_i reflects T_a, the more effectiveness is maximized.

This alternative model has several advantages over previous models of the structure-technology relationship. In addition to providing a synthesis of the congruent and contingent propositions, it resolves several problems and questions enumerated in recent reviews (Barley, 1990; Scott, 1990; Weick, 1990). One of the problems mentioned in these reviews is that the relationship is implicitly static, with little attention given to the process by which the association between structure and technology develops. Here, the relationship is explained in terms of design and implementation processes. As originally proposed by Glisson (1978), these two processes must be separated conceptually to understand the relationship. In the design phase, management creates a version of the core technology (T_d) that it envisions as the most desirable for the organization. This designed technology is influenced to a greater or lesser degree by the available technology (T_a) that reflects the state-of-the-art techniques and the most up-to-date knowledge. The size of the effect of T_a on T_d depends on the extent to which designers incorporate T_a into their design. Softer available technologies that are less determinant and more heterogeneously applied, such as those found in the human services, can be ignored by designers more easily than are harder technologies that are applied more consistently with determinant outcomes. But even with harder technologies, there will be variation in the extent to which designers, because of their resources or their abilities and knowledge, are able to incorporate the available technology into their designs.

In turn, the structure (S_d) is then designed to complement the designers' vision of the technological core (T_d). An important element of the model is that management's conceptualization and design of the technology (T_d) mediates the relationship between the available technology (T_a) and the structural design (S_d). This means that the structure is designed to fit a technological design that is, to some degree, arbitrary rather than designed to fit a "given" available technology.

Macrosocial phenomena that compete with the traditional technological imperative can be introduced in both the design and implementation phases of the process. For example, isomorphic processes have been identified that contribute to similarities among organizations that share a given environment. DiMaggio and Powell (1983) and Galaskiewicz and Wasserman (1989) argue that isomorphic forces such as mimesis are particularly powerful when managers are faced with the type of uncertain technologies and ambiguous goals that characterize human services. In these cases, organizations mimic each other because "actors make their organizations increasingly similar" in their attempts to increase certainty (DiMaggio & Powell, 1983, p. 147). These isomorphic forces can be interpreted in light of the relationships depicted in Figure 9.1. As explained previously, an uncertain available technology results in a weak relationship between the available technology (T_a) and the technology designed by management (T_d). This allows competing environmental forces, such as mimesis, to explain a greater amount of variation in T_d and S_d. Martin and Glisson (1989) provide empirical evidence of structural isomorphism among human service organizations as a function of their geographical location.

The implemented structure (S_i) describes the actual interrelationships among the workers who provide the service. In Figure 9.1, S_i is shown to be a function of the structure designed by management (S_d). However, as between T_d and S_d, the relationship between S_d and S_i is not a simple recursive one. As a result, macrosocial forces can affect the implemented structure regardless of the characteristics of the structural design. For example, population-ecology models offer macrosocial explanations of structural inertia (Hannan & Freeman, 1984; Keats & Hitt, 1988). These models argue that people are attracted to stability and certainty. As a result, people value, support, and contribute to social interactions that are reliably and predictably reproduced. Therefore, under the uncertain conditions that characterize the domain of many human services, structural inertia that resists uncertainty and change in organizations is reinforced whether or not it contributes to effective service outcomes. As predicted by this model, there is empirical evidence that structural rigidity increases as a function of worker tenure and organizational size in human service organizations regardless of effectiveness or the actual characteristics of available technologies (Glisson & Martin, 1980; Martin & Glisson, 1989).

Finally, the implemented technology (T_i) is shown to be a function of both the implemented structure (S_i) and the available technology (T_a). S_i defines the workers' areas of responsibility, the limits on the workers' discretion, and the procedural specifications that direct interactions among workers. As a result, these structural characteristics define and constrain what the workers do, and thus affect the implemented technology. T_a can affect T_i to a greater or lesser extent by workers directly importing the knowledge and skills of the available technology into the organization or by their acquiring it from experience while in the organization. The extent to which workers are able to implement any available technology to which they have access, however, is determined by the structure within which the work is accomplished. Also, as explained in earlier work that examines job characteristics, the relative direct contribution of T_a to T_i depends on the determinacy and certainty of T_a and on the extent to which S_i complements T_a (Glisson & Durick, 1988; Rousseau, 1978).

The Alternative Model
Applied to Human Service Organizations

Glisson (1978) was the first to argue explicitly that the technologies implemented by human service organizations are in a dependent relationship with the structures in which they are embedded. This dependency results from the indeterminate and heterogeneous nature of technologies that attempt to produce cognitive, affective, or behavioral changes in human beings. Such technologies are indeterminate and heterogeneous because the human beings to which the technologies are applied are individualistic and unpredictable, because the technologies do not produce a final "product" that is easily assessed, and because much of the work concerns abstract phenomena such as attitudes, self-concepts, perceptions, and analytical processes. These types of technologies are therefore characterized by a high degree of uncertainty in both implementation and outcome.

The variability of the raw material, the heterogeneity of technological activities, and the low predictability of outcomes all contribute to the susceptibility of human service technologies to organizational influences. Glisson (1978) argues that this is because organizational structures may be designed as if there were little variation in the human beings served by the organization, as if the required technologies were defined and homogeneous, and as if the outcomes were quite predictable. Therefore, the indeterminate and heterogeneous nature of the available technology allows management a great deal of leeway in how they design the technology and the structure that supports it. This means that work and outcomes can be defined in limited ways that inject a deceptive certainty into what are, in reality, uncertain tasks. This has led Glisson and Durick (1988) to describe human service technologies as "vulnerable" to their organizational context. In other words, a human service technology can be defined in a human service organization in the same way that Alice found a word could be defined in Wonderland, "it can mean anything you want it to mean."

Weick's (1990) recent description of the nature of new, developing technologies and the ways in which they are incorporated into organizations, parallels closely the description of human service technologies provided by Glisson (1978) and Glisson and Durick (1988). For example, Weick identifies several properties of new technologies that allow them to be molded in different ways by their organizational context. New and developing technologies, like those found in many human services, are comprised of stochastic events where uncertainty is permanent, continuous events in which workers must emphasize process rather than product, and abstract events that require a high degree of worker imagination, interpretation and inference. As a result, Weick (1990) says that "technology both shapes structure and is itself shaped by structure" (p. 20), and that "technology is both a cause and a consequence of structure" (p. 22). This view complements the model presented in Figure 9.1 showing that the implemented technology is constrained by the implemented structure, and that the implemented structure is a product of managerial design.

Glisson (1978) emphasizes the role of worker discretion in explaining how structural characteristics are translated into technological activities. Glisson explains that management's perceptions of the homogeneity of the clients to be served and the extent to which their presenting problems and required interventions can be anticipated, determines the extent to which management expects workers to exercise discretion in the technological core. If management views clients and their problems as homogeneous and predictable, they view technological activities as requiring little individual worker discretion. This means that workers are expected to encounter few exceptions in their assessments of clients' needs and that they are to apply similar interventive or problem-solving approaches to each client. As explained earlier, there are macro processes that pressure management into creating this type of certainty from an uncertain environment. One response of management to this pressure is to limit worker discretion.

Management's view of the extent to which the technology requires limited worker discretion—that is, the extent to which it can be routinized—then determines the structural characteristics they believe are necessary to support the technology. A technology that is designed to be highly routinized, for example, is maintained by allowing little worker participation in decision making, by creating specific divisions of labor that restrict workers' areas of responsibility, by developing specific procedural specifications to guide worker interaction, and by maintaining a narrow hierarchy of authority. These structural characteristics effectively limit the exercise of worker discretion in their work with clients. Therefore, regardless of the workers' knowledge and skills, or their awareness and understanding of the available state-of-the-art technology, they limit their interventions and problem-solving approaches within the constraints imposed by the structure in which they work. In a reiteration of the qualities that Glisson (1978) and Glisson and Durick (1988) associate with vulnerable technologies, Weick (1990) concludes that, "It does not matter that the operators are more sensitive to nonroutine qualities of the technology that the manager overlooks. Managerial assumptions typically dominate" (p. 37). Compare Weick's conclusions regarding new technologies to the following description of implemented human service technologies.

> The fact that the raw material is human beings does not necessarily indicate that members of service organizations perceive the heterogeneity of their material. The incorporated technology may be more or less routinized and is not constrained to nonroutinization merely because the raw material has many exceptions that cannot all be handled in standardized ways. This quality of the material might not be recognized and the organization may function as if the human beings were homogeneous and predictable. (Glisson, 1978, p. 386)

Summary

A number of problems have plagued three decades of research on the relationship between technology and structure. Among these have been the disparities that exist between the congruent proposition and the contingent proposition, the implicitly static nature of the theoretical models, and the lack of attention to human interpretations and intentions. In response to these problems, an alternative model of the relationship is presented that offers a synthesis of the two interpretations of the technological imperative, provides an explanation of the process by which the relationship between structure and technology develops, and gives specific attention to the human dimension of technology. In addition, answers are proposed to two major unanswered questions. Distinguishing between available and implemented technologies, an explanation is offered of how similar technologies may or may not be associated with similar structures, and of how macrosocial and microsocial forces are entwined in the relationship between structure and technology. Most importantly, it is proposed that the effectiveness of a human service organization is contingent upon the fit between the available state-of-the-art technology and the implemented organizational structure.

References

Barley, S. R. (1990). The alignment of technology and structure through roles and networks. *Administrative Science Quarterly, 35,* 61-103.

DiMaggio, P. J., & Powell, W. W. (1983). The iron cage revisited: Institutional isomorphism and collective rationality in organizational fields. *American Sociological Review, 48,* 147-160.

Fry, L. W. (1982). Technology structure research: Three critical issues. *Academy of Management Journal, 25,* 532-552.

Galaskiewicz, J., & Wasserman, S. (1989). Mimetic processes within an interorganizational field: An empirical test. *Administrative Science Quarterly, 34,* 454-479.

Glisson, C. (1978). Dependence of technological routinization on structural variables in human service organizations. *Administrative Science Quarterly, 23,* 383-395.

Glisson, C., & Durick, M. (1988). Predictors of job satisfaction and organizational commitment in human service organizations. *Administrative Science Quarterly, 33,* 61-81.

Glisson, C., & Martin, P. Y. (1980). Productivity and efficiency in human service organizations as related to structure, size and age. *Academy of Management Journal, 23,* 21-37.

Hage, J., & Aiken, M. (1969). Routine technology, social structure, and organization goals. *Administrative Science Quarterly, 14,* 366-375.

Hall, R. H. (1963). The concept of bureaucracy: An empirical assessment. *American Journal of Sociology, 69,* 32-40.

Hall, R. H. (1987). *Organizations: Structures, processes, and outcomes.* Englewood Cliffs, NJ: Prentice-Hall.

Hannan, M. T., & Freeman, J. (1984). Structural inertia and organizational change. *American Sociological Review, 49,* 149-164.

Hunt, Raymond G. (1970). Technology and organization. *Academy of Management Journal, 13,* 235-252.

Keats, B. W., & Hitt, M. A. (1988). A causal model of linkages among environmental dimensions, macro organizational characteristics, and performance. *Academy of Management Journal, 31,* 570-598.

Khandwalla, P. N. (1974). Mass output orientation of operations technology and organizational structure. *Administrative Science Quarterly, 19,* 74-97.

Martin, P., & Glisson, C. (1989). Social welfare organizations in three locales: Societal culture and context as predictors of perceived structure. *Organization Studies, 10,* 353-380.

Mohr, L. B. (1971). Organizational technology and organizational structure. *Administrative Science Quarterly, 16,* 444-459.

Perrow, C. (1967). A framework for the comparative analysis of organizations. *American Sociological Review, 32,* 194-208.

Rousseau, D. M. (1977). Technological differences in job characteristics, employee satisfaction, and motivation: A synthesis of job design research and sociotechnical systems theory. *Organizational Behavior and Human Performance, 19,* 18-42.

Rousseau, D. M. (1978). Characteristics of departments, positions, and individuals: Contexts for attitudes and behavior. *Administrative Science Quarterly, 23,* 521-540.

Scott, W. R. (1990). Technology and structure: An organizational level perspective. In P. S. Goodman & L. S. Sproull (Eds.), *Technology and organizations.* San Francisco: Jossey-Bass.

Stanfield, G. G. (1976). Technology and organizational structure as theoretical categories. *Administrative Science Quarterly, 21,* 489-493.

Thompson, J. D. (1967). *Organizations in action.* New York: McGraw-Hill.

Weick, K. E. (1990). Technology as equivoque: Sensemaking in new technologies. In P.
    S. Goodman & L. S. Sproull (Eds.), *Technology and organizations*. San Francisco: Jossey-
    Bass.
Woodward, J. (1958). *Management and technology*. Problems of Progress in Industry
    Series, No. 3. London: HMSO.
Woodward, J. (1965). *Industrial organization*. London: Oxford University Press.

PART IV
Working in Human
Service Organizations

The predominance of women as human service workers has significant consequences on the valuation and compensation of their work and on their working conditions. In Chapter 10, Dressel presents a sobering analysis of the reasons for and implications of welfare work as a female-dominated occupation. She attributes the disproportionate representation of women in social welfare work to dominant patriarchal ideologies that are also responsible for the underrepresentation of women in administrative positions. Adding a Marxist perspective on the deskilling of labor, Dressel argues that despite the efforts to professionalize social work, there are powerful economic forces leading to the deskilling of welfare work where women are concentrated. Finally, she proposes that the patriarchal ideology that welfare work is altruistic, calling for self-sacrifice and is therefore the domain of women, has resulted in their exploitation.

There is increasing recognition that working in the human services is potentially very stressful, because it is emotional work requiring the use of the self as an integral part of the service delivery process. McNeely, in Chapter 11, presents an extensive review of studies on job satisfaction in human service organizations, especially public, with particular attention to the gender and ethnicity of the workers. The emerging picture is indeed complex. A persistent finding in predicting job satisfaction, for both women and men, is the degree of job monotony and dullness. Another consistent finding is that women earn less than men. Also, women express more often concerns about the underutilization of their skills, and feelings of excessive pressures. As expected, African Americans are more likely to report racial discrimination as a source of job dissatisfaction, and they also tend to be underrepresented in higher rank positions. As McNeely stresses, regardless of gender and ethnicity, situational conditions such as lack of participation in decision making, work overload, favoritism, inadequate pay, and a hostile political environment are probably the most critical factors determining job satisfaction.

CHAPTER 10

Patriarchy and Social Welfare Work[1]

PAULA L. DRESSEL

Social Welfare Work as "Women's Work"

Welfare work[2] is a female-dominated occupation undergirded by patriarchal ideologies. Specifically, the ideologies that see women as nurturers and men as providers within the family wage system rationalize the preponderance of women in social welfare work. The task of helping people coincides with normative expectations of women's nurturant and expressive functions in a gender-based societal division of labor (Parsons & Bales, 1953). This explains, in part, the disproportionate representation of women in social welfare. Organizers of welfare work viewed it as an extension of nurturing skills and domestic expertise into extrafamilial arenas (Baum, Hyman, & Michel, 1976; Bolin, 1973; Kadushin, 1958; Kravetz, 1976; Vandiver, 1980). For example, in 1831 the Union Benevolent Association of Philadelphia resolved that women would make better friendly visitors than men because they are "more sympathetic, more self-denying, gentler" than men, and because they are better equipped, by virtue of their own domestic responsibilities, to "encourage every effort to make home a pleasant and attractive place" for the poor (quoted in Rauch, 1975, p. 245). Jane Addams, a pioneer of the settlement house movement in the late nineteenth century, justified women's welfare activities as their effort to make their communities and the world "more 'homelike' " (Vandiver, 1980, p. 26). In sum, as emotional labor, or work that appeals "to the heart, not the mind" (Simpson & Simpson, 1969, p. 203), social welfare work has been viewed as an appropriate occupation for women (Hochschild, 1983: Rose, 1983). It is curious that these gender-based descriptions of social welfare activities ignore other components of welfare work, such as critical thinking, analytical decision making (Meyer, 1980) and social control (Piven & Cloward, 1971).

critical thinking

analytic decision making

social control

Within the social welfare industry, men and women tend to do different kinds of work based on normative expectations for both genders. From the beginning of large-scale organized charitable activities, there has been a noticeable division of labor between male and female direct-service practitioners. For example, in her description of friendly visitors in Philadelphia in 1880, Rauch (1975, p. 245) notes:

> Woman's special sphere was the moral; by implication, she was not to be concerned with such crass material questions as wages, working conditions, and even the dispensation of relief. As in the family, the special charges of ladies bountiful were other women, children, the aged, and the sick; by implication, they were to avoid the idle, profligate, intemperate, and other immoral poor, particularly if they were men.

Instead, many of women's early charity activities took forms such as making flower bouquets for the poor and afflicted (Rauch, 1975), protecting women and neighborhoods from prostitution (Baum et al., 1976; Ross, 1978), and imparting moral lessons and domestic science to women in poor families (Baum et al., 1976; Ehrenreich & English, 1978; Ross, 1978). In some cases women who performed what we now think of as casework functions did not make the decisions about the dispensation of financial assistance to poor families. Rather, male administrators and male-dominated advisory committees made these important decisions (Becker, 1961; Rauch, 1975). In other cases, these agencies separated women entirely from issues of financial aid (Baum et al., 1976; Ross, 1978).

Gender-based distinctions between practitioners are just as evident in the 1960s, 1970s, and 1980s. The varied activities performed under the umbrella of social welfare work are typically categorized as casework, group work, and community organization. Within these classifications, women are more likely to be caseworkers, while men are more likely to be community organizers (Brager & Michael, 1969; Fanshel, 1976; Kadushin, 1976; Kravetz, 1976; Sauber, 1965), and the latter specialization is more highly paid than the former (e.g., Stamm, 1968). Within casework, men are more likely to perform functions related to corrections, substance abuse, and occupational social work, while women provide services for families and children (Annual Report to the Trust, 1984; Kadushin, 1976).

Besides the influence of ideologies about women's proper work, the disproportionate representation of women in social welfare work is also related to the key normative assumption underlying the family wage system—that is, that a man's income alone will be sufficient to support an entire family (see Ehrenreich & Piven, 1984). Mens' social responsibility for the economic subsistence of their families presumably freed women from wage labor and enabled them to render their emotional labor as volunteers. Early charitable organizations viewed such volunteer work as superior to paid work because of the commonly held belief that charity and love could not be purchased. Further, many early volunteers were women of upper-income families whose social position would not allow them to accept money for their labors (Vandiver, 1980). Even with the development of the paid social work profession in this century, the work has been underpaid, in part, because it is seen as women's work within a political economy that perpetuates the ideology of the family wage system. Since the early 1900s, social welfare work has provided modestly paid work to a growing number of women who are single, widowed, and divorced, as well as to women whose wages are necessary supplements to their husbands' incomes. The wages obtained through social welfare work have offered only marginal financial security for the many women whose subsistence depends upon their own employment (Hardcastle & Katz, 1979, Table 23).

Table 10.1 documents the overrepresentation of women in social welfare work from the earliest available statistics in 1920 through 1980. To be sure, the types of women recruited to social welfare practice have changed over the last century, but their overrepresentation has not.[3] Furthermore, while social welfare institutions have not been the largest employers of women historically—falling far short of occupations such as clerical work, retail sales, nursing, teaching, and private household work—the growth of the social welfare enterprise in the past two decades has increasingly opened up work opportunities for women. However, the numerical dominance of women in social work has not translated into authority, power, and pay equity or equality.[4]

Like many other work settings in advanced capitalist societies, social welfare organizations are organized hierarchically. Access to higher levels of the organization, with their accompanying privileges and power, is differentially available according to gender (Halaby, 1979; Wolf & Fligstein,

Table 10.1 Women and Men In Social Welfare Work, 1920-1980

		1920[a]	1930[b]	1940[c]	1950[d]	1960[e]	1970[f]	1980[g]
Total	N =	41,078	29,424	69,677	76,890	133,051	231,927	499,090
Women	N =	26,927	23,231	44,809	53,220	76,164	147,525	337,389
Men	N =	14,151	6,193	24,868	23,670	56,887	84,402	161,701
Women	% =	65.6	79.0	64.3	69.2	57.2	63.6	67.6
Men	% =	34.4	21.0	35.7	30.8	42.8	36.4	32.4

SOURCE: a. U.S. Department of Commerce, Bureau of the Census. (1923). Chapter 2, Table 4. Figures are for "Religious, charity, and welfare workers" age 10 and over.
b. U.S. Department of Commerce, Bureau of the Census. (1933). Chapter 7, Table 2. Figures are for "Social and welfare workers" age 10 and over.
c. U.S. Department of Commerce, Bureau of the Census. (1943). Volume 3, Part 1, Table 62. Figures are for "Social welfare workers" age 14 and over.
d. U.S. Department of Commerce, Bureau of the Census. (1956). Volume 4, Part 1, Chapter B, Table 3. Figures are for "Social and welfare workers, except group" age 14 and over.
e. U.S. Department of Commerce, Bureau of the Census. (1964). Volume I, Part 1, Chapter D, Table 205. Figures are for "Social, welfare, and recreation workers" age 14 and over.
f. U.S. Department of Commerce, Bureau of the Census. (1973). Volume 1, Part 1, Section 2, Table 223. Figures are for "Social workers" and "Welfare service aides" age 16 and over.
g. U.S. Department of Commerce, Bureau of the Census. (1982). Volume 1, Chapter D, Part 1, Section A, Table 278. Figures are for "Social workers" and "Welfare service aides" age 16 and over.

1979; Wright, Costello, Hachen, & Sprague, 1982). Since the beginning of paid welfare work in the United States, men have been overrepresented in administrative positions. For example, early accounts of white-dominated and Jewish charity organizations in the 1800s show that supervisory and administrative roles—the domain of men—were the only paid positions; direct service provision—the domain of women—was a purely volunteer endeavor (Baum et al., 1976; Becker, 1961; Rauch, 1975). Moreover, in Philadelphia in the late 1800s, women who wished to volunteer as friendly visitors actually had to pay one dollar to the charity organization to become members of the visitors corp (Rauch, 1975). Women "provided a cheap source of labor for male philanthropists unwilling to support professional social workers" (Rauch, 1975, p. 253). Men headed the NAACP and the National Urban League—two major Black humanitarian organizations founded in the early 1900s— and they dominated the administrative hierarchics of these organizations. The women's clubs that arose in the late 1800s to foster benevolent activities (Baum et al., 1976; Davis, 1981) were the only charitable settings where women held most of the executive positions.

Table 10.2 shows that since 1950, men have been increasingly overrepresented in administrative positions within social welfare organizations (also see Fanshel, 1976; Kadushin, 1976; Kravetz, 1976). Szakacs

Table 10.2 Percentage of Women and Men in Social Welfare Administration, 1950-1984

	1950[a]	1960[b]	1977[c]	1984[d]
Female administrators as percentage of all female social welfare workers	16	15	29	13
Male administrators as percentage of all male social welfare workers	33	29	43	30

SOURCES: a. U.S. Department of Labor, Bureau of Labor Statistics, Division of Wages and Industrial Relations. (1952). Table D-2. Nationwide survey of social welfare workers.
b. U.S. Department of Labor, Bureau of Labor Statistics. (1960). Table 2 and p. 11. Nationwide survey of social welfare workers.
c. Hardcastle and Katz. (1979). Table 12, Survey of members of National Association of Social Workers.
d. National Association of Social Workers. (1984). Tables 30-33. Survey of members of National Association of Social Workers.
NOTE: Statistics are not directly comparable across years because of different data bases. All percentages are rounded.

(1977, p. 12) reports that after the Second World War men began replacing women in administrative positions at the rate of 2% per year. She also provides striking examples of recent displacement of women within member agencies of the Family Service Association of America (FSAA), and the Child Welfare League of America (CWLA). Between 1957 and 1976, the percentage of FSAA agencies directed by women fell from 60% to 20%; female-headed agencies of the CWLA declined from 36% in 1966 to 19% in 1976. Further, in 1976, men headed 91% of Federally Funded Community Health Center agencies; in that same year the National Jewish Welfare Board reported 99% of its agencies were directed by men. Quite clearly, men have more power with administrative hierarchies of social welfare organizations.

It is likely that men will continue to control administrative positions in welfare work for several reasons. First, men have been more likely to enroll in the administrative track of Master of Social Work (MSW) programs (e.g., Jennings & Daley, 1979; Szakacs, 1977). Second, men have been more likely to obtain administrative jobs as entry work (e.g., Jennings & Daley, 1979), and men who begin in direct-service positions have been more likely to be promoted to supervisory and administrative positions (e.g., Jennings & Daley, 1979; Szakacs, 1977). Third, an increasingly acceptable credential for available administrative jobs is a graduate degree in business or public administration—fields that tend to be dominated by men (Patti & Maynard, 1978). The appropriateness of alternative credentials decreases the likelihood that women with MSW degrees will compete successfully for administrative positions. Finally, since representing one's agency to decision makers beyond the service organization is a central function of social welfare administrators (Brager & Michael, 1969; Wilensky & Lebeaux, 1958), the predominance of men in social welfare administration is also likely to continue as long as men are viewed as more powerful and effective in relationships with others in the community.

Men also dominate the field of social work education. In 1981, only 22% of deans and directors of schools and departments of social work were women. At the faculty level, 57.8% of all assistant professors, 39.6% of all associate professors, and 26.9% of all full professors were women (Rubin, 1982a). [5] Further, men disproportionately authored articles in professional social work journals since the 1950s (Faver & Fox, 1984; Kirk & Rosenblatt, 1980, 1984; Rosenblatt, Turner, Patterson, & Rolloson, 1970), and have held the leadership positions in the major professional organization, the National Association of Social Workers (Belon & Gould, 1977; Mahaffey, 1976).

Thus sex-based job segregation within social work has existed historically and continues to exist today. Women have not only performed different work than men within the social welfare industry, but they also have been increasingly underrepresented in administrative positions in social welfare bureaucracies and social work education. However, as we will now see, women's subordination within the social work occupation has not been limited to exclusion from administrative positions and filling lower-paid specializations, but instead, their subordination has been furthered by changes within the social welfare labor process itself.

Patriarchy Within the Social Welfare Labor Process

In his now classic piece on the transformation of work under advanced capitalism, Braverman (1974) analyzed changes in the labor process that furthered the subordination of the *working class* to capital during this century. While Braverman was interested solely in the domination and subordination of the *working class*, I believe that the same dynamics reproduce gender relations under capitalism and further the domination and subordination of women by men in the work place.

Braverman's analysis focused on the restructuring and deskilling of the labor process of private-sector work during the twentieth century. He identified two factors that brought about this transformation: (1) the division of work in the labor process according to the "Babbage principle"; and (2) the organization of the labor process using Taylor's principles of scientific management.

The "Babbage principle"—what Braverman calls "the general law of the capitalist division of labor"—expresses the reduced cost of production through the division of the labor process into different processes requiring different levels of skill. Dividing the work allows the employer to purchase the degree of skill necessary to perform each individual process—no more and no less. In this way, "dividing the craft cheapens its individual parts," and hence, lowers the wage bill and the overall cost of production. A cult of efficiency in production spurred employers to divide the labor process into ever more specialized and repetitive tasks that required less and less skill.

[margin note: Babbage principle]

While the division of work according to the Babbage principle initiates the deskilling of work, the organization of the labor process using Frederick Winslow Taylor's "principles of scientific management" completes the transformation and degradation of work under monopoly capitalism. The first principle—"the dissociation of the labor process from the skills of the workers"—involves management accumulating all knowledge formerly possessed by workers, and reducing this knowledge to a set of rules, laws, formulae, and so forth that can then be executed in a rote manner without reference to the underlying theory of work (Braverman, 1974, p. 113). The second principle—"the separation of conception and execution"—moves all brain work from the shop or office floor to the planning department so that management has a monopoly over the knowledge of the labor process as a whole (Braverman, 1974, p. 114). Finally, the third principle—management's "use of this monopoly over knowledge to control each step of the labor process and its mode of execution"—completes the transformation and degradation of work, and the transfer of control over the labor process from workers to management.

[margin note: Transfer of control over the labour process from workers to management]

The use of the Babbage principle and Taylor's principles of scientific management in the work place significantly affected workers, both in terms of the nature of their work, and the degree of control they exercised over it. Work tasks became routinized and deskilled, while the organization of work became hierarchical in terms of power, prestige, and income. As Wright et al. (1982) show, women and racial/ethnic men tend to fill the lesser-skilled, lower-paid positions in this transformed work place, while white men hold most managerial and high-skilled positions.

Braverman's analysis focused primarily on private-sector industrial work, and the effects of the transformation of work on the progressive subordination of the working class to capital. However, his insights are useful also for understanding how patriarchy operates within the social welfare labor process. Now let us examine the use of the Babbage principle and Taylor's principles of scientific management in the transformation of the social welfare labor process historically, and the effects of this transformation on the relations of domination and subordination between the sexes within this occupation.

Historically, the drive to "professionalize" social work reflects the application of Taylor's principles of scientific management with a distinctive anti-feminine bias to the labor process that produces human services. Efforts to professionalize social work began following the Civil War. The objective of the so-called "scientific philanthropists" of the period was to make charity "a matter of the head as well as the heart" (Bremner, 1956, p. 168). This involved applying objective criteria to the determination of charity eligibility and receipt, thereby increasing the efficiency of welfare work. As one proponent of scientific philanthropy remarked, "There must be no sentiment in the matter. It must be treated as a business scheme" (Bremner, 1956, p. 171). Growing emphasis on rationality, science, and administration represented an attempt to "defeminize" social work by infusing it with "male" qualities (Chafetz, 1972, p. 8). Indeed, the business principles adopted by various charity organizations were expected to "giv[e] form to the chaotic charitable sentiments sometimes floating in the minds of women" (Zaretsky, 1982, p. 205). Consistent with gender-typed beliefs, a paid cadre of men was to bring order to the efforts of the predominantly female volunteer force of friendly visitors. Baum et al. (1976, p. 176) note that "the men who transformed Jewish social work from an avocation into a profession assumed that 'leader' and 'male' were synonymous." In short, at this early point in social welfare work's history, male workers performed paid professional tasks, while women served as volunteers. Later this arrangement transformed into the overrepresentation of men in social welfare administration and the overrepresentation of women in casework.

A second thrust toward professionalization came at the beginning of the twentieth century with the development of training programs in social work at the New York School of Philanthropy (later Columbia University), the University of Chicago, Fisk University, Howard University, Smith College, and Atlanta University, and so forth. Bolin (1973, p. 13) argues that the trend for specialized social work education

> meant a "masculinization" of the profession in terms of values—an emphasis on specialization as opposed to integration, professionalism as opposed to voluntarism, and rationalism as opposed to emotionalism. The acceptance of these values seemed to indicate that for social work to improve its status it had to adopt the masculine values of the society.

The interest in raising the status of social welfare work to a profession once again gained momentum in the 1950s. At that time, practitioners increased their efforts to recruit men to the occupation (Kravetz, 1976; Scotch, 1971; Szakacs, 1977). This effort reinforced the gender-based division of labor: a disproportionate number of men were recruited to or soon rose to the administrative ranks of social service organizations.[6] As a result "a greater share of the work . . . is planned, supervised, and directed by men" (Grimm & Stern, 1974, p. 703) and, it should be added, executed by women.

Proletarianization—the organization of work around manual tasks that are externally structured and controlled (Glenn & Feldberg, 1977) —results from use of the Babbage principle and Taylor's principles of scientific management to deskill the labor process.[7] As I will now show, the social welfare labor process has been increasingly proletarianized historically, and women have disproportionately borne the brunt of the negative consequences of this process.

The use of universal criteria for evaluating client cases in order to remove personal prejudices from practice allows for more efficient processing of client-related decisions and standardizes the application of casework techniques. As a result, caseworkers have less discretion[8] and supervisors can more readily monitor their work. Further, as casework becomes reduced to the standardized application of formulae and techniques dictated by social welfare administrators, educational requirements for casework positions can be decreased, and, correspondingly, wages will decline. The downgrading of some aspects of social welfare work through the deskilling process has occurred during periods when political decision makers want to cut the cost of social welfare programs. For example, the current domestic fiscal crisis in the United States has accelerated the deskilling of social welfare work, particularly direct service provision—the domain of women.

Several significant changes in social welfare practice since the mid-1960s illustrate how deskilling has occurred within the occupation. Since welfare institutions exist within and underwrite a capitalist political economy, it is not surprising that they have undergone many of the same work trends that Braverman described in private sector production. One change gaining momentum is the automation of certain aspects of social welfare work. While computerized data collection will undoubtedly improve functions such as budgetary accounting and client tracking, supervisors are also using the computer to study and monitor workers' time utilization and progress (Boyd, Hylton, & Price, 1978; Schoech & Arangio, 1979), and personnel are using it to perform client intake procedures (Vondracek et al., 1974). Professional social welfare personnel have previously considered intake a strategic occasion to analyze the client's needs through give-and-take conversation with the client (e.g., Zimmerman, 1969). A concurrent change consistent with the Babbage principle is the separation of intake procedures from casework functions (Funiciello & Sanzillo, 1983; Piliavin & Gross, 1977; Vondracek et al., 1974). The presumed benefit of this division of labor is to prevent professional, higher-paid social workers from having to perform what is increasingly viewed as the routine function of client screening, and thus to allow them to perform more complex casework activities with eligible clients. This new division of labor has produced a cadre of mostly women paraprofessional intake workers who perform this routine, low-skilled, low-paid work. In times of fiscal retrenchment, social welfare administrators retain these low-wage paraprofessional employees and expand their responsibility for other activities through "job enrichment" and "job enlargement" (see Braverman, 1974, p. 36-38) while releasing higher-paid professional MSW personnel to cut labor costs (Karger, 1983). In such instances, the social welfare organization benefits at the expense of MSW caseworkers and paraprofessional employees—most of whom are women.

Another change in the division of labor in the social work labor process is the legally mandated separation of income maintenance activities from the provision of social services that occurred in 1967 (Wyers, 1980).[9] This separation produced a two-tiered status system within social welfare work, with income maintenance providers on the bottom. Administrators tend to view the work of income maintenance providers as low-skilled and divorced from professional social work practice since most of their work entails the straightforward application of agency-generated eligibility criteria. Thus, these positions require less education and are low-paid. Not coincidentally, income maintenance workers are mostly women from oppressed racial-ethnic groups (Perlmutter & Alexander, 1978).

A final change that has produced deskilled work at the direct service level where women are clustered is the current job reclassification by state civil service commissions (Karger, 1983; Pecora & Austin, 1983). Reclassification in effect means declassification, or "the reduction in standards of professional education and work-related experience for public social service jobs" (Pecora & Austin, 1983, p. 421). Reclassification frequently involves reducing educational requirements for entry-level social service positions, combining work tasks that eliminate functions requiring higher levels of education, and breaking larger jobs into smaller tasks that presumably can be deskilled. All of these measures result in cost-savings for state budgets by enabling welfare agencies to pay workers—mostly women from oppressed racial-ethnic groups—less than they did before reclassification.[10] Indeed, Meyer (1980, p. 201) argues that racist and sexist practices offer "significant route(s) to economic salvation" in times of fiscal difficulties.

Thus the division of labor according to the Babbage principle and use of Taylor's principles of scientific management are as evident in the deskilling of social welfare work in the public sector as in the private-sector work Braverman analyzed. My examples show that it was women, not men, who suffered further subordination as a result of this deskilling process that reduced labor costs primarily at the expense of female direct-service providers. However, as we will now see, these women themselves play a key role in the maintenance and reproduction of their own subordination within the social welfare labor process.

The Reproduction of Subordination

Underlying the provision of social welfare services is the expectation that welfare workers will be altruistic. Workers are "responsive to a 'dedicatory ethic' " (Pines & Kafry, 1978, p. 499), "sympathetic, understanding, unselfish and helpful to others" (Registt, 1970, p. 11), and have undertaken social welfare work as a "calling" (Cherniss, 1980: Gustafson, 1982; Kadushin, 1974). These occupational expectations are intimately intertwined with the idea of social welfare work as emotional labor and therefore stereotypically "women's work." In addition, they set the stage for the exploitation of women in social welfare agencies.

However useful the orientation of sacrifice is for the profession of social work and for the clients and organizations that benefit from workers' energies, workers' overcommitments to their jobs can adversely affect their personal well-being. Gilligan (1982) argues that self-sacrifice easily becomes self-exclusion and that women historically have shown responsiveness to others at the expense of their own needs. For example, studies comparing male and female professionals have found that women are more likely to be emotionally overextended or exhausted than are men (Maslach & Jackson, 1981; Pines & Kafry, 1981). The flood of studies on burnout among direct service providers who are mostly women suggest that this is the case within social welfare work (see Dressel, 1984 for a summary). The toll that such burnout eventually takes is reflected in workers' symptoms of loss of idealism, feelings of hopelessness, lowered morale, lack of initiative, absenteeism, alcohol and drug use, and physical and emotional exhaustion.

The ethic of altruism in social welfare practice may exploit the tendency of female practitioners toward self-sacrifice. For example, welfare administrators have called upon caseworkers during recent budget cutbacks to do more work with less resources so that clients would not feel the impact of fiscal retrenchment. Hochschild (1983) maintains that because women's identities are more closely allied to the welfare of the group, women who perform emotional labor are susceptible to exploitation. She argues that the danger of women's responsiveness lies in the possibility of developing an "altruistic false self"—that is, they may become alienated from themselves in the ongoing demand to tend to others. The welfare organization benefits from this altruism since productivity is maintained despite funding decreases.

Social welfare workers who are met with unending demands from clients, supervisors, and administrators employ various strategies to manage and cope with job-related stress. Their typical coping strategies involve blaming themselves for the stress rather than the stress-producing work environment. Blaming themselves, they rarely seek to challenge or change their working conditions.

The mechanisms that female social workers use to deal with stress at work are consistent with gender role research on locus of control and attribution theories. Such research shows that women tend to blame themselves for problems and failures they experience at work.[11] For example, Pearlin and Schooler (1978) found that women scored significantly lower than men on the psychological resource of mastery—"the extent to which one regards one's life chances as being under one's control" (Pearlin & Schooler, 1978, p. 5). With regard to occupational coping responses in particular, they found that men were more likely to employ "optimistic action," while women used "selective ignoring" more so than men. In other words, men took action while women took the blame (see also Cloward & Piven, 1979).

Elsewhere (Dressel, 1984) I show that many of the stresses that social welfare workers encounter on a day-to-day basis derived from constraints of social welfare policies and dilemmas of welfare organizations. In other words, the routine sources of caseworkers' difficulties do not lie in their personal characteristics or interpersonal styles. Nevertheless, these workers' patterns of stress management were designed to change themselves and not their work environments. They utilized strategies such as role manipulation (Brager & Holloway, 1978; Dressel, 1984; Levy, 1970; Pines & Maslach, 1978; Wasserman, 1971), role bargaining (Dressel, 1984; Levy, 1970; Pines & Maslach, 1978; Street, Martin, & Gordon, 1979), norm violations (Dressel, 1984; Levy, 1970), and various cognitive realignments (Dressel, 1984; Pines & Maslach, 1978; Wasserman, 1971) to alter their work performances or work orientations in hopes of relieving stress. In effect, they accepted the blame for problems on the job by trying to change themselves. At best, such coping strategies offered temporary relief, but the actual sources of work-related stress remained unchanged and unchallenged. In fact, Pearlin and Schooler's (1978) work suggests that individual actions are not likely to produce any meaningful impact on occupational strains. Rather, these strains usually require collective action for their alleviation (Pearlin & Schooler, 1978).

Social welfare practitioners, like other women involved in emotional labor (Hochschild, 1983), fail to acknowledge that external factors are legitimate sources of their problems at work. One consequence is that women may believe they are unsuccessful because of their own inabilities rather than because of inherent characteristics of the work environment. Believing themselves to be incompetent, they may be reluctant to seek positions with greater responsibilities (O'Leary, 1977). This is an alternative explanation for why women choose to remain in casework rather than seek upward mobility to social welfare administration. Other writers (Brager & Michael, 1969; Chafetz, 1972; and for reviews see Scotch, 1971 and Marrett, 1972) argue that women's preferences for direct contact with clients over activities of organizational maintenance and decision making are responsible for the overrepresentation of men in administrative jobs. Insofar as individualized coping strategies become institutionalized for the largely female welfare worker population, these women may come to accept blame for problems not of their making, lower their own career aspirations, and accommodate themselves to the very arrangements that render them subordinate and exploit their humanitarianism. In short, women's strategies for managing stress on the job often serve to maintain and reproduce patriarchal relations within the social welfare work place.

Notes

1. Excerpt from Dressel (1987). © 1987 by the Society for the Study of Social Problems. Reprinted from *Social Problems*, Vol. 34, No. 3, June 1987, pp. 295-304, by permission.

2. I use the terms *social welfare work, service provision, social work,* and *social service work* interchangeably throughout this chapter. They refer to an "organized system of functions and services under public and private auspices that directly support and enhance individual and social well-being" (Departmental Task Force on Social Work Education and Manpower, 1965, p. 7). The use of this broad definition for social welfare work does not deny existing differences among workers, services, clientele, and auspices. However, such differences are relatively insignificant to the issues raised here.

3. For example, compare Rauch (1975) and Ross (1978) with Hardcastle and Katz (1979).

4. For example, see Belon and Gould (1977), Fanshel (1976), Gripton (1974), Hardcastle and Katz (1979), Meyer (1980), Rytina (1982), Scotch (1971), U.S. Department of Labor (1952, 1960), Williams, Ho, and Fielder (1974), and see Chambers (1986) for a dissenting opinion.

5. Rubin (1982b) argues that the greater percentage of women in lower faculty ranks is associated with a recent increase in the percentage of women earning doctorates and being hired as faculty members. He perceived the differential distribution of men and women across faculty ranks as an indicator of progress, not discrimination.

6. This dynamic is similar to that described by Tuchman and Fortin (1980, 1984) regarding the professionalization of literature.

7. See Kanter (1977) for a discussion of how the emergence of scientific management produced the deskilling and feminization of office work.

8. While Lipsky (1980) noted the opportunity for discretion in decision making at the service delivery level, this latitude may derive more so from the ambiguity inherent in policies that welfare workers implement rather than from formal professional design (Dressel, 1984).

9. Federal relief in the 1930s produced the earliest schism between income assistance and casework activities. Social welfare workers of the period feared loss of their professional status since the administration of relief funds required less skill than casework (Bolin, 1973).

10. That unions representing some social welfare workers have supported reclassification attempts (Karger, 1983) reflects social class and racial schisms among social welfare practitioners (see Dressel, Waters, Sweat, Clayton, & Chandler-Clayton, 1988).

11. See O'Leary (1977) for a summary of conflicting data on this issue.

References

Baum, C., Hyman, P., & Michel, S. (1976). The Jewish woman in America. New York: New American Library.

Becker, D. G. (1961). The visitor to the New York City poor, 1843-1920. *Social Service Review, 35,* 382-396.

Belon, C. J., & Gould, K. H. (1977). Not even equals: Sex-related salary inequities. *Social Work, 22,* 466-471.

Bolin, W. D. W. (1973). Feminism, reform, and social service. Minneapolis: Minnesota Resource Center for Social Work Education.

Boyd, L. H., Jr., Hylton, J. H., & Price, S. V. (1978). Computers in social work practice: A review. *Social Work, 23,* 368-371.

Brager, G., & Holloway, S. (1978). *Changing human service organizations.* New York: Free Press.

Brager, G., & Michael, J. A. (1969). The sex distribution in social work: Causes and consequences. *Social Casework, 50,* 595-601.

Braverman, H. (1974). *Labor and monopoly capital.* New York: Monthly Review Press.

Bremner, R. H. (1956). "Scientific philanthropy": 1873-93. *Social Service Review, 30,* 168-173.

Chafetz, J. S. (1972). Women in social work. *Social Work, 17,* 12-18.

Chambers, C. A. (1986). Women in the creation of the profession of social work. *Social Service Review, 60,* 1-33.

Cherniss, C. (1980). *Staff burnout: Job stress in the human services.* Beverly Hills, CA: Sage.

Cloward, R. A., & Piven, F. F. (1979). Hidden protest: The channeling of female innovation and resistance. *Signs: Journal of Women in Culture and Society, 4,* 651-669.

Davis, A. (1981). *Women, race, and class.* New York: Vintage Books.

Departmental Task Force on Social Work Education and Manpower. (1965, November). *Closing the gap . . . in social work manpower.* Washington, DC: Government Printing Office.

Dressel, P. L. (1984). *The service trap: From altruism to dirty work.* Springfield, IL: Charles C Thomas.

Dressel, P. L. (1987). Patriarchy and social welfare work. *Social Problems, 34,* 294-309.

Dressel, P. L., Waters, M., Sweat, M., Clayton, O., & Chandler-Clayton, A. (1988, June). Deprofessionalization, proletarianization, and social welfare work. *Journal of Sociology and Social Welfare, 15,* 113-132.

Ehrenreich, B., & English, D. (1978). *For her own good: 150 years of the experts' advice to women.* Garden City, NY: Doubleday, Anchor.

Ehrenreich, B., & Piven, F. F. (1984). The feminization of poverty. *Dissent, 31,* 162-170.

Faver, C. A., & Fox, M. F. (1984). Publication of articles by male and female social work educators. *Social Work, 29,* 488.

Fanshel, D. (1976). Status differentials: Men and women in social work. *Social Work, 21,* 448-454.

Funiciello, T., & Sanzillo, T. (1983, Summer). The voter registration strategy: A critique. *Social Policy, 14,* 54-58.

Gilligan, C. (1982). *In a different voice.* Cambridge, MA: Harvard University Press.

Glenn, E. N., & Feldberg, R. L. (1977). Degraded and deskilled: The proletarianization of clerical work. *Social Problems, 25,* 52-64.

Grimm, J. W., & Stern, R. N. (1974). Sex roles and internal labor market structures: The "female" semi-professions. *Social Problems, 21,* 690-705.

Gripton, J. (1974). Sexism in social work: Male takeover of a female profession. *Social Worker, 42,* 78-89.

Gustafson, J. M. (1982). Professions as "callings." *Social Service Review, 56,* 501-515.

Halaby, C. N. (1979). Job-specific sex differences in organizational reward attainment: Wage discrimination vs. rank segregation. *Social Forces, 58,, 108-127.

Hardcastle, D. A., & Katz, A. J. (1979). *Employment and unemployment in social work: A study of NASW members.* Washington, DC: National Association of Social Workers.

Hochschild, A. R. (1983). *The managed heart: Commercialization of human feeling.* Berkeley: University of California Press.

Jennings, P. L., & Daley, M. (1979). Sex discrimination in social work careers. *Social Work Research and Abstracts, 15,* 17-21.

Kadushin, A. (1958). Prestige of social work—Facts and factors. *Social Work, 3,* 37-43.

Kadushin, A. (1974). *Child welfare services.* New York: Macmillan.

Kadushin, A. (1976). Men in a woman's profession. *Social Work, 21,* 440-447.

Kanter, R. M. (1977). *Men and women of the corporation.* New York: Basic Books.

Karger, H. J. (1983). Reclassification: Is there a future in public welfare for the trained social worker? *Social Work, 28,* 427-433.

Kirk, S. A., & Rosenblatt, A. (1980). Women's contributions to social work journals. *Social Work, 25,* 204-209.

Kirk, S. A., & Rosenblatt, A. (1984). The contribution of women faculty to social work journals. *Social Work, 29,* 67-69.

Kravetz, D. (1976). Sexism in a woman's profession. *Social Work, 21,* 421-426.

Levy, G. (1970). "Acute" workers in a welfare bureaucracy. In D. I. Offenbacher & C. H. Poster (Eds.), *Social problems and social policy* (pp. 168-175). New York: Appleton-Century-Crofts.

Lipsky, M. (1980). *Street-level bureaucracy.* New York: Russell Sage.

Mahaffey, M. (1976). Sexism and social work. *Social Work, 21,* 419.

Marrett, C. B. (1972). Centralization in female organizations: Reassessing the evidence. *Social Problems, 19,* 348-357.

Maslach, C., & Jackson, S. E. (1981). The measurement of experienced burnout. *Journal of Occupational Behavior, 2,* 99-113.

Meyer, C. H. (1980). Issues for women in a "woman's profession." In A. Weick & S. T. Vandiver (Eds.), *Women, power, and change* (pp. 197-205). Washington, DC: National Association of Social Workers.

National Association of Social Workers. (1984, October). *Annual report to the trust.* Computer printout. Silver Spring, MD: National Association of Social Workers.

O'Leary, V. E. (1977). *Toward understanding women.* Monterey, CA: Brooks/Cole.

Parsons, T., & Bales, R. F. (1953). *Family, socialization and interaction process.* Glencoe, IL: Free Press.

Patti, R. J., & Maynard, C. (1978). Qualifying for managerial jobs in public welfare. *Social Work, 23,* 288-294.

Pearlin, L. I., & Schooler, C. (1978). The structure of coping. *Journal of Health and Social Behavior, 19,* 2-21.

Pecora, P. J., & Austin, M. J. (1983). Declassification of social service jobs: Issues and strategies. *Social Work, 28,* 421-426.

Perlmutter, F. D., & Alexander, L. B. (1978). Exposing the coercive consensus: Racism and sexism in social work. In R. C. Sarri & Y. Hasenfeld (Eds.), *The management of human services* (pp. 207-231). New York: Columbia University Press.

Piliavin, I., & Gross, A. E. (1977). The effects of separation of services and income maintenance on AFDC recipients. *Social Service Review, 51*, 389-406.

Pines, A., & Kafry, D. (1978). Occupational tedium in the social services. *Social Work, 23*, 499-507.

Pines, A., & Kafry, D. (1981). The experience of life tedium in three generations of professional women. *Sex Roles, 7*, 117-134.

Pines, A., & Maslach, C. (1978). Characteristics of staff burnout in mental health settings. *Hospital and Community Psychiatry, 29*, 233-237.

Piven, F. F., & Cloward, R. A. (1971). *Regulating the poor: The functions of public welfare.* New York: Random House.

Rauch, J. B. (1975). Women in social work: Friendly visitors in Philadelphia, 1880. *Social Service Review, 49*, 241-259.

Registt, W. (1970). *The occupational culture of policemen and social workers.* Washington, DC: American Psychological Association.

Rose, H. (1983). Hand, brain, and heart: A feminist epistemology for the natural sciences. *Signs: Journal of Women in Culture and Society, 9*, 73-90.

Rosenblatt, A., Turner, E. M., Patterson, A. R., & Rolloson, C. K. (1970). Predominance of male authors in social work publications. *Social Casework, 51*, 421-430.

Ross, E. L. (1978). *Black heritage in social welfare 1860-1930.* Metuchen, NJ: Scarecrow Press.

Rubin, A. (1982a). *Statistics on social work education in the United States, 1981.* New York: Council on Social Work Education.

Rubin, A. (1982b). Why do women occupy lower academic ranks: Discrimination or progress? *Social Work Research and Abstracts, 18*, 19-23.

Rytina, N. F. (1982). Earnings of men and women: A look at specific occupations. *Monthly Labor Review, 105*, 25-30.

Sauber, M. (1965). Social work graduates: Salaries and characteristics. *Personnel Information, 8*, 11-18.

Schoech, D., & Arangio, T. (1979). Computers in the human services. *Social Work, 24*, 96-102.

Scotch, C. G. (1971). Sex status in social work: Grist for women's liberation. *Social Work, 16*, 5-11.

Simpson, R. L., & Simpson, I. H. (1969). Women and bureaucracy in the semi-professions. In A. Etzioni (Ed.), *The semi-professions and their organization* (pp. 196-265). New York: Free Press.

Stamm, A. M. (1968). 1967 social work graduates: Salaries and characteristics. *Personnel Information, 11,* 3-7.

Street, D., Martin, G. T., Jr., & Gordon, L. K. (1979). *The welfare industry: Functionaries and recipients in public aid.* Beverly Hills, CA: Sage.

Szakacs, J. (1977). Survey indicates social work women losing ground in leadership ranks. *NASW News, 22*, 12.

Tuchman, G., & Fortin, N. (1980). Edging women out: Some suggestions about the structure of opportunities and the Victorian novel. *Signs: Journal of Women in Culture and Society, 6*, 308-325.

Tuchman, G., & Fortin, N. (1984). Fame and misfortune: Edging women out of the great literary tradition. *American Journal of Sociology, 90*, 72-96.

U.S. Department of Commerce, Bureau of the Census. (1923). *Fourteenth census of the United States, taken in the year 1920, population 1920. Vol. 4: Occupations* (chap. 2). Washington, DC: Government Printing Office.

U.S. Department of Commerce, Bureau of the Census. (1933). *Fifteenth census of the United States, 1930. Vol. 5: General report on occupations* (chap. 7). Washington, DC: Government Printing Office.

U.S. Department of Commerce, Bureau of the Census. (1943). *Sixteenth census of the United States: 1940. Vol. 3: The labor force* (part 1). Washington, DC: Government Printing Office.

U.S. Department of Commerce, Bureau of the Census. (1956). *U.S. census of population: 1950. Vol. 4: Special reports* (part 1, chap. B). Washington, DC: Government Printing Office.

U.S. Department of Commerce, Bureau of the Census. (1964). *U.S. census of population: 1960. Vol. 1: Characteristics of population* (part 1, chap. D). Washington, DC: Government Printing Office.

U.S. Department of Commerce, Bureau of the Census. (1973). *1970 census of population. Vol. 1: Characteristics of the population* (part 1). Washington, DC: Government Printing Office.

U.S. Department of Commerce, Bureau of the Census. (1982). *1980 census of population. Vol. 1: Characteristics of the population* (chapter D). Washington, DC: Government Printing Office.

U.S. Department of Labor, Bureau of Labor Statistics, Division of Wages and Industrial Relations. (1952). *Social workers in 1950: A report on the study of salaries and working conditions in social work—Spring 1950.* New York: American Association of Social Workers.

U.S. Department of Labor, Bureau of Labor Statistics. (1960). *Salaries and working conditions of social welfare manpower in 1960.* New York: National Social Welfare Assembly.

U.S. Department of Labor, Bureau of Labor Statistics, Division of Wages and Industrial Relations. (1952). *Social workers in 1950: A report on the study of salaries and working conditions in social work—spring 1950.* New York: American Association of Social Workers.

Vandiver, S. T. (1980). A herstory of women in social work. In E. Norman & A. Mancuso (Eds.), *Women's issues and social work practice* (pp. 21-38). Itasca, IL: F. E. Peacock.

Vondracek, F. W., Urban, H. B., & Parsonage, W. H. (1974). Feasibility of an automated intake procedure of human services workers. *Social Service Review, 48,* 271-278.

Wasserman, H. (1971). The professional social worker in a bureaucracy. *Social Work, 16,* 89-96.

Wilensky, H. L., & Lebeaux, C. H. (1958). *Industrial society and social welfare.* New York: Russell Sage.

Williams, M., Ho., L., & Fielder, L. (1974). Career patterns: More grist for women's liberation. *Social Work, 19,* 463-466.

Wolf, W. C., & Fligstein, N. D. (1979). Sexual stratification: Differences in power in the work setting. *Social Forces, 58,* 94-107.

Wright, E. O., Costello, C., Hachen, D., & Sprague, J. (1982). The American class structure. *American Sociological Review, 47,* 709-726.

Wyers, N. L. (1980). Whatever happened to the income maintenance line worker? *Social Work, 25,* 259-263.

Zaretsky, E. (1982). The place of the family in the origins of the welfare state. In B. Thorne (Ed.), *Rethinking the family: Some feminist questions* (pp. 188-224). New York: Longman.

Zimmerman. D. H. (1969). Tasks and troubles: The practical bases of work activities in a public assistance organization. In D. A. Hansen (Ed.), *Explorations in sociology and counseling* (pp. 237-266). Boston: Houghton Mifflin.

CHAPTER 11

Job Satisfaction in the Public Social Services
PERSPECTIVES ON STRUCTURE, SITUATIONAL FACTORS, GENDER, AND ETHNICITY

R. L. McNEELY

The purpose of this chapter is to provide insight about the job satisfaction of those employed currently in the public social services, especially insofar as members of racial minority groups and women are concerned. To achieve this objective, relevant literature is reviewed, beginning with a discussion of how several organizational features common to the public social services are related to workers' job satisfaction levels. Some of the job satisfaction implications of several broad situational factors, such as the continuation of budgetary cutbacks imposed by federal and state authorities, are noted and discussed. Detailed is a multisite study of county welfare workers conducted over a span of several years that serves as the basis for much of the information presented in this chapter. The topic of job satisfaction is not merely important because dissatisfied workers provide inferior services; the health, mental health, and social functioning of these workers can be affected substantially by the level of their job satisfaction (McNeely, 1988a; O'Toole, 1973). Following a review of this chapter, readers should have an improved grasp both of factors affecting the job satisfaction of public welfare workers, and of the nature of satisfaction among these workers.

AUTHOR'S NOTE: The author wishes to express his appreciation to Patricia Yancey Martin for her very helpful review of an earlier version of this chapter.

Job Satisfaction Literature

Organizational Structure

Several conclusions pertinent to this chapter may be drawn following a general review of job satisfaction literature. First, much of the focus of this literature is on private sector (business firms) rather than public sector (governmental) organizations. The distinction is important because different forces drive each organizational type. The dependence of public sector organizations on external sources of funding make such organizations more susceptible to the influence of external entities, increasing possibilities for the establishment of conflicting goals. As they are funded by external sources, public sector organizations also are accountable to these sources, meaning that they are required to submit to periodic evaluations and/or governmental monitoring. Public welfare departments must contend with a variety of governmental levels, for example, county commissions, state legislatures, and Congress, all of which are legally authorized to prescribe departmental policies and procedures.

Reacting to external accountability pressures public sector human service organizations tend to have "rational" internal structures that emphasize centralization of authority, standardization of procedures, and codification of rules (P. Y. Martin, 1980). Some studies of these organizations have found centralized authority and formalization of rules and procedures to be related positively to productivity, defined in terms of quantitative outputs, such as the number of clients served during a specified time frame (Glisson & Martin, 1980; Whetten, 1978).

These same bureaucratic conditions are related to lowered job satisfaction among some public sector human service workers (Bonjean, Brown, Grandjean, & Macken, 1982; McNeely, 1983; Whetten, 1978), however, and to greater apathy with regard to clients, in part because professional staff tend to be divorced from decision making (P. Y. Martin & Segal, 1977).[1] Consequently, while professional human service workers have been found to be more "productive" when operating within rationalistic environments, they also have been found to be less effective in treating clients (cf. Fabricant, 1985; Hage, 1974).

Although a degree of standardization in rules and procedures is desirable (Anderson & Martin, 1982), excessive standardization is ineffective because it constrains professional staff, resulting in stifled creativity and diminished chances for the development of innovations and improved methods. In addition, these conditions are ineffective because they are not conducive to the development of human resources which, in turn, serves to enhance long-term organizational survival, growth, and development (cf. Moore, 1979).

Many human service administrators, nonetheless, can be expected to continue trading effectiveness for accountability,[2] because the capacity to demonstrate productivity in "objective" terms is related to maintaining or increasing funding levels, and procuring new funding sources, which also foster organizational survival and growth (Rogers & Molnar, 1976; Solomon, 1986). Given the responsiveness of administrators to multiple accountability pressures, it should not be surprising that several studies have shown public sector professionals to be less job satisfied than private sector professionals (Cacioppe & Mock, 1984; Perry & Porter, 1982; Solomon, 1986), to experience role blurring due to ambiguities or conflicts in organizational goals and policies (Buchanan, 1974; Erera, 1989), and even to rate their jobs as being significantly lower in skill variety, task significance, and autonomy, than jobs occupied by public sector blue-collar workers (Cherniss & Kane, 1987).

A second conclusion to be gleaned from a review of the general job satisfaction literature is that, despite recent growth, there is a comparative paucity of research focused expressly on the human services stratum of workers. This is unfortunate because human service organizations also are not typical of most workplaces as employees are dealing with "raw materials" (human beings) that have great heterogeneity and complexity, and little is known about the technologies applied to achieve the general mission of these organizations; that is, to bring about affective, behavioral or cognitive changes in clients (Glisson, 1978).

As may be inferred from above, many public sector administrators are likely to encourage standardized methods and procedures regardless of client heterogeneity. Under these conditions practitioners required to treat clients as routine objects are confronted with a conflict between professional values emphasizing discretion and autonomy, and bureaucratic norms emphasizing conformity, even though Glisson (1978) has reported that the more routinized the technologies utilized by an organization, the less likely practitioners are to recognize the heterogeneity of their clients. One interpretation of these findings is that routinized methods tend to promote estrangement of workers from clients, resulting in apathetic orientations toward them (Fabricant, 1985), perhaps as one method to reconcile the conflict between values and norms. As Karger (1981) has noted, such conditions are not merely job dissatisfying for workers, they tend to foster the more profound condition of alienation from one's work.

Not all workers are as adversely affected by routinization (Hackman & Oldham, 1980), and since it reduces uncertainty, some studies have shown high routinization to be related to low role overload (Bacharach, Bamberger, & Conley, 1990). Routinized methods, nonetheless, adversely affect a worker's ability to engage in a variety of tasks, and to assign significance to the tasks being performed. Skill variety and task significance are two of several core job satisfaction fostering dimensions that have been identified by decades of research (cf. Butler, 1990; Hackman & Oldham, 1975).

It is desirable for those seeking prescriptions from the general job satisfaction literature to be cognizant of pressures peculiar to the public human services sector. Taken in sum, information reported on organizational conditions creates a somewhat compelling argument that we need to know as much as we can about the determinants of satisfaction and effectiveness for public human service workers. This same information should provide both a perspective and a framework for reflection and conjecture when human services job satisfaction data reported in later sections of this chapter are considered.

Special Populations

Another compelling argument can be made for the need to know about job satisfaction determinants peculiar to women and members of racial minority groups, given their disproportionately high representation in human service employment. More than 65% of all welfare workers are women, and about 20% are members of minority groups (Dressel, 1987).

Yet a third conclusion to be drawn following a review of the literature on human services job satisfaction is that scant attention has been addressed to issues related to gender, race, and ethnicity, and even within the broader satisfaction literature, insufficient work has been done to answer definitively a number of basic questions including whether or not there are consistent job satisfaction differences between the sexes and among the races.

One finding reported often in the literature is that, compared to European-American men, the job satisfaction of women and members of minority groups is influenced to a greater degree by "extrinsic" factors (Loscocco, 1989; Shapiro, 1977). Extrinsic factors focus on issues that are external to the job itself, such as convenience of working hours and pay and fringe benefit levels. Intrinsic factors, on the other hand, refer to a job's inherent features, such as its capacity to confer to workers a sense of challenge, achievement, responsibility, and accomplishment (Herzberg, 1959).

A second oft-reported finding is that women and minorities evidence comparatively high job satisfaction levels despite being in positions of lower rank, and despite earning less (Bartel, 1981; Hodson, 1989; Weaver, 1978). Third, studies report that men are much more concerned about issues related to positional authority, autonomy, and exercising leadership, whereas women are more concerned about having pleasant interpersonal relationships (Beynon & Blackburn, 1972; Quinn & McCullough, 1974; Shinn, Rosario, Morch, & Chestnut, 1984), the cleanliness of the work environment, the convenience of working hours, and the degree to which job pressures are excessive (J. Miller, 1980), presumably because these pressures intrude upon the more important life sphere of the family (Bass & Barrett, 1972; Rainwater, 1984). Although the gap had decreased markedly by the late 1970s (Veroff, 1978), studies continue to report that men are more likely than women to be committed to their work organizations (Glisson, 1989). Several explanations have been used to account for these differences (cf. de Vaus & McAllister, 1991; Moch, 1980), even though the literature is replete with studies that contradict or reinterpret many of these findings, indicate that differences between the sexes often "wash out" after controlling for specified variables, or emphasize that many gender differences are slight.[3]

One set of explanations focuses on job characteristics. Some authors, for example, suggest that women and minorities tend to devalue intrinsic rewards because such rewards are not readily available to them: The jobs both groups tend to occupy are low-status jobs that provide few if any intrinsic satisfactions (Kalleberg & Griffin, 1978). Other authors argue that women and minorities have the same need for intrinsic satisfaction as do other workers, citing as evidence for this view numerous studies reporting their low job satisfaction levels. Similarly, other features of jobs deemed important in predicting the satisfaction of women and minorities is the extent to which they experience social exclusion on the job, and the extent to which they encounter bias in evaluations and promotions (Andrisani & Shapiro, 1978; Konar, 1981; Moch, 1980).

Worker characteristics such as disparate social class backgrounds and differential socialization prior to entry into the work force also have been used to explain job satisfaction differences (J. Miller, 1980). According to this view, expectations are influenced by awareness of job deprivations experienced typically by one's race and gender counterparts. Thus women and members of minority groups will tend to bring to the job different frames of reference than European-American men, causing them both to expect less from their employment and to be satisfied with less (Brenner & Fernsten, 1984; Varca, Shaffer, & McCauley, 1983).

A third explanation, pertinent to women, focuses on the fact that women have more socially sanctioned choices than men on which to base their identities, causing them to experience the work situation differently than men, and to seek job rewards that are different from those sought by men (Becker, 1985). Whereas men tend to recognize themselves and to be recognized by others exclusively in relation to their on-the-job achievements, women may choose either job or family roles as the basis of their achievements. As many women regard the family role as primary, they will place more emphasis on finding intrinsic fulfillment in family versus work roles, and they will evidence increased concerns about extrinsic on-the-job issues such as the degree to which fellow workers are friendly, whether or not their jobs are convenient, and whether or not job-related pressures and demands intrude upon family responsibilities. This view is consistent with the popular notion that many women work mainly to earn "pin" money for family luxuries that could not be provided by the husband's income, and to provide for themselves social contacts outside of the home.[4] As noted by Loscocco (1990), these ideas are shared widely by managers and employers.

Popular stereotypes tend to posit that factors inherent in gender itself explain differences observed between the sexes. If differences reported between the sexes are due to gender itself, one would expect these differences to be reflected in cross-cultural studies of women regardless of nationality and cultural background. As might be anticipated, the literature is consistent in its inconsistency. For example, whereas some studies of individuals from widely divergent cultures have found consistent differences between women and men, even after controlling for education and employment (Norman et al., 1981/1982), other studies have reported considerable gender variation both within countries and among countries, despite also reporting aggregate differences between the sexes in job satisfaction levels and in factors predictive of job satisfaction (de Vaus & McAllister, 1991).

Taken in sum, deficits and inconsistencies in the literature argue for a need to examine race/ethnicity and gender issues specifically within the human services, and to focus these examinations on those who operate under similar conditions, such as workers employed in the public social services. Use of a uniform methodology with a variety of work sites also is desirable, as some of the discrepant findings reported above undoubtedly are due to the vast array of methodological approaches employed in job satisfaction research. Even among workers within the same field, conditions are likely to vary from site to site, as would be the case where minorities in some welfare departments perceive more intense discrimination than those employed elsewhere. Single-site studies are less capable of examining these sorts of differences, again leading to the reporting of discrepant findings.

An additional concern with regard to women and minorities is related to the fact that, along with immigrants, they constitute the fastest growing segment of a shrinking U.S. labor force (Johnston & Packer, 1987). Women and minorities also constitute a disproportionate share of clients receiving public welfare services. Although some question it (Sullivan, 1989), these demographic realities forecast increasing pressure in the human services for the promotion of women and minorities into positions of prominence and leadership. Presently, women and minorities, particularly African-American women, are exceedingly more likely than other employees to occupy the lowest-ranking positions in public welfare work (Dressel, 1987; P. Y. Martin & Chernesky, 1989). Less clear is the extent to which race and gender differences in rank and income can be explained by factors such as education, length of employment, and so forth. Data presented subsequently in this chapter shed light on this issue.

Work Satisfaction: The Broader Context

A final conclusion derived after reviewing the job satisfaction literature is that the vast majority of studies are based on the presumption that satisfaction is a relatively static phenomenon. Most job satisfaction studies report data that amount to "snapshots" in time, ignoring the possible relevance of historical or contemporary influences. Yet, broad forces operating in the economy or in the society can exert considerable influence both on the nature and level of one's job satisfaction (Kalleberg, 1977). This point is particularly pertinent to the public social services, as events taking place over the past decade have had a rather substantial effect on the workplace conditions of those so engaged.

Recent efforts to trim federal funding for human service programs, for example, have exacerbated pressures normally imposed on public welfare workers (cf. Demone & Gibelman, 1984). Between 1980 and 1987 staff of these programs suffered through the effects of more than 60 billion dollars in federal funding cuts initiated by the Reagan administration's retrenchments in services to the poor (Ansberry, 1987). Unforeseeable in the immediate future is any substantive restoration of federal funding (cf. Hasenfeld, 1984) despite increasing recognition within the Bush administration that cutbacks in poverty programs have resulted in rapid social deterioration (DeParle & Applebome, 1991).

Consequently, there is likely to be little abatement any time soon in the austere working conditions experienced by those employed in public social services.

Typical outcomes resulting from budgetary cutbacks have included reduced job security as well as reductions in promotional opportunities, salaries, and in educational travel and subsidies. Shrinking budgets have forced many public human service departments to curtail the breadth of services offered and to achieve reductions in staff through hiring freezes, layoffs, and terminations. Staff reductions often have been accompanied by constricted career opportunities because of the elimination of upper echelon jobs due to funding cuts; in some cases workers occupying the higher occupational ranks in human service agencies have been demoted to lesser positions because of cuts. Demotions, layoffs, and terminations tend to inspire concerns about job security, adding to the morale problems of workers.

The impact of cutbacks have been more pronounced in some states than in others. Sudden tax revenue shortfalls in some "Rust Bowl," midwestern states, for example, eliminated possibilities for the allocation of additional state funds to cushion the impact of trimmed federal budgets. In some cases human services employees were laid off or terminated to bring state budgets into line with sobering tax revenue realities. Indeed, menacing economic conditions resulting in plant shutdowns meant that the number of needy individuals requesting social services increased markedly at the same time the number of staff providing these services was decreasing (cf. Demone & Gibelman, 1984, p. 422).

Higher caseloads do not merely limit the ability of human service workers to provide individualized intervention in accordance with the standards of their training, the ability even to provide therapeutic services is threatened, and workers are required to spend much more of their time filling out paperwork (Fabricant, 1985). Thus another outcome of shrinking budgets has been an increase in routinized procedures for handling clients (Hasenfeld, 1984), making the jobs workers perform more mundane and boring. This problem is compounded by narrowed promotional opportunities, which force many workers to remain for years in jobs they have thoroughly mastered that no longer provide intellectual stimulation. The problem is compounded further by administrators who, following conventional ideas about effective leadership during budget retrenchment periods, tend to react by increasing hierarchical control, defining power and authority more clearly, and by instituting "rational" choice techniques, none of which are likely to take into account the working conditions of staff, and all of which are likely to affect adversely the quality of worklife experienced by the staff (Bombyk & Chernesky, 1985).

Finally, the public image of the social work profession has plummeted so low as to have elicited front-page coverage in a recent edition of *The Wall Street Journal,* in which the point was made that in contrast to the Great Society era, during which social work had a generally higher standing as the professional leader in the War Against Poverty, the image of contemporary social workers has eroded to the point of public disparagement (Ansberry, 1987). Accordingly, it has been reported that in some geographical areas the salaries social workers earn lag behind even those of office clerks (Ansberry, 1987). Both factors are related to job satisfaction, although some studies of human service workers indicate that extrinsic factors such as income and fringe benefits are more salient in predicting the job satisfaction of women than men (McNeely, 1984), and other studies indicate that the degree to which one's occupation (Hawkes et al., 1984b) or place of employment (Gold et al., 1982) is held in high public esteem is most salient in affecting the satisfaction of minority workers.

A variety of questions are raised by conditions described above. Some of these include the following:

(1) Is there a relationship between the extent of budget cuts experienced by public welfare departments and the job satisfaction levels of public welfare workers?
(2) Do factors associated with job satisfaction change during budget retrenchment periods?
(3) Are any factors associated with job satisfaction among public welfare workers related peculiarly to race/ethnicity or gender?
(4) Are rank and income differences related to race and gender explained by factors such as education and length of employment?

Much of the information presented subsequently in this chapter is based on a multisite study conducted over a span of several years. Because it is the foundation for much of what is reported, a brief description follows.

Method and Purpose of the Study

Driven by the wish to know more about the job satisfaction of workers employed in public social services, an ongoing multisite study involving county human service departments located in geographically disparate areas of the nation was begun in 1979. Data were collected from six county welfare departments. Longitudinal data were collected during 1979 and 1981 from Racine County (Racine, WI); retrospective data for 1977 also were collected from this county in 1979. Data were collected in 1983 from Dade County (Miami, FL), in 1984 from Genesee (Flint, MI) and Sacramento (Sacramento, CA) Counties, in 1986 from El Paso County (Colorado Springs, CO) and in 1987 from Fulton County (Atlanta, GA). A mail survey was used to collect information. The study generated 2,198 returned usable questionnaires. The response rate was 52.2%.

Demographic information was solicited focusing upon race, gender, age, length of employment, education, occupational status, and annual earnings before taxes. An instrument designed to yield information on respondents' attitudes about specific working conditions was imbedded into the questionnaire, and two measures of job satisfaction also were included.

The Science Research Associates Attitudes Survey (SRA) was used to capture the attitudes of respondents about a wide range of working conditions including, but not limited to, job dullness/monotony, supervisory and managerial fairness, adequacy of fringe benefits, fairness of pay and promotions, excessiveness of workloads, and so forth (cf. D. C. Miller, 1977). The Index of Job Satisfaction (IJS) focuses upon subjective assessments that yield a measure of overall job satisfaction (cf. D. C. Miller, 1977). The four-item intrinsic satisfaction subscale (MI) of the Morse Index (cf. D. C. Miller, 1977) was used to determine intrinsic satisfaction levels.

Individuals participating in the study also were able to provide additional information by penning extemporaneous comments onto the reverse side of the questionnaire's final page. An analysis of those comments was performed to yield a rank ordering of the concerns expressed. More detailed accounts of the study's methodology may be found elsewhere (cf. McNeely, 1988a).

Gender

Job Satisfaction

Although one publication emerging from this study reported that female human service workers were significantly more satisfied than males (McNeely, 1984), it was based on an analysis of data from a single site. Findings generated by an examination of the study's six sites indicate no consistent differences between the sexes on either overall or intrinsic job satisfaction levels. These discrepant findings (as well as discrepant findings and reversals in findings reported below) have implications that will be commented upon in the Concluding Remarks section of this chapter.

The satisfaction of human service workers, like that of other workers (Doering, Rhodes, & Schuster, 1983), increases with age (McNeely, 1988a). Both older women and older men were significantly more satisfied than younger workers. Presuming the data reflect career cycle changes rather than differences among generations of workers, young human service workers can expect increased satisfaction as they look to the decades ahead.

Job Dullness/Monotony

A consistent finding is the salience for both women and men, of job dullness/monotony, in predicting satisfaction. When multisite analyses were performed this predictor generally emerged as the single best predictor of satisfaction for both sexes, regardless of age, occupational rank, or income. These findings are similar to those reported following a national study of human service workers conducted by Jayaratne and Chess (1983; 1982/1983), in which job challenge was the best predictor of satisfaction both for men and women. In light of these findings, the reader may wish to contemplate pressures for human service departments to adopt highly routinized methods and procedures, previously discussed, and likely long-term effects on workers of such routinization.

Use of Abilities

Another rather consistent finding is the comparative importance, in predicting women's satisfaction, of the extent to which jobs provide workers with opportunities to use their abilities. Data generated by the study indicate this predictor to be much more pervasive across occupational categories among women, with dissatisfied women, regardless of rank, being significantly more likely than men to report that "I have little opportunity to use my abilities in this organization." Other studies examining women two to three decades ago have documented the importance of skill underutilization in predicting their satisfaction (cf. Andrisani & Shapiro, 1978). Speaking particularly in regard to the human services, authors of recent studies have suggested that, despite proper training, sexism militates against the placement of women into managerial positions, and maintains their exclusion from important informal networks (Kravetz & Austin, 1984).

Speaking more broadly, J. Miller (1980) offers an additional explanation. With no reference to discrimination, she found that men, more than women, tend to be placed in jobs that are compatible with the skills they possess. To some extent this is due to the fact that women, particularly European-American women, are more likely to have punctuated work histories, and to engage in voluntary part-time work (cf. Nardone, 1986). Both tendencies militate against opportunities for promotion and, particularly for college-educated women, placement into jobs that are commensurate with their academic qualifications, resulting in a poorer "fit" among women between the skills they possess and the tasks required by their jobs.

Excessive Pressure/Excessive Expectations

Examined in the aggregate, the satisfaction of female human service workers was affected much more than male satisfaction by perceptions of excessive on-the-job pressure (working hours, office cleanliness, degree to which jobs are tiring, etc.), and of job performance expectations being excessive. Subsequent analyses revealed that concerns about job pressures and performance expectations were most salient for middle-aged (30-54 yrs.) women. Since middle-aged women were affected more strongly than other women by these factors, it was assumed that they constituted the subset of women most likely to be experiencing work-family conflict due to child rearing and other life cycle changes.[5]

At some sites, however, the strength of these predictors were most strongly tied to the satisfaction of female administrators and supervisors, whereas at other sites they were tied most strongly to the satisfaction of female paraprofessionals. If work-family conflict is the most compelling explanation, one would expect professional/managerial women to be consistently less likely than more poorly paid women to report excessive pressure associated with work/family conflicts, due to the greater access of these women to child care and other resources that foster smoother interfacing of work and family roles (Burris, 1991). As this was not the case, perhaps a better explanation is that there are situational factors associated with the different sites that account for the inconsistencies observed in the study.

Whatever the explanation, data obtained for the study indicate a clear gender discrepancy, with female satisfaction, regardless of occupational status, being affected far more than male satisfaction by perceptions of excessive pressure/expectations. These findings are consistent with those reported by Jayaratne and Chess (1983) for human service workers, and by J. Miller's (1980) examination of women more representative of the nation.

Supervisors, Managers, and Promotional Opportunities

One report emerging from this study indicated that male satisfaction was affected more than female satisfaction by perceptions of their administrative superiors (McNeely, 1984). An examination of data obtained from all of the study's sites, however, indicates no clear gender differences in the importance of these perceptions. Perceptions about competence, fairness, the concern of superiors for subordinates, and the willingness, particularly by executives, to communicate with staff, and so forth, were important for both sexes. Men, on the other hand, do appear to be more affected than women by the closeness of supervision they experience, the extent to which they perceive promotional opportunities, and by whether or not they have the ability to exercise judgment on the job. These findings are very consistent with J. Miller's (1980) report that men are much more satisfied when in decision-making jobs of positional authority allowing the exercise of leadership. Whether or not supervision was so "close" as to militate against autonomy (use of initiative, thought, and independent judgment) was very central in predicting male satisfaction, whereas the quality of supervisory exchanges was much more important to women.

Pay and Fringe Benefits

Examined in the aggregate, *concerns* about income and fringe benefits were more salient predictors of women's satisfaction. Among women, however, the importance of these predictors diminished as occupational rank increased, and they were most strongly associated with the satisfaction levels of younger females (less than 30 yrs.). These findings appear to support the notion, discussed above, that the job characteristics of women (and minority groups) encourage greater focus on extrinsic factors, as low ranking women and younger women tend to earn less than other workers. Nonetheless, the absolute importance of concerns about pay issues was quite weak, and *actual* income differences among respondents were not predictive of their satisfaction levels (McNeely, 1988c).

Other Factors

African-American women were the most satisfied, both on overall and intrinsic satisfaction, followed respectively by Hispanic- and European-American women. As reported by other studies documenting racial differences among female human service workers (Wright, Wesley-King, & Berg, 1985), married European-American women were more job-satisfied than other European-American women, but marital status was not predictive of satisfaction either for African Americans or Hispanics (McNeely, 1987b).

When rank and income were examined, women were found to earn less and be disproportionately placed in lower status positions, even when educational background and employment longevity were taken into account. In some cases such discrepancies are slight, however, as occurred when an examination was restricted to human service workers who were at least 40 years of age. The study revealed that only 2% of the variance in income among these workers was accounted for by gender (McNeely, 1989a).

Finally, differences observed between the sexes diminish when examinations are restricted to those of high occupational rank. Males and females occupying these positions (administrators, supervisors) appear to become similar in the extent to which their satisfaction is predicted by perceptions of executive managerial competence, fairness, ability to facilitate "smooth running" of the organization, and so forth.

Race/Ethnicity

African Americans

Examined in the aggregate, African-American human service workers were significantly more satisfied than European-American workers, both on overall and intrinsic satisfaction, regardless of occupational rank (McNeely, 1989a). Subsequent analyses indicated that racial differences in satisfaction levels were attributable to the county locations within which respondents were employed, rather than to the race of the respondents, with satisfaction between the races within the human service departments being patterned very differently. Efforts to interpret these findings suggested that situational factors peculiar to the various employment sites offered the most reasonable explanations.

One explanation focuses upon the degree to which respondents perceived that they had been victimized by racism within their departments. The least satisfied African Americans, for example, were located in a site within which significant racial strife had occurred recently regarding layoffs, with minority employees feeling that they had been targeted unfairly.

A second explanation is consistent with H. Fox and Lefkowitz's (1974) suggestion that some race-linked job satisfaction differences may be related to the racial status of those in chief executive roles, given reports that minority employees experience more stress in organizations that are run by European Americans (Bush, 1977). Thus it should not be surprising that the present study of human service workers found African Americans employed in departments headed by African Americans to be significantly more satisfied than other African-American workers. In contrast, *the satisfaction of European Americans* appeared unrelated to the racial status of the executive director. The pattern of their satisfaction *corresponded perfectly to the degree to which their employment sites had experienced funding cuts, with those in departments experiencing the harshest cuts being the most dissatisfied* (McNeely, 1988d).

Although similar to other workers in the importance of job dullness as a predictor of satisfaction, the satisfaction of African Americans (particularly females) was predicted strongly by the degree to which they felt affiliated with their work organizations. Similarly, the degree to which superiors solicited their input and made it evident that the input was valued tended to be stronger predictors for African Americans than for other employees. These findings are quite consistent with those of other studies, indicating that African Americans experiencing workplace social exclusion from other races report less satisfaction. Specifically, African Americans who find themselves in segregated work groups are less satisfied (Moch, 1980), although Konar (1981) suggests that factors responsible for the segregation (i.e., on-the-job discrimination), rather than the physical segregation itself, is the most likely explanation for depressed satisfaction levels. African Americans who provide accounts of work experience have emphasized repeatedly the adverse effects of race-linked isolation on the job (E. Jones, 1973), and race-linked exclusion from informal social groups that fraternize and network away from the office (Taylor, 1982).

Both males and females were affected substantially by their perception of the fairness of promotional patterns, and the extent to which they felt jobs would be available for them to fulfill career aspirations.

Taken in sum, the factors identified thus far (e.g., organizational strife related to race, "belongingness" to the organization, promotional fairness) *suggest the salience of perceived discrimination as key in predicting the satisfaction of African Americans.* Other robust predictors are consistent with literature previously reviewed: The satisfaction of African-American females was predicted strongly by whether or not they regarded job expectations as being excessive, and male satisfaction was predicted strongly by the degree to which they felt able to exercise judgment.

Contrary to much of the job satisfaction literature (a great deal of which is based on individual examinations of single sites that cannot determine differences *among* sites), these findings suggest that factors associated with individual workplaces may be more salient in determining satisfaction levels than are other factors, such as the bringing to the job of different frames of reference.

African-American human service workers earned less than European-American workers, even when occupational status, education, and length of employment were taken into account. Among all human service workers, African-American and other minority women are the most poorly paid and they experience disproportional representation in lesser status positions, even when years of schooling and employment tenure are controlled.

Asian Americans

Following a review that revealed no references to Asian Americans in the human services job satisfaction literature, the author of this chapter was prompted to disaggregate his sample so that Asian Americans could be examined (McNeely, 1987a). Unfortunately, the limited number ($N = 68$) of Asians in the study group did not permit separate analyses for ethnicity: Separate examinations of Chinese, Japanese, Koreans, and others might have revealed important intergroup differences.

Results indicated no significant differences in the job satisfaction levels of Asian-American workers compared to other workers.[6] The pattern of variables that were predictive of satisfaction, however, were different. *The single best predictor for Asians, a variable that was virtually unrelated to the satisfaction of other workers, was whether or not they perceived that "Most of the 'higher-ups' are friendly toward employees."* This finding mirrors other research conducted on Asians (native Asians *and* Asian Americans) wherein it has been reported that Asian cultural values (particularly Japanese values) lead these workers to expect, value, and be more job satisfied when there are paternalistic personal ties between superiors and subordinates (Cole, 1979; Lincoln, Hanada,

& Olson, 1981). Unlike other workers, personal ties and job satisfaction increase for these workers as hierarchical differentiation (tall status hierarchies) and organizational size increase. As noted by Lincoln et al. (1981), these findings have important implications for commonly held Western assumptions that tend to emphasize the universal desirability of "egalitarian" (horizontally differentiated) organizational forms.[7]

Similar to other human service workers, the satisfaction of Asian Americans was predicted strongly by whether or not they perceived their jobs as being dull and monotonous, and whether or not they felt able to use their abilities on the jobs. These workers, however, were less affected by perceptions of excessive pressure and expectations, a finding consistent with that of other studies reporting some Asian groups to prefer superiors who make heavy demands so long as these superiors evidence personal interest in employees (Marsh & Mannari, 1976, p. 194). Other findings indicated that Asian Americans both earned less and were represented disproportionately in nonprofessional human services positions despite having attained more years of schooling than their non-Asian counterparts, and despite having lengthier employment tenure. These findings are consistent with national norms, however, wherein Asian Americans have higher educational attainment, lengthier service to the employer, work more hours per week, work more weeks per year, yet still earn less than European Americans (Sandefur & Pahari, 1989; Takaki, 1985).

Hispanic Americans

Another group about which little is known in the human services is Hispanic Americans. Unlike Asian Americans, a sample of Hispanics ($N = 124$) composed of roughly equal percentages of Cuban- and Mexican- Americans were found to have significantly higher job satisfaction levels than non-Hispanics, both on overall and intrinsic satisfaction (McNeely, 1989b). In their study of Hispanic workers, Hawkes et al. (1984b) reported that in contrast to the average European American who measures his or her status primarily in terms of attained or potential income, the job satisfaction of Hispanics is predicted far more strongly by the degree to which an occupation is held in high esteem, regardless of job income. Noted as a dramatic finding, they reported that job satisfaction was highest among Hispanics when occupational status was high and income low, indicating that occupational status rather than income status is the most highly regarded prestige dimension among these workers (Hawkes et al., 1984b, p. 386). Within Hispanic communities, having full-time nonseasonal employment with fringe benefits in a relatively clean professional setting may be more likely to generate respect, perhaps accounting for the high satisfaction levels of Hispanic employees engaged in comparatively low paying public welfare work.

Similar trends were observed in the pattern of variables predictive of satisfaction for Hispanics and non-Hispanics. Both groups were affected most substantially by perceptions of job dullness/monotony, they both were influenced by assessments of the extent to which they were able to use their abilities on the job, and both were affected by perceptions of on-the-job pressure. Compared to non-Hispanics, Hispanic satisfaction was influenced to a greater degree by perceptions of managerial competence, whereas satisfaction among non-Hispanics was predicted more strongly by the extent to which these respondents felt affiliated with their workplaces.

The most discrepant findings when comparisons were made between the two groups were observed for upper-echelon (administrative, supervisory, professional) Hispanic and non-Hispanic females. Whereas predictors of satisfaction for non-Hispanic women conformed generally to the patterns reported within this chapter, the satisfaction of upper-echelon Hispanic women was affected most by whether or not their supervisors were able to get employees to work together as a team, and whether or not they felt free to talk with superiors when they had complaints (McNeely, 1987b).

The relationship to job satisfaction of these variables for similarly employed African- and European-American female workers was quite low, suggesting that Hispanic women may be a distinctive subgroup of the larger group of females occupying professional, supervisory, and administrative positions. Alternatively, these findings may be due to an artifact of the sample that appears to be consistent with national norms in public welfare work. Among high echelon women, Hispanics had served the fewest years within their departments. McIlwee (1982) has shown that female newcomers in nontraditional positions (in this case professional and higher positions) are especially appreciative of co-worker cooperation. Thus executive directors are urged to consider the historical representation within their departments of minority employees in high echelon positions.

As was the case with other minority groups, Hispanics were disproportionately placed in positions of low rank, and earned less than non-Hispanics. However, after controlling for education, occupational rank, and length of employment, statistically significant income differences applied primarily to those who were more highly educated and most recently employed; that is, the greatest income discrepancies between

Hispanics and their European-American counterparts were experienced by recently employed professional Hispanics (McNeely, 1989b).

Race, Gender, Earnings, and Occupational Rank

As noted previously, differences in income by race and gender are evident in the public social services. Table 11.1 indicates that European-American males earn the highest incomes. Whereas African-American males report the next highest income level, the standard deviation for this group is larger than that of any other group, suggesting that while some of these individuals are faring quite well, others are faring quite poorly. Although the table does not report data disaggregated for education, length of employment, and occupational rank, significant income discrepancies remain even when these variables are taken into account, and patterns evident in the table remain the same (McNeely, Blakemore, & Washington, in press). Male European Americans occupied 40% of all administrative positions, and 21% of all supervisory positions, even though they comprised only 15.7% of the sample.[8] Both European-American males and females were more likely than their same-sex counterparts to hold jobs of high rank, and African American males were less likely than either European- American or Other males to hold high ranking jobs. Those experiencing the harshest conditions in public welfare work are African American and Other women. They earned the least, and were least likely to occupy professional or higher status positions, even when education and employment length were controlled (observed differences significant at $P < .002$ or less, for all employee groups stratified by education/employment length).

Situational and Other Factors

The extemporaneous comments of human service workers also were examined. One finding emerging from this portion of the study was that complaints increased by an average of 250% following the onset of federal funding cuts. Another observation was that workers at the sites least affected by the funding cuts expressed the fewest complaints. Third, *perceptions that job expectations were excessive became both more pronounced and more pervasive across occupational categories following the enactment of cuts,* and the importance of these perceptions in predicting

Table 11.1 Race, Gender and Income[a](All Occupational Groups)

Population Group	N	$\bar{x}$	Sd	Scheffe Contrasts[b]	F-value	Sig. of F-value
Entire Sample	1914[c]					
1. Afro-American females	435	20143	6305.7			
2. Afro-American males	75	24278	10142.3	1,5		
3. Euro-American females	870	22673[d]	6363.6	1,5	46.01	< .001
4. Euro-American males	302	27356	8827.3	1,2,3,5,6		
5. Other females	160	19686	6527.9			
6. Other males	72	21124	5857.6			

NOTES: a. Reported income figures are based on computations converting grouped data into dollar figures according to Blalock's recommended procedure (Blalock, 1960, pp. 50-53). Dollar figures are presented merely to aid readers in interpreting data. F-tests and Scheffe contrasts are based on analyses of grouped data. Thus the procedure utilized yielded the most conservative estimates of income differences.
b. Scheffe contrasts (Kachigan, 1986, p. 315) denote pairs of groups significantly different at $p \leq$ .05. For example, the numbers "1" and "5" are reported for African-American males. This indicates that the mean income of these males is significantly different than that of groups 1 (African-American females) and 5 (Other females).
c. Excludes Racine County employees for whom income data were not collected.
d. The earnings data reported in Table 11.1 understate the true income of European-American females as a much higher percentage of these workers, compared to other workers, were employed voluntarily in part-time jobs.

male satisfaction increased. Also, both men and women became more concerned about job security issues, *suggesting* not only *that factors associated with work satisfaction are influenced by budgetary retrenchment,* but that predictors of satisfaction become more similar for males and females under these conditions.

Sites were rank ordered according to the degree to which they had been affected by budget reductions. Aggregate job satisfaction levels corresponded perfectly to the ranking, with the most satisfied workers being employed in the least affected sites, and the most dissatisfied workers being employed at the sites affected most harshly by the cuts (McNeely, 1988d).

These findings suggest that broad situational factors, such as the current era of budgetary retrenchment, may be affecting adversely the satisfaction of human service workers. Such a conclusion, however, must be regarded with caution. As the study was not a laboratory experiment, no examination of the "pure" effects of retrenchment could be undertaken, and it is possible that factors other than funding levels could explain the observations reported in the preceding paragraph.

Images of the adverse "dust and smoke" conditions under which some contemporary public human service workers are operating were derived most clearly from the examination of their written comments.

In descending order, these comments focused upon: Concerns about management; work overloads; favoritism and/or discrimination in promotions or layoffs; inadequate pay, incentives, and perks; and poor environmental working conditions, including faulty equipment.

Concerns About Management

The most common expressions of discontent regarding management focused on managerial "remoteness" from line workers, managerial failure to solicit decision-making input from workers, perceptions that administrators appear to be concerned only about their own advancement, and perceptions that administrators lacked imagination, sympathy for employees experiencing problems, and competence. The most common complaint was expressed by the following comment: "Wouldn't it be wonderful if bosses asked our opinion, after all we deal with our problems all of the time and know better how to get results."

Work Overloads

The most upsetting work overload reported by respondents focused upon paperwork demands.[9] In the words of a 42-year-old female social service worker, "There are times when the paperwork makes me want to scream." Complaints about surging caseloads constituted the next most frequently reported source of concern about overloads, particularly in situations where managerial expectations of workers were not modified as caseloads increased.

Favoritism/Discrimination:
Concerns About Promotions

Surprisingly, there were virtually no remarks about discrimination or sexual harassment against women. Tensions associated with promotions and layoff policies perceived as being racially discriminatory, instead, were reported frequently ("The county has consistently eliminated jobs designed especially to help minority clients"), followed by complaints made by European-American males that female and minority employees were benefiting unfairly from affirmative action policies ("White males are never going to be promoted again . . . They are becoming an acceptable target without any legal rights"). Particularly galling for many employees, regardless of sex, were declining opportunities for advancement, as noted by one respondent:

There is no career ladder to speak of. Recently our bureau chief told us two positions had "disappeared." Apparently they were lost, like someone loses a wallet. (Female social services worker, 39 yrs. of age)

Inadequate Pay, Incentives, and Perks

A rather pervasive perception among all but those in the highest positions is that pay levels are too low, particularly given the amount of work that must be performed. Six respondents suggested the need for comparable worth policies to address pay equity issues for women regarded as occupationally segregated, such as eligibility workers. Other concerns focused upon the absence of financial or other incentives for meritorious work, and privileges associated with status differentials ("Top management parks next to the building"). Supervisors appeared particularly affected when their efforts were not verbally praised by superiors, although an analysis revealed that complaints about not being regarded as valuable employees and of not being given financial or honorific rewards increased as employees became more administratively distant from top management. Some workers commented on their inability to derive feelings of pride in their work because of public attitudes.

Poor Environmental Working Conditions

A good deal of irritation was expressed about computer incompatibility, deficient computer programs, and inadequate operator training. Substantial distaste was expressed by employees working in office modules as opposed to offices with floor-to-ceiling walls. Many female employees expressed concerns about having to walk unaccompanied after normal working hours to distantly located parking facilities situated in dangerous areas, of having to share rest room facilities with clients—"many of whom are ill"—and of the desirability to have internal facilities for lunch and break periods in order to avoid walking in dangerous neighborhoods. Child protective service workers, in particular, expressed fears about having to make dangerous client contacts without adequate back-up. Additionally, complaints about poor ventilation, overcrowding, poor lighting, and of offices decorated with orange-colored walls or motifs of "gas chamber green," were common. One eligibility worker commented: "The OSHA inspector said this is the type of building that's marginal . . . but he was only here two hours, and my supervisor had to get him medication for his headache before he left." A data coding operator suggested: "We need proper pens that don't dribble ink all over government forms."

Concluding Remarks

Not captured in the comments above is the fact that many human service workers, despite the variety of problems they encounter, truly enjoy their jobs, feeling that they are both challenging and rewarding while allowing them to do something of genuine value for other people. An office manager noted: "My job is very fulfilling, especially during the busy periods." An eligibility worker indicated: "All we really need is to be respected and supported and understood by management! When this is done, difficult clients become a challenge, and the job is O.K." As is the case in any employment setting, the morale of those less satisfied can be improved by instituting effective policies and programs (cf. McNeely, 1988b; McNeely & Fogarty, 1988), and job satisfaction may be restored following budget cuts in a relatively short period (McNeely, Feyerherm, & Johnson, 1986).

Regardless of race or gender, a key morale enhancing factor that hopefully has been evident throughout this discussion is the opportunity for workers to participate meaningfully in decision making, or at least have their input seriously considered. In itself this can help to address the boredom that appears to be pervasive among human service employees who are dissatisfied. On this point it should be noted that although participation in decision making conveys to workers a sense that their opinions and, therefore, they are of value to the organization, a particular form of participation is associated with the performance of high quality work. Workers allowed discretion in the execution of *their* jobs are more likely than those participating in policy development to perform high quality work (Whiddon & Martin, 1989).

Also hopefully evident is the importance of situational factors—factors peculiar to the sites within which workers are employed—in predicting satisfaction. Efforts to address factors peculiar to a worksite may be more important in raising morale than other efforts focused on factors that characterize the race or gender groups in the aggregate, although executives certainly must be sensitive to any influences that appear to be generally common to the race and gender groups. At the same time it is important to recognize that findings reported for aggregated groups of workers, even when restricted to specific race and gender subgroups, mask important individual differences in motivation and life-cycle changes.

It is also important to consider an implication of the numerous contradictions and reversals in findings reported previously. To some extent these reversals and contradictions are due to the variety of noncomparable instruments and methods used by different researchers examining job satisfaction. But they are also due to numerous factors which often vary in unknown ways across different sampling frames. For example, J. Martin and Hanson (1985) have shown that primary wage-earning women are more concerned about extrinsic rewards, whereas secondary earners are more concerned about intrinsic satisfaction, more likely to seek out jobs that provide comfort and convenience, and inclined to eschew jobs high in material rewards (cf. J. Martin & Shehan, 1989). Sampling frames composed disproportionately of one of these groups, therefore, will generate findings that contradict those obtained from a sample with disproportionate representation from the other group.

Although these comments may help in countenancing the many contradictions and reversals found in the work satisfaction literature, of greater importance is their implication for those who steward the public social services. The implication is that *effective administrators will not need merely to be knowledgeable of conditions peculiar to their particular organizations, and factors associated broadly with the aggregated race and gender groups, they also will need to be sensitive to differences in the motivational characteristics and life-cycle stages of individuals.*

Such sensitivity enables executives and others seeking to improve satisfaction both to recognize and appropriately act upon the needs of individual workers as those needs unfold and change over time. Among other things this means that workers need to be provided with choices within the organization in the conditions of their employment. As noted by one respondent:

> I work $\frac{1}{2}$ time so I enjoy my job more because of this. I was working full-time until one month ago. I appreciate the fact that I was allowed to work $\frac{1}{2}$ time although it took me 3 months to convert. (Female welfare eligibility worker, 28 years of age.)

Organizations that do not allow for part-time employment possibilities, job sharing, flexible scheduling, and so forth, are not likely to be regarded as positively as those that do.

Finally, executives and others wishing to improve satisfaction must be aware that restoring and maintaining satisfaction requires recurring efforts; such efforts should be regarded as a dynamic rather than static process.

Our previous discussion about the effect of powerful external forces in influencing executives to make the most "rational" decisions might lead one to conclude that the above is unlikely to occur. However, an optimistic point regarding the tendencies of administrators is that interest is growing within the general population about quality work life and workplace democracy concerns which, in turn, is generating increasing pressure for greater executive sensitivity to job satisfaction issues. This is particularly so in that a growing body of literature supports the effectiveness (assessed in terms of performance, quality, cost efficiency, productivity, etc.) of implementing quality-work-life initiatives. In addition, the extent to which forecasts predicting increased future competition for highly trained workers are accurate for the human services also will bear on administrative receptiveness. Organizations with job-satisfied workers will be better positioned to attract and retain desirable employees.

Employees are the most important resource of human service agencies (cf. Hasenfeld, 1984). The coming relative shortage of young workers (compared to the late 1970s, a 26% decrease in the number of high school graduates is forecasted for the early 1990s) will soon create increased competition for employees and increased difficulty in retaining experienced staff (Lawlor, 1991). Additionally, increases in the number of two-earner families participating in the work force will generate increased pressure from both working spouses for part-time work, innovative child-care arrangements, job sharing, flexible scheduling, and other quality-work-life programs. As has been the case in other countries confronted with an increasing percentage of women participating in a declining pool of labor, American employers will become more receptive to the implementation of innovations (cf. Foy & Gordon, 1976). They are likely to have few other rational choices.

Notes

1. Despite survey evidence (Whiddon & Martin, 1989) indicating that professional human service workers desire more participative decision making (PDM), and studies indicating that PDM is related to increased performance and other positive organizational outcomes (Daly, 1990; Greenberger & Strasser, 1986; Malka, 1989; Packard, 1989),

PDM can be associated with role conflict and role overload (Bacharach, Bamberger, & Conley, 1990), and increased organizational tension (Austin, 1989). In addition, not all forms of PDM are related to positive organizational outcomes (Cotton, Vollrath, Lengnick-Hall, & Froggatt, 1988; Leana, Locke, & Schweiger, 1990), and similar to many other motivational strategies, PDM is likely to be most effective among employees with high growth needs (cf. Hackman & Oldham, 1980).

2. Confronted with a policy proposal that permits participative decision making which, if implemented, is likely to enhance staff development and long-term organizational well-being, a human service executive will recognize that sanctioning the policy may have the effect of absorbing staff time that otherwise could be deployed to the generation of accountability-related quantitative outputs, such as "numbers of clients served." As this arguably is the executive's "rational" choice, it explains the observation of an astonished investigator who reported that: "One striking finding concerns the actual managerial behavior in the human service agencies. Contrary to widespread belief, participatory management is not practiced in most of the (thirty) organizations in our study" (Malka, 1989, p. 61).

3. These studies indicate, for example, no significant job satisfaction differences between men and women when intervening variables such as education, occupational status, and organizational context are controlled, that women are not less committed than men to their work organizations, that women (particularly when wage-earning status is taken into account) and minorities are not less "intrinsically" oriented, that both groups are *less* job satisfied than Caucasian men, in part due to discrimination, and that many of the gender- or race-related differences reported in the literature do not constitute meaningful differences (Gold, Webb, & Smith, 1982; A. P. Jones, 1977; Loscocco, 1990; Loscocco & Spitze, 1991; J. Martin & Shehan, 1989; O'Reilly & Roberts, 1973; Sauser & York, 1978; Voydanoff, 1980).

4. Despite women's increasing labor force participation and demands by women for equal opportunities and pay occurring during the 1970s, widely disseminated information, such as a 1980 Roper Organization survey, has reinforced these notions. The survey indicated that 58% of working women reported they were employed in order to bring in extra money, to have something interesting to do, or that they did not know why they were working (M. F. Fox & Hesse-Biber, 1984).

5. For example, a younger middle-aged woman is likely to be engaged in balancing work and family (especially child rearing) demands, whereas an older middle-aged woman may be confronted simultaneously with children leaving the nest, parental caretaking, the death or imminent death of a parent, the onset of menopause, and with a husband experiencing mid-career crisis. *An important implication to this point is that what workers need and expect from their jobs does not remain constant over the life cycle.* Life-cycle events confronting workers shift personal priorities, causing changes in needs and expectations, and attitudinal changes occurring over the course of a life span also spawn differences in what workers wish to derive from their jobs.

6. This finding was a bit surprising as studies of some Asians, notably Japanese and Japanese Americans, have been rather consistent in demonstrating these workers to have lower job satisfaction levels than either non-Asian Americans or Europeans, arguably (cf. Lincoln, Hanada, & Olson, 1981) because they expect more from their work organizations than the latter groups (Cole, 1979). Thus the differential frame-of-reference assumption, which suggests that minority workers will have high satisfaction levels because they expect less, is not supported by these data.

7. While Japanese organizations tend to be highly differentiated vertically, they nonetheless are characterized by substantial informal participation in decision making, limited role differentiation and task generalization in the division of labor, and personalized interpersonal relations (Cole, 1979).

8. Some social work writers have suggested that the profession and schools of social work deliberately have developed men for leadership positions in order to legitimize social service agencies to members of powerful external publics, many of whom regard women as ill-suited to management (Patti, 1984, p. 27).

9. Bernard, Butler, and Eisenberg reported in 1979 that eligibility workers participating in their study were forced to utilize more than 2,000 pages of information as the basis for making decisions, and that in one year alone more than 1,100 pages of new information and directives were generated.

References

Anderson, W., & Martin, P. Y. (1982). Bureaucracy and professionalism in the social services. *Journal of Social Service Research, 5*(3/4), 33-51.

Andrisani, P., & Shapiro, M. (1978). Women's attitudes toward their jobs: Some longitudinal data on a national sample. *Personnel Psychology, 31*(1), 15-34.

Ansberry, C. (1987, January 5). Burgeoning caseloads, cuts in funding beset public social workers. *Wall Street Journal*, p. A1.

Austin, D. M. (1989). The human service executive. *Administration in Social Work, 13*(3/4), 13-36.

Bacharach, S., Bamberger, P., & Conley, S. (1990). Work processes, role conflict, and role overload. *Sociology of Work and Organizations, 17*(2), 199-228.

Bartel, A. P. (1981). Race differences in job satisfaction: A re-appraisal. *Journal of Human Resources, 16*(2), 291-294.

Bass, B., & Barrett, G. (1972). *Work, man and organizations: An introduction to industrial and organizational psychology*. Boston: Allyn & Bacon.

Becker, G. (1985). Human capital, effort and the sexual division of labor. *Journal of Labor Economics, 3*, 533-558.

Bernard, S., Butler, B., & Eisenberg, D. (1979). Policy overload: The plight of the public assistance worker. *Administration in Social Work, 3*(2), 197-232.

Beynon, H., & Blackburn, R. (1972). *Perceptions of work: Variations within a factory.* Cambridge, UK: Cambridge University Press.

Blalock, H. (1960). *Social statistics.* New York: McGraw-Hill.

Bombyk, M., & Chernesky, R. (1985). Conventional cutback leadership and the quality of the workplace: Is beta better? *Administration in Social Work, 9*(3), 47-56.

Bonjean, C., Brown, B., Grandjean, B., & Macken, P. (1982). Increasing work satisfaction through organizational change: A longitudinal study of nursing educators. *Journal of Applied Behavioral Science, 18*, 357-369.

Brenner, O., & Fernsten, J. (1984). Racial differences in perceived job fulfillment of white-collar workers. *Perceptual and Motor Skills, 58*(2), 643-646.

Buchanan, B. (1974). Government managers, business executives, and organizational commitment. *Public Administration Review, 34*, 339-347.

Burris, B. (1991). Employed mothers: The impact of class and marital status on the prioritizing of family and work. *Social Science Quarterly, 72*(1), 50-66.

Bush, J. (1977). The minority administrator: Implications for social work education. *Journal of Education for Social Work, 13,* 15-22.

Butler, B. (1990). Job satisfaction: Management's continuing challenge. *Social Work, 35*(2), 112-117.

Cacioppe, R., & Mock, P. (1984). A comparison of the quality of the work experience in government and private organizations. *Human Relations, 37,* 923-940.

Cherniss, C., & Kane, J. (1987). Public sector professionals. *Human Relations, 40*(3), 125-136.

Cole, R. E. (1979). *Work, mobility, and participation: A comparative study of American and Japanese industry.* Los Angeles: University of California Press.

Cotton, J., Vollrath, D., Lengnick-Hall, M., & Froggatt, K. (1988). Employee participation. *Academy of Management Journal, 13,* 8-22.

Daly, A. (1990). *Perception of influence and job satisfaction* (mimeo, 24 pp.). New Brunswick, NJ: Rutgers University, School of Social Work.

Demone, H., & Gibelman, M. (1984). Reagonomics: Its impact on the voluntary not-for-profit sector. *Social Work, 29*(5), 421-427.

DeParle, J., & Applebome, P. (1991, January 29). Ideas for helping the poor abound, but consensus is wanting. *The New York Times,* pp. A1, A12.

de Vaus, D., & McAllister, I. (1991). Gender and work orientation: Values and satisfaction in western Europe. *Work and Occupations, 18*(1), 72-93.

Doering, M., Rhodes, S., & Schuster, M. (1983). *The aging worker: Research and recommendations.* Beverly Hills, CA: Sage.

Dressel, P. L. (1987). Patriarchy and social welfare work. *Social Problems, 34,* 294-309.

Erera, I. (1989). Role ambiguity in public welfare organizations. *Administration in Social Work, 13*(2), 67-82.

Fabricant, M. (1985). The industrialization of social work practice. *Social Work, 30*(5), 389-395.

Fox, H., & Lefkowitz, J. (1974). Differential validity: Ethnic groups as a moderator in predicting job performance. *Personnel Psychology, 27*(2), 209-223.

Fox, M. F., & Hesse-Biber, S. (1984). *Women at work.* Palo Alto, CA: Mayfield.

Foy, N., & Gordon, H. (1976). Worker participation: Contrasts in three countries. *Harvard Business Review, 54,* 71-83.

Glisson, C. A. (1989). The effect of leadership on workers in human service organizations. *Administration in Social Work, 13*(3/4), 99-116.

Glisson, C. A., & Martin, P. Y. (1980). Productivity and efficiency in human service organizations as related to structure, size and age. *Academy of Management Journal, 23*(1), 21-37.

Glisson, C. A. (1978, September). Dependence of technological routinization on structural variables in human service organizations. *Administrative Science Quarterly, 23,* 383-395.

Gold, R. S., Webb, L. J., & Smith, T. K. (1982). Racial differences in job satisfaction among white and black mental health employees. *Journal of Psychology, 111*(2), 255-261.

Greenberger, D., & Strasser, S. (1986). Development and application of a model of personal control in organizations. *Academy of Management Review, 11,* 164-177.

Hackman, R., & Oldham, G. (1975). Development of the job satisfaction diagnostic survey. *Journal of Applied Psychology, 60,* 159-170.

Hackman, R., & Oldham, G. (1980). *Work redesign*. Reading, MA: Addison-Wesley.

Hage, J. (1974). *Communication and organizational control: Cybernetics in health and welfare settings*. New York: John Wiley.

Hasenfeld, Y. (1984). The changing context of human services administration. *Social Work, 29*(6), 522-529.

Hawkes, G. R., Guagnano, G., Accredolo, C., & Helmick, S. (1984a). The influence of work and non-work factors on job satisfaction for Mexican-American male workers. *Rural Sociology, 49*(1), 117-126.

Hawkes, G. R., Guagnano, G., Accredolo, C., & Helmick, S. (1984b). Status inconsistency and job satisfaction: General population and Mexican-American subpopulation analyses. *Sociology and Social Research, 68*(3), 378-387.

Herzberg, F. (1959). *The motivation to work*. New York: John Wiley.

Hodson, R. (1989). Gender differences in job satisfaction. *Sociological Quarterly, 30*(3), 385-399.

Jayaratne, S., & Chess, W. (1982-1983, Fall/Winter). Some correlates of job satisfaction among social workers. *Journal of Applied Social Sciences, 7*, 1-17.

Jayaratne, S., & Chess, W. (1983). Job satisfaction and turnover among social work administrators: A national survey. *Administration in Social Work, 7*(2), 11-22.

Johnston, W., & Packer, A. (1987). *Workforce 2000: Work and workers for the twenty-first century*. Indianapolis: Hudson Institute.

Jones, A. P., James, L., Bruni, J., & Sells, S. (1977). Black-white differences in work environment perceptions and job satisfaction and its correlates. *Personnel Psychology, 30*(1), 5-16.

Jones, E. (1973). What is it like to be a black manager. *Harvard Business Review, 51*, 108-116.

Kachigan, S. (1986). *Statistical analysis*. New York: Radius Press.

Kalleberg, A. (1977, February). Work values and job rewards: A theory of job satisfaction. *American Sociological Review, 42*, 124-143.

Kalleberg, A., & Griffin, L. (1978). Position source of inequity in job satisfaction. *Work and Occupations, 5*, 371-400.

Karger, H. J. (1981, June). Burnout and alienation. *Social Service Review, 55*, 270-283.

Konar, E. (1981). Explaining racial differences in job satisfaction. *Journal of Applied Sociology, 66*(4), 522-524.

Kravetz, D., & Austin, C. (1984). Women's issues in social service administration. *Administration in Social Work, 8*(4), 25-38.

Lawlor, J. (1991, May 13). Experts: Workplace to be more flexible. *USA Today*, p. 10B.

Leana, C., Locke, E., & Schweiger, D. (1990). Fact and fiction in analyzing research on participative decision making: A critique of Cotton, Vollrath, Froggatt, Lenick-Hall, and Jennings. *Academy of Management Review, 15*(1), 137-146.

Lincoln, J., Hanada, M., & Olson, J. (1981). Cultural orientations and individual reactions to organizations: A study of employees of Japanese-owned firms. *Administrative Science Quarterly, 26*(1), 93-115.

Loscocco, K. (1989). The instrumentally oriented factory worker: Myth or reality? *Work and Occupations, 16*, 3-25.

Loscocco, K. (1990). Reactions to blue-collar work: A comparison of women and men. *Work and Occupations, 17*(2), 152-177.

Loscocco, K., & Spitze, G. (1991). The organizational context of women's and men's pay satisfaction. *Social Science Quarterly, 72*(1), 3-19.

Malka, S. (1989). Managerial behavior, participation, and effectiveness in social welfare organizations. *Administration in Social Work, 13*(2), 47-65.

Marsh, R., & Mannari, H. (1976). *Modernization and the Japanese factory*. Princeton, NJ: Princeton University Press.

Martin, J., & Shehan, C. (1989). Education and job satisfaction: The influence of gender, wage-earning status, and job values. *Work and Occupations, 16*(2), 184-198.

Martin, J., & Hanson, S. (1985). Sex, family wage earning status and satisfaction with work. *Work and Occupations, 2*, 91-109.

Martin, P. Y. (1980). Multiple constituencies, dominant societal values, and the human service administrator. *Administration in Social Work, 4*(2), 15-27.

Martin, P. Y., & Chernesky, R. H. (1989). Women's prospects for leadership in social welfare: A political economy perspective. *Administration in Social Work, 13*(3/4), 117-143.

Martin, P. Y., & Segal, B. (1977). Bureaucracy, size and staff expectations for client independence in halfway houses. *Journal of Health and Social Behavior, 18*, 376-390.

McIlwee, J. (1982). Work satisfaction among women in nontraditional occupations. *Sociology of Work and Occupations, 9*(3), 299-355.

McNeely, R. L. (1983). Organizational patterns and work satisfaction in a comprehensive human service agency: An empirical test. *Human Relations, 36*(10), 957-972.

McNeely, R. L. (1984). Occupation, gender and work satisfaction in a comprehensive human services department. *Administration in Social Work, 8*(2), 35-47.

McNeely, R. L. (1987a). Job satisfaction and other characteristics of Asian American human service workers. *Social Work Research and Abstracts, 23*(4), 7-9.

McNeely, R. L. (1987b). Predictors of job satisfaction among three racial/ethnic groups of professional female human service workers. *Journal of Sociology and Social Welfare, 14*(4), 115-136.

McNeely, R. L. (1988a). Age and job satisfaction in human service employment. *The Gerontologist, 28*(2), 163-168.

McNeely, R. L. (1988b). Five morale-enhancing innovations for human service settings. *Social Casework, 69*(4), 204-214.

McNeely, R. L. (1988c). Job satisfaction differences among three age groups of female human service workers. *Journal of Aging Studies, 2*(2), 109-120.

McNeely, R. L. (1988d). Recisions, organizational conditions and job satisfaction among black and white human service workers: A research note. *Journal of Sociology and Social Welfare, 15*(3), 125-134.

McNeely, R. L. (1989a). Gender, job satisfaction, earnings, and other characteristics of human service workers during and after midlife. *Administration in Social Work, 13*(2), 99-115.

McNeely, R. L. (1989b). Job satisfaction and other characteristics among Hispanic American human services workers. *Social Casework, 70*(4), 237-242.

McNeely, R. L. (1989c). Race and job satisfaction in human service employment. *Administration in Social Work, 13*(1), 75-93.

McNeely, R. L., Blakemore, J., & Washington, R. O. (in press). Race, gender, occupational status, and earnings in county human service employment. *Journal of Sociology and Social Welfare*.

McNeely, R. L., Feyerherm, W., & Johnson, R. E. (1986). Services integration and job satisfaction reactions in a comprehensive human resource agency. *Administration in Social Work, 10*(1), 39-53.

McNeely, R. L., & Fogarty, B. (1988). Balancing parenthood and employment: Company receptiveness to innovations. *Family Relations, 37*(2), 189-195.

Miller, D. C. (1977). *Handbook of research design and social measurement.* New York: David McKay.

Miller, J. (1980). Individual and occupational determinants of job satisfaction: A focus on gender differences. *Sociology of Work and Occupations, 7*(3), 337-366.

Moch, M. (1980). Racial differences in job satisfaction: Testing four common explanations. *Journal of Applied Psychology, 65*(3), 299-306.

Moore, L. (1979, May-June). From manpower planning to human resources planning through career development. *Personnel,* pp. 9-16.

Nardone, T. J. (1986). Part-time workers: Who are they? *Monthly Labor Review, 109*(2), 13-19.

Norman, D. K., et al. (1981-1982). Sex differences and interpersonal relationships. *Aging and Human Development, 14*(4), 291-306.

O'Reilly, C., & Roberts, K. (1973). Job satisfaction among whites and non-whites: A cross-cultural approach. *Journal of Applied Psychology, 57*(3), 295-299.

O'Toole, James. (Ed.). (1973). *Work in America: Report of a Special Task Force to the Secretary of Health, Education and Welfare.* Cambridge: MIT Press.

Packard, T. (1989). Participation in decision making, performance, and job satisfaction in a social work bureaucracy. *Administration in Social Work, 13*(1), 59-73.

Patti, R. (1984). Who leads the human services? *Administration in Social Work, 8*(1), 17-29.

Perry, J., & Porter, L. (1982). Factors affecting the context for motivation in public organizations. *Academy of Management Review, 13,* 182-201.

Quinn, R., & McCullough, M. (1974). *Job satisfaction: Is there a trend.* Manpower Research Monograph 30. Washington, DC: U.S. Department of Labor, Manpower Administration.

Rainwater, L. (1984). Mothers' contribution to the family money economy in Europe and the United States. In P. Voydanoff (Ed.), *Work and family* (pp. 73-88). Palo Alto, CA: Mayfield.

Rogers, D. L., & Molnar, J. (1976). Organizational antecedents of role conflict and role ambiguity in top-level administrators. *Administrative Science Quarterly, 21,* 598-610.

Sandefur, G., & Pahari, A. (1989). Racial and ethnic inequality in earnings and educational attainment. *Social Service Review, 63*(2), 199-221.

Sauser, W. I., & York, C. M. (1978). Sex differences in job satisfaction: A re-examination. *Personnel Psychology, 31*(3), 537-547.

Shapiro, E. (1977). Racial differences in the value of job rewards. *Social Forces, 56*(1), 21-30.

Shinn, M., Rosario, M., Morch, H., & Chestnut, D. (1984). Coping with job stress and burnout in the human services. *Journal of Personality and Social Psychology, 46*(4), 864-876.

Solomon, E. (1986). Private and public sector managers: An empirical investigation of job characteristics and organizational climate. *Journal of Applied Psychology, 71,* 247-259.

Sullivan, T. (1989). Women and minority workers in the new economy. *Work and Occupations, 16*(4), 393-415.

Takaki, R. (1985). Is race insurmountable. In Van Horne (Ed.), *Ethnicity and the workforce*. Milwaukee: University of Wisconsin, Milwaukee Urban Corridor Consortium.

Taylor, A. (1982, December 6). The myth of the black executive. *Time*, p. 53.

Varca, P. E., Shaffer, G., & McCauley, C. D. (1983). Sex differences in job satisfaction revisited. *Academy of Management Journal, 26*(2), 348-353.

Veroff, J. (1978, April). *Psychological orientations to the work role: 1957-1976*. Paper presented at the Radcliffe Pre-Centennial Conference, Radcliffe College, Cambridge, MA.

Voydanoff, P. (1980). Perceived job characteristics and job satisfaction among men and women. *Psychology of Women Quarterly, 5*(2), 177-185.

Weaver, C. N. (1978). Sex differences in determinants of job satisfaction. *Academy of Management Journal, 21*(2), 265-274.

Whetten, D. (1978). Coping with incompatible expectations: An integrated view of role conflict. *Administrative Science Quarterly, 23*, 254-271.

Whiddon, B., & Martin, P. Y. (1989). Organizational democracy and work quality in a state welfare agency. *Social Science Quarterly, 70*(3), 667-686.

Wright, R., Wesley-King, S., & Berg, W. E. (1985). Job satisfaction in the workplace: A study of black females in management positions. *Journal of Social Service Research, 8*(3), 65-79.

PART V
Client-Organization Relations

When clients interact with the human service organization an exchange relation is initiated. The clients are looking to the organization to provide them with needed services, and the organization recognizes that the clients are valuable to its existence and survival. Nonetheless, one of the intrinsic characteristics of such an exchange relation is that it starts out as a very unbalanced relationship. Generally, each individual client is more dependent on the services of the organization than the organization is dependent on the client as a resource. This creates a power disadvantage for the client which is even more pronounced when the client has few alternative options, and when the organization has a monopoly over its services—a common pattern in the human services. Having power over clients means that, effectively, the workers have considerable discretion in how they can serve them. Consequently, client-organization relations in the human services are influenced by the twin forces of power and discretion. In Chapter 12, I explore the role of power in determining the nature of client-organization relations. Using a power-dependence model, I argue that when workers have a power advantage they use it to advance their own work values and interests. I suggest that because power is distributed unequally among agencies and clients, agencies with more power can use it to buttress their own position and improve the quality of their practices, resulting in an unequal distribution of quality practice. Similarly, clients with more power have greater access to quality practice, thus perpetuating social inequality. I see client empowerment as one strategy to overcome the inequality of practice.

Handler, in Chapter 13, examines the issue of discretion. Recognizing that it is inevitable in the human services, he poses the question whether discretion can be made to be a positive rather than a negative force in shaping client-organization relations. This can be done if the power advantage that produces discretion is not exploited. Handler proposes that the protection of the client can be achieved through the developing of morally sound trusting relations between workers and clients, and such relations arise when both the worker and the client work together to produce *common goods*, that is, simultaneously benefitting both of them. Handler concludes with a discussion of the conditions that give rise to empowerment of clients, a theme explored in Part VI.

CHAPTER 12

Power in Social Work Practice[1]

YEHESKEL HASENFELD

The role of power in social work practice has been generally understated despite its importance to the course and outcome of the clinical process. This paper examines the sources of power of workers and clients, and, by using a power-dependence perspective, it explores the consequences of power on social work practice. It is argued that, in most instances, the effectiveness of social work practice is predicated on the enhancement of the power resources of the client. Client empowerment strategies are proposed as the core tasks of social work practice.

The Neglect of Power in Practice Theory

The quality of the relationship between the worker and the client has been axiomatically accepted as the cornerstone of effective practice. Studies of clinical effectiveness have repeatedly demonstrated that, irrespective of the intervention technology, a major determinant of the effectiveness of practice is the quality of this relationship (Freiswyk et al., 1986; Orlinsky & Howard, 1978). Not surprisingly, much of the emphasis in social work practice theory is on the formation of a relationship that is voluntary, mutual, reciprocal, and trusting. Although there is a tacit recognition that the relationship may not be symmetrical owing to the power of the worker, this factor tends to be understated in practice theory. For example, in their influential life-cycle model of social work practice, Germain and Gitterman (1980) argue that "the client-worker relationship is transactional. . . . client and worker roles shift from

259

those of subordinate recipient and superordinate expert . . . to roles permitting greater mutuality and reciprocity in interaction" (Germain & Gitterman, 1980, p. 15). Garvin and Seabury (1984) take it a step further and define clients as

> persons who come for help to a social agency and who expect to benefit directly from it; who determine, usually after some exploration and negotiation, that this was an appropriate move; and who enter into an agreement—referred to as a contract—with the social worker with regard to the terms of such service. (Garvin & Seabury, 1984, p. 82)

Notice that although they recognize that the client must transact with a social agency and must negotiate a service agreement, both of which are processes that involve the use of power, the implication is that in most instances mutuality of interest will prevail and that power differences will be neutralized. Moreover, although they acknowledge its role, power does not enter into their model of direct practice. Put differently, although social work practice theory recognizes that the worker typically exercises considerable power over the client, the impact of power on the clinical relationship and outcome generally remains understated. There are, of course, some notable exceptions. In her seminal paper on the worker-client authority relationship, Studt (1959) emphasized the importance of authority, as one form of power, in social work practice. Her position was recently echoed by Palmer (1983), who noted the desire of social workers to disassociate themselves from power. The neglect of the concept of power is common to most helping professions. Heller (1985, p. 17) remarks that "the most striking oversight in the field of psychotherapy has been the great neglect of power."

Power as an Integral Component of Social Work Practice

The inescapable fact is that workers and clients use power to influence the helping relationship in some very fundamental ways. Specifically, workers use their power resources to influence the behavior of their clients, and these power resources therefore become the major tools in shaping the helping process (Feld & Radin, 1982; Pincus & Minahan, 1973). Social work practice theory acknowledges that professional social workers have several sources of power, ranging from coercive to normative, but only three are considered most appropriate. First, social workers rely on power of expertise, which is derived from their access to and command of specialized knowledge. Second, they use referent power or persuasion, which emanates from their interpersonal skills, partic- 2 . ularly their ability to develop empathy, trust, and rapport with the client. Third, they evoke legitimate power, which is an appeal to dominant cul- 3 . tural values and authoritative norms.

Nonetheless these sources of power are secondary to the primary source of power used by social workers, namely, the resources and services controlled by the organization or agency in which they are employed. Because social work is primarily an agency-based practice, the organization determines how resources will be allocated and to whom. The roots of the power of social workers are not only in expertise and interpersonal skills but also in the fact that they are members of an organization that controls critical resources needed by the client. The power of the agency is reinforced by the fact that clients must yield some control over their own fate to the agency when seeking help from it (Coleman, 1974).

The Power of the Service Agency

Practice theory generally does not address the power of the agency over the role performance of the workers. There is an implicit assumption that the professionalism and expertise of the workers will provide them with sufficient autonomy to guard against organizational intrusion into the helping process. Nonetheless, as pointed out by various researchers, the performance of social workers is significantly determined by the organizational context in which they work (Epstein & Conrad, 1978; Toren, 1973). Much of the power of the organization over its workers is invisible and operates through its standard operating procedures. The agency, in effect, controls the decision-making processes of its workers by constraining the type of information they will process, by limiting the range of alternatives available to them, and by specifying the decision rules for choosing among the alternatives.

By constraining the decision-making processes of its workers the agency makes sure that its core activity—the delivery of services—maintains, strengthens, and reinforces its operative goals. These goals, in turn, represent the interests of those who control the key resources of the agency (Hasenfeld, 1983). Such interests may, and often do, represent the professional values and norms of the social workers and may also incorporate the interests of the clients. Nonetheless, the values and interests of any individual worker or client are subordinated to and shaped by organizational policies that take precedence and are enforced by a collective power generally greater than the power of either the individual worker or the client. Public welfare workers, for example, quickly realize that they lack sufficient agency resources to meet the needs of their clients. Recognizing that as individual workers they have little power to change the situation, they develop personal coping mechanisms such as capitulation, withdrawal, specialization, or self-victimization (Sherman & Wenocur, 1983).

It is important to emphasize that the power of the agency is influenced by the environment in which it is located. Political, economic, and cultural factors greatly affect how the resources of the agency will be used. A "humane" agency, in which the needs of the clients are integrated in its operative goals, can exist only when key groups in its environment endorse and support such values.

Recognizing that social work practice is agency based, Weissman, Epstein, and Savage (1983) have proposed to augment traditional therapeutic skills with organizational skills, which they see as equally important in helping people in an agency context. They conceptualize these additional skills in the form of roles that are "framed by an organizational perspective [that] provides the clinical social worker with access to the array of problem-solving resources agencies provide" (Weissman, Epstein, & Savage, 1983, p. 7). Among the roles they identify are (a) the diagnostician, who utilizes in the assessment process not only personality or ecological theory but also an organizational theory to identify the barriers to effective functioning; (b) the expediter, who can get things done for the client, particularly in the organization, mostly through bargaining; (c) the case manager, who plans, coordinates, and monitors client services; (d) the advocate, who tries, on behalf of the client, to break down organizational barriers to access to services; (e) the program developer, who uses feedback from clients to initiate, plan, and implement new programs to improve service effectiveness; and (f) the organizational reformer, who attempts to change organizational structure and the processes that impede service effectiveness. In articulating these roles, the authors attempt to demonstrate the close interrelation between clinical and therapeutic skills and the organizational skills associated with these roles. In contrast to other theorists, they accord the agency its rightful place in the practice process and try to derive practice principles that fully acknowledge the ubiquity of the agency into the worker-client relationship.

The difficulty with this approach is that it does not fully account for the role of power, that is, the power of the agency, of the worker, and of the client in shaping the practice process. While they clearly attempt to formulate practice principles that reduce the power gap between agencies and clients, the lack of a systematic theory about the role of power in worker-client relations renders this approach too limited and somewhat simplistic. Therefore I propose a model of worker-client relations in which power assumes a central role.

A Power-Dependence Perspective

What motivates the worker and client to interact? This seemingly obvious question becomes less trivial if we reject the often implicit professional assumption that there is a mutuality of interests between the worker and the client. It is commonly assumed that, since clients want help and agencies wish to provide help, they share a common goal. In fact, however, the interests of the worker and the client are determined by their respective systems. Like all living systems, the agency and the client want to maximize their own resources while minimizing the costs of attaining them. Therefore a person becomes a client in order to get needed services and tries to do so with minimal personal costs. The agency, via the worker, engages the client in order to obtain resources controlled by him or her while minimizing organizational costs. It is this exchange of resources that makes both systems interdependent. For example, a person needing financial assistance will initiate an encounter with the welfare department in order to get maximum aid with as little harassment as possible. The workers representing the department need the client to justify the agency's mandate, and thus their own position, but try to conserve personal and agency resources in processing the client.

What governs this relationship, and particularly the ability of each party to optimize its interests, is the power each brings to the exchange. We say that A has power over B when A has the potential to obtain favorable outcomes at B's expense (Emerson, 1962). Moreover, the power of A over B indicates the dependence of B on A. The amount of power A has over B is a direct function of the resources A controls and B needs and an inverse function of the ability of B to obtain these resources elsewhere. Thus, the amount of power the welfare worker has over the client is a direct function of the client's need for financial aid and an inverse function of the client's ability to obtain the aid elsewhere. Similarly, the amount of power the client has over the agency is a direct function of how much the agency needs the resources controlled by the client and an inverse function of the agency's ability to obtain these resources elsewhere. It is quite obvious from this definition that agencies having a monopoly over services wield considerable power over clients. In this instance we say that the agency has the power advantage over the client because the client needs the agency more than it needs him or her. In contrast, potential clients having extensive personal resources (e.g., income and education) or highly desirable attributes (e.g., youth, verbal skills, and intelligence) wield significant power, particularly if the agency needs their resources. Clients with extensive resources have greater choices in selecting the agency, the worker, and the mode of intervention. They may, therefore, have a power advantage over the agency.

A power advantage does not imply that it will always be used to obtain favorable outcomes at the expense of the other party. There are values and norms that govern the use of power. The welfare worker, for example, is bound by departmental rules and regulations that define how the worker can use his or her power. Moreover, the worker is also socialized to a set of professional norms and ethics that ensure such power will not be abused. In general, the institutionalization of professional values and ethics emphasizing the rights of clients comes in recognition of the potentially exploitable power advantage professionals have over clients.

From this perspective, social work practice is actually an exchange of resources in which the power-dependence relationships between the worker and the client are being played out. The social work contract reflects the terms of the exchange—what is being exchanged and how—as determined by the power-dependence relationships.

The ideal model of social work practice, while acknowledging the power gap between the worker and the client, assumes that the mutuality of interests and the contractual relationship between the worker and the client will reduce the gap and result in a power balance. To quote Loewenberg (1983, p. 138), "The power gap may be unavoidable, but most social workers, just as most of their colleagues in other helping professions, think that it is undesirable and that it should be reduced as much as possible." However, it can be argued that it is precisely such a power differential that enables workers to engage in social intervention. Yet social work practice tends to understate the importance of power in shaping worker-client relations because of the assumption that the interests of the client and the worker are compatible.

The power-dependence perspective also recognizes that the exchange relationship may be either voluntary or involuntary for each party. The degree of choice available to each party, as noted earlier, is a key determinant of the power-dependence relationships between the client and the worker. For example, when the client is coerced to interact with the agency, as in the case of involuntary commitment to a mental hospital, the client is at a significant power disadvantage. Even when the patient may formally consent to treatment, the extreme power disadvantage does not give him or her a real choice. Patients, of course, can band together in informal groups to counteract some of the consequences of the power imbalances they experience, but they cannot eliminate them.

Social work practice tends to ignore involuntary interaction since most social work techniques assume that the client has the right of self-determination. In reality, in many social services, particularly those for vulnerable groups such as children, the poor, or the chronically ill, worker-client relationships are involuntary. Again, in social work practice theory we encounter reluctance to admit and often denial that many worker-client relationships are involuntary. To illustrate, Garvin and Seabury state (1984, p. 84), "In a sense, there is no such thing as an involuntary client as we defined a client as a person or persons who accept a contract for social work services." They reach such a conclusion because they, like others, assume that a contract is based on mutuality of interests and equality of power between the worker and the client. They fail to recognize that the client may accept the contract for lack of other alternatives or may pretend to accept the contract with no intention of adhering to it. Indeed, what the contract does is confirm the power-dependence relationships between the worker and the client. Therefore what is normally taken for granted in social work practice theory, namely, mutuality of interest and symmetry of power, is made problematic in this perspective.

In this framework, social work intervention techniques, such as enhancing the client's awareness through confrontation and interpretation or modifying the client's behavior through reinforcement and modeling, are actually utilizations of power by the worker to elicit desired outcomes from the client. In a broader sense, the worker uses power resources as means of influence to bring about desired changes in the client in accordance with the agency's interests.

Gaining and Using Power Advantage
in Social Work Practice

There is generally an asymmetry of power between the agency and the client, and therefore between the worker and the client, that is maintained through the structure of social services. First, most agencies are not directly dependent on their clients for procurement of resources. Typically, funds are obtained from third parties who are not the direct recipients of the services. Second, the demands for services often outstrip their supply. Third, many agencies have a quasi-monopoly over their services. Within the agency, the asymmetry is reinforced by the worker's monopoly of knowledge and by limiting the client's access to other workers, making the continuation of services contingent on the client's compliance, and limiting the client's options for alternative services. The same organizational power that shapes the decision-making processes of the worker also influences the decision-making processes of the client while in the agency.

The power advantage of the agency and worker shapes the social work process in several distinct ways. As noted earlier, the agency uses its power to set the parameters of the social work process in a manner that maintains and strengthens the interests of the organization. It does so primarily through its control over the intake, processing, and termination of clients. First, the agency will prefer clients who reflect positively on the evaluative criteria used by the key external legitimizing and funding bodies. Scott (1967) found that agencies for the blind prefer young over old blind clients because the former evoke greater sympathy among donors. Similarly, the agency may prefer clients who are covered by insurance. Second, the agency will prefer clients who conform to its moral assumptions about human behavior. Roth (1972) noted that emergency room staff delay treatment of patients who appear to be morally inferior, such as welfare recipients, the homeless, and alcoholics. Third, the agency will select clients whose attributes affirm and fit its dominant service technologies. Link and Milcarek (1980) found that patients selected to individual and group therapies in New York State psychiatric hospitals were the youngest, most competent, most communicative, and most motivated. Finally, the agency will send clients into different service routes as a way to maintain the efficiency of its operations.

Social workers may also use their power advantage to enhance their work values and interests. Heller (1985, pp. 109-122) argues that power is used by psychotherapists in every aspect of their work, including controlling the environment in which they see their patients, defining the agenda of the psychotherapeutic session, determining interaction patterns with the patient, and controlling the onset and termination of the psychotherapeutic process. By using power to control most aspects of the helping process, social workers aim to substantiate their personal and professional moral and practice ideologies.[2] They do so to protect, in effect, the enormous investment and commitment they have made in their moral and professional socialization. Social workers obviously rely on scientific knowledge to justify their activities and modify their tactics when they fail to achieve the desired outcomes. Nonetheless, they rarely step out of the boundaries of their basic moral and professional ideologies, and they use their power to protect such boundaries.

The power of the worker is a critical element of the social work process and a determinant of its successful outcome. Heller suggests that power enables therapists to initiate the intervention process, to enhance the therapeutic relationship, to become an identificatory figure for the client, to foster confidence and hope, and to manage the interaction process effectively (Heller, 1985, pp. 151-157). Power resources are indispensable when the aim of the clinical intervention is to achieve attitudinal and behavioral changes in the client (Kelman, 1965).

Clients are not without power resources that they can use to negotiate favorable outcomes. Clients may possess resources that are sought after by the agency (i.e., they may possess "desirable" attributes); they may have a broad range of alternative service providers to choose from; they may have knowledge and expertise regarding the services they seek; and they may have support of larger collectivities with which they are affiliated whose power resources can be mobilized on their behalf, such as kin and friendship networks, trade unions, or civic and business associations. Clearly, clients with power resources, particularly income and education, are better able to obtain the services they want and are more likely to influence the social work process to suit their needs and interests. This is manifested, first and foremost, in the choices they have in selecting agencies and workers. The ability to choose and, particularly, the range of available choices are the core of power.

For both the agency and the worker, access to power resources means having a greater potential to provide superior services. Actualizing such potential depends on the extent to which the interests of those controlling these power resources are compatible with the interests and needs of clients. I propose that such compatibility is more likely to occur when there is a power balance between workers and clients.

The Inequality of Practice
and the Practice of Inequality

In a society such as ours, characterized by considerable social inequality, the distribution of power among agencies and clients is inherently unequal. Agencies are differentiated by the amount of resources they possess and the control they have over their environment. Urban hospitals, for example, are stratified according to the resources at their disposal, including the quantity and quality of medical personnel and facilities, and their ability to select their patients. These factors result in an unequal distribution of medical services, and as Milner (1980) has shown, high-quality hospitals are able to maintain their superior position by relying on low-quality hospitals where they can "dump" their undesirable patients. Thus more powerful social service agencies are able to use their advantage to buttress their own power, partly through their ability to invest in and maintain superior practice, and partly by selecting desirable clients who ensure service effectiveness. Hence the dynamics of power are such that they perpetuate an unequal distribution of quality practice, unless checked and controlled by countervailing powers, such as government intervention.

Within the agency, an analogous process occurs. Workers with more power are better able to control the conditions of their work. They too can use their power advantage to improve the quality of their practice by having, for example, control over the type and number of clients they serve and by having greater access to sources of knowledge and expertise. Being able to provide superior practice in turn strengthens their power. Hence even within the agency there are forces that, unless checked, accentuate the inequality of practice.

The unequal distribution of power resources among clients, a reflection of social class differences, also results in unequal access to quality services. It is not surprising, therefore, that poor clients tend to receive poor services. One of the most striking consequences of the inequality of practice is that clients from low socioeconomic groups are more likely to interact with social service agencies whose primary function is social control and surveillance rather than prevention and rehabilitation. Nowhere is this pattern more apparent than in services for children and youths. Children from low socioeconomic groups and oppressed minorities are much more likely to be placed in out-of-home facilities, to be routed to the juvenile justice system, and to be cared for in social control institutions (Kriesberg et al., 1986). This pattern repeats itself in diverse sectors of the social welfare systems, such as in services to low-income female heads of households or in treatment of the mentally disabled (Sarri, 1984).

The use of power advantages by agencies, workers, and clients results not only in the inequality of practice but, what is more important, in the practice of inequality as well. Access to power resources enables both clients and workers to maintain and reinforce their power advantage by controlling the nature of the practice itself. The differential ability to control the process and content of social work practice in turn perpetuates the practice of social inequality.

Empowerment as the Cornerstone of Social Work Practice

Because power is such a central element in social work practice and yet is largely neglected in the formulation of practice principles, a major shift is necessary in current theory and practice. If we view social work practice as an exchange of resources, social work effectiveness, then, is predicated on the reduction of the power imbalance between workers and clients—specifically on increasing the client's power resources. What is needed, therefore, is to place client empowerment at the center of social work practice. The perspective I advocate calls for a revision of social work practice theory in a way that defines the major function of social work as empowering people to be able to make choices and gain control over their environment. The distinctiveness of social work and its practice theory and principles can be achieved only if it embraces empowerment as its domain rather than emulating other helping professions.

Social work practice that focuses on increasing the power resources of the client requires a shift in orientation from person- to environment-centered practice. Kagle and Cowger (1984) point out that in a person-centered practice there is a much greater tendency to blame the clients for their problems. In contrast, Gambrill (1983) proposes that,

> if you believe that the problems result from the transactions between people and their environments and that the individual himself is a rich source of resources, then you will attend to personal assets and will examine the social context within which the person exists to determine the extent to which it could be altered to achieve outcomes. (Gambrill, 1983, pp. 205-206)

The structural approach to social work practice proposed by Middleman and Goldberg (1974) offers the beginnings of an empowerment-based

practice because it presupposes that "large segments of the population
—the poor, the aged, the minority groups—are neither the cause of,
nor the appropriate locus for, change efforts aimed at lessening the
problems they are facing." It follows that the main function of social
workers is to "help people to connect with needed resources, negotiate
problematic situations, and change existing social structures where
these limit human functioning and exacerbate human suffering" (Middleman & Goldberg, 1974, pp. 26-27).

A theory of empowerment is based on the assumption that the
capacity of people to improve their lives is determined by their ability
to control their environment, namely, by having power (Pinderhughes,
1983). Being powerless results in both loss of control and negative self-
evaluation. Focusing on the latter, Solomon (1976, p. 19) defines empowerment as a "process whereby the social worker engages in a set
of activities with the client or client system that aim [sic] to reduce the
powerlessness that has been created by negative valuations based on
membership in a stigmatized group." My conception is at once broader
and more fundamental: Empowerment is a process through which
clients obtain resources—personal, organizational, and community—
that enable them to gain greater control over their environment and to
attain their aspirations.

There are four principal ways in which clients can gain power over
the social services environment: (a) by reducing their need for specific
resources and services; (b) by increasing the range of alternatives through
which they can meet their needs; (c) by increasing their value to those
elements in the environment whose services and resources they need;
and (d) by reducing the alternatives available to the elements in the
environment whose services and resources they need. These four principles are the building blocks of a theory of empowerment. It is important to recognize that empowerment must occur on at least three levels.
First, it must be undertaken at the worker-client level and be directed
at improving the client's power resources. Second, it must also occur
at the organizational level, aiming generally at harnessing the agency's
power advantage to increasingly serve the needs of the client. Third,
it must occur at the policy level so that the formulation and enactment
of policy decisions are influenced by those directly affected by them.

At the worker-client level, some of the strategies to increase the
clients' power resources directly might include (a) providing clients
with greater information about the agency and its resources, and particularly about the clients' entitlements; (b) training clients to assert and
claim their legitimate rights in the agency; (c) increasing clients' knowl-

edge and expertise in handling their needs; (d) enhancing the personal skills of the clients to manipulate their environment effectively to achieve desired outcomes; (e) increasing the clients' resources through coalescence with significant others (Longress & McLeod, 1980); (f) teaching clients when threats or disruptions may be effective tactics in obtaining needed resources; (g) linking clients to a supportive social network that can lend them resources, reduce their dependence on the agency, or that can help the clients to negotiate better their environment; and (h) using the workers' own power resources, such as information, expertise, and legitimacy, to obtain needed benefits or services.

Harnessing organizational resources on behalf of clients requires that clients become a key interest group affecting organizational policies. Clearly, in the current structure of social services this is not the case. Nonetheless, social workers can play a significant role in affecting these policies if they subordinate their own interests to those of their clients and represent them effectively. One of the avenues available to social workers for influencing organizational policies and procedures is the selection of practice technologies. The agency is generally dependent on the knowledge and expertise of social workers in choosing such technologies. The workers can therefore use their professional power to endorse adoption of empowerment-based practice technologies (see, for example, Rose & Black, 1985). Second, social workers can use their professional power to influence the agency to adopt accountability measures that are based on empowerment principles. In contrast to accountability measures based on social control, these measures evaluate the extent to which staff activities successfully increase the client's power resources rather than the client's conformity to prescribed behaviors. Such measures may include the degree of fairness and equity in the provision of services, the freedom of clients to determine their service needs and objectives, and the extent to which intervention technologies focus on mobilizing resources for the client and on environmental changes. The incorporation of evaluations by clients is also an important element of empowerment-based accountability.

An effective implementation of such a system of accountability invariably circumscribes the discretion of workers by limiting their activities so that the empowerment of clients is ensured. As noted by Handler (1979), professional discretion may actually disempower clients when its exercise results in discriminatory, unequal, and unfair practice. Therefore limiting worker's discretion to conform to the principles of client empowerment is an important step in attaining these principles.

Finally, social workers can organize within the agency as an interest group advocating on behalf of their clients. Through such organization, social workers can provide mutual support to colleagues and reinforce shared values. More important, they can more effectively mobilize power resources to influence agency policies and procedures.

Making social service agencies more responsive to their clients necessitates, ultimately, changes at the social policy level. The point of such policy changes is to increase the clients' control over resources needed by the agency and to increase the availability of alternative sources for the services controlled by the agency. The transfer of power from the agency to the clients will require some drastic changes in the policies and the resultant structure of social service agencies. Such a transfer may require several approaches: (a) Give the clients greater control over the fiscal resources of the agency. Currently, clients have little say about the allocation of such resources to the agencies that serve them. By giving them control over such resources (for example, through vouchers) they are transformed into an important interest group. (b) Organize clients into an advocacy group so that the agency will be required to interact with the clients as a collectivity rather than only as individuals. As a collectivity, clients can articulate common goals and be more effective in expressing their views and in negotiating with the agency. (c) Break up, when appropriate, the monopoly of the agency over services by creating alternative programs.

These strategies require social workers to engage in political activities that transcend the boundaries of their own agencies and professional specializations. The leadership role that social workers have taken in voter registration drives in the human services and in organizing clients to lobby for better services is a pertinent example. That leadership represents the commitment of the social work profession to social action. Such a commitment, often neglected in the rush of the profession to adopt the latest developments in clinical practice, must be reintegrated in social work practice because it is only through these political activities that the tension between agency goals, client needs, and professional values can be reduced (Withorn, 1984).

Conclusion

I have argued that social work practice theory tends to understate the importance of power as a key factor shaping the process and outcome of the client-worker relationship. Such a theoretical bias arises because of the underlying assumption that there is a compatibility of interests between the client and the worker. I have shown, however, that, once this assumption is removed, power emerges as an inherent element in social work practice. To understand and analyze its function I have proposed a power-dependence perspective that views social work practice as an exchange of resources between clients and workers; the terms of the exchange are determined by the respective power resources of the client and the worker. I have further proposed that social work practice theory must shift its emphasis from a person-centered practice to one that takes as its core activity the formulation of strategies to empower clients. The essence of these strategies is to create a balance of power between social service agencies and clients. These strategies call for redefining the role of the social worker, harnessing agency resources on behalf of clients, and, most important, reorganizing social service agencies. Bertha Reynolds, one of the great pioneers in social work practice, advocated client-controlled agencies as the means for achieving such a power balance. On the basis of her experience in the United Seamen's Service, she wrote:

> If this membership control seems shocking to some social workers who believe that they are responsible to nobody but their own conscience before God, it is useful to be reminded, as were the personal service workers at the National Maritime Union Hall, that in a social agency there is interposed between the caseworker and God a Board of Directors whose interests are more remote from those of the clients than are the interests of officials elected by their fellow members. . . . Responsibility of a caseworker to an organized group which is at once her board of directors and her clientele is, in part, a responsibility of knowing what the members want in the way of help. Being close to their daily lives, in an association with their own organization so that they feel free to say what they think, is an immense advantage. (Reynolds, 1951, pp. 59-60)

Social workers should follow the tradition of Bertha Reynolds by taking a leadership role in planning, mobilizing resources, and organizing alternative social service agencies that are increasingly based on the sharing of power between workers and clients. It is through such a partnership that the profession will be able to retain its distinctive identity and mobilize its constituencies to counter the attacks on the welfare state.

Notes

1. Reprinted from *Social Service Review, 61,* (3), September, 1987, pp. 469-483. © by the University of Chicago. All rights reserved. Used by permission.

2. By *practice ideology* I mean "formal systems of ideas that are held in great tenacity and emotional investment, that have self-confirming features, and that are resistant to change from objective rational reappraisal" (Rapoport, 1960, p. 269).

References

Coleman, J. (1974). *Power and the structure of society.* New York: W. W. Norton.

Emerson, R. (1962). Power-dependence relations. *American Sociological Review, 27,* 31-41.

Epstein, I., & Conrad, K. (1978). The empirical limits of social work professionalism. In R. C. Sarri & Y. Hasenfeld (Eds.), *The management of human services.* New York: Columbia University Press.

Feld, S., & Radin, N. (1982). *Social psychology for social work and the mental health profession.* New York: Columbia University Press.

Freiswyk, S. H., Allen, J. G., Colson, D. B., Coyne, L. F., Gobbard, G. O., Horowitz, L., & Newsome, G. (1986, February). Therapeutic alliance: Its place as a process and outcome variable in dynamic psychotherapy research. *Journal of Consulting and Clinical Psychology, 54,* 32-38.

Gambrill, E. (1983). *Casework: A competency-based approach.* Englewood Cliffs, NJ: Prentice-Hall.

Garvin, C., & Seabury, G. (1984). *Interpersonal practice in social work.* Englewood Cliffs, NJ: Prentice-Hall.

Germain, C. B., & Gitterman, A. (1980). *The life model of social work practice.* New York: Free Press.

Handler, J. T. (1979). *Protecting the social service client: Legal and structural controls on official discretion.* New York: Academic Press.

Hasenfeld, Y. (1983). *Human service organizations.* Englewood Cliffs, NJ: Prentice-Hall.

Heller, D. (1985). *Power in therapeutic practice.* New York: Human Sciences Press.

Kagle, J. D., & Cowger, C. D. (1984, July-August). Blaming the victim: Implicit agenda in practice research? *Social Work, 29,* 347-352.

Kelman, H. C. (1965). Compliance, identification, and internationalization: Three processes of attitude change. In H. Proshansky & B. Seidenberg (Eds.), *Basic studies in social psychology.* New York: Holt, Rinehart & Winston.

Kriesberg, B., Schwartz, I., Fishman, G., Eisikovitz, Z., Guttman, E., & Joe, K. (1986). *The incarceration of minority youth.* Minneapolis: University of Minnesota, Hubert Humphrey Institute.

Link, B., & Milcarek, B. (1980, September). Selection factors in the dispensation of therapy. *Journal of Health and Social Behavior, 21,* 279-290.

Loewenberg, F. M. (1983). *Fundamentals of social intervention* (2nd ed.). New York: Columbia University Press.

Longress, J. T., & McLeod, E. (1980, May). Consciousness raising and social work practice. *Social Casework, 61,* 276.

Middleman, R., & Goldberg, G. (1974). *Social service delivery: A structural approach.* New York: Columbia University Press.

Milner, M., Jr. (1980). *Unequal care.* New York: Columbia University Press.

Orlinsky, D. E., & Howard, K. I. (1978). The relation of process to outcome in psychotherapy. In S. Garfield & A. Bergin (Eds.), *Handbook of psychotherapy and behavior change* (2nd ed.). New York: John Wiley.

Palmer, S. E. (1983, March-April). Authority: An essential part of practice. *Social Work, 28,* 120-125.

Pincus, A., & Minahan, A. (1973). *Social work practice: Mode and method.* Itasca, IL: F. E. Peacock.

Pinderhughes, E. B. (1983, June). Empowerment for our clients and for ourselves. *Social Casework, 64,* 331-346.

Rapoport, R. (1960). *Community as a doctor.* London: Tavistock.

Reynolds, B. C. (1951). *Social work and social living.* New York: Citadel Press.

Rose, S. M., & Black, B. L. (1985). *Advocacy and empowerment: Mental health care in the community.* Boston: Routledge & Kegan Paul.

Roth, J. A. (1972, March). Some contingencies of the moral evaluation and control of clientele: The case of the hospital emergency service. *American Journal of Sociology, 77,* 839-856.

Sarri, R. C. (Ed.). (1984). *The impact of federal policy change on working AFDC women and their children.* Ann Arbor: University of Michigan, Institute for Social Research.

Scott, R. A. (1967, Winter). The selection of clients by social welfare agencies: The case of the blind. *Social Problems, 14,* 248-257.

Sherman, W. R., & Wenocur, S. (1983, September-October). Empowering public welfare workers through mutual support. *Social Work, 28,* 375-379.

Solomon, B. B. (1976). *Black empowerment.* New York: Columbia University Press.

Studt, E. (1959, January). Worker-client authority relationship in social work. *Social Work, 4,* 18-28.

Toren, N. (1973). The structure of social casework and behavioral change. *Journal of Social Policy, 3,* 341-352.

Weissman, H., Epstein, I., & Savage, A. (1983). *Agency-based social work.* Philadelphia: Temple University Press.

Withorn, A. (1984). *Serving the people: Social services and social change.* New York: Columbia University Press.

CHAPTER **13**

Dependency and Discretion

JOEL F. HANDLER

Discretion has emerged from the shadows. Always known, grudgingly tolerated, it is now celebrated. In law and administration, traditional ways of doing business are giving way. Top-down, bureaucratic, hierarchical regulation is to be replaced by decentralization, bargaining, and flexibility. Alternative dispute resolution—various alternatives to formal adjudication—is now an industry: there are numerous and multiple forms of "informal justice" structures, a large scholarly literature, and public and foundation support; it has a name: "ADR." Trends in the law are reflected in feminist theory and ethical philosophy. Modern and postmodern philosophers argue for conversation, for dialogue, and for community, rather than governing relationships through rules.[1]

Discretion is ubiquitous, hence difficult to define.[2] Basically, it involves the existence of choice, as contrasted with decisions dictated by rules. A common example involves law enforcement. The police officer exercises choice as to whether to invoke authority and how much; the prosecutor decides whether to prosecute. Similar choices are available to many regulatory agencies—whether to cite violations or institute other kinds of actions. The opposite would be situations where the officer feels that there is no choice, that the rules dictate a particular decision. This is a theoretical distinction, and it should not be exaggerated. While it is probably true that in a great many situations, officers do feel that they are bound by rules, many important discretionary decisions are made by low-level eligibility workers, tax auditors, licensing officials and other kinds of bureaucrats (Kagan, 1984).

276

Discretion is everywhere in the bureaucracy (Smith, 1981; Winkler, 1981). Choice has been exercised in the framing of the rules, and quite often, officials conceal their choices behind the *excuse* of a rule (Lipsky, 1980). In any event, in the relationships that I will be discussing in this chapter—those involving human service agencies—the distinction is not important—the officials—doctors, social workers, teachers, mental health workers—have lots of choice.

Discretion, especially in its contemporary manifestations, has been attacked on both substantive and procedural grounds. As compared to the idealized version of the rule of law, where parties have equal access and the court applies neutral rules evenhandedly, it is argued that discretion allows for the bargaining away of publicly defined normative standards and may further disadvantage the weak and the powerless. With regulation, for example, negotiated resolutions will fall short of substantive goals; without procedural protections and the clear application of substantive rights, the powerless will be even more victimized by employers, landlords, merchants, and bureaucrats.[3]

The contemporary literature extolling discretion generally ignores distribution issues. It is more or less assumed that the parties are relatively equal; the issue is how can the parties better relate to each other. With rare exceptions (Brodkin, 1986, 1987), there has been little systematic consideration of how discretion would work when there are serious inequalities. This chapter focuses on the unequal relationship. Specifically, I am concerned with discretion when a dependent person is dealing with a large-scale public bureaucracy. Discretion gives the official a choice. Choice, at least normatively, should be based on a careful weighing of the interests and needs of the client in relation to public considerations. Discretion contemplates a conversation within a normative framework, but dependent people are often at a serious disadvantage. They lack the information, the skills, and the power to persuade. The official has the unfair advantage.

It is for these reasons that the advocates for the powerless have been so opposed to discretion. My argument is different. Discretion is inevitable, especially in most human service agencies. It ought to be approached positively and creatively; but ways have to be sought to insure that power advantages are not exploited, that effective bargaining does in fact take place, and that both parties meaningfully participate in the choices that are to be made. However, before getting to solutions, the issues have to be examined more closely. How is power exercised in the bureaucratic setting? And what do we mean by participation?

The Manifestations of Power

def.
power

The standard definition of power is: A has power over B to the extent that she can get B to do something that B would not otherwise do.[4] At first blush, the definition seems unproblematic, especially in the context of the dependent bureaucratic client. The client, as the price of receiving something that is needed, has to do something that the official insists upon. The model assumes an objective conflict of interest; there is a direct exercise of power and a knowing albeit unwilling submission. In theory, the legal rights regime has a response to this situation. If the official acted contrary to law, then the dependent person has a right to challenge the exercise of power and a neutral third party will order a remedy.

Suppose, however, that the client willingly submits? Has there been an exercise of power if B *appears* to do what A wants? Now the situation becomes more problematic. What does consent mean in a hierarchical, dependent relationship? Can we take the client's position at face value? Steven Lukes, in *Power: A Radical View* (1974), addressed the problem of power and quiescence. Lukes argued that there are three dimensions of power. The one-dimensional approach is the example given above where A gets B to do something she otherwise would not have done. This dimension focuses on observable behavior (Dahl, 1986; Gamson, 1968, p. 3; Polsby, 1963, p. 55); it assumes that grievances and conflicts are recognized and acted upon, that participation occurs within decision-making arenas that are more or less open, at least to organized groups, and that leaders, or decision makers, can be studied as representatives of these groups. Nonparticipation, or inaction, then, is not a political problem; "the empirical relationship of low socioeconomic status to low participation gets explained away as the apathy, political inefficacy, cynicism or alienation of the impoverished" (Gaventa, 1980, p. 7; see also Gamson, 1968, p. 46). Quiescence lies in the characteristics of the victims; it is not constrained by power.

The two-dimensional view of power seeks to meet this last point. Bachrach and Baratz (1962) argued that power has a "second face" by which it is not only exercised upon the participants within the decision-making arenas but also operates to exclude participants and issues altogether; that is, power not only involves who gets what, when, and how, but also who gets left out and how (Bachrach & Baratz, 1962, 1970; Gaventa, 1980, p. 9). Some issues never get on the political agenda—for example, pollution in a company-dominated town, or the failure of southern Blacks to register and vote prior to the 1965 Voting Rights Act.

3 dimensions of power

1.

2

2.

Quiescence is not because of the lack of grievances; the study of power has to consider the barriers to even expressing grievances.

Lukes argues that the two-dimensional view does not go far enough; it fails to account for how power may effect even the *conception* of grievances. The absence of grievances may be due to a manipulated consensus. Furthermore, the dominant group may be so secure that they are oblivious to anyone challenging their position. This is the third dimension of power. A exercises power over B, not only by getting him to do what he does not want to do, but "he also exercises power over him by influencing, shaping or determining his very wants" (Lukes, 1974, p. 23).

An important characteristic of the third-dimensional view is that it is not confined to looking at the exercise of power in an individualistic, behavioral framework; rather, it focuses on the various ways, whether individual or institutional, by which potential conflicts are excluded. It is much more sociological than either the one- or perhaps the two-dimensional views. Under the third dimension, two theoretical approaches are combined—the hegemonic social and historical patterns identified by Gramsci (1971) and the subjective effects of power identified by Edelman (1988).

What are the mechanisms of power in the three dimensions? In the first dimension are the conventional political resources used by political actors—votes, influence, jobs. The second dimension adds what Bachrach and Baratz call the "mobilization of bias." These are the rules of the game—values, beliefs, rituals, as well as institutional procedures—that systematically benefit certain groups at the expense of others. The mobilization of bias operates not only in the decision-making arenas but primarily, through "nondecisions" whereby demands are "suffocated before they are voiced, or kept covert; or killed before they gain access to the relevant decision-making arena; or failing all of these things, maimed or destroyed in the decision-implementing stage of the policy process" (Bachrach & Baratz, 1970, p. 43). Quiescence can be the product of force or its threat, co-optation, symbolic manipulation, or the silent effects of incremental decisions or institutional inaction (Gaventa, 1980, p. 15).

The mechanisms of power in the third dimension are the least understood. Here is where power is influenced by social construction of meaning, language, myths, symbols, and legitimation (Gaventa, 1980, p. 15-16). Third-dimensional mechanisms of power not only include the control of information and socialization processes, but also fatalism, self-deprecation, apathy, and the internalization of dominant values and beliefs—the psychological adaptations of the oppressed to escape the subjective sense of powerlessness. Voices become echoes rather than grievances and demands. Political consciousness and participation are reciprocal and reinforcing; those who are denied participation will not develop political consciousness. In Paulo Freire's words, dependent societies develop a "culture of silence" that, in turn, lends legitimation to the dominant order. If voices do emerge, they are especially vulnerable to manipulation by the powerful (Freire, 1985; Gaventa, 1980, pp. 15-16).

The three-dimensional view of power poses significant methodological problems (Gaventa, 1980, p. 25). How can one tell whether B would have *thought* and *acted* differently? There is a real issue of imputing interests and values to the voiceless. In real life, the methodological issues may not, in fact, be that severe in many situations. If there are major inequalities in social relations, at least as a first step one should not assume that quiescence is natural but seek other explanations. In less obvious situations, Gaventa suggests a number of steps to try to explain the inaction. He would look to the historical development of the apparent consensus to see how the situation was arrived at and how the consensus has been maintained. He would look at the processes of communication and socialization and the relationship between the ideologies and beliefs. There may be comparative examples with different power relationships. However,

> if . . . no mechanisms of power can be identified and no relevant counterfactuals can be found, then the researcher must conclude that the quiescence of a given deprived group is, in fact, based upon consensus of that group to their condition, owing for instance, to differing values from those initially posited by the observer. (Gaventa, 1980, p. 25)

Power in Human Services Agencies

Hasenfeld, in *Power in Social Work Practice* (1987), describes the exercise of power from a political economy perspective. The traditional view of social work practice theory views the client-caseworker relationship as voluntary, mutual, reciprocal, and trusting; traditional theory tends to underestimate unequal power relationships by assuming that in most relationships natural power advantages will be neutralized through the voluntary mutuality of interests. In contrast, Hasenfeld argues that the principal source of social worker power derives from the resources and services controlled by the agency. Workers are members of organizations, and it is the organizations that determine how their resources are to be allocated. If the clients want these resources, then they must yield at least some control over their fate. In addition, workers have other sources of power: expertise, persuasion, legitimacy, specialized knowledge, and interpersonal skills.

A great deal of organizational power is exercised through its standard operative procedures—the type of information that is processed, the range of available alternatives, the decision rules. The agency is concerned with maintaining and strengthening its core activity—the delivery of services. The environment matters; goals represent the interests of those who control the key resources of the agency, which may or may not incorporate professional norms and/or the interests of the client. In public agencies, which chronically lack the resources to meet demand, social workers develop various personal coping mechanisms such as withdrawal and client victimization.

Hasenfeld rejects the concept of mutuality of interests—that agencies and clients share the common goal of helping the client—in favor of a transactional approach. The interests of the client and the agency are determined by their respective systems. Each wants to maximize its own resources while minimizing costs. A person becomes a client to obtain needed resources but tries to do so with a minimum of costs; the social worker needs the resources controlled by the client while minimizing personal and agency costs. The relationship is governed, then, by the power that each person has over their own interests (Gamson, 1968, p. 93). Agencies that have a monopoly of services exercise considerable power over clients. On the other hand, clients can exercise power if they possess desirable characteristics. Thus the exchange relationship between the client and the agency can be voluntary or involuntary, depending on the degree of choice that each possesses. Furthermore, even in situations where social workers possess considerable power, that power may not necessarily be used. There are rules and regulations, and workers in varying degrees are influenced by professional norms and values. But in any event, the traditional social work practice theory assumption of client self-determination is largely untrue for vulnerable groups. There, relationships tend to be involuntary. The asymmetrical power relationship between the agency and the client, and hence between the worker and the client, is maintained throughout the structure of social services. Social workers increase the power advantage through their monopoly of expertise, limiting client access to other workers, making the offer of services conditional on compliance, and limiting options for alternatives.

Agency processes reflect the evaluative criteria of the external funding and legitimating sources. The more powerful the agency, the more it will use its advantages to maintain its position. Within the agency, the more powerful workers are better able to control the conditions of their work. In this way, the dynamics of power perpetuate the unequal distribution of quality practice. Poor clients tend to receive poor services. This results not only in an inequality of practice, but, Hasenfeld argues, the practice of inequality.

the Practice of inequality

The distinguishing characteristic of a human service agency is its technology (Hasenfeld, 1983, chap. 5). These agencies are designed to change people; thus the technology not only requires knowledge of the complexities of human behavior, but it is also a *moral* system. As Hasenfeld points out, clients are invested with moral and cultural values that define their status. The processes of the organization—intake, intervention, and termination—are crucially shaped by the workers' moral evaluation of the client. The technology is based on a conception of human nature, and this conception is reinforced through the selection, processing, and evaluation of the clients. Workers develop ideologies that seek confirmation in self-fulfilling prophecies by screening incompatible information and resisting change or reappraisal. The workers select and deal with those clients that will serve their interests—either to confirm their ideologies or comport with the demands of their working conditions, or both. Since technologies and resources are limited, the attributes of the clients who *enter* are important to organizational success. Thus organizations seek to attract desirable clients and screen out the undesirable. Although public agencies are often limited in their ability to pick and choose, they employ other mechanisms for acceptance and rejection. Hasenfeld describes the selection and processing of clients as "typification," which is a pervasive feature in the exercise of field-level discretion. The organization identifies client characteristics in terms of diagnostic labels that then determine the service response. Agency perceptions of the client's moral character are often determinative. Is the client responsible for his or her condition and is the client amenable to change? Is the client morally capable of making decisions? The answers to these questions, in turn, determine the workers' moral responsibility to the client. The social construction of the client's moral character will have a decisive impact on the treatment that the client receives; thus the constructed moral character becomes reinforcing.

Labeling

The three dimensions of power are consistent with the political-economy perspective of social worker-client relations. The first dimension is the paradigm of liberal, legal adversarial relations. A dependent person applies for welfare; a condition of aid is a behavioral change—for example, a work assignment—which the person would prefer not to do, but feels is the price of receiving assistance. Assume that the agency is acting illegally—the client may be legally exempt from the work requirements, the agency failed to follow required procedures (e.g., evaluation, offers of training, etc.), or adequate day care was not available. The client knows of the illegality but needs the aid, has no other adequate alternative, but lacks the resources to challenge the agency. Or, the client has available competent legal services and does challenge the agency. This is the first dimension of power—there is an objective event—individualized conflict and empirical evidence as to who won what under what circumstances.

Suppose, however, that the client acquiesces in the condition. Assume that the client is of the same frame of mind—that is, she would prefer not to work. It may be that the agency is acting legally; in this case, the decision has been made legislatively and the agency is not exercising its discretion but is following a rule. The client is now precluded from voicing a grievance, certainly in this forum, but probably not in any other arena as well. This would be a case of the second dimension. There is a grievance but the woman has been effectively precluded from contesting the decision. There are other ways in which the second dimension of power can operate. The agency may be operating illegally, the woman feels her grievance, but lacks the resources with which to pursue her remedy or for some other reason feels that it would be either useless or even counterproductive to pursue her remedy. She may, for example, fear retaliation (Handler, 1986). These are examples of the second dimension of power because even though there is no objectively observed conflict, there is a grievance. One could empirically verify not only the grievance, but also the reasons for quiescence.

There are also several variations on the third dimension of power—where the absence of conflict is due to a manipulation of consensus, where A shapes and determines the very wants of B. The very idea of welfare as an *entitlement* is of recent vintage. Prior to the legal rights revolution of the 1970s, welfare was considered a gratuity, something that was offered on the terms and conditions of the grantor, much as private charity is given today. Given the extremely low level of legal challenges in social welfare programs, one questions even now how far the concept of entitlement has penetrated the consciousness of the disadvantaged (Handler, 1986, chap. 2). There is very little support for the idea that one is *entitled* to a minimum level of support without any corresponding obligations.[5] To the extent that the applicant for assistance has internalized these values—the obligations of work, responsibility, and welfare—then the dominant group has prevented even the conception of the grievance. This view of power is not individualistic; it is much more historical and institutional.

The social and historical patterns and the subjective effects identified by Gramsci (1971) and by Edelman (1971) are deep rooted and pervasive. Both the powerful and the powerless carry into the relationship their respective characters and self-conceptions, their root values, nurtured through immediate as well as past social relationships. Who they are and where they come from—class, race, childhood, education, employment, relations with others, the everyday structures of their lives, their very different social locations—crucially affect their languages, social myths, beliefs, and symbols—how they view themselves, their world, and others, which produce vastly different meanings and patterns in their encounters. How does the staff-professional view herself in a full, deep context and the person sitting across the desk? How does the client view herself, in her context, and the person sitting across from her? It is no surprise that social welfare clients either fail to pursue their grievances or even to conceptualize a grievance. The structures of their social life shape their identities and direct their behavior (Molotch & Boden, 1985).[6]

The difficult problem comes in empirically verifying the third dimension. When there is quiescence, how do we know whether the consent is genuine or manipulated? How does the researcher (the dominant group) avoid imputing her values, the social construction of meaning, to the quiescent? An approach that I will use will be to analyze the issue of trust. Hasenfeld argues that the core of the worker-client relationship in human service organizations is trust, treating clients as subjects rather than objects. What I will argue is that if there is trust, then we can be more confident that the consent is genuine. If there is quiescence without trust, then I will argue that the consent is problematic.

Dependency and Trust

Trust is as ubiquitous as discretion. As a form of social organization, it is used whenever there are principals and agents, whenever we invest resources, responsibility, or authority in others (Barber, 1983; Shapiro, 1987). We trust strangers as well as intimates; trust, it is said, is necessary to reduce the complexities of life (Luhmann, 1980, p. 4). Annette Baier (1986) draws a distinction between merely relying on the dependable habits of others and trusting; the latter relies on *good will*. When one relies on another's good will, one becomes vulnerable; but although there is the opportunity to do harm, one does not expect this to happen. We place ourselves in this vulnerable position because we need the help of agents to achieve or maintain things that we value—our lives, our health, our children, our property. Trust also involves discretion; we trust our agents to use their competence in our best interests, which also means that they have the ability to conceal their mistakes or their ill will under the pretense of honest judgment. Trust can be unconscious or cultivated.

Baier distinguishes trust from contract. Making contracts and promises includes trust, but contract does not capture the full variety and moral dimensions of trust. Contracts are mainly used by adults who are more or less equal in power; Baier is interested in trust relations with dependent people—children, servants, wives, and slaves.

Baier argues that trusting relationships are not necessarily morally decent; they can also be morally rotten. How can one tell the difference? Baier proposes a moral test in terms of *expressibility*—can the trust relationship survive the knowledge the parties are relying on to continue the relationship? The example she uses is an old-fashioned husband and wife where the wife is entrusted to care for the child. As long as there are not radical disagreements as to child-rearing practices, the husband can trust the wife to use her discretion. The trust, however, would be undermined if there were serious conflicts in values and the husband knew that the wife was willing to sacrifice his interests for hers. Trusting is rational. If the husband knew that the wife was only conforming to avoid sanctions, then he would rely on threats rather than trust. Similarly, the wife would only conform as long as she thought that keeping the trust would produce more of the benefits that she and the child were interested in than breaking the trust. In other words, rational trust can exist in a variety of situations where the parties are, in fact, quite suspicious of each other; threats and concealments would keep the trust going. This would be a "morally rotten" trust. Under the expressibility test, knowledge of what the other is relying on weakens the relationship. Conversely, with a moral trust, knowledge would strengthen the relationship—"the other's love, or concern for some common good or professional pride in competent discharge of responsibility" (Baier, 1986, p. 256).[7]

Trust, under Baier's more expansive concept, alters power relationships. The most basic, elemental trust is between infant and parent; it is trust that does not have to be won, but can be destroyed. Even though this is an example of extreme dependency and unequal vulnerability, Baier argues that it is still to some extent mutual; the parent is "vulnerable to the child's at first insignificant but ever-increasing power, including power as one trusted by the parent" (Baier, 1986, p. 242).[8] The goods that the parent supplies are nutrition, shelter, clothing, health, and love. The child can expect the parent to keep supplying these goods because the goods that the parent supplies are also goods to the parents— they are *common goods*. Harm to these goods would be self-harm. Trust and vulnerabilities between the parent and child become more mutual over time, and eventually, adult children may become responsible for their parents; but this latter relationship, however contractual or not it may be, does not transform the initial trust into a contractual exchange. The childhood relation may be a moral reason, says Baier, for taking care of one's parents, but it is not consideration. Trust, then, between unequal participation does not necessarily have equality as its goal; what is does have, under the expressibility test, is equal moral agency.[9]

Baier's expressibility test connects Hasenfeld's definition of the client-worker relationship in human service organizations with the empirical problems of the third dimension of power. The core of the relationship, argues Hasenfeld, is trust whereby the worker treats the client as a subject, not an object. The empirical problem of the third dimension of power involves the issue of what appears to be manipulated consent that suffocates even the conception of a grievance. There are situations where expressibility meets both objections; if the true reasons for the relationship are disclosed and the relationship is thereby strengthened, then the client is closer to a subject and consent seems more genuine and less manipulated.

Some Empirical Examples

There are examples where powerful officials enter into conversations with dependent people, where information and decision-making authority is shared, where dependent people become partners, in effect, in the exercise of discretion. There is an alteration in power relations.[10]

Most of the time informed consent in health care is a fiction: it is a legal, bureaucratic hurdle that the physician has to negotiate. The task of the physician is to get the parent to sign the form to avoid malpractice liability. There is no real communication. Power has not changed. The paradigmatic example is the surgeon presenting the consent form the night before surgery (Katz, 1984). Informed consent works differently with the chronically ill. There, the task of the physician is to get the patient to come to *understand* and *accept* the chronic condition and to *participate* in the therapy. Renal dialysis patients are a prominent example. Here, patients become knowledgeable; they become very active in their treatment: they often speak in jargon and diagnose their own problems; and doctors listen. Patients are encouraged to learn about alternatives and are given real choice. Physicians, in these circumstances, are more successful than when patients only passively comply (Lidz & Meisel, 1983).

Another example involves special education. Many handicapped children were either excluded from schools, or were improperly classified and segregated, so that their lives were wasted. The Education for All Handicapped Children Act (1972) granted all handicapped children the right to an "appropriate" public education but left it to the local participants to decide what the content of that education was to be. Schools would decide on the specific programs but parents were given the right of informed consent before a child was to be selected for diagnosis, evaluation, and placement in a special education program. Evaluation and the placement decision had to take place in a conference in which the parents had the right to attend and participate. If the parent disagreed with any decision, there were two administrative appeals (the district and the state) with the right of judicial review.

In most jurisdictions, the procedural innovations do not work. There are strong incentives to routinize the process and place and keep a child in available slots. Most parents, especially those from lower socioeconomic classes, lack the ability to participate. In addition to psychological burdens, the parents lack the necessary information and resources. The result is that participation and consent are formalities only. School officials decide cases beforehand, parents are presented with the staff recommendations, the consent forms are ritualistically signed. What we have is the classic case of either the second or third dimension of power. There is the subtle implication that the child or the parent is at fault. Parents who have grievances are overpowered; many have no idea that there are alternatives; doubts as to the wisdom of the powerful are not even raised (Handler, 1986, chap. 3; Heller, Holtzman, & Messick, 1982).

The Madison (WI) School District has a vastly different relationship with the parents—one that is based on trust (in Baier's sense), that treats parents as subjects, where power relations are altered, and where consent appears to be genuine." The district made three moves that serve as the foundation for their approach. The first was ideological; the parents had to be part of the *solution* to the task of educating handicapped students; if students were to be successful in school *and* in life outside and after school, then the parents had to be both *knowledgeable* and *active* participants; the school could not do it alone. Second, the technology was uncertain; therefore, diagnosis and treatment had to be flexible and experimental. By taking uncertainty seriously, the district lowered the level of potential conflict; participants can feel comfortable in agreeing to a course of action knowing that it will be open to renegotiation. Parents are given the opportunity to participate, but they lack the resources. The third move was to supply parent advocates—lay people who were experienced in the process (usually they were parents of handicapped children)—to help the parents. The parent advocates were to advise the parents as to the range of alternative services and programs, and that the parents could get independent evaluations; they would counsel them, accompany them to the meetings, and help them in the negotiations with the school people. The parent advocates were to introduce conflict deliberately, to ask questions that parents were afraid to ask or didn't know how to ask. A genuine dialogue involves questioning, listening, and openness. The parents not only had to feel comfortable with the decisions; they also had to be *active* participants in the plan. Quiescence—the standard practice in other school districts—was not enough. There were other things necessary to make the Madison approach work: social movement activity—parent groups, training sessions, and outings, all designed to decrease alienation and share information. The parents had access to independent experts who were welcome in the conferences.

In this system, the parents are considered subjects, not objects, the foundation of the relationship is reciprocal trust, power relationships have been altered, and consent appears to be genuine. The school has to get the parent involved; they would not do this unless they had confidence in the parent—that the parent understood what was expected, was capable, and would be active. A parent would not agree to this *and* perform in the manner that the school system considered necessary unless he or she understood and trusted the school people. Moreover,

since the plans were tentative and experimental, always subject to renegotiation, the conversations had to continue. The teachers needed the
active, understanding participation of the parent through the school
life of the child.[12]

The parents were still parents and the teachers were still teachers;
there were no redistributions of income and changes in social class. In
real life, there were still great imbalances of power. Each brought with
them their vast cultural differences. Yet, in this relationship, the parents
approached equal moral agency. Trust based on good will, where Baier's
test of expressibility would strengthen the trust relationship, altered
power relations. The parent was given information and responsibility;
she was empowered.

The parent was not only changed vis-à-vis the teacher, she herself was
also changed. The ability to take more control over her life and the fate
of her child means that there was a change in her self-conception, in her
views about herself. Changes in practices necessarily mean a change
in one's ideologies. Ideology defines experiences and constructs reality. Events become socially meaningful when they are interpreted.[13]
The empowerment of the parent, in this transaction, was both transformative and constitutive.

Another example may be found in some demonstration programs
providing community-based care programs for the frail, elderly poor.
These programs are designed to provide cheaper, more effective care to
people who are at risk of becoming nursing home residents. The clients
are typically very old, single women who need help in a variety of
activities of daily life—transportation, chore services, nutrition, bath-
ing, toileting, and health needs. For most of the elderly in this situation,
home care is provided by a spouse or other family; but for those without such supports or where the support is having great difficulty in
helping, there will be rapid deterioration and the client will have to be
institutionalized unless this care is provided.

I have been researching several voluntary and for-profit agencies in
the Los Angeles area that are operating community-based care programs. While the programs vary, basically the agencies recruit clients,
provide case management, and contract for services according to need.
Most of the services are for the routine, mundane tasks of daily living—
the most popular service is home help. If available, the agencies work
with family. For a variety of reasons, the agencies have to enlist the active cooperation of the clients. Those who are familiar with the elderly
know that it is no small matter to get the elderly to participate in
service programs; not infrequently they are fearful, confused, or have

a determined, sometimes counterproductive, sense of independence. These agencies, however, have to do more than get the clients merely to accept the services that are offered. The clients have to be engaged— for example, they have to interview the home help aides, supervise their work, and report to the agencies on the quality of the performance, and if necessary discharge the workers. The agencies assist in various ways, but they simply do not have the resources to provide this kind of close supervision. They rely on the clients, and where available, family members, to provide the necessary information. As a result, instead of being passive recipients of services, the clients become active participants in the selection and supervision of a variety of services. They become part of the solution. This is often a difficult transition. It is accomplished through careful, patient conversations; clients (and family) are slowly brought along; confidences are established; gradually, agency staff and clients and family begin to rely on each other. There is cooperation based on understanding and trust.

These are examples where consent appears to meet the objections raised in the third dimension of power. In order for the dominant person—physician (of the chronically ill), teacher, or case manager—to perform the professional task, the dependent person has to become an active, understanding participant. I stress the word *understanding* because the professional relies on the dependent person for accurate information and judgment. To get this kind of participation, the dependent person has to have discretion, the ability to consider alternatives. At least in some respects, this satisfies the empirical concerns about the third dimension of power. Here, potential conflicts (alternatives) are considered. We also have the kind of trust that Baier (1986) is talking about; under the expressibility test, if the reasons for the relationship are disclosed, the relationship would be strengthened. Power has been altered both instrumentally and constitutively. The self-conceptions, the ideologies, of the empowered persons have been changed. As equal moral agents, the dependent person has a different conception of self, of the professional, and of the relationship.

These examples may be contrasted with instrumental cooperation. There are many cooperative relations that are strictly instrumental, where expressibility is used to clarify the benefits and costs of dealing rather than fighting. Knowledge here is not of *common goods* such as mutual respect, love, good will, and professional pride. Cooperation is not the common good; it is only instrumental to reducing costs; if the costs to one of the parties begins to exceed benefits, then cooperation ceases. Cooperation can be based on trust or fear—as long as there is clear information. In these situations, power relations are not altered. Cooperation is neither constitutive nor transformative. With the chronically ill, the parents, and the frail, elderly poor, while there was no change in economic and social positions, power was altered; the patient and the client moved from a dependent person to an equal moral agent. The change on the part of the dependent people was constitutive in the sense that their ideologies changed—their conception of themselves and their relationships with the professionals.

How much change, and how significant? The transformative empowerment that occurs in these situations is partial in that it may only apply to the particular transactions between the clients or patients and the professionals. Further, it may not apply to the full range of alternatives; the clients (as well as the professionals) may be constrained within an unduly limited set of alternatives. The middle-class professionals work within bureaucracy; the clients are still dependent people. Even though they seemed to do well in their associations with the agencies, they are still dependent people. One would hope that the moral values developed in these relationships would have effects in other arenas—that doctors, teachers, and social workers would be more responsive to dependent people who come their way, and, similarly, that dependent people would use their enhanced self-conception in their other relationships, but this is uncertain. So we are talking about meeting the objections of the third dimension of power in an important, but nevertheless selected area; in other areas, in other relationships between agencies and clients, and in other relations with these very same people, power may still be exercised in the conventional manner. The participatory examples are enclaves, alternative practices, within larger, hierarchical structures.

Moreover, the relationships may also be transitory. In the medical area, it has been verified that when the chronically ill become acute care patients, they and their physicians revert to the traditional role. With both the parents and the frail, elderly poor, the professionals have to work constantly to maintain active, understanding participation.

These limitations should not be surprising. Lawyers especially put too much faith in the relevance and durability of process, but process is always molded by substantive events. Partial relationships may be necessary for autonomy; even communitarian philosophers worry about social distance (MacIntyre, 1984, pp. 142-143; Unger, 1975, p. 279). The task is to discover the conditions that will facilitate the creation and nurturing of empowerment in discretionary dependent relationships, not to search for some magical procedural formula.

Conclusion: Structuring Empowerment

There are four conditions for the empowerment of dependent people in the discretionary relationships that I have identified. First, there must be changes in professional norms. In Baier's (1986) examples, dependent people become equal moral agents through love, mutual respect, altruism, and professional pride. Many have argued for such values in client-bureaucracy relations, such as informed consent in health care (Katz, 1984) and social work (Simon, 1986). In the examples that I used there were the humanistic values of mutual respect and professional pride. Patients, parents, and clients were reconceived as subjects rather than objects.

Second, the technology must lend itself to shared decision making. Participation is usually justified in process terms—autonomy, dignity, and respect. These are values in and of themselves. But I think that something more is necessary; there has to be substantive benefits from cooperation. This is the third condition—what I call *reciprocal concrete incentives*. In the three examples, the professional could not perform her task unless the patient or client participated as an equal moral agent, that is, *actively* cooperated on the basis of understanding and trust. Although I distinguished these examples from instrumental cooperation, these examples also had strong instrumental elements. While they were more than instrumentalist, I want to emphasize that instrumentalism is at the base. Because the power relationship is so unequal when dependent people are dealing with large-scale public agencies, unless there are strong, reciprocal, concrete incentives, including financial incentives,[14] I do not believe that the humanistic values of mutual respect, love, altruism, and professional pride would be enough to sustain equal moral agency, at least in the long run. In the examples that I used, active, understanding participation was necessary if the physician or case manager were to perform satisfactorily *their* professional task. More than reciprocal concrete incentives are required—they are a necessary but not sufficient condition—but they are required. Power must serve the interests of the powerful; that is not disputed (Lukes, 1986, p. 5). But in these examples, the interests are even better served by empowering the client.

The idea of reciprocal concrete incentives increase the client's value to the worker and thereby encourages change in the power relationship. With reciprocal incentives, if the client fails, the worker fails; thus the worker has a professional *stake* in empowerment. This is not consistent with changes in professional norms and ideologies; but since professional norms and ideologies are often used to manipulate or suffocate grievances, the presence of reciprocal concrete incentives gives one more confidence about the meaning of consent.

Dependent clients, too, need resources. Psychological burdens, of course, will vary; some clients will be able to take advantage of the opportunities being offered, but others will not. Although in my examples the professionals provided information and support, it would seem that in many other situations, social movement groups would be necessary. This would be a fourth condition. Groups provide solidarity, encouragement, and information. They show the clients that they are not alone, that others share their burdens; they can collectivize grievances. Groups can provide training and experts. Clients need groups in order to be able to participate. This means that the bureaucracy also needs the groups if it is to get the kind of client participation that it wants. The professional task is reconceptualized so that clients are part of the solution, but in order for clients to participate, client groups have to be part of the solution as well.

The fact of discretion is inevitable in the modern social welfare state, and as long as government and large-scale agencies are serving and regulating the disadvantaged, then the consequences of unfair power in the exercise of discretion must be addressed. The solutions of the legal system—the reduction of discretion through the application of tightly drawn legal rules, and the enforcement of those rules through procedural due process, that is, the assertion of the rule of law—has limited application, especially since procedural due process protections are such a problematic remedy for the vast majority of dependent people. Instead, discretion must be addressed more positively, more creatively; ways have to be explored that will restructure relationships to empower dependent clients. This requires changes in professional ideologies, redesigning reciprocal incentives, and providing resources to clients so that they can participate. Still, one must proceed cautiously. The examples that I have outlined are special and fragile. While they may indicate beginnings, it must not be forgotten that they exist in small corners of large-scale, hierarchical structures.

Notes

1. There is by now a considerable literature on all of these topics. Some representative examples include: regulation: Bardach & Kagan (1982), Stewart (1986); alternative

dispute resolution: Abel (1982), Carrie Menkel-Meadow, (also on the practice of law); feminist theory: Olsen (1984), Sunstein (1988), West (1988); jurisprudence: Habermas (1986), Luhmann (1986), Tuebner (1986); modern/postmodern philosophy: Bernstein (1985), Cornell (1985). The relationship between these various developments and discretion is more fully discussed in Handler (1990).

2. For recent discussions of discretion, see Brodkin (1987), Adler & Asquith (1981).

3. There is also a considerable literature attacking discretion in informal justice. See, for example, Abel (1982, 1985), Delgado (1985).

4. While this may be a common, and for our purposes useful, definition of power, there is in fact no agreement on the various meanings of power. According to Talcott Parsons, "Power is one of the key concepts in the great Western tradition about political phenomena. It is at the same time a concept on which, in spite of its long history, there is, on analytical levels, a notable lack of agreement both about its specific definition, and about many features of the conceptual context in which it should be placed. There is, however, a core complex of its meaning having to do with the capacity of persons or collectivities 'to get things done' effectively, in particular when their goals are obstructed by some kind of human resistance or opposition" (Parsons, 1986, p. 94). The Lukes volume contains a series of essays on various approaches to power. At the end of the introduction, Lukes says: "[I]n our ordinary unreflective judgments and comparisons of power, we normally know what we mean and have little difficulty in understanding one another, yet every attempt at a single general answer to the question has failed and seems likely to fail" (Lukes, 1986, p. 17). For a discussion of power, see Clegg (1989).

5. See, for example, Hartmann (1987, pp. 33, 58), and Mead (1986). For a discussion of the current consensus on work and welfare reform, see Handler and Hasenfeld (1991).

6. There is a vast theoretical and empirical literature dealing with the problems of lack of rights consciousness. See, for example, Felstiner, Abel, & Sarat (1980-1981); Bumiller (1988); Handler (1986, chap. 2).

7. Baier's (1986, pp. 259-260) definition of trust is as follows: "trust is morally decent only if, in addition to whatever else is entrusted, knowledge of each party's reasons for confident reliance on the other to continue the relationship could in principle also be entrusted—since mutual knowledge would be itself a good, not a threat to the other goods. To the extent that mutual reliance can be accomplished by mutual knowledge of the conditions of that reliance, trust is above suspicion, and trustworthiness a nonsuspect virtue."

8. This conception of reciprocal power relations within an example of extreme dependency seems to fit Foucault's (1986, p. 234) conception of the nature of power: "Power must be analyzed as something that circulates, or rather as something that only functions in the form of a chain. It is never localized here or there, never in anybody's hands, never appropriated as a commodity or piece of wealth. Power is employed and exercised through a net-like organization. And not only do individuals circulate between its threads; they are always in the position of simultaneously under-going and exercising this power. They are not only its inert or consenting target; they are always also the elements of its articulation. In other words, individuals are the vehicles of power, not its points of application."

9. Baier's (1986) view of trust seems very close to Hannah Arendt's (1986) concep-tion of power, which is the ability to agree upon a common course of action in uncon-strained communication. See Arendt (1986) and Habermas (1986a, pp. 59-74, 75-93).

10. The examples are more fully discussed in Handler (1986, 1990).

11. The Madison example is discussed in detail in Handler (1986, chap. 4).

12. Consider the following quote from a lower-class parent: "Our family has never been criticized, they've never said, 'you're failing him.' They've encouraged us to allow him to do more and try more, and not to be afraid. They've convinced us he can do more than we think he can do" (Handler, 1986, p. 79).

13. "There is no social world except as it is lived and experienced, and events become socially meaningful only when they are interpreted. . . . [Thus] ideology is constitutive, in that ideas about an event or relationship defined that activity, much as the rules about a game define a move or a victory in that game" (Merry, 1986, p. 254).

14. In all three examples, the patient, parent, and client *shared* the work. Cooperation and trust would be much more difficult if financial incentives were perverse. Surgeons, most of the time, are not paid to talk.

References

Abel, R. (Ed.). (1982). *The politics of informal justice* (Vols. 1, 2). New York: Academic Press.

Abel, R. (1985). Risk as an area of struggle. *Michigan Law Review, 83,* 772.

Adler, M., & Asquith, S. (Eds.). (1981). *Discretion and welfare.* London: Heinemann Educational Books.

Arendt, H. (1986). Communicative power. In S. Lukes (Ed.), *Power* (pp. 59-74). New York: New York University Press.

Bachrach, P., & Baratz, M. (1962). The two faces of power. *American Political Science Review, 56,* 947-952.

Bachrach, P. & Baratz, M. (1970) *Power and poverty: Theory and practice.* New York: Oxford University Press.

Baier, A. (1986, January). Trust and antitrust. *Ethics, 96,* 231-260.

Barber, B. (1983). *The logic and limits of trust.* New Brunswick, NJ: Rutgers University Press.

Bardach, E., & Kagan, R. (1982). *Going by the book: The problem of regulatory unreasonableness.* Philadelphia: Temple University Press.

Bernstein, R. (1985). *Beyond objectivism and relativism: Science, hermeneutics, and praxis.* Philadelphia: University of Pennsylvania Press.

Brodkin, E. (1986). *The false promise of administrative reform: Implementing quality control in welfare.* Philadelphia: Temple University Press.

Brodkin, E. (1987). Policy politics: If we can't govern, can we manage? *Political Science Quarterly, 102,* 571.

Bumiller, K. (1988). *The civil rights society: The social construction of victims.* Baltimore, MD: Johns Hopkins University Press.

Clegg, S. (1989). *Frameworks of power.* Newbury Park, CA: Sage.

Cornell, D. (1985). Toward a modern/postmodern reconstruction of ethics. *University of Pennsylvania Law Review, 133,* 291.

Dahl, R. (1986). Power as the control of behavior. In S. Lukes (Ed.), *Power* (pp. 37-58). New York: New York University Press.

Delgado, R. (1985). Fairness and formality: Minimizing the risk of prejudice in alternative dispute resolution. *Wisconsin Law Review,* 1359.

Edelman, M. (1971). *Politics as symbolic action: Mass arousal and quiescence.* Chicago: Markham.

Edelman, M. (1988). *Constructing the political spectacle.* Chicago: University of Chicago Press.

Felstiner, W., Abel, R., & Sarat, A. (1980-1981). The emergence and transformation of disputes: Naming, blaming, claiming . . . *Law & Society Review, 15,* 631.

Foucault, M. (1986). Disciplinary power and subjection. In S. Lukes (Ed.), *Power* (p. 234). New York: New York University Press.

Freire, P. (1985). *Pedagogy of the oppressed.* New York: Continuum.

Gamson, W. (1968). *Power and discontent.* Homewood, IL: Dorsey Press.

Gaventa, J. (1980). *Power and powerlessness: Quiescence and rebellion in an Appalachian valley.* Urbana: University of Illinois Press.

Gramsci, A. (1971). *Selection from the prison notebooks.* New York: International Publishers.

Habermas, J. (1986). Hannah Arendt's communications concept of power. In S. Lukes (Ed.), *Power* (p. 79). New York: New York University Press.

Habermas, J. (1986). Law as medium and law as institution. In G. Tuebner (Ed.), *Dilemmas of law in the welfare state* (pp. 203-220). Berlin: Walter de Gruyter.

Handler, J. (1986). *The conditions of discretion: Autonomy, community, bureaucracy.* New York: Russell Sage.

Handler, J. (1987-1988). The transformation of aid to families with dependent children: The Family Support Act in historical context. *New York University Review of Law & Social Change, 16,* 457-533.

Handler, J. (1990). *Law and the search for community.* Philadelphia: University of Pennsylvania Press.

Handler, J., & Hasenfeld, Y. (1991). *The moral construction of the poor and welfare reform.* Newbury Park, CA: Sage.

Hartmann, H. (1987). Changes in women's economy and family. In B. Lourdes & C. Stimpson (Ed.), *Women, households, and the economy* (pp. 33-58). New Brunswick, NJ: Rutgers University Press.

Hasenfeld, Y. (1983). *Human service organizations.* Englewood Cliffs, NJ: Prentice-Hall.

Hasenfeld, Y. (1987, September). Power in social work practice. *Social Service Review,* 469-483.

Heller, K., Holtzman, W., & Messick, S. (Eds.). (1982). *Placing children in special education: A strategy for equity.* Washington, DC: National Academy Press.

Kagan, R. (1984). Inside administration law. [Book review.] *Columbia Law Review, 84,* 816.

Katz, J. (1984). *The silent world of doctor and patient.* New York: Free Press.

Lidz, C., & Meisel, A. (1983). Informed consent and the structure of medical care. In *President's Commission for the Study of Ethical Problems in Medicine and Biomedical and Behavior Research* (vol 2, pp. 349-53). Washington, DC: Government Printing Office.

Lipsky, M. (1980). *Street-level bureaucracy: Dilemmas of the individual public services.* New York: Russell Sage.

Lukes, S. (1974). *Power: A radical view.* London: Macmillan.

Lukes, S. (Ed.). (1986). *Power.* New York: New York University Press.

Luhmann, N. (1980). *Trust and power.* New York: John Wiley.

MacIntyre, A. (1984). The virtues, the unity of a human life and the concept of a tradition. In M. Sandel (Ed.), *Liberalism and its critics* (pp. 125, 142-143). Oxford: Basil Blackwell.

Mead, L. (1986). *Beyond entitlement: The social obligations of citizenship.* New York: Free Press.

Menkel-Meadow, C. (1984). Toward another view of legal negotiation: The structure of problem solving. *UCLA Law Review, 31,* 754.

Merry, S. (1986). Everyday understandings of the law in working class America. *American Ethnologist, 13,* 254.

Molotch, H., & Boden, D. (1985). Talking social structures: Discourse, domination and the Watergate hearings. *American Sociological Review, 50,* 273-288.

Olsen, F. (1984). Statutory rape: A feminist critique of rights analysis. *Texas Law Review, 63,* 387.

Parsons, T. (1986). Power and the social system. In S. Lukes (Ed.), *Power* (p. 94). New York: New York University Press.

Polsby, N. (1963). *Community power and political theory.* New Haven, CT: Yale University Press.

Shapiro, S. (1987). The social control of impersonal trust. *American Journal of Sociology, 93,* 623-658.

Simon, W. (1986). Rights and redistribution in the welfare system. *Stanford Law Review, 38,* 1431.

Smith, G. (1981). Discretionary decision-making in social work. In M. Adler & S. Asquith (Eds.), *Discretion and welfare* (pp. 47-68). London: Heinemann Educational Books.

Stewart, R. (1986). Reconstitutive law. *Maryland Law Review, 46,* 86.

Sunstein, C. (1988). Feminism and legal theory. [Book review.] *Harvard Law Review, 101,* 826.

Tuebner, G. (1986). After legal instrumentalism? Strategic models of post-regulatory law. In *Dilemmas of law in the welfare state* (pp. 299-325). Berlin: Walter de Gruyter.

Unger, R. (1975). *Knowledge and politics.* New York: Free Press.

West, R. (1988). Justice and gender. *University of Chicago Law Review, 53,* 1-72.

Winkler, J. T. (1981). The political economy of administrative discretion. In M. Adler & S. Asquith (Eds.), *Discretion and welfare* (pp. 82-134). London: Heinemann Educational Books.

PART VI
Empowerment of Clients

While the idea of empowerment is now in vogue, it is an elusive concept. It is used both as a justification to dismantle human service organizations in the name of giving clients greater control over their lives, and as a rallying cry to develop more services for dependent clients. In Chapter 14, Gottlieb expands on the feminist perspective of empowerment, especially on the idea that the "personal is political." She argues that when social workers continue to use an individual pathology model, they actually perpetuate the status quo. Gottlieb then presents examples of several alternative empowerment strategies in mainstream human service organizations. They may include a nonstereotyped view of women, social action complementing individual coping, and use of peers. She suggests that human service organizations can be restructured in ways that do empower their clients.

Gutiérrez, in Chapter 15, points out that, historically, the organization and structure of human services resulted in the disempowerment of ethnic minorities. This was manifested through structural barriers to access, typification and tracking of clients, but most importantly through an ethnocentric orientation. In order to respond more effectively to the needs of ethnic minorities, Gutiérrez presents a series of empowerment strategies ranging from the creation of ethnic sensitive services to establishment of ethno-conscious services.

CHAPTER 14

Empowerment, Political Analyses, and Services for Women

NAOMI GOTTLIEB

An important contribution of the women's movement is the analysis embedded in the phrase, "the personal is political," that is, that the personal circumstances of women are largely determined by the stereotyping and discrimination that have constrained their position in society. Thus, both individual and social change are necessary and interconnected. A related contribution of the women's movement has been to highlight the issue of women's relative powerlessness. This chapter takes those two issues—the political analysis of the condition of the individual woman and strategies for empowerment—and pursues the argument that organizations providing social work services should consider the application of those factors to all their work with women clients.

I will argue that the individual problems of many women clients are largely determined by societal forces. By and large, social workers do not use such a political analysis in their work with women clients nor is the issue of power for women, both in society and in the social work relationship, raised when women receive services. Women in both corners of the service relationship are affected by the societal definitions and oppression of women, although many members of both groups avoid seeing those effects. The thesis of this chapter is that services may be improved when women clients and women social workers can both act, with an increased sense of personal power, on their awareness of the political analysis of their circumstances.

The discussions are based on feminist ideology and analysis and re-present a specific value base. Social work is grounded in a number of values, one of which is to help clients break down barriers in order to attain a quality life (P. Brown, 1981). This chapter is within that social work tradition.

The organizational issues that frame these discussions focus on the use of alternative practice technologies (Hasenfeld, 1983) and the impor-tance of the power differential in the interaction between client and worker (Hasenfeld, 1987; Smith & Siegel, 1985). Staffs of human service agencies regularly work within some form of practice ideology to which they have a strong commitment. Feminist practice technologies are not unique in that respect nor in the fact that, similar to other technologies, the practices are based on a belief system and not necessarily, to this point, on grounded knowledge demonstrating their effectiveness. What may be unique to feminist practice technologies is that the practitioner often makes that technology and its ideology explicit in the encounter with the client and actively attempts to lower the power differential between herself and her client. The chapter offers examples of this process as well as some organizational implications when such approaches are incorporated into the services of social work agencies.

The focus will be largely on the interactions between women clients and women social workers in mainstream organizations since this is the usual configuration for services for women clients. Feminist organi-zations have made major contributions to the development of new ap-proaches to women (Gottlieb, 1980; Kravetz & Jones, 1991; Martin, 1990) but most women clients continue to receive services in conventional settings. The other reason for this focus is to demonstrate that innova-tive approaches can be instituted in settings that do not purport to be feminist or women-centered.

My argument is that the two major issues under consideration here —political analyses of personal problems and empowerment of women clients—can enhance whatever else occurs in the course of service delivery and therefore should be considered in administrative deci-sions about service programs. This discussion is also directed to staffs of agencies because they have the concomitant responsibility to press for those conditions that will lead to better services for their clients.

The recommendation for a political analysis of gender is not meant to create an image of a social worker intent on convincing someone else of the "truth" in a heavy-handed manner. As later examples will illustrate, enabling a woman client to see the political aspects of her situation can take many forms, as can the management of the use of power by the client.

Following a discussion of the rationale for this chapter's major premises, examples will be given of services incorporating these perspectives. These examples will demonstrate feminist practice principles in work with women and can suggest ideas to both administrators and staff about feasible organizational changes to improve services for women clients.

Political Analysis and Personal Empowerment

Political Analysis of Individual Problems

Three of the most frequent problems that women clients face—domestic violence, depression, and poverty—illustrate a gender-based political analysis. Women are the majority of the victims of interpersonal violence (U.S. Department of Justice, 1983), they are much more vulnerable to depression than men (Nolen-Hoeksema, 1990) and they are overrepresented among the poor—this last is particularly true among women of color (Pearce & McAdoo, 1981; Zopf, 1989). The usual explanations of these phenomena do not reflect the belief that women's personal and social conditions are shaped by gender-biased political forces (Bricker-Jenkins & Hooyman, 1986).

A number of factors are central to the fact that women are the vast majority of abuse victims. Men are expected and encouraged to be dominant and aggressive in this society and messages are everywhere that violence resolves conflicts. Women are socialized to regard the roles of wife and mother as primary. Women are the guardians of the family's emotional well-being and are expected to hold the family together at whatever cost. These are some of the circumstances that increase women's vulnerability to violence in the home.

A political analysis of the prevalence of serious depression in women leads to the question: Are societal conditions such that women, as a group, are more likely to be depressed? Seligman's studies (1975) imply that persons who have less sense of autonomy and control in their lives are more vulnerable to depression. Women are not trained to exercise interpersonal or public power (indeed, socialization emphasizes the mediator and nonassertive role), and are economically and socially dependent on men.

Women's poverty is a complex phenomenon but we know that women are by and large segregated in a small number of low-paid, dead-end occupations. Because of this restricted choice of jobs, most women are not only underpaid but underemployed. The wage gap between men and women persists and continues to be considerably wider than in most other industrialized countries (Hewlett, 1986).

In most situations when a woman client brings these and other problems to social workers, we help the woman cope on an individual basis. This lack of attention to wider social causation and to the connection between political forces and personal pain, briefly discussed here, holds a particular irony for social work. We are the one professional group who state with pride that we do, in fact, see the connection between the individual and her/his societal conditions. But, as later discussion will maintain, the political analysis of gender is hampered by strong resistances among both women and men.

Personal Empowerment

This discussion of empowerment for women clients is grounded in three assumptions. The first is that it is to the advantage of women, whatever problem they bring to social workers, to increase their sense of power and control over the circumstances of their lives. Second, gaining such control and using power are enhanced by an understanding of the political aspects of those adverse circumstances. The third assumption is that women can and should develop the skills to use that power, individually and collectively, to try to change the troublesome conditions of their lives.

Taking the responsibility for empowering clients is a necessary task for social workers but one that is not engaged in by many of them. As a profession, we tend to think that our well-articulated commitment to self-determination is an assurance that we are giving power and control to the client. Because we rarely discuss the issue of the power differential in the social work encounter (Hasenfeld, 1987), we convince ourselves that we have the client's interest at heart and may find ourselves engaged in persuasion and manipulation to encourage the client to accept "our assessment of what ought to be done" (Abramson, 1985, p. 391). In the situation of a conflict between client and worker as to diagnosis and intervention decisions, honoring the client's conception of what is in his or her own good creates a dilemma for the worker. In those circumstances, the cultivation of even a "garden-variety" self-determination, much less full empowerment, becomes problematic.

The sticky issue is that for women social workers to encourage such a political understanding of power in their clients, they must, of necessity, have dealt with these insights themselves. In a negative sense, the woman social worker would find it difficult to talk with her client about the restrictions and oppression of women in society if she had not considered how these phenomena relate to herself as a woman. In a positive sense, she can engage herself more fully with her client if she has come to some clear convictions herself about the political effects of sexism and sex discrimination on her own life. Such a stance, however, entails a significant transformation in women social workers and there are enormous barriers to doing this.

Barriers to Political Analyses

Awareness of the oppression of women in society is a subject area qualitatively different from other sensitivities a social worker may develop. The white, heterosexual professional can be aware of the effects of racism and homophobia but can still maintain some distance from those effects because her or his ethnicity and sexual orientation is a shield against the internal acceptance of other people's oppression. Discrimination and oppression on the basis of gender is another matter. Each of us is profoundly affected by gender-role socialization and the politics of gender. The dynamics of power differentials between men and women and sexist assumptions in our lives can be so ingrained that we cannot see them readily, and in fact we may not want to do so (Bernard & Gottlieb, 1987).

In addition to these personal considerations, it is difficult to change entrenched intellectual views. For example, the educational arm of the profession has had limited success in changing educational practices. For more than a decade, the Council of Social Work Education has mandated attention to sexism and content on women in the curriculum and scholarly literature about these issues has become more and more readily available (Simon, 1988). Yet, it is fair to conjecture that most social work graduates come to their jobs without the perspective that this chapter advocates (Lincoln & Koeske, 1987; Weiner, 1988).

Hasenfeld (1987) describes the crucial role played by line staff in human services agencies. Since administrators must allow for the staff's autonomous actions with clients, staff control information given to the client as well as the reports on clients to the administration. Thus the attitudes and beliefs of women social workers (the majority of line staff) determine, in large part, the nature of the services women clients will receive. Their views about the position of their women clients in society are central to their work with those women.

The Consequences of the Status Quo

When women social workers do not grasp the societal aspects of women's problems, the focus continues to be on individual causation and individual solution to women's problems. The difficulties that the client brings to the social worker are considered her individual ones; there is pathology that needs to be addressed, requiring the help of an expert. Within this model of individual pathology, the impact of society and the client's survival strategies are lost to view. Workers will act on the assumption that the traditional relationship between men and women is not the problem. The worker has not disturbed either her own or her client's basic views of women in society and has "overtly and/or covertly . . . contribute[d] to the status of these entrenched societal norms in [her] practice" (P. Brown, 1981, p. 218). Keeping clients ignorant of important social forces related to their gender denies them access to much pertinent information on which to act autonomously (Abramson, 1985). Workers may not serve women clients well when the power dimension in their own lives is not understood. As a consequence, workers may not encourage the client to develop and use her own power to improve her life condition.

A woman client may also be aware that social workers offering direct services, including her own worker, are not in administratively powerful position in agencies. P. Brown (1981, p. 219) asks, "What kind of statement does the social work profession make when about two-thirds of the administrative positions are held by men and the ratio declining?" That statement comes across to clients in direct and indirect ways and erodes the possibility that the social worker she consults will be a model and advocate for the client's assertion of power.

With these consequences of the lack of attention to political analyses and empowerment (for both clients and workers) as background, examples of alternate services describe different modes of intervention.

Services to Counteract Gender Oppression

The examples described now are culled partly from the writings of feminist social workers, but include other reports as well, all drawn from practice in mainstream settings. The case studies illustrate different principles of social work practice, each of which is meant to counteract the negative effects of traditional views of women. The discussion is organized around those principles. The case studies also detail how political analyses and empowerment strategies are implemented. The case examples demonstrate, as anticipated earlier in this chapter, that the importance of a political awareness does not require a series of lectures to clients about women's role in society nor does empowerment mean some version of "storming the barricades." Various modes of empowering are used, attuned to the client situation, that show that there are many ways to increase client's understanding of the impact of society's expectations of and restrictions on women, and many avenues in which to develop powerful actions by women to improve their circumstances. However, the emphasis on a political analysis, rather than a woman's particular problem, is not meant to imply that attention to the individual situations of women is ignored. The oppression of women takes general forms and is usually pervasive, but each individual woman reacts idiosyncratically to that barrage, and she requires parallel attention to her individual needs. The case examples illustrate the interconnection between the two approaches.

The emphasis in these case examples is on different types of intervention based on the two principles of political analysis and empowerment. The primary purpose is to illustrate the possibilities of alternative approaches in mainstream agencies. The outcomes for the clients are also discussed and represent anecdotal descriptions of positive results. Extensive future work remains to test whether these interventions, compared with conventional social work practice, serve women more effectively.

Organizational issues will also be evident in these case examples, particularly related to the consequences of alternative practice technologies. In human services organizations, staff have the task of changing the status of clients in some way (Hasenfeld, 1983), for example, to a more effective parent, to a more reasonable marital partner, to a more efficient user of limited funds. Workers use their position of power to do this, albeit often in a benign way. In the process, they make moral judgments about their clients and their need to change. The worker is seen as the expert and the client as the "object" of the work. The emphasis is usually on the individual client and her individual circumstances. As the following case illustrations will demonstrate, the use of feminist practice technologies assume different perspectives as to definitions of the problems and a different distribution of power.

A Nonstereotyped View of Women

Because a stereotyped view of women is used as a rationale for a large set of sexist practices—about work, family issues, health care and the legal system among others, defining women differently can be a key to developing more appropriate social services for them.

In a community mental health setting, Wedenoja (1991) used a feminist approach to help a mother of a seriously mentally ill adult son develop a different conception of her responsibilities for her son. In the field of mental illness, there is a sorry tradition of mother-blaming. Problems in the family, and particularly schizophrenia, are "either the mother's fault, her responsibility to solve or both" (Wedenoja, 1991, p. 179). Wedenoja's client had assumed the blame for her son's condition, particularly for his continuing dependence on her, and had accepted the criticism of others around her for both his condition and her overprotectiveness of him. Some of Wedenoja's multifaceted approach overlapped with conventional services—for example, referral to a self-help group and for education about current theories of mental illness—but there were aspects that reflected the use of a gender-specific political analysis.

Wedenoja talked with her client about the history of mothers being blamed for a family member's mental illness. This helped the client to challenge the attitudes of others, including mental health professionals and family members, and to discontinue personalizing their assumptions. This approach was complemented by the self-help group experience. There, she heard other women talk of having accepted the blame, some of whom had relinquished their feelings of guilt and shame.

Wedenoja also discussed with her client two societal issues that had direct bearing on this woman's situation: the assumption that women must assume the major tasks of caregiving, although that care is not valued by society, and the lack of social policies and programs that might support women caregivers. Wedenoja recognized the value of the client's caregiving, and at the same time encouraged the client to acknowledge her personal limitations and needs. She supported the client's challenges, both individual and in the group, to the lack of societal support for her circumstances. More self-protective and non-self-blaming behaviors subsequently characterized the client's encounters with both family and professionals.

Social Action Complementing Individual Coping

Trying to raise children in an inner-city, low-income neighborhood plagued by inadequate housing, racism, drug abuse, and crime can be a brutal experience for single mothers of color. Attempting to help those mothers deal with their children's school problems can be daunting and depressing for social workers. Gutiérrez (1991) and her associates, working within the constraints of a child development center, devised a several-step plan to address first, the individual child-rearing concerns of a group of low-income single mothers, mostly Hispanic and African American, and then to help the women to move toward a societal explanation for their children's school problems, leading to social action to change school conditions.

Initially, support groups helped the women identify the source of their problems as family stress, dangerous neighborhoods, and an inadequate school system. In subsequent skill-building groups, the women learned more effective parenting behaviors (Schaeffer & Gutiérrez, 1980). The women also learned skills in group facilitation and in the final stage of intervention, the social action phase, the group was client-led. When concerns about the educational system arose repeatedly, the group, with the workers' support, initiated a class-action suit against the board of education. The case was subsequently won, and had a positive impact on children throughout the city. Gutiérrez (1991, p. 210) comments:

> This example indicates how in less than one year, these women moved from feeling overwhelmed by their young children to feeling capable of confronting the city board of education. . . . Although these women set out to learn how to become more effective parents, they quickly became interested in having an impact on those external conditions that made their role so difficult.

This example illustrates the enhancement of the strengths of women to move into the political arena—the appropriate context for resolving some of their problems. There are also some lessons about the possibilities for worker empowerment. Gutiérrez and her associates decided to devise interventions that would aid this group of women to challenge the powerlessness in their lives and to learn to advocate for themselves. The workers needed to innovate within agency limitations in order to do this. They were realistic about the leeway they had within the major agency's requirement that they serve a specific number of clients. Empowering themselves to innovate within those limits contributed in turn to the empowerment of their clients.

Strategies for Empowerment of the Least Powerful

In Cathy Jay McDermott's (1989) account of a resident rights campaign in a nursing home for the elderly, she makes no mention of gender politics. Yet the great majority of nursing home residents are women and by virtue of ageist sexism, those residents are among the least powerful groups in our society. The strategies McDermott reports are clearly applicable to women, as is her assessment of the harmful effects of the usual treatment of patients in nursing homes.

Ordinarily, residents are given little control over their lives. Autonomous behavior is discouraged and dependency encouraged. Depression is prevalent and tied to institutional helplessness. Dependency, lack of autonomous control, and depression characterize the lives of many women and so strategies that address those problems are central to the well-being of women, particularly old women.

The purpose of the innovation McDermott (1989) describes was to empower nursing home residents to gain control over their lives and improve their mental health. The particular strategies included: education of both residents and staff to resident rights; a celebration of those rights, fashioned like a political campaign and under the complete control of the residents; emphasis on residents as mature adults; development of group cohesion among the residents for the continued assertion of those rights. As a result of these activities, the residents demanded and received more respect from the staff in many practical aspects of their daily lives and became more confident in independent decision making. Significantly, the residents showed an increase in their "levels of activity, sociability and motivation . . . [and] as the literature indicates, these conditions enhance self-esteem and mental clarity and reduce depression and mortality rates" (McDermott, 1989, p. 156).

These innovations were instituted in a mainstream health care system, with all the trappings and constraints of the medical model. One can assume an overworked staff and physically and mentally restricted residents, as is true of many nursing homes. The example illustrates the potential for change even in those constricting circumstances, bringing with it the possibility not only for increased independence and respect for women, but more dramatically than most situations, an actual increase in women's life expectancy.

The Use of Peers for Empowerment

In an urban children's hospital, Gary (1991) describes the use of peer advocates in services to mothers of abused children. The case also indicates the value of moving from a traditional view of women, as noted earlier. That shift in thinking forms the background to Gary's example. She describes a change in her own view of the responsibility of a mother for her child's abuse and a subsequent alteration in services to the woman, with positive results. Along with most of her colleagues and similarly with respect to many other instances of child abuse, Gary assumed that the abused child in the family she describes was the central client and she viewed the woman primarily as the child's caretaker. She therefore assumed that the mother was the primary person responsible to see that the child was no longer abused, even though her husband was the perpetrator of the abuse. Gary was angry and frustrated with her when the mother could not even acknowledge her husband's abuse of her child. Only when Gary could perceive the woman as being an individual separate from this expected family role, did she understand the woman's own fear of abuse to herself as well. She could then begin the process of helping the woman to protect herself first, and then the child.

The program of "dual advocacy"—protection for both the child and the mother—was initiated by a group of staff members at this children's hospital as a result of this shift in thinking about the mother's role. An important part of this program is the use of a peer advocate—a woman who is herself a survivor of abuse that both she and her children have experienced. The peer advocate has lived through the dilemmas of leaving or staying with an abusive situation and is also familiar with community resources from a client's perspective. Use of such peer advocacy accomplishes an additional purpose—the valuing, the use, and the enhancement of the strengths of women survivors.

Gary (1991, p. 24) outlines many of the issues grounding the dual advocacy/peer advocate model:

> Initial primary focus on the child's medical and social condition: the mother's seeming ambivalence or fear of her partner, thus confusing staff and causing them to blame her; the mother's need for intense, nonjudgmental support which staff who are directly involved in the care of severely injured child may not be able to provide; feelings of inadequacy and hopelessness on the part of child protection and hospital social workers, causing them to look beyond the mother to the foster care system for the child's care; constant interdisciplinary collaborations with legal counsel and other staff to protect both the child and mother and to find them housing, welfare and child care resources; and the need for strong advocacy for the mother, without which she may be immobilized and misjudged.

In this case example, the mother, with the help of the advocate, found courage to change her previous denial and to acknowledge that her husband had battered both herself and her child. With the advocate, she went to court to secure an order of protection, went through the necessary procedures at the hospital to bar her husband from visiting, and decided to be a witness in criminal proceedings against her husband.

The example shows that valuing women's strengths, in this instance the peer advocate to begin with and later, the client herself, can result not only in positive actions for client protection, but the abatement of frustration and anger on the part of professional staff as well. Another significant result of this program has been a considerable decrease in foster home placements, because children can remain at home with their mothers, both free and safe from violence. Gary (1991, p. 23) reports that "in a recent review of 46 advocacy cases, only two children have been placed in temporary foster care."

Similar use of peer support for women is reported in work with homeless women (K. Brown & Ziefert, 1990), with battered women (NiCarthy, Merriam, & Coffman, 1984), and as part of the Gutiérrez example described above. Peer support, especially in self-help groups, has been widely used for both men and women. However, among the differences noted between mixed-gender and women-only groups, particularly feminist-oriented groups, two are of significance here. Walker (1987, p. 9) comments that "female groups tend to encourage greater exploration of the social determinants of personal problems rather than emphasize solely interpersonal problems." Burden and Gottlieb (1987, pp. 35-36) assert that feminist group work encourages "the reduction of the power differential between leader and group members. . . . and resocializes [women] to take risks, be leaders and trust in their own judgment about the world."

Clients as Instructors in Empowerment

Each of the instances discussed so far have focused on the initiative taken by the social worker in empowering the client and/or raising the consciousness of women clients about gender politics. The process can proceed in the other direction as well. In fact, when it does so, there is further strengthening of the women clients who become the instruments for staff changes.

The example offered by Liddie (1991) describes such a reversed educational process. The project she discusses is a program for mothers of children in an urban day center. The project had a wider purpose than just the daily care of young children and was meant to develop self-help groups for the mothers, including strategies for social action and community change. In the project, the mothers were successful in establishing a food co-op, a great benefit to this group of low-income women, and they also participated in a march on City Hall to protest day-care cuts. However, it was the social action directed at the program itself that illustrates the mothers' impact on the staff.

In their ongoing groups within the project, the mothers frequently complained about feeling overburdened by the expectations of the day-care staff. They felt harassed about criticisms of their children's manner of dress or unruly behavior, of their inconsistencies in dropping off or picking up their children, and of their parenting skills in general. The mothers also felt they were not part of the decision making about their children's care at the center. Liddie and her associates helped these women plan for an expression of these concerns in a joint meeting with the staff and secured the staff's cooperation for this problem-solving session. The results were twofold: First, there were changes in staff attitudes and behaviors toward the mothers as well as a greater recognition on the staff's part of the strengths of these women. Second, "the group served as an impetus for staff members themselves to confront the director and the board members regarding issues directly related to their work within the program" (Liddie, 1991, pp. 141-142). One could conjecture that the staff's previous feelings of powerlessness might have been translated into criticisms of the children's mothers, and that finding their own power to advocate for themselves also resulted in better services for the children.

Organizational Implications of Feminist Practice Technologies

This chapter's discussions and examples constitute recommended changes in services to women based on a political analysis of gender and increased empowerment of clients. As noted earlier, such a stance is congruent with a basic value of the social work profession to change unjust conditions. This chapter has argued that grounding services to woman in that perspective has a positive impact on the client's individual problem, on the social conditions that contribute to that problem, and on the professional competence of the worker.

The discussion assumes that both workers and agencies need to change in order to empower women to improve their life circumstances

(Pinderhughes, 1983). Part of that change must be within staff social workers so that, in their encounters with their women clients, they can teach and model skills in using power and in self-advocacy (Hegar & Hunseker, 1988). The chapter has focused on the particular issues that affect the ability of women staff to do this and offered cases to demonstrate positive outcomes for women clients when women staff assure that political analyses and strategies for empowerment are part of how services are delivered.

There are a number of organizational implications embedded in these case examples. First, in each instance, the workers introduced an alternative practice technology within the framework of a traditional human services agency. Even with the constraints of the medical model of a nursing home, changes in staff actions there considerably increased the autonomy and self-respect of the residents. Without challenging the basic structure of the agencies in which they worked, Wedenoja proceeded to help a mother alter her conception of herself as a mother of a mentally ill son; Gutiérrez and her associates acted on their conception of their clients as potential social change activists; Gary introduced a peer advocate to aid a mother of an abused child and, in the process, changed her own view of the mother's responsibility; Liddie and her day-care teacher associates learned from a group of clients, reversing the usual power and teaching dynamics. None of these staff members had to change the basic structure of their organizations in order to change their own work. Indeed, Gutiérrez reported that her group was careful to abide by certain policies of the agency—such as numbers of clients seen—as they went about changing their approach to the group of women.

In each of these instances, more power was given to the client and several processes were involved in that transfer. First, the workers redefined their client(s) as not totally and individually responsible for their circumstances and thereby mitigated the client's tendency toward self-blame. They helped the women to learn, in Hyde's (1989, p. 152) words, "to reject self-blame and to embrace collective actions that target structural barriers."

Although there was little evidence that the workers engaged in a political discourse with their clients about women's place in society and the political implications of their individual problems, the workers acted on those beliefs by leading clients away from an individual analysis and emphasis. The results were a greater sense of autonomy (McDermott), important social action (Gutiérrez), change in relationships with staff (Liddie), self-respecting action to protect herself from abuse (Gary), and a refusal to accept the blaming finger of others (Wedenoja). Hasenfeld (1983) writes of the tendency of staff in human services organizations to make moral judgments of clients, often to assume that clients are morally deficient. By redefining the core of the problem and by acting on client strengths and not pathology (Weick, Rapp, Sullivan, & Kisthardt, 1989), the basic judgments in these case examples were changed. The worker was no longer the unquestioned expert making such moral judgments but rather, as Hyde (1989) suggests, a respecter of the client as the "expert" in her own survival.

A second aspect of the power transfer is its potential effect on the workers' interactions with their clients. When women social workers help women clients to see beyond an individual causation and individual solution to their problems, they have themselves become more aware of the political implications of women's problems. Because of this, there is more of a tendency to see their commonalities with their clients and less of a tendency to see them as "objects" of service. Vladeck (1980) asserts that fraternal solidarity may lead to higher quality human services. In the same vein, sisterly solidarity results when women social workers understand their commonalities with their clients as similarly oppressed persons in this society. This may lead workers to attribute a greater sense of social worth to their clients, reversing a tendency to devalue clients and thus to make them more vulnerable to control.

The third implication of the worker's greater respect for the client and willingness to encourage autonomy and empowerment relates to the issue of trust. In many worker-client interactions, trust is based on the client's willingness to accept the worker's expertise and well-meant intentions. Hasenfeld (1983) writes of the importance of such trust and the need to bring this about by reason and not coercion. In the examples cited, I would conjecture that trust was based on a set of different dynamics. When staff create conditions of greater autonomy and self-direction in a nursing home; when workers engage with clients in redefining the problem as that of the day-care staff or the city's board of education; when workers acknowledge the value and power of a client's peer; and in each instance, when workers believe in the ability of the client to take action, then trust between client and worker appears to have a more solid base than a blind belief that the worker is on her side. The phenomenon of trust implied in these examples comes from an appreciation of the client's potential, especially to act independently of the worker in broader social arenas.

Finally, an outcome of giving greater power to the client may be less burnout for the worker. Gary, Liddie, and Gutiérrez write of their frustrations in helping women who have experienced multiple pressures in the care of children, including the protection of a child from abuse. As the workers sought other explanations and other solutions to the women's problems, they themselves became less frustrated. They could see the women take hold of their problems, redefine them, and take more self-protective actions—in Liddie's instance, the women use their new found power to empower other staff; in Gutiérrez's example, they took on the board of education; in Gary's case, the client acted against an abusive husband to protect her child and herself.

Dressel (1987) comments that women workers tend to do the emotional labor with clients in social service agencies, in contrast to the greater likelihood that men will do the managerial tasks. Because women have a tendency to blame themselves when things go wrong (as they often do in the day-to-day work with clients), they are particularly vulnerable to stress. When more women workers engage in feminist practice technologies, there may be multiple positive results: when workers act on a political understanding of their client's problems, they are also more likely to make a political analysis of their own workplace and personal situations and are less prone to self-blame; when they encourage their clients toward independent actions based on client strengths, they are less likely to be frustrated by the intractability of client problems; when they more correctly diagnose the client's problems, value their client more highly and are willing to challenge the agency culture, they are less likely to "reinforce and reproduce their own subordination" (Dressel, 1987, p. 295).

There are a few further organizational implications to the use of feminist practice technologies. When social workers use the "personal is political" analysis in work with clients, they are also more likely to engage in practice at both the micro and macro practice level. In recent years, there has been much dissatisfaction expressed about the false dichotomy between interpersonal and organizational practice. Undergraduate social work programs have been strong proponents of a generalist approach for years and many graduate programs have been redesigning their programs along such lines. If a worker sees that her client's problem is both personal and political, then work is called for at both levels. In this perspective, the needs of the client may encourage workers to be more versatile and more helpful to all clients.

There is another implication about how agencies as a whole may change. The point was stressed earlier that, in the case examples, workers changed their mode of practice without disturbing the basic agency structure. But there is another, more encouraging long-term possibility. Hasenfeld (1983) comments on the tendency for agencies to select those service technologies that are congruent with the ideological preferences of their staff. One might conjecture therefore that as more women social workers adopt the perspective advocated in this chapter, the organizations in which they work may very well follow suit.

A final issue is related to the call for more women administrators. Many authors have advocated for the increase in numbers of women administrators in social work agencies (Belon & Gould, 1977; Chernesky, 1980; Weil, 1987). Most of the arguments have appropriately centered on the issue of equity and a needed difference in administrative style that women may bring. Here, I want to stress another argument pertinent to this chapter's thesis.

Using the rationale of effective service to clients (i.e., the bottom line in social work), I would argue that more women administrators could mean a greater likelihood that services to women clients would be grounded in a political analysis of gender. There is no guarantee of this, of course. However, Martin and Chernesky (1989) offer some encouraging examples from the political arena. They comment that "all women elected (or appointed) to office do not vote as feminists, but they are aware of women's problems of combining paid work and family obligations" (Martin & Chernesky, 1989, p. 136). They also note that one of the qualities present in states with the most progress in comparable worth enactment was the greater proportion of women in the state houses of representatives. If the same dynamics operated in human services agencies, women clients would benefit in the long run. If there were more women administrators, women social workers and their clients would have role models of women in power. One would also expect that women administrators would be more likely than male administrators to implement a feminist analysis of women's circumstances.

Conclusion

In this chapter, I have argued the necessity for a gender-based political analysis in all work with women, presented some practice examples to illustrate this perspective, and considered some of the organizational issues in the use of feminist practice technologies. Obviously, I believe that women clients would benefit if all staff could incorporate the values and strategies discussed here and if all social work administrators would take responsibility for assuring this. This belief will be greatly strengthened as empirical work supports the efficacy of these approaches.

References

Abramson, M. (1985). The autonomy-paternalism dilemma in social work practice. *Social Casework, 66*(7), 387-393.

Belon, C. J., & Gould, K. (1977). Not even equals: Sex related salary inequities. *Social Work, 22*(6), 466-471.

Bernard, L. D., & Gottlieb, N. (1987). Conditions for non-sexist education. In D. Burden & N. Gottlieb, *The woman client* (pp. 13-24). New York: Tavistock.

Bricker-Jenkins, M., & Hooyman, N. (1986). *Not for women only.* Silver Spring, MD: National Association for Social Workers.

Brown, K., & Ziefert, M. (1990). A feminist approach to working with homeless women. *Affilia: Journal for Women in Social Work, 5*(1), 6-20.

Brown, P. (1981). Women and competence. In A. Maluccio (Ed.), *Promoting competence in clients* (pp. 213-235). New York: Free Press.

Burden, D., & Gottlieb, N. (1987). Women's socialization and feminist groups. In C. Brody (Ed.), *Women's therapy groups* (pp. 24-39). New York: Springer.

Chernesky, R. (1980). Women administrators in social work. In E. Norman & A. Mancuso (Eds.), *Women's issues and social work practice* (pp. 241-262). Itasca, IL: F. E. Peacock.

Dressel, P. (1987). Patriarchy and social welfare work. *Social Problems, 14*(3), 294-309.

Gary, L. (1991). Feminist practice and family violence. In M. Bricker-Jenkins, N. Hooyman, & N. Gottlieb (Eds.), *Feminist social work practice in clinical settings* (pp. 19-32). Newbury Park, CA: Sage.

Gottlieb, N. (1980). *Alternative social services for women.* New York: Columbia University Press.

Gutiérrez, L. (1991). Empowering women of color: A feminist model. In M. Bricker-Jenkins, N. Hooyman, & N. Gottlieb (Eds.), *Feminist social work practice in clinical settings* (pp. 199-214). Newbury Park, CA: Sage.

Hasenfeld, Y. (1983). *Human services organizations.* Englewood Cliffs, NJ: Prentice-Hall.

Hasenfeld, Y. (1987). Power in social work practice. *Social Service Review, 6*(3), 469-483.

Hegar, R. L., & Hunzeker, J. M. (1988). Moving toward empowerment-based practice in public child welfare. *Social Work, 33*(6), 499-502.

Hewlett, S. (1986). *A lesser life.* New York: William Morrow.

Hyde, C. (1989). A feminist model for macro-practice: Promises and problems. *Administration in Social Work, 13*(3/4), 145-181.

Kravetz, D., & Jones, L. (1991). Feminist practice in feminist service organizations. In M. Bricker-Jenkins, N. Hooyman, & N. Gottlieb (Eds.), *Feminist social work practice in clinical settings* (pp. 233-249). Newbury Park, CA: Sage.

Liddie, B. (1991). Relearning feminism on the job. In M. Bricker-Jenkins, N. Hooyman, & N. Gottlieb (Eds.), *Feminist social work practice in clinical settings* (pp. 131-146). Newbury Park, CA: Sage.

Lincoln, R., & Koeske, R. D. (1987). Feminism among social work students, *Affilia: Journal for Women in Social Work, 2*(1), 50-57.

Martin, P. (1990). Rethinking feminist organizations. *Gender and Society, 4*(2), 182-206.

Martin, P., & Chernesky, R. (1989). Women's prospects for leadership in social welfare: A political economy perspective. *Administration in Social Work, 13*(3/5), 117-143.

McDermott, C. J. (1989). Empowering the elderly nursing home resident: The resident rights campaign. *Social Work, 34*(2), 155-157.

NiCarthy, G., Merriam, K., & Coffman, S. (1984). *Talking it out: A guide to groups for abused women.* Seattle: Seal Press.

Nolen-Hoeksema, S. (1990). *Sex differences in depression.* Stanford, CA: Stanford University Press.

Pearce, D., & McAdoo, H. (1981). *Women and children: Alone and in poverty.* Washington, DC: National Advisory Council on Economic Opportunity.

Pinderhughes, E. (1983). Empowerment for our clients and for ourselves. *Social Casework, 64*(5), 331-338.

Schaeffer, M., & Gutiérrez, L. (1980). *Parents as therapists.* Paper presented at the New York Association for the Learning Disabled Annual Conference, New York.

Seligman, M. E. P. (1975). *Helplessness: On depression, development and death.* San Francisco: Freeman.

Simon, B. (1988). Social work responds to the women's movement. *Affilia: Journal for Women in Social Work, 3*(4), 60-68.

Smith, A., & Siegel, R. (1985). Feminist therapy: Redefining power for the powerless. In L. B. Rosewater & L. Walker (Eds.), *Handbook of feminist therapy.* New York: Springer.

U.S. Department of Justice, Bureau of Justice Statistics. (1983). *Report to the nation on crime and justice: The data.* Washington, DC: Office of Justice Programs.

Vladeck, B. C. (1980). *Unloving care: The nursing home tragedy.* New York: Basic Books.

Walker, L. (1987). Women's groups are different. In C. Brody (Ed.), *Women's therapy groups* (pp. 3-12). New York: Springer.

Wedenoja, M. (1991). Mothers are not to blame: Confronting cultural bias in the area of serious mental illness. In M. Bricker-Jenkins, N. Hooyman, & N. Gottlieb (Eds.), *Feminist social work practice in clinical settings* (pp. 179-196). Newbury Park, CA: Sage.

Weil, M. (1987). Women in administration: Curriculum and strategies. In D. Burden & N. Gottlieb (Eds.), *The woman client* (pp. 92-110). New York: Tavistock.

Weick, A., Rapp, C., Sullivan, W. P., & Kisthardt, W. (1989). A strengths perspective for social work practice. *Social Work, 34*(4), 350-354.

Weiner, A. (1988). Are BSW students sexist. *Affilia: Journal for Women in Social Work, 3*(1), 69-78.

Zopf, P. E. (1989). *American women in poverty.* Westport, CT: Greenwood Press.

CHAPTER 15

Empowering Ethnic Minorities in the Twenty-First Century
THE ROLE OF HUMAN SERVICE ORGANIZATIONS

LORRAINE M. GUTIÉRREZ

Demographic projections suggest that as our nation moves into the twentieth century, our society will increasingly comprise minorities of color. This is due in part to increased immigration of individuals from Asia and Latin America, as well as the higher fertility rates of Latinos and other people of color. These trends will require changes in all of the institutions in our society, but particularly those human service organizations that have been organized to meet the needs of vulnerable populations (Chau, 1990; Dodd & Gutiérrez, 1990; McAdoo, 1982; Ozawa, 1986; Sarri, 1986).

Although minorities of color—African American, Native American, Hispanic, and Asian American—are increasing in numbers, statistics suggest that they have gained little in respect to social and economic status or political power (Sandifur & Pahari, 1989). Therefore, their minority status in our society remains characterized by social exclusion, economic oppression, and lack of direct access to sources of power (Carpenter, 1980; McAdoo, 1982; Ozawa, 1986; Washington, 1982). Although the specific ethnic and racial groups encompassed by this umbrella term differ from one another in respect to culture and history, they share some similarity due to their experiences as ethnic minorities. As a group, people of color disproportionately experience the effects of racism and classism in our society. They are hampered by average earnings lower than that of whites, by overrepresentation in low status occupations, and by a low average level of education. Correspondingly, people of color are underrepresented in positions of power within our government, corporations, and nonprofit institutions (McAdoo, 1982; National Committee on Pay Equity, 1988; Ozawa, 1986; Sandifur & Pahari, 1989).

These statistics suggest some ways in which the powerlessness of this group has very direct and concrete effects on daily experiences. Lack of access to many social resources is both a cause and an effect of powerlessness (Mizio, 1981; Solomon, 1976). In 1980 the percentage of people of color living in poverty ranged from one and one-half to three and one-half times the percentage of whites: 21% of all African Americans, 10% of all Asian Americans, 16% of all Hispanics, and 19% of all Native Americans were earning 75% of the poverty level in comparison with 6% of the white population (U.S. Department of Commerce, 1982). Updates since the 1980 census indicate similar trends (Ozawa, 1986). Therefore, people of color are more likely than whites to suffer from conditions of poor or no housing, insufficient food and clothing, inadequate access to health and mental health services, and location within low-income and physically deteriorating communities.

These demographic projections have contributed to concern within the corporate sector and among policymakers regarding our ability as a nation to manage the increasing ethnic and racial diversity while creating mechanisms to ensure that people of color are able to participate in and contribute to our society (Johnston, 1987; Ozawa, 1986; Sarri, 1986). A number of scholars have argued that human service organizations can play a particularly crucial role in creating a society in which diversity can contribute to our strength as a nation by improving the human capital potential of people of color through improved access to quality health care, education and support services. This investment in ethnic minorities could reverse trends that suggest that we could become a nation of poor minority children and youth and older whites, neither group being capable of producing the economic resources necessary for supporting existing social services or other social goods (Ozawa, 1986; Sarri, 1986; Williams, 1990).

Business and industry have begun to respond to the challenges of increasing workplace diversity and of a work force that may not have the necessary education or skills. For example, some large corporations are beginning to develop remedial education and literacy programs while others are engaging in partnership programs with local school districts. In contrast, there has been little discussion among human service organizations regarding the challenges these demographic trends present. Although the field of education has begun to respond, there has been little recognition within the field of social services of these trends or adequate exploration of ways in which they will deal with the increasing need for services by ethnic minorities and how they can play a role in the empowerment of these groups in order to achieve greater equity.

Human service organizations are those institutions in our society that have been developed to deal with a wide range of human needs. Their "principal function is to protect, maintain, or enhance the personal well-being of individuals by defining, shaping, or altering their personal attributes" (Hasenfeld, 1983, p. 1). Further distinguishing human services organizations from other types of bureaucracies is their focus on changing and working with people and social groups, and their mandate to protect and promote the welfare of their client populations. Some examples of human services organizations are schools, health clinics, child protective services, mental health programs, and community centers.

Human services organizations exist in a web of interactions with the larger social environment, which affect their support and ability to function. They are particularly vulnerable to changes in the economic and political power structures that can increase or diminish support for particular social programs, and to demands from client or community groups that can affect their credibility, status, and survival. The purpose of this chapter is to explore ways in which human service organizations can begin to more effectively meet the demographic challenges of the twenty-first century. It will focus primarily on those human service agencies designed and developed to provide social services, which have been less responsive to these changes than those that provide health or educational services. It begins with a review of the literature that has looked at this challenge from the perspective of people of color, their needs, strengths, and histories. It then moves into a discussion of common approaches to meeting the needs of minority populations and of the strengths and shortcomings of these approaches. A final section looks at the literature on organizational empowerment and proposes ways in which human services organizations can be recreated not only to meet the needs of minority groups, but also to more effectively advance the development of a more equitable society.

Social Services and Ethnic Minorities

Although this chapter is framed in respect to demographic trends that suggest that the proportion of people of color in our population is increasing, the need for social service organizations to serve this group is not new. In fact, given the overall lower status, fewer economic options, and higher stress experienced by minority groups, they have always had a disproportionate need for social services. How have human services organizations responded to ethnic and racial diversity within the client population in the past and what does this suggest for our future?

The literature on social services for people of color suggests that most social service organizations have fallen short in meeting their needs. Although minorities are overrepresented in agencies with a strong social control function, such as the criminal justice and child welfare systems, they are underrepresented in agencies of a more voluntary and preventive nature, such as mental health clinics or counseling centers (Flaskerud, 1984; Hasenfeld, 1983; Morales, 1981; Olson, 1982; Rogler, 1982; Sarri, 1986; Stehno, 1982; Takeuchi, Leaf, & Hsu-Sung, 1988). These trends can best be understood as symptomatic of ways in which minority groups interface with the larger social services system.

Barriers to Services

A number of studies have begun to identify how barriers to service impede the ability of members of minority groups to access existing social services. They have identified such barriers both within social agencies and within populations of color. The importance of these barriers varies within and between different ethnic minority groups dependent on nativity, age, income, and education. For example, one cross-ethnic study found that Caucasians were the least likely to perceive service barriers, while those ethnic minorities with the fewest social resources perceived the most barriers (Takeuchi et al., 1988).

A number of *structural barriers* have been identified that can limit the access of people of color to voluntary agencies. Barriers that affect all four ethnic minority groups include location of services, cost, and knowledge of services (Die & Seelbach, 1988; Land, Nishimoto, & Chau, 1988; Lee, 1986; Lorenzo & Adler, 1984; Parker & McDavis, 1989; Starret, Mindel, & Wright, 1983; Watkins & Gonzales, 1982). Asian Americans and Hispanics, particularly first generation or the elderly, are also affected disproportionately by the availability of bilingual and bicultural services and prefer social workers from their own ethnic background (Land et al., 1988; Lee, 1986; Lorenzo & Adler, 1984; Pomales & Williams, 1989; Rogler, Malgady, Constantino, & Blumental, 1987; Starret et al., 1983; Watkins & Gonzales, 1982). Within the African-American community, where awareness of existing social services is high relative to other minority groups (Neighbors & Taylor, 1985; Parker & McDavis, 1989), the older, poorer segments of the population are more likely to utilize social services (Broman, Neighbors, & Taylor, 1989; Neighbors & Taylor, 1985).

Research has also identified *characteristics within minority groups* that may inhibit the use of social service agencies. Cultural beliefs regarding problem definition and help seeking may discourage contact with service providers outside of the family or ethnic community (Die & Seelbach, 1988; Flaskerud, 1984; Lee, 1986; Pomales & Williams, 1989; Rogler, 1982; Starret et al., 1983). Underutilization can also be due to feelings of shame or mistrust due to negative interactions between social service agencies and the particular minority community (Carpenter, 1980; Lee, 1986; Parker & McDavis, 1989). The existence of social supports, such as extended family networks, family associations, tribal councils, or churches, can also account for some underutilization, although current research suggests that among African Americans and Hispanics these social supports more typically complement, rather than substitute for, services received from agencies (Jackson, Neighbors, & Gurin, 1986; Starret et al., 1983; Starret, Wright, Mindel, & Tran, 1989).

Client Typification and Tracking

For those minority clients who do enter social service agencies, the practices and procedures of agencies may discourage their use or lead to client typification based on race or ethnicity. Agency practices that discourage use include waiting lists, intrusive intake procedures, or rigid eligibility requirements (Lorenzo & Adler, 1984; Parker & McDavis, 1989; Takeuchi et al., 1988). Although these procedures may not be developed to restrict access, they may result in engaging only the most motivated and resourceful clients.

Client typification is a mechanism used by human service organizations to ensure that clients are provided with the services they need. At its best it can have a triage function, in which clients are provided with the most appropriate services; however, errors in typification can lead to a mismatch between client needs and the services provided. There is evidence that this is likely to occur when service providers base their assessments and interventions on the client's race or ethnicity (or any other status characteristic), hence on preexisting biases rather than on stated needs. A number of studies on the helping process suggest that this frequently occurs within social service organizations. Research on minority mental health (Good & Del Vecchio Good, 1986; Rogler et al., 1987) has begun to identify ways in which mental health services for minorities are affected by biases inherent in the technology developed for assessment and treatment. For example, the DSM-III provides no procedure for assessing the meaning of an individual's symptoms in relation to his or her culture. Research on children in foster care describes minority children as more neglected, in terms of service plans and permanency planning, than white children (Olson, 1982). The literature on the perceptions of helping professionals reports a tendency of human service workers to view the problems of minority clients as related to mental illness and to recommend treatment rather than social support or changes in life-style (Flaskerud, 1984). This can be especially pronounced when the worker and client are of different racial backgrounds (Franklin, 1985).

These tendencies within human service organizations can account in part for the overrepresentation of people of color in involuntary agencies. If minority children in the child welfare system are less likely to receive preventive or permanency planning services, they are more likely to spend their lives in foster care or group homes (Olson, 1982). If people of color with mental or emotional distress are unable to access counseling services, they may later come in contact with the system when their symptoms are more severe and are then viewed as requiring institutionalization, rather than counseling and community support.

Responses to Racial and Ethnic Diversity

Ethnocentrism in Human Services

The tracking and typification of minorities are symptomatic of the historically ethnocentric orientation of most social service organizations. The ethnocentric perspective is one that considers, either explicitly or implicitly, the norms, values, and needs of the majority culture to be the most desirable (Chau, 1990; Gallegos, 1982; Morales, 1981). This perspective places little or no value on the unique experiences of minority populations and may approach the cultures of ethnic and racial minorities as the basis of many of the problems faced by these groups.

There is ample evidence that the ethnocentric perspective has been the dominant orientation of most social services. In its most damaging forms, ethnocentrism has manifested itself in social service organizations as the provision of segregated services (Stehno, 1982), in the deportation of "aliens" (Moore & Pachon, 1985), or in "Americanization" programs that resulted in the loss of culture and community (Carpenter, 1980). For example, social service organizations have been instrumental in the removal of Native American children from their families into boarding schools or white foster families, which resulted in the break up of families, communities, and the loss of language and cultural heritage (Cross, 1986). Similarly, during the Depression of the 1930s, social service agencies in the southwest spearheaded efforts to "repatriate" people of Mexican descent in order to reduce public assistance costs. This resulted in more than 400,000 people of Mexican descent, a large percentage of them American citizens, being sent to Mexico and separated from their homes, families, and sources of employment (Moore & Pachon, 1985).

The impact of less direct, more insidious, forms of ethnocentrism has been damaging as well. The presence of some ethnic groups, such as Asian Americans, has been ignored by service planners and providers (Lee, 1986). Some ethnic groups and their needs have been overlooked based on the notion that they "take care of their own" or may not respond well to the treatments offered at agencies (Land et al., 1988; Lee, 1986; Starret et al., 1983). Rather than looking at ways in which existing agency procedures, structures, or treatments can be altered to better respond to the needs of ethnic minorities, the ethnocentric approach assumes that the "problem" in accessing and using services exists in the client group and that it is their responsibility to change.

Ethnic Sensitive Services

Within the past 20 years, criticisms by communities of color led to the development of the ethnic sensitive approach to social service organizations and programs (Chau, 1990; Devore & Schlesinger, 1987; Gallegos, 1982; Scott & Delgado, 1979). The goal of the ethnic sensitive or ethnic competent approach is to create or recreate programs and organizations that will be more responsive and responsible to the culture of minority groups. Training for cultural competence and the delivery of ethnic sensitive services requires understanding of one's own personal attributes and values, gaining knowledge about the culture of different groups, and developing skills for cross cultural work (Chau, 1990; Gallegos, 1982). It is based on the notion that the nature of our society is multicultural and that positive gains can result from learning about different cultural groups and incorporating culture into agency procedures, structures, and services (Devore & Schlesinger, 1987; Gallegos, 1982).

This approach has contributed to different thinking by some service providers regarding communities of color. Rather than teaching solely from the perspective of common human needs, training in social work and other helping professions is placing increasing emphasis on ways in which the needs, values, and beliefs of different cultures can be viewed as equally valid (Mizio, 1981). Rogler et al. (1987) provide one framework for conceptualizing how culturally relevant, ethnic sensitive services can be developed and implemented.

Access to Services. The first stage focuses on increasing access to services, especially at an early phase of distress, as one way to prevent further problems and the need for more expensive services. This would involve removing or reducing the impact of many of the barriers to services discussed in the previous section. Some methods for increasing accessibility include: hiring bilingual or bicultural staff (Arroyo & Lopez, 1984; Lorenzo & Adler, 1984; Watkins & Gonzales, 1982), identifying and working with lay providers such as ministers or spiritual leaders for outreach and consultation (Humm-Delgado & Delgado, 1986; Land et al., 1988; Manson, 1986), and involving community leaders in agency programs, especially in an outreach capacity (Arroyo & Lopez, 1984; Humm-Delgado & Delgado, 1986).

Tailoring Interventions. The second level involves selecting existing treatments to fit the culture and reality of the group in question. This requires learning about the culture of the ethnic minority group and then critically appraising the services that are provided and considering which methods might fit best into the ethnic minority community, their level of acculturation, structure, and other important factors. For example, if the local ethnic minority community is primarily low income, they will require more concrete service, training, and education regarding their rights or methods for self advocacy (Devore & Schlesinger, 1987; Mizio, 1981; Washington, 1982). With many ethnic groups, in which extended family networks are influential, family counseling or family network interventions may be viewed as more compatible with their methods for dealing with emotional distress than individual counseling (Rogler et al., 1987).

Modification of Services. A third level is the modification of agency procedures, structure, and service delivery systems to improve the fit with the culture of the client group. This will often require the creation of new programs and services and hiring full-time professional staff from the minority community. For example, Rogler et al. (1987) have developed "*Cuento* therapy" for use with Hispanic children, as an extension of how Puerto Rican families have traditionally communicated important values and ideas to children through folk tales—*Cuentos*. Rather than carrying out a traditional play therapy session, a counselor trained in *Cuento* therapy would work with children around the discussion of characters in *Cuentos* who are experiencing similar problems and conflict. Other examples include work with Chinese Americans that integrates traditional medicine with counseling (Lorenzo & Adler, 1984), services for African Americans that engage extended family systems (Devore & Schlesinger, 1987), or use of traditional "talking circles" in the treatment of Native Americans (Manson, 1986).

The Organization Development Model. Although organizations may attempt to integrate new ethnically relevant or competent services into existing structures without modifying them, they will eventually find that if the program is to be successful, modifications and changes in existing policies, personnel, and procedures will be necessary (Scott & Delgado, 1979). Most often, organizations have attempted to create ethnically competent services through organizational development or specialized program approaches.

The organizational development (OD) model attempts to make changes within existing human services organizations through consultation, research, and training (Resnick & Menafee, 1989). The goal is to create a structure, policies, and procedures within the agency that support the creation and provision of ethnically competent services. An OD approach requires sanction and support from all decision makers in the agency in order for work to be effective and to achieve maximum change (Jones, 1989; Kelley, McKay, & Nelson, 1985).

Two examples from the literature describe ways in which an OD approach can be implemented. Jones (1989) describes one OD method for the implementation of cultural sensitivity training for social work with African Americans. By beginning training with a clear commitment from board, administration, and staff to changing their approach to working with African Americans, the cultural sensitivity program led to a critical analysis of the agency's programs and structure. This created a new structure in which African Americans were hired into more staff positions and given greater voice within the agency. Similarly, Kelley et al. (1985), in describing OD with a Native American agency, found that working with the board, administration, and staff of this organization in a collaborative fashion contributed to the empowerment of workers by enlarging their roles and encouraging professional development. This change in the staff roles improved both direct client services and the agency's status in the community.

The Specialized Program Model. The specialized program model involves the development of a program within a larger social service organization to meet the needs of a specific ethnic or racial group (Arroyo & Lopez, 1984; Olmstead, 1983; Scott & Delgado, 1979; Watkins & Gonzales, 1982; Zambrana & Aguierre-Molina, 1987). This allows an organization to concentrate its efforts to serve a particular population, though it can also have the effect of marginalizing the needs and priorities of the target group. A successful specialized service is one that can create and provide effective ethnic sensitive services while influencing agency wide change.

An example of one way a specialized program can influence agency policy is provided by Olmstead (1983), who describes how a small unit to train minority social work students within a child welfare agency with a predominantly white staff had profound effects on the services of the agency. Although it was the intention of the agency to provide specialized services to minorities and to train students, administration and staff soon found that the ethnic minority students brought a different perspective to the agency. Their critiques contributed to a change in the orientation of the agency toward greater connection with ethnic minority communities, the use of ethnic sensitive approaches to direct service work, and a new affirmative action policy that resulted in a greater participation of people of color on the board and in professional staff positions (Olmstead, 1983).

Scott and Delgado (1979) describe and analyze ways in which the implementation of a program to service the Hispanic population moved from marginalization and ineffectiveness to success. Initial efforts to create a specialized program through the incorporation of Hispanic paraprofessionals into a primarily white mental health agency resulted in the marginalization of the program, conflict between the minority workers and white supervisors, and a failure to provide effective services. It was only when the agency hired a bilingual/bicultural Hispanic administrator to design and implement the program that it was successful in creating an effective program that was accepted by both the Hispanic and social service communities. This demonstrates that unless the administration of specialized services is located within or near the center of power in an organization, it is likely to remain marginal and its effectiveness limited.

Ethnic sensitive programs and services were developed in response to criticisms by ethnic minority communities that existing social service agencies were irrelevant and unresponsive to the needs of people of color. Although the development of the ethnic sensitive approach to social services has led to changes in the training and thinking of individual service providers and the creation of new programs, it is not an adequate response to the challenges related to the low status and power of ethnic minorities as a group. The examples cited above suggest that if OD or specialized services do not lead to structural changes in organizations and a greater participation of people of color in the governance of the agency, efforts toward change can be mostly symbolic and marginal (Gutiérrez, 1990; Mizio, 1981; Morales, 1981; Solomon, 1976; Washington, 1982). If human service organizations are to work to improve the overall social status of ethnic minorities they must also develop ways to contribute to the empowerment of these groups. The ethnoconscious approach, which combines an ethnic sensitive orientation and an empowerment perspective on practice, holds promise for creating empowering services, programs, and organizations.

Ethno-Conscious Services

Empowerment practice in social service aims to increase personal, interpersonal, or political power so that individuals, families, and communities can take action to improve their situations. It has become a popular concept in the social work, community psychology, and health care fields as a means for addressing the problems of powerless populations and for mediating the role powerlessness plays in creating and perpetuating social problems (Gutiérrez, 1990; Hasenfeld, 1987; Pinderhughes, 1983; Solomon, 1976; Zimmerman, in press). Empowerment is a process of change that can occur on the individual, interpersonal, organizational, or political level. Individual empowerment means developing a sense of personal power, while interpersonal empowerment involves developing the ability to affect others (Dodd & Gutiérrez, 1990; Hirayama & Hirayama, 1985; Sherman & Wenocur, 1983). The organizational level of empowerment refers to the development of organizations' ability to contribute to the empowerment of individuals and communities (Gerschick, Israel, & Checkoway, 1989; Hasenfeld, 1987; Prestsby, Wandersman, Florin, Rich, & Chavis, 1990; Zimmerman, in press). Empowerment on the political level involves developing the ability to work with others to change social institutions (Fagan, 1979; Kahn & Bender, 1985; O'Connell, 1978).

Ethno-conscious services are those that attempt to impact all four levels of empowerment with people of color. They are based on the assumption that social service programs should take a "mezzo-level" approach to their work by (1) making efforts to both assist in the development of individuals and families and impact on the social conditions that contribute to the problems they experience, (2) working with the clients and community to develop a sense of personal control and an ability to influence the behavior of others, and (3) establishing equity in the distribution of resources (Biegel & Naperste, 1982; Frumpkin & O'Connor, 1985; Mizio, 1981; Morales, 1981; Rappaport, 1981; Washington, 1982). The ultimate goal of this approach is to work with people of color and their communities to increase their power within the context of cultural values, symbols, and strengths (Kelley et al., 1985).

Ethno-conscious social services are oriented toward empowerment rather than remediation or adjustment of individual clients and can contribute to the creation of organizations that encourage the empowerment of consumers and workers. Empowerment-based services differ from traditional programs by equalizing the power between service providers and clients: utilizing small groups; accepting the client's definition of the problem; identifying and building upon the client's strengths; raising the client's consciousness of issues of class and power; actively involving the client in the change process; teaching specific skills; using mutual aid, self help, or support groups; encouraging clients to exercise their personal power within the context of the organization; and mobilizing resources or advocating for clients (Gutiérrez, 1990; Hasenfeld, 1987; Pinderhughes, 1983; Solomon, 1976; Zimmerman, in press).

Research on organizational empowerment suggests that the ways in which social service organizations are structured can have an effect on individual and community empowerment. The ability of individual workers to share their power with clients and engage in the range of interventions required for empowerment practice can be dependent on the support they receive for this type of work and their own feelings of personal power. Social service organizations that contribute to the disempowerment of workers may undermine their ability to empower clients and communities because in response to feelings of powerlessness, many social service workers may become ineffective, hostile towards clients, apathetic, or "burned out" (Mathis & Richan, 1986; Pinderhughes, 1983; Sherman & Wenocur, 1983). Organizations that empower workers through participatory management, the ability to make independent decisions about their work, communication and support from administrators, and opportunities for skill development can be more capable of empowering clients (Bredeson, 1989; Gerschick et al., 1989; Zimmerman, in press).

Examples of Ethno-Conscious Services. What examples of ethno-conscious services exist in the literature? The most integrated approach to ethno-conscious services is that of the alternative, ethnic agency. The ethnic agency is a human service organization organized by ethnic minorities to serve the needs of a specific community. As such it faces the challenges both of organizational maintenance and meeting the primary group functions of the ethnic group (Jenkins, 1989; Kelley et al., 1985). Ethnic agencies often emerge organically from within the ethnic community in order to meet social service needs and usually have some commitment to impacting community issues and problems (Jenkins, 1989; Uriarte & Merced, 1985). Therefore, they have an explicit goal of empowering the community in which they work (Gutiérrez, 1986).

Ethnic agencies exist within all communities of color. The literature documents the presence of child-care centers (Jenkins, 1989), senior citizen programs, youth-oriented programs (Zambrana & Aguierre-Molina, 1987), mental health programs (Solomon, 1976), and health care clinics (Lee, 1986) that have been developed to meet the needs of specific minority communities. However, it is the multiservice center that may best exemplify the work of ethnic agencies.

Within ethnic minority communities, multiservice centers have been developed by community organizations to try to meet a variety of needs —often as a reaction to the fragmentation of the existing social service system and out of a desire to reduce service barriers. These agencies are similar in structure, programs, and purposes to settlement houses in that they offer a range of services and present themselves as community centers.

In her research on ethnic agencies, Jenkins (1989) found that most of them incorporate ethnic factors into their programming, ideology, and staff composition. From the perspective of ethno-conscious services, ethnic considerations need to be integrated into all these dimensions in order for an organization to be most effective. El Centro de la Raza, in Seattle, WA, is one example of an effective ethnic multiservice center. The agency was founded in 1972 when a group of Latino activists occupied an empty school building. They demanded that the city of Seattle rent the building to their group so that they could develop a center for the Latino community (Johansen, 1972). In the ensuing years,

El Centro de la Raza has developed into a large and complex organization with the goal of empowering the minority population of Seattle. Their orientation toward services is that of working with individuals, families, groups, and the community to increase their choices, power, and influence. Services of the agency include a child-care program, case management and advocacy, senior citizen nutrition, English as a second language (ESL), job training, and a food bank. El Centro also has a community development and social action department that is involved in bringing together ethnic communities, encouraging agency/community linkages, and political advocacy in the United States and in Latin America. Because there is no identifiable "barrio" in Seattle and because they see themselves as involved in an effort to bring together members of all four ethnic minority groups, El Centro is located in a multiethnic community and its programs and services are open to all. The organization is perceived by many as successfully balancing the often competing goals of providing social services while working toward social change (Hessburg, 1987).

An analysis of El Centro and other ethnic agencies that have successfully worked toward empowerment suggests that their effectiveness is influenced by their horizontal and vertical ties within the community, as well as the strength of their leadership (Gutiérrez, 1986). El Centro has developed strong horizontal ties by engaging the community in cultural events and involving the community in the assessment of needs, as volunteers, and in agency governance. This has contributed to tremendous community support that has allowed the agency to survive despite fluctuating financial and political support. Within the past decade, El Centro has developed increasingly strong vertical ties with funding organizations and state and local governments through the participation in human services networks and political advocacy. As a result, it has become more successful in receiving financial support for programs and services while maintaining a role as an advocate for the ethnic minority population of Seattle.

Although the ethnic agency exemplifies ways in which social service organizations can work toward empowerment, it is not the only mechanism of ethnic-conscious services. The literature on empowerment suggests that social service organizations involved in developing ethnic sensitive services can move toward an ethno-conscious perspective by incorporating program elements that focus on increasing client power (Hasenfeld, 1987). This chapter and the other literature on empowerment provide many examples of the characteristics and structure of empowerment based services. From an organizational perspective, empowerment will also require involving members of the ethnic minority community as decision makers with equal power in developing and administering any programs or services. It will also require giving voice and power to clients and members of the ethnic minority community who can provide input regarding program development and implementation. Finally, ethno-conscious services are based on principles of participatory management, where mechanisms for client, community, and worker feedback and participation are built into the organization (Gerschick et al., 1989; Zimmerman, in press).

Conclusion

The demographic challenge of the twenty-first century is to develop more effective means for all social institutions to handle increasing ethnic and racial diversity. Research on the experiences of ethnic minorities within social service organizations suggests that existing organizational structures have mirrored and perpetuated conditions of inequality and powerlessness. The movement toward developing ethnic sensitive services, which places a value on the experiences, norms, and expectations of people of color, has been the predominant method for responding to ethnic diversity in a positive, rather than oppressive, way. However, this chapter points out ways in which this approach falls short in addressing the larger agenda of increasing the power of ethnic minorities so that they achieve greater equity and are no longer disproportionately hampered by conditions of poverty and discrimination. An ethno-conscious approach to structuring and providing social services is proposed here as one means of moving beyond sensitivity and toward empowerment. However, the creation of more ethno-conscious, empowerment-based organizations is dependent on the ability of existing social service administrators to create programs in which people of color are full participants in their creation, staffing, and administration.

References

Arroyo, R., & Lopez, S. (1984). Being responsive to the Chicano community: A model for service delivery. In B. White (Ed), *Color in a white society* (pp. 63-73). Silver Spring, MD: National Association of Social Workers.

Biegel, D., & Naperste, A. (1982). The neighborhood and family services project: An empowerment model linking clergy, agency, professionals and community residents. In A. Jeger & R. Slotnick (Eds.), *Community mental health and behavioral ecology* (pp. 303-318). New York: Plenum.

Bredeson, P. (1989, October-November). Redefining leadership and roles of school principals: Responses to changes in the professional worklife of teachers. *High School Journal*, pp. 9-20.

Broman, C., Neighbors, H., & Taylor, R. (1989). Race differences in seeking help from social workers. *Journal of Sociology and Social Welfare, 16*(3), 109-123.

Carpenter, E. (1980). Social services, policies, and issues. *Social Casework, 61,* 455-461.

Chau, K. (1990). A model for teaching cross cultural practice in social work. *Journal of Social Work Education, 26,* 124-133.

Cross, T. (1986). Drawing on cultural tradition in Indian child welfare practice. *Social Casework, 67,* 283-289.

Die, A., & Seelbach, W. (1988). Problems, sources of assistance, and knowledge of services among elderly Vietnamese immigrants. *The Gerontologist, 28,* 448-452.

DeVore, W., & Schlesinger, E. G. (1987). *Ethnic sensitive social work practice (2nd ed.).* Columbus, OH: Merrill.

Dodd, P., & Gutiérrez, L. (1990). Preparing students for the future: A power perspective on community practice. *Administration in Social Work, 14,* 43-62.

Fagan, H. (1979). *Empowerment: Skills for parish social action.* New York: Paulist Press.

Flaskerud, J. (1984). A comparison of perceptions of problematic behavior by six minority groups and mental health professions. *Nursing Research, 33*(4), 190-197.

Franklin, D. (1985). Differential clinical assessment: The influence of class and race. *Social Service Review, 59,* 44-61.

Frumpkin, M., & O'Conner, G. (1985). Where has the profession gone? Where is it going? Social work's search for identity. *Urban and Social Change Review, 18*(1), 12-19.

Gallegos, J. (1982). The ethnic competence model for social work education. In B. White (Ed), *Color in a white society* (pp. 1-9). Silver Spring, MD: National Association of Social Workers.

Gerschick, T., Israel, B., & Checkoway, B. (1989). *Means of empowerment in individuals, organizations, and communities: Report on a retrieval conference.* Ann Arbor: University of Michigan, Program on Conflict Management Alternatives.

Good, B., & Del Vecchio Good, M. (1986). The cultural context of diagnosis and therapy: A view from medical anthropology. In M. Miranda & H. Kitano (Eds.), *Mental health research and practice in minority communities: Development of culturally sensitive training programs* (pp. 1-28). Rockville, MD: National Institute of Mental Health.

Gutiérrez, L. (1986, March). *Alternative services and community organization.* Paper presented at the National Symposium on Community Organization and Social Administration, Miami, FL.

Gutiérrez, L. (1990). Working with women of color: An empowerment perspective. *Social Work, 35,* 149-154.

Hasenfeld, Y. (1983). *Human service organizations.* Englewood Cliffs, NJ: Prentice-Hall.

Hasenfeld, Y. (1987). Power in social work practice. *Social Service Review, 61,* 469-483.

Hessburg, J. (1987, October 23). 15th Anniversary of a man's dream: Helping Latinos. *Seattle Post-Intelligencer*, p. B1.

Hirayama, H., & Hirayama, K. (1985). Empowerment through group participation: Process and goal. In M. Parenes (Ed.), *Innovations in social group work: Feedback from practice to theory* (pp. 119-131). New York: Haworth.

Humm-Delgado, D., & Delgado, M. (1986). Gaining community entree to assess the service needs of Hispanics. *Social Casework, 67*, 80-89.

Jackson, J., Neighbors, H., & Gurin, G. (1986). Findings from a national survey of Black mental health: Implications for practice and training. In M. Miranda & H. Kitano (Eds.), *Mental health research and practice in minority communities: Development of culturally sensitive training programs* (pp. 91-116). Rockville, MD: National Insitute of Mental Health.

Jenkins, S. (1989). The ethnic agency defined. In D. Burgest (Ed.), *Social work practice with minorities*. Metuchen, NJ: Scarecrow Press.

Johansen, B. (1972, October 22). Chicanos were following slogan, "power to the people." *Seattle Times*, p. B6.

Johnston, W. (1987). *Workforce 2000: Work and workers for the 21st century*. Indianapolis: Hudson Institute.

Jones, R. (1989). Increasing staff sensitivity to the black client. In D. Burgest (Ed.), *Social work practice with minorities*. Metuchen, NJ: Scarecrow Press.

Kahn, A., & Bender, E. (1985). Self help groups as a crucible for people empowerment in the context of social development. *Social Development Issues, 9*(2), 4-13.

Kelley, M., McKay, S., & Nelson, C. (1985). Indian agency development: An ecological practice approach. *Social Casework, 66*, 594-602.

Land, H., Nishimoto, R., & Chau, K. (1988). Interventive and preventive services for Vietnamese Chinese refugees. *Social Service Review, 62*, 468-484.

Lee, J. (1986). Asian-American elderly: A neglected minority group. *Journal of Gerontological Social Work, 9*(4), 103-116.

Lorenzo, M., & Adler, D. (1984). Mental health services for Chinese in a community health center. *Social Casework, 65*, 600-609.

Manson, S. (1986). Recent advances in American Indian mental health research: Implications for clinical research and training. In M. Miranda & H. Kitano (Eds.), *Mental health research and practice in minority communities: Development of culturally sensitive training programs* (pp. 51-90). Rockville, MD: National Insitute of Mental Health.

Mathis, T., & Richan, D. (1986, March). *Empowerment: Practice in search of a theory*. Paper presented at the Annual Program Meeting of the Council on Social Work Education, Miami, FL.

McAdoo, H. (1982). Demographic trends for people of color. *Social Work, 27*, 15-23.

Mizio, E. (1981). Training for work with minority groups. In E. Mizio & A. Delaney (Eds.), *Training for service delivery to minority clients* (pp. 7-20). New York: Family Service Association of America.

Moore, J., & Pachon, H. (1985). *Hispanics in the United States*. Englewood Cliffs, NJ: Prentice-Hall.

Morales, A. (1981). Social work with third world people. *Social Work, 26*, 48-51.

National Committee on Pay Equity. (1988). In P. Rothenberg (Ed.), *Racism and sexism: An integrated study* (pp. 69-75). New York: St. Martin's.

Neighbors, H., & Taylor, R. (1985). The use of social service agencies by black Americans. *Social Service Review, 59*, 258-268.

O'Connell, B. (1978). From service delivery to advocacy to empowerment. *Social Casework, 59*(4), 195-202.

Olmstead, K. (1983). The influence of minority social work students on an agency's service methods. *Social Work, 28,* 308-312.

Olson, L. (1982). Services for minority children in out-of-home care. *Social Service Review, 56,* 572-585.

Ozawa, M. (1986). Nonwhites and the demographic imperative in social welfare spending. *Social Work, 31,* 440-445.

Parker, W., & McDavis, R. (1989). Attitudes of Blacks toward mental health agencies and counselors. In D. Burgest (Ed.), *Social work practice with minorities* (pp. 14-25). Metuchen, NJ: Scarecrow Press.

Pinderhughes, E. (1983). Empowerment for our clients and for ourselves. *Social Casework, 64,* 331-338.

Pomales, J., & Williams, V. (1989). Effects of level of acculturation and counseling style on Hispanic students, perceptions of counselor. *Journal of Counseling Psychology, 36,* 79-83.

Prestsby, J., Wandersman, A., Florin, P., Rich, R., & Chavis, D. (1990). Benefits, costs, incentive management and participation in voluntary organizations: A means to understanding and promoting empowerment. *American Journal of Community Psychology, 18,* 117-149.

Rappaport, J. (1981). In praise of paradox: A social policy of empowerment over prevention. *American Journal of Community Psychology, 9*(1), 1-25.

Resnick, H., & Menefee, D. (1989). *Organization development in social work: A human service partnership.* Paper presented at the Annual Program Meeting, Council on Social Work Education, Chicago.

Rogler, L. (1982). A barrier model for Hispanic mental health research: New techniques for the psychiatric evaluation and psychotherapy of Hispanic children. *Research Bulletin: Hispanic Research Center, 5*(4), 1-3.

Rogler, L., Malgady, R., Constantino, G., & Blumental, R. (1987). What do culturally sensitive services mean? The case of Hispanics. *American Psychologist, 42,* 565-570.

Sandifur, G., & Pahari, A. (1989). Racial and ethnic inequality in earnings and educational attainment. *Social Service Review, 63,* 199-221.

Sarri, R. (1986). Organizational and policy practice in social work: Challenges for the future. *Urban and Social Change Review, 19,* 14-19.

Scott, J., & Delgado, M. (1979). Planning mental health programs for Hispanic communities. *Social Casework, 60,* 451-456.

Sherman, W., & Wenocur, S. (1983). Empowering public welfare workers through mutual support. *Social Work, 28*(5), 375-379.

Solomon, B. (1976). *Black empowerment.* New York: Columbia University Press.

Starret, R., Mindel, C., & Wright, R. (1983). Influence of support systems on the use of social services by the Hispanic elderly. *Social Work Research and Abstracts,* 35-40.

Starret, R., Wright, R., Mindel, C., & Tran. T. (1989). The use of social services by Hispanic elderly: A comparison of Mexican American, Puerto Rican and Cuban elderly. *Journal of Social Service Research, 13*(1), 1-25.

Stehno, S. (1982). Differential treatment of minority children in service systems. *Social Work, 27,* 39-45.

Takeuchi, D., Leaf, P., & Hsu-Sung, K. (1988). Ethnic differences in the perception of barriers to help seeking. *Social Psychiatry and Psychiatric Epidemiology, 23,* 273-280.

Uriarte, M., & Merced, N. (1985). Social service agencies in Boston's Latino community: Notes on institutionalization. *Catalyst, 5,* 21-34.

U.S. Department of Commerce. (1982). *1980 Census of the population. Vol. 1: Characteristics of the population.* Washington, DC: U.S. Department of Commerce.

Washington, R. (1982). Social development: A focus for practice and education. *Social Work, 27,* 104-109.

Watkins, T., & Gonzales, R. (1982). Outreach to Mexican Americans. *Social Work, 27,* 68-73.

Williams, L. (1990). The challenge of education to social work: The case of minority children. *Social Work, 35,* 236-242.

Zambrana, R., & Aguierre-Molina, M. (1987). Alcohol abuse prevention among Latino adolescents: A strategy for intervention. *Journal of Youth and Adolescence, 16*(2), 97-113.

Zimmerman, M. (in press). Empowerment: Forging new perspectives in mental health. In J. Rappaport & E. Seidman (Eds.), *Handbook of community psychology.* New York: Plenum.

PART VII

The Effectiveness
of Human Services

An often voiced criticism of human service organizations is that they are ineffective, and various indicators are presented, some contradictory, to support such arguments. Part of the difficulty with the concept of effectiveness is the many connotations it can evoke, especially in the case of human service organizations. This is because these organizations often have multiple and conflicting goals, their products are mostly intangible (e.g., improvement in quality of life); and their technologies are indeterminate. In Chapter 16, D'Aunno examines these issues and explores several organizational models to assess effectiveness. These range from rational systems to multiple constituency models. D'Aunno proposes that each model springs from a particular organizational perspective and its underlying assumptions about the nature of the organization. He proposes that the appropriateness of each model depends on the stability and measurability of the assessment criteria to be used.

Grusky and Tierney, in Chapter 17, present an empirical study of effectiveness, using a systems perspective to evaluate the effectiveness of county mental health care systems. The virtue of their approach is their emphasis on the entire mental health sector serving the chronically mentally ill rather than on a single organization. Moreover, they show how the four measures of effectiveness— comprehensiveness, coverage, quality, and coordination—are interrelated, thus capturing the idea of the effectiveness of the service system. Indeed, these measures could differentiate the counties studied in terms of their relative effectiveness.

CHAPTER 16

The Effectiveness of Human Service Organizations
A COMPARISON OF MODELS

THOMAS D'AUNNO

Many groups internal and external to human service organizations are affected by their performance and take an active interest in their effectiveness and efficiency. For example, insurers, employers, and other groups that pay for health care are demanding that hospitals decrease their costs and at the same time maintain or improve the quality of care they provide. In the past several years, rising health care costs have led to increased scrutiny of hospital performance (Scott & Shortell, 1988). And, the same is true for a variety of other human service organizations.

Given widespread concern about the performance of human service organizations, researchers have given a great deal of attention to the concept of organizational effectiveness. This concept has much intuitive appeal. Groups that have investments in an organization ask, How well is it meeting my needs and interests? How well is it performing? In short, is it effective?

As a result, dozens of books and articles have attempted to define— and develop models to assess—organizational effectiveness (e.g., Cameron & Whetten, 1983; Friedlander & Pickle, 1968; Georgopoulos, 1986; Goodman & Pennings, 1977; Price, 1968; Steers, 1975; Yuchtman & Seashore, 1967; Zammuto, 1982). Unfortunately, there is still little agreement about the definition and measurement of organizational effectiveness. Indeed, there are multiple models of organizational effectiveness, each with a somewhat different definition of *effectiveness* and varying criteria to assess it.

Cameron and Whetten (1983) and others (Scott, 1987) argue that a key reason why there are so many approaches to defining and assessing organizational effectiveness is that there are so many different models of organizations. In other words, each conceptualization of what an organization is entails a conceptualization about what effectiveness means. Scott (1987, p. 319) summarizes this view well: "Quite diverse conceptions of organizations are held by various analysts, and associated with each of these conceptions will be a somewhat distinctive set of criteria for evaluating the effectiveness of organizations."

The existence of multiple models of effectiveness is not necessarily a problem. In fact, several researchers consider such diversity a strength because it fosters a more complex view of organizations (e.g., Morgan, 1980; Weick, 1977). I agree with this perspective but, at the same time, I argue that we need closer analysis of the relationships among various models of organizational effectiveness (e.g., Cameron, 1986; Zammuto, 1984). Such analysis is not likely to show the superiority of one model of effectiveness over other models (e.g., Bluedorn, 1980; Connolly, Conlon, & Deutsch, 1980). Rather, following Cameron (1986), I propose that comparisons among different types of effectiveness models are needed in order to identify the conditions under which a particular model or combination of models may be more useful than others.

In short, this chapter argues that by developing knowledge of how models of organizational effectiveness vary and relate to each other, we can better apply them more usefully in research on human service organizations. The chapter is divided into three sections: a brief discussion of particular problems in analyzing the effectiveness of human service organizations; a discussion and comparison of central models of effectiveness; and an analysis of the conditions under which such models may be usefully applied.

Problems in Assessing the Effectiveness of Human Services

Human service organizations have some relatively distinctive features that make assessing their effectiveness especially difficult. Further, the distinctive features of human service organizations may make some models of effectiveness more useful than others. These features are briefly noted here to provide background for a comparison of effectiveness models.

Perhaps the most important distinguishing feature of human service organizations is that people are their "material" or "inputs" (Hasenfeld, 1983). This fact has several consequences for such organizations and assessments of their effectiveness. First, the technologies that human service organizations use tend to be indeterminate. That is, knowledge of means-ends relationships in service technologies is limited. This is due in part to the inherent complexity of human nature: means to address people's social and health needs often are beyond the reach of current scientific knowledge (for example, as is the case in trying to find a cure for HIV infection). Further, there are methodological problems involved in attempting to develop adequate treatment technologies for people. For example, extraneous factors other than the service or treatment influence clients' behavior. As a result, it is difficult to determine the extent to which services are achieving their desired effects. Similarly, the components of many service organizations are often loosely coupled, making it difficult to determine the contribution of any single service or unit to the overall effectiveness of an organization (Hasenfeld, 1983).

Finally, because ours is a pluralistic society, public values and views about the roles and work of human service organizations often are ambiguous and changing. Moreover, external groups often place competing or conflicting demands on service organizations. As a result, human service organizations face turbulent and hostile environments. Assessments of effectiveness are not only difficult to conduct in such environments, but they also tend to have short life spans because the criteria of effectiveness shift rapidly (Quinn & Cameron, 1983).

Models of Organizational Effectiveness

This section examines and compares three models of organizational effectiveness: a goal-attainment model, multiple constituency (MC) models, and an institutional theory model. These approaches vary considerably in their assumptions and in their measures of organizational effectiveness. As a result, they nicely illustrate a range of conceptual approaches to effectiveness. And, though each has its weaknesses, I will argue that each also has important strengths.

Goal Attainment Model

One of the most well-known and widely critiqued approaches to organizational effectiveness is the goal attainment model. This model posits that organizations are effective to the extent that they accomplish their stated goals. The model is based on the theory that organizations are rational systems that exist to achieve desired ends. In this view, organizational behavior consists of actions performed by purposeful actors whose efforts are coordinated to achieve their ends as efficiently as possible (Scott, 1987).

Analyses of effectiveness based on this view of organizations begin by specifying organizational goals and then proceed to measure the extent to which such goals are achieved. Measures typically include the quantity and quality of goods or services produced and the efficiency with which goods or services are produced.

To illustrate, consider an application of a goal attainment approach to drug abuse treatment organizations. These organizations are relatively small (an average of 11 full-time equivalents), mostly private nonprofit (although there are also publicly owned and private for-profit organizations), and mostly funded with state and federal grants. Further, staff members use a combination of various types of individual (e.g., behavioral) and group therapy to treat client problems ranging from alcohol abuse to cocaine addiction.

Consider two measures of goal attainment for these drug abuse treatment organizations: the percentage of an organization's clients in the last year who ended treatment (1) free from the use of drugs; (2) meeting their treatment goals. We found that these two measures correlate .52 in a national random sample of 575 treatment organizations (McCaughrin, Price, & Klingel, in press).

Several points are important to note about these two measures of goal attainment. First, we developed these measures based on case studies and interviews with managers; that is, we began specifying organizational goals primarily by asking influential organization members what their goals were. This approach is problematic, of course, when different groups of organization members (e.g., managers versus staff members) have conflicting goals for the organization or for themselves, or when goals are unclear, difficult to measure, or changing.

Indeed, in the case of drug abuse treatment there is often conflict about appropriate organizational goals (D'Aunno, Sutton, & Price, 1991). On the one hand, there is the belief that the only valid goal for treatment and for treatment organizations is for clients to become, and remain, totally abstinent from drug use. This view is promulgated by the well-known and influential self-help group, Alcoholics Anonymous, which believes that drug abuse is a disease that can be cured only by abstinence. On the other hand, there are those who believe that clients can return to moderate use of drugs once the underlying cause of excessive drug use is addressed. Such underlying causes include, for example, work stress, marital problems, physical health problems, adolescent rebellion, and so on.

Goal conflict and goal ambiguity may explain why the correlation between the percentage of clients ending treatment drug-free and the percentage of clients meeting treatment goals is not higher. This correlation might be higher if being drug-free were the only, or even the most important, goal for treatment. But there are other important treatment goals, such as clients being able to deal with stressful situations in adaptive ways that do not involve excessive drug use.

Another difficult question is, How high should the percentages be on these measures for an organization to be considered "effective"? In other words, what is the yardstick of success? Should funding agencies continue to support organizations in which less than 50% of the clients end treatment without meeting their treatment goals? Or, is even a 30% rate very good with this difficult client group? (It turns out that, on average, 53% of clients met treatment goals in these organizations and 45% of clients ended treatment drug-free.) There are, of course, several ways to address these questions. One could compare an organization's current performance to previous years and look for improvement; organizations could be compared to each other, checking statistically for outliers; or, some acceptable range of scores could be established arbitrarily on the basis of expert opinion. All of these approaches have advantages and disadvantages, and the goal attainment approach has been criticized because it provides little or no basis for choosing among them (Hannan & Freeman, 1977; Hasenfeld, 1983).

Despite the weaknesses of a goal attainment approach, researchers often find that measures of goal attainment are useful to include in an effectiveness assessment. Such measures may uncover goal conflict and goal ambiguity that were not known. Further, at least some organizational constituents may be concerned with aspects of goal attainment. Finally, the goal attainment approach is most useful to the extent that organizations have goals that are: measurable or observable; relatively few in number; and widely agreed on (Cameron, 1986; Hasenfeld, 1983).

Multiple Constituency Models

The multiple constituency (MC) approach has been proposed as an alternative to previous approaches to organizational effectiveness, especially the goal and systems approaches noted above (Connolly et al., 1980; Tsui, 1990; Wagner & Schneider, 1987; Zammuto, 1982, 1984). Though there are several variations of the MC approach (see Zammuto, 1984, for a comparison of MC approaches), they share the view that an organization is effective to the extent that it at least minimally satisfies the interests of multiple constituencies associated with it. The common underlying assumption of MC approaches is that organizations depend on various groups for resources and, ultimately, for survival. Thus unless organizations can at least minimally satisfy such groups, they will withdraw their support, causing organizational decline and, possibly, death. In other words, a political economy perspective (Hasenfeld, 1983; Wamsley & Zald, 1976; Zald, 1970) underlies MC approaches.

The term *constituency* refers to groups or individuals holding preferences or interests pertaining to the focal organization (Tsui, 1990). The term *stakeholder* has been used synonymously with constituency (e.g., Blair & Fottler, 1990; Freeman, 1984). For example, the constituents or stakeholders of a hospital include: its employees, board members, medical staff members, regulatory groups, patients and their families, private and public insurance groups and other groups that pay for services (e.g., employers), and referring physicians.

Using MC approaches involves at least two steps (Pfeffer & Salancik, 1978, p. 84). The first task is to identify constituents. Second, the satisfaction of various constituents with organizational performance is assessed. Additional steps also have been included in MC models. For example, some MC models ascertain the criteria that constituents use to evaluate a focal organization; further, criteria can be rank-ordered in terms of their importance to a constituent. Other MC models rank the importance of power of each constituent relative to the focal organization. This allows evaluators to weigh the consequences of meeting or not meeting each constituent's needs.

MC approaches vary both in how they identify an organization's constituents and in how they deal with conflicting views among constituents (Zammuto, 1984). One variant of MC approach addresses these issues from a power perspective (e.g., Goodman & Pennings, 1977; Pfeffer & Salancik, 1978). In this view, one identifies the constituents of an organization first by tracing its exchanges of valued and scarce resources. Groups that hold such resources potentially have a good deal of power over the focal organization (Emerson, 1962;

Thompson, 1967) and, as a result, they should be included in an assessment of effectiveness. Further, the preferences of the most powerful constituents should be weighed most heavily when constituents have conflicting evaluations of an organization's performance: Without the support of powerful providers of resources organizations cannot survive.

In contrast, a second MC variant, proposed by Zammuto (1982), takes an evolutionary perspective. The perspective is "evolutionary" in the sense that it focuses on environmental changes and organizational adaptation to such changes over time. Zammuto (1982) argues that organizations and their environments are evolving and that effectiveness must be viewed within the context of change. As a result, constituent preferences at one point in time are insufficient for assessing organizational effectiveness because they do not take long-term changes in environments into account. That is, effective performance at one point in time may become ineffective as environmental demands change.

To the extent this is true, questions of whose preferences should be satisfied at any given point in time are not as important as questions of how divergent preferences can be satisfied in the long run (Zammuto, 1984). In other words, this model emphasizes that evaluations of effectiveness should not only take constituents' preferences into account but also should consider changes in organizational environments. The model focuses on the processes of becoming effective rather than on static evaluations of effectiveness (Zammuto, 1982, 1984).

In sum, MC models vary in their assumptions about how to identify constituents and about how to value their preferences. Nonetheless, for the most part the models share the view that organizational effectiveness should be defined and assessed according to the preferences of key constituents.

An MC Model of University Hospitals

MC approaches can be illustrated in a recent study of university hospitals that my colleagues and I conducted (D'Aunno, Hooijberg & Munson, 1991; Munson & D'Aunno, 1987, 1989). University hospitals are among the most complex human service organizations. This complexity stems from their three-part mission: teaching, research, and patient care. Meeting each part of this mission requires university hospitals to relate to several groups. For example, the teaching role involves the hospital with universities; in fact, most university hospitals are owned by universities and, as a result, hospital managers are responsible to university administrators and trustees. Moreover, when the universities are public institutions (as most of them are) both the university and the hospital are subject to state laws and a variety of state offices. In addition, other important constituents concerned with the hospital's educational mission include medical school faculty members and students, interns, and residents.

The research role means that the hospital, in collaboration with faculty members and research staff, must depend on biomedical research funding agencies as well as the federal Food and Drug Administration, which regulates medical procedures and pharmaceutical medications. Finally, patient care entails contact with insurance companies and other groups that pay for care, licensing/accreditation bodies, patients and their families, and various groups of health care professionals, some of whom are employees (e.g., nurses) and some of whom are community-based (e.g., referring physicians).

Each of these major constituents focuses on a different aspect of hospital performance, although they certainly share some concerns too. From patients' point of view, for example, university hospitals are effective to the extent that they provide a high quality of care. University administrators worry about the financial performance of hospitals that, if poor, can threaten the financial status of the university itself. Medical school faculty members focus on the hospital's ability to help them train students and attract research grants. Table 16.1 shows correlations among six measures of university hospital effectiveness that reflect the concerns of different constituents.

The data to develop the measures of patient and employee satisfaction and quality of care were gathered from chief executive officers, university vice-presidents and medical school deans at 76 university hospitals using telephone surveys. In addition, financial data were gathered from Medicare records and the National Institute on Health; data on educational performance came from the National Residency Matching Program.

If we applied a power perspective to these measures of effectiveness, we would focus most on the measures of medical school research funds and hospital financial performance. These measures reflect how well the hospital is meeting the expectations of its two most powerful constituents, university administrators (and, if it is a public university, state administrators) and medical school faculty. Employee satisfaction, in contrast, is of less concern to these constituents. Thus hospital effectiveness would be judged more on the basis of how well the hospital met the expectations of the university administrators and medical school faculty than on how well the needs of employees were satisfied.

Table 16.1 Correlations Among Six Measures of University Hospital Effectiveness

	(1)	(2)	(3)	(4)	(5)
(1) Medical School Research Funds					
(2) Quality of Undergraduate Education	.75*				
(3) Quality of Care in University Hospital	.22*	.36*			
(4) Patient Satisfaction in University Hospital	.06	.20*	.65*		
(5) University Hospital Employee Satisfaction	.14	.17	.41*	.56*	
(6) University Hospital Financial Viability	.09	.18	.13	.10	.05

NOTE: *$p < .05$

There are positive, but low, correlations between the measure of employee satisfaction and the measure of medical school research funds (.14) and the measure of hospital financial performance (.05). These correlations indicate that hospitals that satisfy the preferences of employees do not necessarily satisfy the preferences of more powerful groups, and vice versa. It is also important to note that the measures of medical school research funds and hospital financial performance correlate only .09. This indicates that hospitals are not simultaneously meeting the interests of both of these two powerful groups. A "pure" application of a power perspective might attempt to resolve this conflict by determining which of these groups is most powerful and assessing hospital effectiveness accordingly. Nonetheless, these data point out the complexity involved in applying a multiple constituency power perspective to a human service organization. Similar results were obtained by Friedlander and Pickle (1967) in their widely cited study that correlated satisfaction measures from seven constituents (e.g., owners, customers, suppliers) of 97 business firms.

An evolutionary perspective would take the data in Table 16.1 into account, but would focus more on stability and change in the data. That is, how are constituents' preferences and their interrelations likely to change over time? For example, might the preferences of employees become critical to the hospital if there are labor shortages (e.g., as in past shortages of nurses) that threaten to close units? If so, effectiveness would depend on hospitals' ability to adapt by recruiting and retaining employees.

Evaluation of MC approaches

MC approaches clearly have their strengths and weaknesses. In these approaches, judgments of effectiveness are based on the values and preferences that individuals and groups hold for an organization (Cameron, 1986). This leads to several problems for researchers applying this perspective, some of which were identified above. They include:

(1) Values and preferences vary from one group to another, and it is difficult to resolve such conflicts.
(2) A group's preferences are sometimes difficult to identify, even for the group itself.
(3) Preferences vary over time.
(4) Contradictory preferences are sometimes held by a group.
(5) How to identify constituents to participate in an assessment is often ambiguous.

Despite these weaknesses, MC models are attractive because they are, at heart, pragmatic. They provide researchers with a set of guidelines to follow in assessing organizational effectiveness. Further, the guidelines are flexible and can be adapted to a variety of circumstances. As Cameron (1986) points out, organizational effectiveness is primarily a problem-driven concept; MC approaches can be adapted to the problem of interest. Researchers can use MC approaches, for example, to draw comparisons about the relative effectiveness of several organizations of a given type, as illustrated above in the example with a national sample of university hospitals. A hospital's financial performance could be analyzed, for instance, by determining if it differs significantly from the mean of the entire sample. Similarly, the financial performance of subgroups of hospitals (e.g., urban versus rural) could be contrasted with each other. Another strength of MC approaches is that they take a diverse group of constituents into account, thus reducing the possibility that important conflicts among constituents' preferences will be ignored. In other words, identifying conflict among constituents is important even if MC approaches vary or are weak in guiding efforts to resolve such conflicts.

It is interesting to compare a goal attainment approach with MC approaches to effectiveness. The goal attainment approach has the virtue of parsimony: It has narrower and fewer effectiveness criteria than MC approaches simply because it does not consider all of the preferences of an organization's constituents. Rather, the goal attainment approach assumes that constituents are primarily concerned with how well the organization is meeting its stated goals. But this assumption is not often valid. As noted, some constituents are likely to be concerned with goal attainment but they certainly hold other preferences too.

Institutional Theory and Effectiveness

A thorough introduction to institutional theory would be useful for understanding its application to organizational effectiveness. Such an introduction is, however, beyond the scope of this chapter and can be found in Scott (1987) and Zucker (1987). Here, I will focus on a few key assumptions of the theory, relate them to organizational effectiveness, and illustrate the approach using data from drug abuse treatment organizations.

Institutional theorists argue that widely held beliefs and rules in the environments of organizations often influence their structure and behavior irrespective of their technologies and resource exchanges (Scott, 1987; Zucker, 1987). When organizations face environments characterized by strong belief systems and rules, survival and effectiveness depend more on the legitimacy acquired from conforming to widely held expectations than on efficient production (DiMaggio & Powell, 1983; Meyer & Rowan, 1977).

In other words, institutional theorists distinguish between two kinds of environmental pressures that organizations face. On the one hand, organizations face pressures for efficiency and effectiveness in the production of goods or services. Such pressures are particularly strong when (1) there are high levels of competition among organizations and (2) consumers and other interested external groups can readily measure the efficiency or effectiveness of an organization's production of goods or services (e.g., the quality of a service).

On the other hand, organizations face pressures to conform to expectations about how they should behave. Such pressures are particularly strong for organizations whose outputs or outcomes are difficult to measure. That is, there are many organizations that produce goods or services whose quality or price is hard for consumers to evaluate (e.g., hospitals, schools). As a result, there are not well-developed "markets" for these organizations in the traditional economic sense of the term *market*. And, such organizations are not rewarded so much for efficiency or effectiveness in production because their efficiency and effectiveness (e.g., quality) are too difficult to assess. Rather, such organizations are rewarded for looking like we expect them to look: Do they have structures and processes that conform to our expectations? The emphasis is on measures of structure and process (isomorphism) rather than on measures of outcomes or outputs (Donabedian, 1966).

Further, institutional theorists argue that conformity to widely held expectations makes organizations legitimate in the view of society, and legitimacy brings external support, including funds and other resources, that organizations need to survive. Finally, institutional theorists argue that human service organizations typically face more pressures for conformity to widely held beliefs than demands for efficiency or effectiveness in production (Meyer & Scott, 1983). How much competition, for example, does a drug abuse treatment organization face for clients? Are there reliable and valid measures of efficiency or quality in the production of drug abuse treatment services? To what extent do external groups reward these organizations for efficiency or quality in their work? These questions certainly can be posed for other human service organizations (Hasenfeld, 1983).

An institutional theory approach to effectiveness thus focuses on the extent to which organizations are conforming to widely held expectations about their structure and processes. The less that organizations deviate from societal norms for them, the more likely that they will be viewed as legitimate and rewarded with continued resource support. In short, institutional theory equates organizational effectiveness with resource acquisition and survival that, in turn, depend on conformity in structure and process, and the legitimacy conformity bestows on organizations.

To illustrate, consider assessing the effectiveness of drug abuse treatment organizations. As noted above, one widely held and influential set of beliefs about drug abuse treatment is the AA model. In this view, alcoholism and substance abuse are believed to be diseases that can be treated only when clients abstain completely from alcohol and drugs and take responsibility for helping themselves. All clients have the same problem and all can be treated through the same methods. Effective treatment can begin only after individuals recognize that they are ill and have the desire to recover. Further, clients are always "recovering" because their continued good health depends on complete abstinence. Support for recognizing one's illness and continued recovery comes from recovering alcoholics or drug addicts who have had personal experience with trying to remain abstinent.

For organizations that adopt the AA model, AA beliefs shape the organization of treatment services. Complete abstinence from drugs or alcohol is typically a prerequisite for admission to treatment, and clients are closely monitored for compliance. Ex-addicts or alcoholics are hired as counselors because they have firsthand knowledge of AA's 12 "steps to recovery."

In contrast, another relatively widely held set of beliefs can be termed a psychosocial model of drug abuse treatment. In this view, drug abuse problems develop in part because of stressful events in a person's environment (e.g., work stress, death of a spouse) and in part because of failure to cope with such events. Maladaptive responses are thought to include substance abuse, depression, and anxiety. Effective treatment consists of altering environmental demands and modifying coping responses, for example, by helping a person to relax, become assertive, or express emotions to others.

These beliefs, similar to AA beliefs, shape the organization of treatment services for organizations that adopt them. These organizations hire professionals (e.g. psychiatrists, psychologists, social workers), rather than ex-addicts, who are trained to diagnose sources of stress and maladaptive responses. A central belief is that professionals should diagnose clients using psychological tests or classification systems such as the Diagnostic and Statistical Manual (DSM-III) of the American Psychiatric Association. These diagnostic approaches, as noted above, are not espoused by AA, which believes that all clients have the same problem and can be treated with the same methods. In contrast, these diagnostic approaches are endorsed by professional associations (e.g., the American Psychiatric Association), accreditation bodies (e.g., the Joint Commission on Accreditation of Health Care Organizations), and financing groups (e.g., Blue Cross).

In short, drug abuse treatment organizations often face conflicting beliefs about how to treat their clients. That is, the AA and psychosocial approaches differ in their prescriptions about who should treat clients (ex-addicts and recovering alcoholics versus professionals), how to assess clients' problems (all have the same disease versus use of DSM-III and similar diagnostic approaches), and the goals of treatment (complete abstinence versus coping with underlying causes of drug abuse).

Moreover, we have focused on mental health centers that diversified to provide drug abuse treatment services. Prior to diversification, these mental health centers faced an environment that emphasized traditional psychosocial models of treatment for mental health clients. After diversification, however, these organizations began providing both mental health and drug abuse treatment services. We thus termed them "hybrids." As a result of diversification, hybrids were exposed to AA beliefs that conflicted with their traditional beliefs about treatment.

This situation poses interesting and important questions for an institutional theory perspective of organizational effectiveness. What responses do organizations make to conflicting beliefs held by external groups? And, what are the consequences for their external support? In other words, if conformity to external demands is the key for acquiring legitimacy and resources needed for survival, what happens to organizations that face conflicting external demands? In this case, we hypothesized that hybrids would adopt only a few AA practices (e.g., hiring ex-addicts) to satisfy AA groups, but they would retain many of their traditional mental health practices (e.g., use of DSM-III) to maintain external support from the mental health sector.

Results from regression and multinomial probit analyses of data from a national random sample of 90 hybrids show that they deviated from traditional mental health practices more than we anticipated (D'Aunno, Sutton, & Price, 1991). Hybrids combined hiring practices (i.e., emphasized hiring both ex-addicts and professionals), adopted abstinence as a treatment goal, and used DSM-III less consistently than traditional mental health centers. Further, the results show that hybrids that deviated from traditional mental health practices received less external support (e.g., funds) from mental health sector sources. Thus the results support the institutional theory perspective that environmental actors reward organizations that conform to their expectations about appropriate structure and process.

Evaluation of an Institutional Theory Approach to Effectiveness

An institutional theory perspective on effectiveness has both similarities and dissimilarities to MC approaches. Similar to MC approaches, an institutional perspective emphasizes the preferences of important external constituents as the key to organizational effectiveness. The central assumption is that satisfying such preferences will enable organizations to be viewed as legitimate and hence acquire resources that, at a minimum, ensure their survival. An institutional view, however, extends MC approaches by hypothesizing what the preferences of such constituents are, that is, conformity with their beliefs about structure and process. In other words, an institutional perspective suggests that researchers can assess effectiveness by examining how well organizations have adopted the symbols, if not the practices, that are valued by important groups in their environments. In contrast, MC approaches are, for the most part, silent about the content of constituents' preferences and how they are met.

It is important to point out that human service organizations may have activities that are only loosely coupled (Orton & Weick, 1990) to the practices and symbols they adopt for external groups. For example, some drug abuse treatment units have adopted the language of AA's 12 steps, without adopting many of the actual practices prescribed by

AA. In this case, what the units say about their treatment practices is loosely coupled to their actual practices. Institutional theory draws attention to such loose coupling and enables researchers to understand how external support may be maintained in the absence of data measuring efficiency or attainment of other goals.

An institutional view thus differs substantially from a goal attainment approach to effectiveness. The latter emphasizes organizational outcomes or outputs, while institutional theorists argue that for most human service organizations outcomes and outputs are too difficult to evaluate and are, hence, not the focus of attention for external groups.

In my view, theory-specific approaches to organizational effectiveness, such as the institutional theory approach, have the advantages of parsimony and specificity. The institutional theory approach illustrates this point. This perspective not only informs the selection of constituents for an assessment of effectiveness, it also informs managers and researchers about constituents' preferences. On the other hand, the crucial question for theory-specific approaches to organizational effectiveness is obvious: How good is the theory that underlies the approach and its effectiveness criteria?

Moreover, there are as many theory-specific approaches to organizational effectiveness as there are theories of organizations. It turns out that there are now many such theories, each with some, but not substantial, empirical support. Thus it seems important to consider a strategic approach to questions of defining and assessing the effectiveness of human service organizations. The strategy I propose is similar to strategies proposed elsewhere, especially by Cameron (1986), Cameron and Whetten (1983) and Hasenfeld (1983). That is, we ought to consider analyzing the conditions under which single or even combined approaches are most useful.

A Contingency Approach to Organizational Effectiveness

Two assumptions underlie the contingency approach discussed below. First, it is assumed that organizational effectiveness is primarily a problem-driven concept that is closely tied to the empirical contexts that organizations face (Cameron, 1986). Because empirical contexts vary so widely, we ought to ask which organizational theory or model of effectiveness best fits a particular circumstance rather than attempt to build or apply a single model of effectiveness for all organizations.

Second, based on the MC approaches discussed above, I assume that one should not overlook the multiple constituencies that are typically involved with organizations. This assumption does not argue that all constituents should be treated equally; it merely asserts that researchers can learn something about organizational performance by understanding the preferences of as many constituents as possible.

I do not argue, however, that we should approach the assessment of constituents' preferences in an entirely atheoretical or simple empirical fashion. Rather, the key is to inform our understanding of the criteria that various constituents are likely to use to evaluate an organization. That is, we ought to try to understand what constituents want and what models of effectiveness will be useful prior to conducting a full-scale assessment. This preliminary diagnostic work can be done first by recognizing that constituents' preferences are likely to vary along several dimensions and, second, by drawing from available organizational theory. Important dimensions along which constituents' criteria are likely to vary include: (1) the extent to which the performance criteria are measurable; (2) the extent to which criteria held by different groups are shared; and (3) the extent to which criteria are stable over time (see Table 16.2). Depending on how constituents' preferences are likely to vary on these dimensions, different organizational theories might be used to inform an assessment of organizational effectiveness.

This contingency approach can be described as follows. First, as Hasenfeld (1983), Thompson (1967), and others have pointed out, the performance criteria that groups hold for organizations vary along the dimension of measurability. I argued, for example, that it is difficult to measure the quality or efficiency of services produced by drug abuse treatment organizations. Thus constituents of these organizations typically use criteria that are low on this dimension. Consider, in contrast, how much easier it is to measure the performance of an office that processes social security applications by counting the number that are completed in an interval.

A second way that performance criteria vary is in the extent to which they are shared by constituents. The example of university hospitals (Table 16.1) showed that though some criteria are shared by constituents, it is often the case that various constituents hold different criteria for an organization's performance. Further, the example of drug abuse treatment organizations shows that performance criteria can directly conflict (i.e., how to assess and treat clients and the goals for treatment conflict in the AA and psychosocial models). Finally, performance criteria and organizational environments vary in their stability; they

Table 16.2 A Contingency Approach to Assessing Organizational Effectiveness

Assessment Approach	Suggested for Use When Assessment Criteria Are:
Rational systems models (e.g., goal attainment; transaction cost analysis)	measurable, stable, shared
Systems models	measurable and stable, but not shared
Multiple constituency power models; resource dependence model; political economy models	measurable and stable, but conflict with each other across groups
Multiple constituency evolution models; life-cycle models	measurable and changing; either shared or conflictual
Institutional theory models; other organizational models focusing on symbolism	difficult to measure; not shared or conflictual; changing

can change rapidly and substantially in content or they can evolve slowly or even remain the same for long time periods (Zammuto, 1984). These dimensions are not intended to be exhaustive. But, they illustrate three major ways in which constituents' preferences for performance can vary.

Depending on how constituents' performance criteria vary on these dimensions, different organizational theories may be useful to inform understanding of their criteria. For example, to the extent that performance criteria are measurable, shared by constituents, and stable, rational systems models of organizations are likely to be useful in defining and measuring organizational effectiveness (Hasenfeld, 1983). Rational systems models, as noted above, include the goal attainment approach; another rational system model is transaction cost analysis (Williamson, 1975, 1981). Specifically, the goal attainment approach emphasizes the quantity, quality, and efficiency of organizational outputs, while the transaction cost approach focuses on factors that affect the efficiency of organizations' exchanges of resources with external groups, including clients.

These emphases are appropriate when performance criteria are measurable, shared, and stable, but they are less appropriate under other conditions. For example, when performance criteria tend to be measurable and stable, but they are not shared by various constituents, a systems approach might be useful. In other words, Hasenfeld (1983, p. 209) points out that in such conditions, "various and often disparate components and activities of the organization, important to different providers, will be assessed simultaneously."

When performance criteria are measurable and stable but conflict with each other, multiple constituency power models or other organizational models based on a power perspective (e.g., resource dependence, Pfeffer & Salancik, 1978) will be useful to researchers. That is, when different constituents have conflicting preferences for organizational performance, one would expect the more powerful groups to prevail. Thus an assessment of effectiveness would do well to rank-order the preferences and power of each constituent; such rankings would allow evaluators to narrow their attention to criteria that are most important to an organization's resource acquisition and survival.

When performance criteria are measurable and changing, MC evolution models and organizational life-cycle models (e.g., Cameron & Whetten, 1981; Kimberly & Miles, 1980; Quinn & Cameron, 1983) will be useful for assessments of effectiveness. These perspectives emphasize change in organizations and their environments and the importance of organizational adaptation for effectiveness and survival. Further, these perspectives can address issues of conflicting constituent preferences. Quinn and Cameron (1983) found, for example, that criteria of effectiveness shifted over the course of organizational life cycles. What was defined as effective performance in one stage (e.g., birth) was contradictory to effectiveness in another stage (e.g., formalization and control stage). The key point is that organizations experience transitions and, when they do, assessments of effectiveness need to be informed by appropriate models of organizational change.

Thus far, we have considered approaches to assessing effectiveness when performance criteria are relatively measurable. As noted above, however, it is often the case for human service organizations that criteria are not well defined and are difficult to measure. Hasenfeld (1983) asserts that when criteria are not directly measurable, but they are shared among constituents, satisficing will occur. That is, organizations and their constituents will settle for indirect or proxy measures of performance. For example, the Health Care Financing Administration, which is responsible for administering the Medicare program, has released data on the mortality rates at every hospital in the nation that receives Medicare payments. These rates are intended to be measures of quality of care for consumers. The rates, however, are clearly only proximal measures of hospital performance and, indeed, in some cases may be misleading. But mortality rates must suffice until better measures are developed.

When performance criteria are difficult to measure and not shared or are conflictual, symbolic approaches to effectiveness are useful (Hasenfeld, 1983). In this case, organizations will attempt to satisfy constituents' conflicting demands using symbols that are not directly related to the substance of organizational activity. In so doing, managers can give the appearance of conforming to external demands without making changes in organizational practices that would be disruptive. Thus models of organizations that focus on symbols, symbolic interaction, impression management, and related issues could usefully inform assessments of effectiveness. For example, the use of institutional theory in these conditions was illustrated above. Indeed, Hasenfeld (1983) has termed this an institutional mode of organizational evaluation.

Conclusions

This chapter has compared alternative approaches to defining and assessing the effectiveness of human service organizations. I have argued that certain approaches or combinations of approaches may be more appropriate than others depending on key dimensions of the empirical context in which organizations operate. In other words, following Hasenfeld (1983), Cameron (1986) and others, I argued for a contingency approach to organizational effectiveness. Such an approach may benefit researchers of human service organizations. It is clear that interest in the performance of human service organizations will increase in the next several years as resources continue to be scarce. A contingency approach to effectiveness may prove more important than ever.

References

Blair, J. D., & Fottler, M. D. (1990). *Challenges in health care management.* San Francisco: Jossey-Bass.

Bluedorn, A. C. (1980). Cutting the Gordian knot: A critique of the effectiveness tradition in organization research. *Sociology and Social Research, 64,* 477-496.

Cameron, K. S. (1986). Effectiveness as paradox: Consensus and conflict in conceptions of organizational effectiveness. *Management Science, 32*(5), 539-553.

Cameron, K. S., & Whetten, D. A. (1981). Perceptions of organization effectiveness across organizational life cycles. *Administrative Science Quarterly, 26*, 525-544.

Cameron, K. S., & Whetten, D. A. (Eds.). (1983). *Organizational effectiveness: A comparison of multiple models.* New York: Academic Press.

Connolly, T., Conlon, E. M., & Deutsch, S. J. (1980). Organizational effectiveness: A multiple constituency approach. *Academy of Management Review, 5*, 211-218.

D'Aunno, T. A., Hooijberg, R., & Munson, F. C. (1991). Decision making, goal consensus and effectiveness in university hospitals. *Hospital and Health Service Administration, 36*(4), 505-523.

D'Aunno, T. A., Sutton, R. I., & Price, R. H. (1991). Isomorphism and external support in conflicting institutional environments: The case of drug abuse treatment units. *Academy of Management Journal, 34*(3), 636-661.

DiMaggio, P., & Powell, W. W. (1983). The iron cage revisited: Institutional isomorphism and collective rationality in organizational fields. *American Sociological Review, 48*, 147-160.

Donabedian, A. (1966). Evaluating the quality of medical care. *Milbank Memorial Fund Quarterly, 44*, 166-188.

Emerson, R. M. (1962). Power-dependence relations. *American Sociological Review, 27*, 31-41.

Freeman, R. E. (1984). *Strategic management: A stakeholder approach.* Boston: Pitman.

Friedlander, F., & Pickle, H. (1968). Components of effectiveness in small organizations. *Administrative Science Quarterly, 13*, 289-304.

Georgopoulos, B. (1986). *Organization structure, problem solving and effectiveness: A comparative study of hospital emergency services.* San Francisco: Jossey-Bass.

Goodman, P. S., & Pennings, J. M. (Eds.). (1977). *New perspectives on organizational effectiveness* (pp. 146-184). San Francisco: Jossey-Bass.

Hannan, H. T., & Freeman, J. (1977). The population ecology of organizations. *American Journal of Sociology, 82*, 929-964.

Hasenfeld, Y. (1983). *Human service organizations.* Englewood Cliffs, NJ: Prentice-Hall.

Kimberly, J. R., & Miles, R. H. (Eds.). (1980). *The organizational life cycle.* San Francisco: Jossey-Bass.

McCaughrin, W. C., Price, R. H., & Klingel, D. M. (in press). Effective outpatient drug abuse treatment organizations: Program features and selection effects. *International Journal of the Addictions.*

Meyer, J., & Rowan, B. (1977). Institutionalized organizations: Formal structure as myth and ceremony. *American Journal of Sociology, 83*, 340-363.

Meyer, J. W., & Scott, W. R. (Eds.). (1983). *Organizational environments.* Beverly Hills, CA: Sage.

Morgan, G. (1980). Paradigms, metaphors, and puzzle solving in organizational theory. *Administrative Science Quarterly, 25*, 605-622.

Munson, F. C., & D'Aunno, T. A. (1987). *The university hospital in the academic health center: Finding the right relationship.* Washington, DC: Association of Academic Health Centers/Association of American Medical Colleges.

Munson, F. C., & D'Aunno, T. A. (1989). Structural change in academic health centers. *Hospital and Health Service Administration, 34*(3), 413-426.

Orton, J. D., & Weick, K. E. (1990). Loosely coupled systems: A reconceptualization. *Academy of Management Review, 15*(2), 203-223.

Pfeffer, J., & Salancik, G. R. (1978). *The external control of organizations.* New York: Harper & Row.

Price, J. L. (1968). *Organizational effectiveness.* Homewood, IL: Irwin.

Quinn, R. E., & Cameron, K. S. (1983). Organizational life cycles and shifting criteria of effectiveness. *Management Science, 9,* 33-51.

Scott, W. R. (1987). The adolescence of institutional theory. *Administrative Science Quarterly, 32,* 493-511.

Scott, W. R., & Shortell, S. M. (1988). Organizational performance: Managing for efficiency. In S. M. Shortell & A. D. Kaluzny (Eds.), *Health care management.* New York: John Wiley.

Steers, R. M. (1975). Problems in the measurement of organizational effectiveness. *Administrative Science Quarterly, 20,* 546-558.

Thompson, J. D. (1967). *Organizations in action.* New York: McGraw-Hill.

Tsui, A. S. (1990). A multiple-constituency model of effectiveness: An empirical examination at the human resource subunit level. *Administrative Science Quarterly, 35,* 458-483.

Wagner, J. A., & Schneider, B. (1987). Legal regulation and the constraint of constituency satisfaction. *Journal of Management Studies, 24,* 189-200.

Wamsley, G. L., & Zald, M. N. (1976). *The political economy of public organizations.* Bloomington: Indiana University Press.

Weick, K. E. (1977). Re-punctuating the problem. In P. S. Goodman & J. M. Pennings (Eds.), *New perspectives on organizational effectiveness* (pp. 193-225). San Francisco: Jossey-Bass.

Williamson, O. E. (1975). *Markets and hierarchies.* New York: Free Press.

Williamson, O. E. (1981). The economics of organization: The transaction cost approach. *American Journal of Sociology, 87,* 548-577.

Yuchtman, E., & Seashore, S. E. (1967). A system resource approach to organizational effectiveness. *American Sociological Review, 32,* 891-903.

Zald, M. N. (1970). A framework for comparative analysis. In M. N. Zald (Ed.), *Power in organizations* (pp. 221-261). Nashville, TN: Vanderbilt University Press.

Zammuto, R. F. (1982). *Assessing organizational effectiveness: Systems change, adaptation, and strategy.* Albany: SUNY Press.

Zammuto, R. F. (1984). A comparison of multiple constituency models of organizational effectiveness. *Academy of Management Review, 9*(4), 606-616.

Zucker, L. G. (1987). Institutional theories of organizations. *Annual Review of Sociology, 13,* 443-464.

CHAPTER **17**

Evaluating the Effectiveness of Countywide Mental Health Care Systems[1]

OSCAR GRUSKY

KATHLEEN TIERNEY

Mental health service delivery systems have become increasingly complex as the number and types of treatment modalities and service providers have increased. As noted by Tessler and Goldman (1982), there is a national need for better information on the properties of these systems. Reliable and valid measures of key mental health local delivery system elements do not exist. A need exists for measures of service coverage, quality, comprehensiveness, and system coordination or integration. Such instruments should be simple and adaptable to a range of settings. These measures would contribute to knowledge of the consequences of interorganizational relations and could help state and local officials improve service delivery.

This chapter addresses this problem. New system effectiveness measures are developed and applied to a set of eight carefully selected counties, four urban and four rural, situated in a state in the northwest United States.

AUTHORS' NOTE: This research was supported by the National Institute of Mental Health (MH-38887 and MH 14583; O. Grusky, P.I.). We are very grateful for the assistance of the following post-doctoral scholars in the senior author's NIMH-supported services research training program who participated in the pretest, data collection, and in other ways: Bonnie Berry, Lee Clarke, Robert Fiorentine, Carol Gardner, Chris Grella, Matthew Lynes, Kathleen Montgomery, Keiko Nakao, Margaret Spanish, William Staples, and Patricia Ullman. Research assistance on this project was ably carried out by Amalya Oliver and Leah Robin. Finally, we deeply appreciate the cooperation of the state mental health division, the county authorities, and the individual respondents. A revised version of this chapter was presented at the meeting of the American Sociological Association, Atlanta, 1988.

A simplified conceptual model is posited. According to this model county or community service systems consist of two basic stakeholder groups: service providers and service recipients. Service providers are organization directors or administrators who are responsible for managing the service system or running agencies that provide services or are case managers whose main task is to link service recipients to the system. Service recipients consist primarily of clients or patients and constitute a set of agencies or organizations that are responsible for administration and service provision, adapt to the environmental circumstances of the county milieu, and influence the internal organizational culture and structure of these agencies, which, in turn, influence how the staff perform their case management and therapeutic tasks. These circumstances and the content of the services provided assist in shaping the clients' and the family members' of clients view of the county service system, their participation in the system, and hence their various outcomes.

Background

Recent years have seen a proliferation of community treatment for individuals with mental health problems. Several trends in the organization of services for the mentally ill have produced a clear need for research on local delivery systems, particularly those systems serving seriously mentally ill persons. A partial list of these trends includes: (1) radical shifts in state hospital inpatient censuses and lengths-of-stay; (2) the growth of new kinds of organizations serving the mentally ill, such as board-and-care homes, "locked" nursing facilities, and private, proprietary psychiatric hospitals; (3) changes in the parties responsible for paying for mental health services, with the increasing use of Social Security benefits and a growth in coverage by private insurance companies; and (4) a trend toward decentralization of mental health policy-making and planning, with more autonomy given to states, counties, and local communities. In general, the picture nationwide is one of increasing variety and complexity in mental health delivery systems, with the attendant likelihood of uneven quality, fragmentation of services, and high costs. The organization and effectiveness of local delivery systems has particularly clear implications for seriously mentally ill persons, a population with a potential for high and long-term service utilization.

Reliable information on the experience of the seriously mentally ill population in the mental health delivery system is badly needed. It has been estimated that there are approximately three million adults who suffer severe mental disability; about one half of this population can function in the community (Goldman, Gattozzi, & Taube, 1981; Robins et al., 1984). Since deinstitutionalization, a major need for this group has been the provision of adequate community support services (CSSs). In a recent review paper, Ashbaugh, Leaf, and Manderscheid (1983) identified several major categories of system barriers facing this group. First, professionals responsible for care, friends, families, and neighbors of the seriously mentally ill are pessimistic about the mentally ill person's chances for clinical improvement. Second, despite evidence that alternative care is consistently more effective than hospitalization (Kiesler & Sibulkin, 1987), the rate of mental hospitalization is increasing for this group. Federal funding policies discourage community services for the seriously mentally ill, despite the fact that 25% of all hospital days are for mental illness. Third, there is a serious problem of fragmentation and lack of coordination of services at the local, state, and federal levels. Fourth, there is a need for knowledge about how to deliver services to this population.

The National Institute of Mental Health (NIMH) Community Support Program (CSP) (Carling, 1984; Stroul, 1982) is an innovative program developed in response to trends in the organization of psychiatric services such as those discussed above, to ensure integrated services and continuity of care for seriously mentally ill adults. As Kiesler and Sibulkin (1987) have observed, detailed knowledge is needed of how CSP program elements are implemented at the local level and how effectively communities are currently serving this population. Such data are important for two reasons. First, they can serve as the basis for systematic generalizations about what factors encourage effective service delivery, thus providing guidance for persons responsible for upgrading services. Second, they can provide a context for understanding and interpreting client outcome data.

Our approach to evaluating service system effectiveness may be understood within the following framework. Both the key service components and the notion of system, which requires interorganizational coordination, are policies developed by NIMH, and more or less accepted by CSPs and CSSs. They therefore constitute system goals. *Thus, county or local service system effectiveness refers to the degree to which that unit provides the key service components to the population intended to receive them, the quality of the services provided, and the extent to which services are coordinated.*

Major Dimensions of CSS Performance

CSP program documents emphasize three different intermediate system-change goals for local CSSs. First, because services for these clients are known to be deficient, emphasis is placed on increasing the number and kinds of services available for seriously mentally ill persons. Second, program developers stress the need to reduce system fragmentation and bring about more collaboration and cooperation among caregiving organizations. Third, CSSs are seen as needing to involve more segments of the community in working with clients and mobilize community resources to make the needs of seriously mentally ill persons a higher priority. We developed instruments to assess each of these three aspects of CSP performance.

The developers of CSP recognized that without a broad, comprehensive service base, seriously mentally ill persons would be less able to adjust successfully in the community and be more likely to return to the hospital. Further, they believed local systems should be able to respond, not only to the needs of clients, but also to family and community concerns. To this end, providing or encouraging the development of 10 forms of assistance, known as key service components, were seen as a major objective for local CSSs. This approach to services was modeled on the "balanced service system" formulated by the Joint Committee on Accreditation of Hospitals (1981), which emphasizes the need for both specialized mental health care and a range of supportive services in mental health systems. The 10 essential components identified by CSP included diverse services and activities such as identifying and doing outreach with clients; helping clients get basic income assistance, food, and shelter; psychosocial and vocational rehabilitation services; supportive services to families; protection of clients' rights; and crisis services.[2]

One obvious criterion for assessing CSSs is the extent to which these services are being provided to seriously mentally ill persons. Several aspects of service delivery are important. One question involves how many of these key services are actually being provided. A community may offer a number of services but lack the ability to provide crucial crisis services, for example. Another distinction concerns how many of the eligible potential service recipients are receiving services. Certain services may be widely available and reaching the majority of the individuals who need them. On the other hand, because of a lack of resources or an insufficient commitment to providing care, some other services may be offered to a relatively small segment of the target population. A third issue concerns the quality of the services that are offered. Communities and service systems can differ on all three dimensions. To take these different aspects of service availability into account, we developed three measures: (1) service comprehensiveness, or the number of services available in the community; (2) service coverage, or the proportion of the potential client population that is actually receiving the service; and (3) service quality. A fourth and final issue concerns the interrelation of services, that is, the extent to which they are coordinated or fragmented.

Methods

Eight counties situated in a state of the northwest were studied. A ninth county was used to pretest the interview instruments and insure adequate test-retest reliabilities. Half of the counties were urban and half rural, a total of 364 face-to-face interviews were conducted, approximately 45 in each site. Four stakeholder groups were interviewed in about the same proportion in each county: 156 organization directors/ administrators, 49 case managers, 77 family members, and 82 seriously mentally ill clients.

Organization directors were selected by a snowball sampling technique. The director of the lead agency was asked to identify the 10 most important organizations that provide mental health services for chronically mentally ill adults in the county. The directors of these 10 were then called and asked to do the same. The size of the network was arbitrarily limited to 20 in each county by using two criteria, frequency of nomination and sector (mental health, health, public social agencies, residential care, job training, public safety/law enforcement, and consum- er advocacy). The goal was to have at least one representative of each sector.

Case managers usually constituted about the total number in their county and were employed by the lead mental health agency in the county. The state followed NIMH Community Support program guidelines and established a core mental health agency that was responsible for coordinating the care system and seeing that case management services were provided.

Family members were selected with the assistance of case managers and local advocacy organizations.

Selection of clients was done with the assistance of case managers using two criteria: (1) clients had to meet the state's definition of "Priority #1" clients, meaning that they were chronically mentally ill adults at risk of hospitalization, and (2) they were capable of communicating in an interview situation. Clients were 95% Caucasian, 59% male, median age was 38, had a median annual income of $2,846, 95% were on medication, and averaged 4.6 hospitalizations. Most were diagnosed as schizophrenic. Table 17.1 presents information on the social characteristics of respondents.

Four measures of system effectiveness were used: service comprehensiveness, coverage, quality, and coordination. The procedures used to assess the first three of these components was part of the interview called the key service components. The key service components items are based on NIMH guidelines for Community Support Systems, which are to provide a range of essential services or functions (such as outreach, help in applying for entitlements, mental health services, and so on). The respondent is presented in serial fashion with 13 cards, each of which describes a different service component. The descriptions of service components retain the actual language used by the NIMH. In order to assist clients and laypersons a short summary of each component is included on the card, such as "Safeguard legal rights of clients," "Seek out clients in need of services," and so forth. Respondents are then asked a number of questions about each service identified on the cards.[2]

Findings

Service Comprehensiveness

Service comprehensiveness refers to the number of services identified as present in the county. Respondents are asked whether or not each service exists in their county. The maximum score a county can receive is 13, that is, a score of 1 for each identified service. Subjective reports at the existence of services are not necessarily evidence that such services actually exist. Some time ago the noted social psychologist W. I. Thomas observed that "If men define situations as real, they are real in the consequences." At the same time, however, if clients and family members are unaware of the existence of services, that is, believe they do not exist in their community, they are obviously unlikely to avail themselves of these services. Hence, a subjective measure of service

Table 17.1 Selected Social Background Characteristics of Respondents (N=349)*

	Organization Directors (N = 141)		Case Managers (N = 49)		Families (N = 77)		Clients (N = 82)	
	#	%	#	%	#	%	#	%
Sex								
Male	100	71	28	57	24	31	48	59
Female	41	29	21	43	53	69	34	41
Race								
Caucasian	137	97	46	94	76	99	78	95
Black	4	3	2	4	—	—	3	4
Asian	—	—	1	2	1	1	1	1
Age								
under 20	—	—	—	—	—	—	1	1
20-29	1	1	3	6	2	3	21	26
30-39	38	27	30	61	5	7	25	30
40-49	51	36	8	16	8	9	15	18
50-59	38	27	5	10	26	34	15	18
60-69	11	8	3	6	26	34	4	6
70-over	1	1	—	—	10	13	1	1
N.A.	1	1						
Education								
4-8 yrs	—	—	—	—	3	4	1	1
9-11	1	1	—	—	12	15	11	13
12-H.S. Grad	7	5	—	—	21	27	27	33
Some College	16	11	5	10	22	29	31	38
Bachelor's	31	22	10	20	10	13	7	9
Some Grad School	19	13	6	12	3	4	—	—
Master's	57	40	23	47	4	5	4	5
Ph.D.	5	4	5	10	2	3	—	—
M.D.	10	4	—	—	—	—	—	—
N.A.							1	1

NOTE: *There were 364 interviews conducted and a total of 349 individuals were interviewed. Some organizations provide services for more than one county. In these cases the director was interviewed more than once.

comprehensiveness has important implications for the delivery of mental health services.

Table 17.2 presents the findings. First, we discovered that the eight counties differ significantly on this measure. The analysis of variance that compared the average number of services across the eight sites was statistically significant at less than .0001. As Table 17.2 shows, the average

Table 17.2 Service Comprehensiveness Ratings: Average Number of Services Identified as Present by Four Stakeholder Groups

County	Case Managers	Organization Directors	Clients	Families	All	N
		Stakeholder Groups				
A	12.70	12.05	9.40	12.20	11.67	49
B	12.90	12.15	11.00	10.80	11.80	50
C	12.50	12.00	9.92	9.80	11.18	51
D	12.75	11.35	11.10	10.30	11.18	44
E	12.00	8.20	7.67	5.43	7.76	38
F	12.50	9.63	9.00	6.80	9.09	43
G	12.67	11.10	8.70	8.10	9.95	43
H	13.00	11.00	8.18	10.40	10.46	46
All counties	12.69(49)	10.93(156)	9.39(82)	9.38(77)	10.49	364

NOTE: *Thirteen key services were described individually on cards and the respondent was asked whether or not each service existed in their county. Hence, the maximum score was 13. Two-way analysis of variance results are: Main effects, $F = 15.79$, $p < .0001$.
Main effect of stakeholder type, $F = 22.83$, $p < .0001$.
Main effect of county, $F = 10.43$, $p < .0001$.

number of services identified by the respondents as present in their county varied from about 8 in County E, to about 12 in county B. A second major finding shown in Table 17.2 is the existence of pronounced differences between rural and urban counties. Not surprisingly, more services are identified as present in urban than in rural counties. This is what we would expect since urban counties typically have more resources, such as organizations, people that are professionally skilled, and funds, than do rural counties.

A third significant finding demonstrated in Table 17.2 is that availability of mental health services differs between the four stakeholder groups ($p < .0001$). Human service delivery systems have two main stakeholder groups, service providers and service recipients. Organization directors and administrators and case managers are components of the service provider group in the systems studied while clients and families are the chief components of the service recipient group. Service providers identify more services than service recipients. Specifically, case managers identify the next largest number, followed by clients, while families identify the smallest number of services.

The differences between stakeholder reports of the number of services available in their county is in part due to differing role definitions. Case

managers are responsible for connecting clients to services and therefore tend to have a great deal of information about service availability. Of
course, they do not necessarily know about the exact nature of some of
those services because they may never have referred clients to some
agencies or if they have they may not have received direct reports from
clients about those services. We note two interesting features about
case managers' reports. First, there is very little variation among case
managers. In all counties the case managers know the most about
services or at least report the existence of more services than other
stakeholder groups. Second, their belief that a large number of services
are present may reflect a tendency to overestimate the availability of services. In the same way, the relatively low reports of family members with
regard to service availability reflects their particular system role definition. Not being fully integrated into the system or occupying a peripheral
role with regard to that system, family members are not privy to a great
deal of information. Hence, they may underestimate service availability.

Both the differences between counties and the differences within
counties between stakeholders are striking. For example, County A is
noteworthy because it has a very strong family advocacy organization.
Accordingly, we find that families identify more services in that county
than do families in any other county. In fact, families in County A identify
more services on average than do agency or organization directors in
their county, a situation found in no other county studied. Overall we
found that families know relatively less about services that are present
in their county than other groups. If the County A situation is suggestive of a trend, then it would seem that this situation is related to the
low level of organization of this stakeholder group. The more organized families are the more knowledge of the system they are likely to
have. The other relatively poorly organized component of the system
is, not surprisingly, the clients, who also identify many fewer services
than do service providers. Knowing that services exist is significant,
since if one is not aware of the existence of a service, he or she may be
unlikely to seek out that service when in need of it.

Service Coverage

Service coverage was the second subjective index of system effectiveness examined. This refers to respondents' perceptions of the number of persons who need a particular service who are actually getting
it. Here also measurement was based on the key service components.
For each service described on the card, respondents were asked whether
all, most, some, few, or none of those in need of the service in their county

Table 17.3 Service Coverage Rankings for 13 Services by County[a]

County	*a*	*b*	*c*	*d*	*e*	*f*	*g*	*h*	*i*	*j*	*k*	*l*	*m*	Average Rank
D	1	3	5	1	1	1	3	3	1	3	3	1	2	2.2
F	4	2	2	3	3	2	1	2	2	1	2	2	5	2.4
H	2	5	1	4	2	3	4	1	4	6	3	5	1	3.2
E	5	1	3	5	5	4	2	4	3	2	1	3	6	3.4
A	2	6	3	1	4	5	5	5	8	5	6	6	4	4.6
G	7	4	6	7	6	6	6	7	5	4	5	4	3	5.4
B	6	7	7	8	6	7	7	6	6	7	7	7	7	6.8
C	8	8	8	6	8	8	8	8	7	8	8	8	8	7.8

Above the service columns: Service[b]

NOTE: a. There were five ties. In all cases counties were assigned the same rank.
b. Services were as follows: (a) client outreach, (b) basic services such as food, income entitlement, medical care, (c) mental health care, (d) crisis assistance, (e) help in setting goals, (f) living skills such as medication use, shopping, hygiene, (g) social skills, (h) job assistance, (i) housing, (j) support to families, (k) persuade organizations such as churches to help, (l) protect legal rights, and (m) case manager services.

were receiving it. Table 17.3 presents the main findings. This table presents the average score on the service coverage item for respondents in each of the eight counties. Analysis of variance is used to test the significance of the differences between the counties' scores. The eight counties differ significantly on 10 of the 13 services on which they were compared. The only services that did not discriminate between the counties to a statistically significant extent were (d) crisis assistance; (j) support to families; and (k) community organizations. We do not know why these services did not discriminate.

Table 17.3 also ranks each county in terms of its effectiveness with regard to service coverage for each service. For example, the first service is outreach or "identify clients" and the table reveals that County D is the most effective of the eight counties on this measure while County C is the least effective.

Table 17.3 presents the rankings for each of the eight counties for each of the service coverage items. If one assumes that coverage of all 13 services is important for system effectiveness, and that therefore services should be weighted equally on this dimension, then an average rank is a useful measure of service coverage effectiveness. By this approach County D is the most effective county and County C is the least effective. Although an urban county, D, is ranked first, the second, third, and fourth highest ranked counties are all rural (F, H, and E). The fifth-ranked county is urban (A), but the sixth is rural (G). The two least effective counties on this index are both urban counties (B and C).

Service Quality

The third system effectiveness dimension we assessed based on the 13 key service components is service quality. There may be a great many services in a community, and most people in need of those services may be receiving them, but the quality of these services may vary considerably. Respondents were asked in the case of each service to "Rate the quality of the service?" (Excellent, very good, good, fair, poor, very poor). Analysis of variance reveals that county scores are significantly different for 8 out of 13 services; identify clients, basic services, living skills, social skills, job assistance, housing, support to families, and legal rights of clients. Table 17.4 summarizes the data on service quality by presenting the quality rankings for each county on the 13 service components. An average rank across the 13 components is also presented. Although County D again comes out on top and County C is tied with two other counties for the bottom spot, the range of service quality is considerably less than on service coverage. Additionally, even counties that rank low overall are seen as doing a good job of providing some services. For example, even though County C's overall rating is in the bottom half of counties, it ranks first on the quality of its social skills training.

Service Coordination

Coordination has been defined as "the process whereby two or more organizations execute and/or use existing decision rules that have been established to deal collectively with their shared task environment" (Rogers & Whetten, 1982). Coordination unlike cooperation is deliberate and involves a collective or system purpose. Coordination is a crucial aspect of CSS functioning and is an essential prerequisite to providing services for clients so as to insure continuity of care. We have devised a method of measuring coordination that uses respondents' perceptions of the service system. Respondents were asked to indicate the extent to which they agree with each of six statements that refer to aspects of the county's service system that bear on coordination. In order to deal with acquiescence response set some of the items are worded negatively. The following are examples of items that comprise the coordination scale: "The agencies that serve chronically mentally ill persons in this county are not getting the services they need because no agency takes the lead to see that things get done." Analyses of pilot study data indicated that these six scale items showed acceptable test-retest reli-

Table 17.4 Service Quality Rankings for 13 Services by County[a]

County	a	b	c	d	e	f	g	h	i	j	k	l	m	Average Rank
D	1	1	3	4	2	2	3	4	1	2	1	1	2	2.1
A	3	2	4	1	1	1	4	1	2	1	8	7	1	2.8
B	2	3	1	2	3	5	2	3	4	5	5	5	3	3.3
H	5	4	5	3	4	4	8	5	5	8	6	3	4	4.9
F	6	7	7	8	5	6	7	2	3	4	2	6	8	5.5
C	7	8	2	6	8	7	1	7	8	3	4	8	6	5.8
E	4	5	6	5	7	8	5	6	7	7	7	4	5	5.8
G	8	6	7	7	6	3	6	8	5	6	3	2	7	5.7

NOTE: a. There were two ties. In all cases counties were assigned the same rank.
b. Services were as follows: (a) client outreach, (b) basic services such as food, income entitlement, medical care, (c) mental health care, (d) crisis assistance, (e) help in setting goals, (f) living skills such as medication use, shopping, hygiene, (g) social skills, (h) job assistance, (i) housing, (j) support to families, (k) persuade organizations such as churches to help, (l) protect legal rights, and (m) case manager services.

abilities. The Cronbach Alpha for item consistency in the study population is .711.

In general terms, the coordination scale concerns the ability of agencies serving chronically mentally ill clients to work well together, avoid disputes, eliminate conflicting rules and requirements for service eligibility, and provide a range of needed services to the target population. In an analysis similar to those described above on service comprehensiveness, coverage, and quality, the eight counties were ranked in terms of mean stakeholder ratings on the coordination items. Table 17.5 shows the results of this analysis. While scores on these items have a relatively small range (about 2.3 to about 2.9), analysis of variance indicates that the difference between sites is significant.

These data reveal several interesting patterns. First, all sites were rated moderate to good on coordination, suggesting that stakeholders recognize that an effort is being made in accordance with CSP principles to provide integrated systems of care in the counties studied. Second, it is often argued and seems intuitively correct that coordination problems (fragmentation, conflict, lack of clarity about leadership) are more common in urban communities than in rural settings. However, our data indicate that this may not be the case with regard to programs for chronically mentally ill persons in CSS sites. Urban sites perform better on this dimension than rural sites ($p = .033$). In fact, of the

Table 17.5 Ranking and Means on Coordination Scale by County[a]

| | Urban | | | | Rural | | | | |
	A	B	C	D	E	F	G	H	All
Mean	2.74	2.76	2.57	3.07	2.8	2.56	2.46	2.87	2.71
S.D.	.47	.62	.54	.45	.57	.60	.60	.48	.57
N	41	38	45	38	22	31	32	35	282
Rank	(4)	(3)	(6)	(1)	(5)	(7)	(8)	(2)	

NOTE: a. N was reduced because only respondents who answered five or more coordination scale items were included. One was Analysis of Variance F \min Ratio = 4.805, p < .0001.

four highest-ranking communities on these measures, three are urban sites. The only high-ranking rural site is County H and the only low-ranking urban site is County C.

Stakeholder and Urban-Rural Differences

Although space does not permit detailed analysis, a few additional comments on stakeholder and urban-rural differences are in order. We have already noted that stakeholder and urban-rural differences were found with regard to service comprehensiveness. Stakeholder groups also differed significantly in their perception of service coverage ($p = .009$) and service quality ($p = .001$). In both cases, case managers and clients reported greater service coverage and quality than did organization directors and families. This may be because these two groups occupy roles that place them closest to mental health services, that is, case managers are service providers themselves and probably perceive many services because of their boundary-spanning role. They have contacts with a broad range of community agencies. Since clients are already in the system and hence have access to services, they too may exaggerate their availability. Both groups may report services as of high quality because of self-interest as system participants.

The four stakeholder groups did not differ with regard to their perceptions of service coordination. It is hard to know how to interpret this. This was the only effectiveness dimension that did not discriminate stakeholder groups (see Table 17.6).

In terms of urban-rural differences on the four effectiveness dimensions, urban counties scored higher than rural counties on three of the four indicators: comprehensiveness ($p < .0001$), quality ($p < .0001$), and coordination ($p = .033$). On the other hand, the rural sites scored higher than the urban sites on coverage ($p = .022$). It may be that rural sites, because of their small population, can identify and serve a greater

Table 17.6 Mean Scores on Effectiveness Indicators for Stakeholder Groups

| | | Effectiveness Indicators | | |
	Comprehensiveness	Coverage	Quality	Coordination
Organization Directors	10.92	3.13	3.97	2.72
Case Managers	12.69	3.35	4.40	2.79
Families	9.37	3.11	4.16	2.67
Clients	9.39	3.35	4.24	2.64
F-Ratio	22.93	3.92	5.37	.600
p-Level	< .0001	.009	.001	.615

proportion than urban sites of severely mentally ill persons in need. Also, many people migrate to urban areas in order to obtain services and hence increase service demand in urban areas. On the other hand, the superior resources and professional skills typically available in urban sites may account for greater service comprehensiveness, quality, and coordination. These differences are provocative and require further exploration.[3]

Relationship Between the Dimensions of System Effectiveness

Several interesting findings emerged from examination of the zero order Pearson correlation coefficients between the four effectiveness measures we have called service comprehensiveness, coverage, quality, and coordination (see Table 17.7).

A small but statistically significant positive correlation ($r = .267, p < .0001$) was found between service comprehensiveness and service quality. Counties seen as providing many services for the severely mentally ill are more likely than those seen as providing fewer services to have the quality of their services rated highly. This is counterintuitive since one *might* assume that offering a large number of services would dilute service quality. Yet the opposite is the case.

A second finding was a modest positive correlation ($r = .393, p < .0001$) between service coverage and service quality. This relationship also might be considered surprising because one might assume that meeting the needs of a larger rather than a smaller proportion of persons would interfere with service quality. Instead what is found is that the greater the number of persons in need who presumably are getting services the better the quality of the services that are provided.

Other significant findings are the positive correlations between service coordination and comprehensiveness ($r = .257, p < .0001$), and the

Table 17.7 Mean Scores on Effectiveness Indicators for Urban and Rural Counties

| | | Effectiveness Indicators | | |
	Comprehensiveness	Coverage	Quality	Coordination
Urban Counties	11.46	3.14	4.27	2.77
Rural Counties	9.38	3.29	3.97	2.63
p-level[a]	< .0001	.022	< .0001	.033

NOTE: a. By T-test

even stronger positive relationships between coordination and coverage ($r = .372, p < .0001$) and coordination and quality ($r = .538, p < .0001$). These positive correlations are consistent with the notion that the NIMH's set of essential services when appropriately coordinated form an interrelated package of services, and furthermore, that it is both desirable and feasible to provide the full range of services at the county level and provide adequate coordination and coverage without sacrificing quality of mental health care.

Overall, five of the six zero-order correlations are significant. Only the relationship between coverage and comprehensiveness is not significant and is negative ($r = -.024$). The fact that the four-service system effectiveness indicators are generally interrelated is encouraging and supportive of the conceptual scheme and research techniques we have developed. However, it should be noted that although there is a significant correlation, at the same time, the four services are conceptually and practically not one and the same. The correlations are modest in size. We could not tap system effectiveness with a single measure and hence there is a need for all four (and probably more) dimensions.

It should also be noted that the relationship between the effectiveness measures and client outcome measures must be systematically studied. An ultimate clinical criterion of system effectiveness resides in longitudinal client measures that demonstrate a relationship between system structure and functioning and client improvement or decline.

Summary and Conclusions

The main findings reported above are, as follows: (1) The primary criteria of service system effectiveness identified, namely, comprehensiveness, coverage, quality, and coordination, differentiated the eight counties studied. This suggests they are useful primary criteria for assessing CSSs. (2) The four effectiveness indicators, although tapping different dimensions of service system performance, are in five of six cases intercorrelated. We have found patterns such that some counties tend to score high and some score low on most of these indicators, thereby suggesting that they can be used to identify exemplar service systems. The indicators also appear to be consistent in many cases with qualitative information gathered on the characteristics of these service systems. (3) The effectiveness indicators also differentiated the four main stake-holder groups in suggestive ways. For example, service providers report significantly more services as present in the county than do service recipients, a finding consistent with the former group's role which enables them to obtain greater information about the presence of services. In addition, we discovered that case managers and clients, the two groups that in some respects have the most intimate knowledge of the service system, perceive greater service coverage and service quality than do family members or organization directors. We also found that stakeholders do *not* differ in their evaluation of the extent to which services are coordinated in their county. (4) Finally, we found that urban counties differ significantly from rural counties on the four dimensions of service system effectiveness. Urban counties score higher on comprehensiveness, quality, and coordination, while rural counties score higher than urban sites on coverage.

In conclusion, the effectiveness of service delivery systems at the community level is one of the most important questions in the field of mental health services at this time. Most practitioners and researchers agree that service system effectiveness is important and that it is multidimensional and therefore quite complex. Yet there are no agreed upon measures for assessing the functioning of these complicated human services delivery systems. It is evident that the results we have reported about the behavior of local delivery systems are based on small sample studies and hence enjoy more the status of speculations rather than established findings. The study of total systems at the local level is in its infancy. Nevertheless, the problems we have alluded to are now amenable to systematic investigation. We have developed new measures and crude as they may be, they are capable of providing significant new knowledge about improving the functioning of human service delivery systems.

Notes

1. Reprinted form *Community Mental Health Journal*, 25, (1), Spring 1989, pp. 3-20. Used by permission.

2. The original 10 services components of NIMH were expanded to 13 in order to clarify respondent identification of each service.

3. It could be argued that these cross-county differences could be explained by county differences in the relative numbers of the types of stakeholders. However, in unreported two-way analyses of variance we have found that this was not the case.

References

Ashbaugh, J. W., Leaf, P. J., Manderscheid, R. W., et al. (1983). Estimates of the size and selected characteristics of the adult chronically mentally ill population living in U.S. households. In J. R. Greenley (Ed.), *Research in community and mental health* (Vol. 3). Greenwich, CT: JAI Press.

Carling, P. J. (1984). *The National Institute of Mental Health Community Support Program: History and evaluation.* Unpublished report. Rockville, MD: National Institute of Mental Health.

Goldman, H. H., Gattozi, A. A., & Taube, C. A. (1981). Defining and counting the chronically mentally ill. *Journal of Hospital Psychiatry, 32,* 21-27.

Joint Commission on Accreditation of Hospitals. (1981). *Principles of accreditation of community mental health service programs.* Chicago: Joint Commission on Accreditation of Hospitals.

Kiesler, C. A., & Sibulkin, A. E. (1987). *Mental hospitalization: Myths and facts about a national crisis.* Newbury Park, CA: Sage.

Robins, L. N., Helzer, J. E., Weissman, M. M., Orvaschel, H., Gruenberg, E., Burke, J. D., Jr., & Regier, D. A. (1984). Lifetime prevalence of specific psychiatric disorders in three sites. *Archives of General Psychiatry, 41,* 949-958.

Rogers, D. I., Whetten, D. A., & Associates. (1982). *Interorganizational coordination: Theory, research, and implementation.* Ames: Iowa State University Press.

Stroul, B. (1982). *Community support program: Analysis of state strategies.* Boston: Boston University, Center for Rehabilitation Research and Training in Mental Health.

Tessler, R. C., & Goldman, H. (1982). *The chronically mentally ill: Assessing community support programs.* Cambridge, MA: Ballinger.

Index

About the Authors

Andrew Abbott is Professor of Sociology at the University of Chicago. Substantively, his research concerns work and occupations. Methodologically, he has investigated new techniques for the analysis of over-time data.

Joel A. C. Baum is Assistant Professor of Management at the Leonard N. School of Business, New York University. His current research focuses on ecological and institutional processes in organizational environments and taxonomy and evolution. He is conducting a historical study of competition in the Manhattan hotel industry. He is coauthor (with Christine Oliver) of "Institutional Linkages and Organizational Mortality," (*Administrative Science Quarterly*, 36, 1991) and (with Robert J. House) "On the Maturation and Aging of Organizational Populations," in Jitendra V. Singh (Ed.), *Organizational Evolution: New Directions*. He received his Ph.D. in organizational behavior from the University of Toronto.

Thomas D'Aunno (Ph.D., Organizational Psychology, University of Michigan) is Associate Professor of Health Services Management and Psychology at the University of Michigan. His research interests include institutional theory and organizational responses to conflicting and changing external demands. He is currently examining these issues in a national study of drug abuse treatment units funded by the National Institute on Drug Abuse. He has published articles in several management and health care journals, including the *Academy of Management Journal, Academy of Management Review, Medical Care, The Journal of the American Medical Association,* and *The American Journal of Public Health.*

Paula L. Dressel is Associate Professor of Sociology at Georgia State University where she specializes in social problems and the political economy of social welfare. She is the author of *The Service Trap: From Altruism to Dirty Work*, articles in *Social Service Review, The Gerontologist, Social Problems, Journal of Sociology and Social Welfare,* and *Journal of Marriage and the Family,* and chapters in books focusing on both gerontology and social welfare. She is on the board of directors of Aid to Imprisoned Mothers, Inc., a nonprofit community agency providing assistance to the multigenerational families of imprisoned women. Her current writings focus on "Three Generations at Risk."

Charles Glisson earned his doctorate from the George Warren Brown School of Social Work, Washington University, St. Louis. He is currently Professor and Chair, Ph.D. Program in Social Work, University of Tennessee, Knoxville. His current research, funded by a National Institute of Mental Health RO1 research grant, examines the quality and outcomes of services to children who are in the custody of the state, following a major interorganizational restructuring of those services in Tennessee. He has published a text on quantitative methods in social work and numerous chapters and articles on social work research methodology, services to children, and human service organizations.

Naomi Gottlieb, M.S.W., Ph.D., is Professor, School of Social Work, University of Washington. She is editor of *Alternative Services for Women,* and co-editor of *The Woman Client* and *Feminist Social Work Practice in Clinical Settings.* She is a cofounder of *Affilia: Journal for Women in Social Work* and serves as the journal's book review editor. She is coordinator of a curriculum specialization on women at her School of Social Work. She is currently at work on a book for the general public about emotional abuse of women in the workplace.

Kirsten A. Gronbjerg is Professor of Sociology at Loyola University of Chicago, with prior appointments at SUNY, Stony Brook, and Hofstra University. Her primary interests center on public and private social policies and she has authored a number of books, articles, and reports on American welfare policies and the nonprofit sector. Her current interests focus on the interorganizational structure of the human service field, and on the effects of funding changes on the management of nonprofit organizations.

Oscar Grusky is Professor of Sociology, Director, NIMH-supported Postdoctoral Training Program in Mental Health Service System and Evaluation Research, and Director, NIMH-supported Training Program on Psychosocial Issues and Mental Health Services for Persons with AIDS, Department of Sociology, University of California, Los Angeles. He earned his doctorate at the University of Michigan. He has served as Department Chairman at UCLA for five years and as Acting Chairman for one year. He has served on the editorial boards of numerous publications. His current research is concerned with the stigma toward the mentally ill and persons with HIV/AIDS, the assessment of the effectiveness of countywide mental health systems for the seriously mentally ill, and the analysis of organizational factors and their influence on safety in nuclear power plants.

Lorraine M. Gutiérrez (Ph.D., A.C.S.W.) is Assistant Professor of Social Work at the University of Washington, where she coordinates the Specialization on People of Color. Her areas of research and teaching include advanced generalist practice, gender- and ethno-conscious practice, and Latino issues. She has extensive experience in working as a social worker and administrator in multi-ethnic communities in the fields of developmental disabilities, family services, and domestic violence.

Joel F. Handler (J.D., Harvard Law School) is Professor of Law at the University of California, Los Angeles. His primary research interests are in the areas of poverty law and administration, social welfare programs, race, and law reform activities. He has published more than a dozen books and numerous articles on these subjects.

Yeheskel Hasenfeld (Ph.D., University of Michigan) is Professor of Social Welfare at the School of Social Welfare, University of California, Los Angeles. His main research focus has been on the organization of human services with special emphasis on the impact of the environment, and on client-organization relations. He has published several books and many articles in the field, including *Human Service Organizations*, and *Administrative Leadership in the Human Services*. Recently, he has been studying the implementation of welfare-work programs, which is reported in his publication, *The Moral Construction of Poverty: Welfare Reform in America* (with J. Handler).

Cheryl Hyde is Assistant Professor in Human Behavior in the Social Environment at Boston University's School of Social Work. She received her Ph.D., MSW, and Certificate in Labor Relations from the University of Michigan, Ann Arbor. Her areas of interest include the women's movement, the New Right, feminist models for macro practice, multicultural education, and organizational change. At present, she is collaborating on two studies, one addressing the dilemmas of incorporating cultural diversity into social work education and the other focusing on the neglect of social and economic class in social work curricula. Also in progress is a project on the transformative nature of qualitative research as conducted within organizational settings.

Stuart A. Kirk is Professor at Columbia University School of Social Work, where he teaches in the areas of social administration, organizations, research, and mental health. His doctorate in social welfare is from the University of California, Berkeley. He has served on the faculty at the University of Hawaii, University of Kentucky, and the University of Wisconsin. From 1980 to 1987 he was Dean of the School of Social Welfare at the State University of New York at Albany. He is the author of many articles and chapters on research utilization, service delivery, and on labeling in mental health. He has just completed a longitudinal study of burnout among intensive case managements in mental health. His book, *The Selling of DSM: The Rhetoric of Science in Psychiatry*, coauthored with Herb Kutchins, is in press.

Herb Kutchins is Professor of Social Work at California State University, Sacramento. He received his bachelor of arts degree from the University of Chicago and his doctorate from the University of California, Berkeley. He has been on the faculty at Sonoma State University and the University of Hawaii. He is the author of numerous articles on criminal justice, advocacy, mental health, and law and social welfare. In recent years, he has coauthored a dozen articles with Stuart A. Kirk on the sociology of psychiatric diagnosis that have appeared in such journals as *Social Service Review*, *Social Work*, *Health and Social Work*, and *Social Work Research and Abstracts*.

R. L. McNeely, Professor of Social Welfare, University of Wisconsin–Milwaukee, earned his Ph.D. at the Florence Heller School for Advanced Studies in Social Welfare, Brandeis University. He is a Research Fellow of the Gerontological Society of America, and served recently at the University of New Orleans as a Fellow of the American Council on Education. His job satisfaction research interests focus on work-life issues associated with race and gender among public human service employees.

Hillel Schmid (Ph.D.) is Senior Lecturer at the Paul Baerwald School of Social Work at the Hebrew University of Jerusalem. His main areas of interest and research are the adaptation of human service organizations to changing environments, the strategy and structure of organizations, processes of management, integration of organizational theories and policy making in the social services. He has published articles and book chapters on the management of human services.

Jitendra V. Singh is Joseph Wharton Term Associate Professor of Management at The Wharton School, University of Pennsylvania. He is also Research Director-Entrepreneurship at the Sol C. Snider Entrepreneurial Center, The Wharton School. His current research interests center around models of ecological and evolutionary processes in organizations and populations. Among other journals, his research has appeared in *Administrative Science Quarterly, Annual Review of Sociology, Annual Review of Psychology, American Psychological Review, Academy of Management Journal*, and *Academy of Management Review*. He has served on the editorial boards of *Administrative Science Quarterly* and *Academy of Management Journal* and is currently on the editorial review board of *Organization Science*. He received his M.B.A. at the Indian Institute of Management, Ahmedabad, India, and his Ph.D. in organization theory and behavior from the Graduate School of Business, Stanford University. He recently edited *Organizational Evolution: New Directions,* a collection of papers using an evolutionary approach to understanding organizational change, creation, and demise.

Kathleen Tierney is Associate Professor of Sociology and Research Director of the Disaster Research Center at the University of Delaware. Her areas of interest include the social, economic, and policy aspects of natural and technological hazards; social movements and other forms of collective behavior; and the sociology of mental health and mental illness. She has published extensively on those topics in various journals, including *Social Problems, Journal of Health and Social Behavior, Public Administration Review, Sociological Quarterly*, and *The International Journal of Mass Emergencies and Disasters*. She is co-editor (with Russell R. Dynes) of a forthcoming book, *Disaster, Collective Behavior,* *and Social Organization.* She is currently involved in several projects focusing on disasters and community crises, including studies on community disaster recovery and on the organizational aspects and social impacts of catastrophic oil spills.

David J. Tucker is Professor of Social Work, School of Social Work, University of Michigan. Previously he served on the Faculty of Social Science, McMaster University, Hamilton, Ontario, Canada. His research interests include the ecology of human service organizations, the structural analysis of interorganizational service delivery systems, dynamic change process in populations of foster homes, and the critical analysis of selected public policy issues. His accomplishments as an organizational scholar have been recognized with major national and international awards. His publications have appeared in a variety of journals, including *Academy of Management Review, Administrative Science Quarterly, Social Service Review,* and *Canadian Public Policy,* and as chapters in a number of books. He received his Ph.D. in social work from the University of Toronto, Toronto, Ontario, Canada.